The Plantation Ideal

CRITICAL ENVIRONMENTS: NATURE, SCIENCE, AND POLITICS

Edited by Julie Guthman and Rebecca Lave

The Critical Environments series publishes books that explore the political forms of life and the ecologies that emerge from histories of capitalism, militarism, racism, colonialism, and more.

The Plantation Ideal

Landscapes of Extraction in Mozambique

WENDY WOLFORD

University of California Press

University of California Press
Oakland, California

Cataloging-in-Publication data is on file at the Library of Congress.
ISBN 978-0-520-41685-7 (cloth)
ISBN 978-0-520-41686-4 (pbk.)
ISBN 978-0-520-41687-1 (ebook)

GPSR Authorized Representative: Easy Access System Europe,
Mustamäe tee 50, 10621 Tallinn, Estonia, gpsr.requests@easproject.com

34 33 32 31 30 29 28 27 26 25
10 9 8 7 6 5 4 3 2 1

To the people of rural Mozambique,
for whom the struggle continues

The publisher and the University of California Press Foundation
gratefully acknowledge the generous support of the
Ralph and Shirley Shapiro Endowment Fund
in Environmental Studies.

Contents

Illustrations

Acknowledgments

I am reading through this manuscript one last time in my office in Ithaca, New York, while people are dying on the streets in Mozambique. Widespread protests began just after the presidential election in early October 2024. Months of flagrant campaign manipulation followed by a blatantly corrupt counting of the vote led to the unsurprising but still breathtakingly bold announcement that the ruling party's candidate had won the presidency. No one believed the announcement—it is difficult to imagine that even the most dedicated Frelimo supporters believed it, but as Frelimo's grip on the country has weakened over the past decade, the brazenness and violence of the party's efforts to stay in power have grown. The book I have written is not about electoral politics, but the infrastructure of historical injustice I document in it may help to explain how such a rich country could perpetuate such poverty. This book might explain why plans to promote development end up extracting wealth, and it might explain why, after a century of oppression, people have taken to the streets. I dedicate this book to all of the people in Mozambique fighting for a better future against the odds.

·　·　·

This is not a long book, but it has taken me a long time to write. I often doubted whether I would ever finish it. I kept going in part because of the people who gave me their time and shared their experiences and insights; I didn't want that to have been for nothing. I am grateful to everyone I met in Mozambique: people who answered my endless questions, let me into their homes, walked me around their properties, and invited me to meetings and workshops. I can't name all of the people I interviewed or worked with, in part because many of them are cited anonymously in the chapters that follow, and people in positions of power might not want to be associated with this book's message. I am particularly grateful for the passion and insight of the scholars and activists who contributed their thoughts to the final chapter, and who have done so much to create space for genuine alternatives in Mozambique: Máriam Abbas, Teresa Cunha, Bernardo Mançano Fernandes, Anabela Lemos, Uacitissa Mandamule, Boaventura Monjane, Jan de Moor, and Bernhard Weimer. I wrote the final chapter with a Mozambican scholar, Natacha Bruna, who is brilliant and committed to climate and social justice in Mozambique. It has been an honor and a joy to work with her.

In Mozambique, I was affiliated with the Rural Observatory, led by João Mosca, one of the most well-known and respected political economists of rural Mozambique. This book owes much to his guidance. He was the one who insisted on the similarities between contemporary Mozambique and the colonial period. I am also grateful for Sérgio Chichava's advice and support. Sérgio directed the Institute of Socio-Economic Studies in Maputo and welcomed me into its regular seminar series. I benefited immensely from conversations and collaboration with Euclides Gonçalves, who sets a high bar for critical ethnography in rural Mozambique. I was introduced to communities in northern Mozambique by two stalwart rural development practitioners, Dan Mullins and Nicolas Dexter. In Maputo, my family and I spent many happy hours with Nicky Shellens and Besu Yirgu. We had the good fortune to connect with local musician and activist Nery Pires; he welcomed us into the cultural community in Mafalala, where we had the opportunity to work with a lively community of young Mozambicans. In Portugal, I was affiliated with the Center for African and Development Studies at the University of Lisbon under the helpful sponsorship of Joana Pereira Leite. In Lisbon, my oldest son played basketball for Benfica, and a close-knit group of wildly dedicated team parents, particularly Cristina Pereira and José Faria, took us under their wings.

Several students and postdocs have helped me with research and writing over the years, and this manuscript is much better for their thoughtful work. My PhD students are a constant source of inspiration; working with talented new scholars is the reason I became a professor, and they regularly remind me why. Katherine (Kata) Young and Amanda Hickey spent several weeks in Mozambique with me; we had some epic adventures, and I benefited greatly from their research skills and hard work. Ryan Nehring conducted interviews in Maputo and read through decades of *Farmer Gazettes*. Nina Chaopricha organized an endless amount of literature for me. Andrew Ofstehage helped analyze interview data and organize manuscript material. Natacha Bruna read the manuscript through multiple times and provided essential assistance and advice.

In writing this book, I stand on the shoulders of many talented scholars, but I owe a particular debt to James C. Scott, Allan Isaacman, and Cláudia Castelo. Jim Scott's scholarship and generous intellectual curiosity have shaped more than a generation of scholars who have read his work or spent time at the Agrarian Studies Program at Yale University. We lost a huge heart and mind when we lost Jim, but I bet he was curious until the end; he always said you could tell a lot about a society by how they thought about death and treated their dead. I miss knowing that he is in this world. Allen Isaacman and Cláudia Castelo are two of the best historians of Mozambique; I could not have done my work without theirs.

I owe a lot to colleagues who have read drafts of various chapters and heard me talk about the book (for many years). My fellow organizers in the Land Deals Politics Initiative have been mentors and co-conspirators for almost fifteen years. Our unofficial captain, Jun Borras, is an inspiration in everything he does; the academy needs more people like him. I draw on literature and ideas from Ian Scoones, Marc Edelman, and Ben White throughout the book. Ruth Hall has been a friend and inspiration; her work is brilliant and important. She read through the manuscript at a time when I badly needed advice. In Brazil, I rely on the friendship and guidance of two true scholar-activists: Sérgio Sauer and Bernardo Mançano Fernandes. Durba Ghosh and Marina Welker at Cornell invited me to join their writing group when I first got to Cornell; we have been reading each other's work ever since, and their comments on my outlines, chapters, and manuscript were always constructive and smart. My former student and now colleague, Kasia Paprocki, generously read everything I sent her. Her characteristically incisive comments sharpened my arguments considerably. My colleagues in the Contested Global Landscapes project supported by the Institute for Social Sciences at Cornell were instrumental in the early days of this work: Ray Craib, Chuck Geisler, Paul Nadasdy, Sara Pritchard, and Steven Wolf. Participants in the 2018 Social Life of Land workshop (co-organized with my fellow editors and friends, Michael Goldman and Nancy Peluso) offered excellent comments on what became chapter 4 of this manuscript. I have benefited from the scholarship and friendship of many others at Cornell, including Sarah Besky, Rachel Bezner Kerr, Gustavo Flores-Macias, Chuck Geisler, Jenny Goldstein, Gunisha Kaur, Fouad Makki, Tom Pepinsky, Rachel Riedl, Eric Tagliacozzo, and Stephen Yale-Loehr. Phil McMichael is the reason I came to Cornell, and I have followed his work and in his footsteps ever since. Rachel Riedl and the Einaudi Center for International Studies hosted a virtual conference on The Plantationocene for me in 2021, and I am so grateful for all of the participants and conversations in that event. I would also like to thank two anonymous reviewers for UC Press who gave extensive comments on this manuscript, as well as Julie Guthman, whose no-nonsense critiques and advice improved the manuscript greatly. Naja Pulliam Collins is a patient and enthusiastic editor. Philip Sayers and Louise Silberling helped me articulate my ideas at a time when they were still very amorphous.

For most of the time that I have been writing this manuscript, I have served as vice provost of international affairs at Cornell University. I have loved the responsibilities of that position, but they did make it harder to get any writing done! I might not have stayed on were it not for the people. Then Dean Kathryn Boor allowed me to dedicate my limited "faculty time" to my graduate students and my own research; this book would not have gotten written without that gift of time. My colleagues on the Provost Staff Council are dedicated and generous: John Siliciano listened to me go on and on and almost never complained, and I depended on regular "coffee talks" with my fellow vice provosts, Lisa Nishii, Katherine McComas, and Steve Jackson. The staff in Global Cornell are talented and committed; my senior leadership essentially run the place on their own. And the provost, despite an annoying habit of correcting my grammar, has been an inspiring mentor and leader. My assistant Donna Wilczynski has been a friend and a huge support; she never chastised me for taking time away from the office and even celebrated every milestone, although I am sure she wondered why it took so long to finish.

I am grateful to the National Science Foundation (SES-1331265) and the Fulbright Foundation for supporting the research in this book, parts of which have been published in other forms. Two previously published articles were early articulations of my arguments, and I draw from their ideas and text throughout the manuscript: "The Colonial Roots of Agricultural Modernization in Mozambique: The Role of Research from Portugal to ProSavana," *Journal of Peasant Studies* 48, no. 2 (2019): 254–73 and "From Pangaea to Partnership: The Many Fields of Rural Development," *Sociology of Development* 1, no. 2 (2015): 210–32. In chapter 5, the community descriptions come from research that I did with Amanda Hickey and Katherine Young, originally written up as a report for CARE Mozambique in 2014. Finally, chapter 4 is a much-expanded version of a chapter published in the edited volume *The Social Lives of Land* (Cornell University Press, 2024). I am grateful to the anonymous reviewers for their comments on these earlier works and to their publishers for permission to draw on these pieces in this manuscript. All errors of fact or judgment are of course mine.

Last, but by no means least, are the people who have nothing substantive to do with the manuscript but who have kept me going over the years of research and writing. I have the great fortune to live next to fantastic people who feed me, run with me, and listen to me complain: Sarah von Schrader, Anurag Agrawal, Jen Thaler, and Matt Klemm. Rachel Dunifon and Rachel Riedl have been friends, running partners, and sounding boards for everything from party plans to book titles. Julie Guthman (again), James McCarthy, and Amy Ross educate, entertain, and challenge me. But it is of course my family that deserves the greatest acknowledgment. Their laughter, love, and forbearance are on every page of this manuscript. My three boys and husband came with me to Mozambique and Portugal. The kids made friends, went to school, (mostly) learned Portuguese, and asked good questions. My husband took care of all of us, played drums with a local band in Maputo, and photographed everything. He has listened to me describe every chapter of this book (repeatedly, often early in the morning before anyone's coffee has really set in) and more than once convinced me to keep writing. His belief in the project and in me is everything I have needed and arguably more than I deserved.

Introduction

Cultivating Landscapes of Extraction

In 2009, riding a wave of large-scale investments in African land, the leaders of Brazil, Japan, and Mozambique announced an ambitious new project to remake agricultural production in northern Mozambique. Called ProSavana after an earlier trilateral project (Brazil-Japan-United States) in the Brazilian Midwest, each of the three countries had a different part to play. Brazil would contribute scientific research garnered from its 1970s soybean "miracle," Japan would finance new rural development models, and Mozambique would supply the land and labor. Mozambican officials argued that the project would modernize farming in the densely populated northern corridor, turning the country into the global plantation that political leaders, scientific experts, and investors had long envisioned. Modern grain farmers from Brazil were intrigued by the idea of a "new frontier" in Africa, where land and labor were cheap and soybeans and other commodity crops could sail east from the newly renovated, Japanese-funded "bulk grain terminal" at the Port of Nacala, across the Indian Ocean to Asia. In anticipation, two "missions" of Brazilian farmers visited Mozambique, and the three governments established a private fund (the Nacala Fund; see allAfrica 2012) to raise $2 billion in greenfield financing for investments on what was estimated to be roughly 14 million hectares of available land.

Six years later, when I arrived in Mozambique to conduct research on the project, ProSavana had fallen apart, going "into hibernation," as one activist said. The project registered some small successes in plant breeding, scientific training, and local development projects but fell far short of its original goals and certainly never achieved anything like the hoped-for agricultural transformation. There was blame all around: on the investors who never materialized, on the farmers who didn't adopt the new Brazilian varieties and protested the project's lack of transparency, on the foreign scientists who looked down on their Mozambican counterparts, on the politicians who failed to consult the people living in the project area. The project engendered historic, nationwide (if not always unified) protests, and representatives from all three governments scrambled to justify their role, often changing or reversing their initial descriptions of the project. Everyone had a different explanation for why ProSavana had failed, although perhaps the better question was why they thought it was a good idea in the first place. How did ProSavana, with its focus on foreign investment and large-scale, mechanized commodity production for export, come to be seen and defended as a logical use of capital, science, land, and labor in a country where the majority of the population lives in rural areas and goes hungry, farming on small plots of land with hand tools?

The spectacular story of ProSavana is all too familiar in Mozambique. Although plantations across twentieth-century colonial and postcolonial Mozambique have failed to generate sustainable local or national development, they are idealized as forms of production and as pathways to profit and progress. The *plantation ideal*, as I call it in this book, fundamentally shapes science, agriculture, and rural life in the country, with devastating and ongoing consequences. From the royal charter companies under the Portuguese to socialist state farms and agricultural growth corridor megaprojects such as ProSavana, the focus on plantation models of development has meant that for over one hundred years, the global market has taken priority over place-based ecological and human well-being. As I researched ProSavana, it became clear that the similarities with historical projects and a colonial/postcolonial mindset required a longer time frame and a broader analysis. As a result, this book went from a focus on one plantation project to a study of the conditions that gave rise to the desire for plantations as well as the implications of that long-standing desire.

Mozambique is not unique in its quest for plantation profits, as evidenced by the dramatic, global rush for what the World Bank called "Large-Scale Land Acquisitions" (Deininger and Byerlee 2011) in the last two decades (Zoomers 2010; Borras et al. 2011; Wolford et al. 2024), but it does represent an extreme example. Born in the particularities of the Portuguese economy and society in the early 1900s, twentieth-century colonial rule was a militarized form of external occupation for extraction that was "at once the most primitive and the most extreme modality of colonialism" (Anderson 1962a: 89). The Portuguese, whose strength was going places, not making things, saw themselves as particularly adept in ruling over and profiting from their overseas territories. They imagined both landscapes and local residents as sites of extraction, imbuing the plantation model with a sense of inevitability and triumph that disguised their poor economic and social performance. The pursuit of plantations continues today, one hundred years later, under the increasingly authoritarian one-party state, with the support of external corporations, science, and donors. The extractive mechanisms and the brutal depredations of forced labor, export orientation, predictable starvation, and withholding of basic human rights and public services all continue to exist and to shape and twist the boundaries of what it is possible to think and do. A small but powerful group of people favor plantation production because they stand to profit from it and because it is what they *know*. This knowledge has been shaped by over one hundred years of colonial and postcolonial rule, in which plantations generate the conditions for their own reproduction. Plantations call into being large landholders, multinational corporations, investors, and bureaucrats; they fuel ideologies and expectations of development; and they incentivize the production of supportive infrastructure, from roads, land rights, and agronomy textbooks to the organization and administration of government agencies.

Plantations in Mozambique are thus not simple economic organizations, actors, or ideas; they are political-cultural-economic assemblages with deep colonial histories and a tendency to reappear as the solution to the very problems they arguably created. Over time and space, they have been produced by and then produced ways of seeing the world (knowledge, imagination, aspirations) and ways of organizing the world (rules, incentives, institutions). In this book, I describe the way in which plantation aspirations—what I call the plantation ideal—have shaped rural land and life in Mozambique, from the science done to pave the way for new plantation crops to the constant plans for turning local residents into plantation labor, fixing them in place and slotting them into commodity streams as producers or small-scale suppliers (outgrowers or contract farmers).

Colonial visions for East Africa were evident in the way that ProSavana played out (Patel 2012). Contrary to the original roles each country expected to take on, I would summarize their interventions this way:

- Brazil provided scientific research that facilitated extraction by developing and testing new varieties of export crops.
- Japan designed community development projects that offered subsistence-level resources intended to keep rural inhabitants in their place rather than practicing mobile forms of swidden agriculture.

- Mozambique devised new land laws that privileged private investors and created new aggregation schemes to coordinate and motivate local residents, who were expected to do the bulk of the work, whether on their own land or on another's.

With the case of ProSavana as a point of departure, I make two contributions in this book. First, I answer the question, How and why do plantations, which have never produced long-term profits or sustainable development, still dominate the political imaginary in Mozambique as the best strategy for economic growth? Second, I illustrate the consequences of this "plantation ideal" for life on the land in rural Mozambique, focusing on the way that science, external aid, nongovernmental organizations (NGOs), extensionists, and local communities are caught up in and co-produce this plantation ideal. Portuguese Africa is relatively less well studied than other parts of the world or other colonial powers, so the case is instructive in its specificity as well as in comparison to other places and people.

Each of the chapters in this book stands alone, but they are best read in conversation with one another. Chapter 2 is perhaps overlong, with more history than most people will want, but colleagues in Mozambique have told me it contains useful information that many in the country do not know, so I have kept in much of the detail. People not specifically interested in twentieth-century Mozambique could skim this chapter, but I hope everyone will read the last chapter, which is co-written with a brilliant young Mozambican scholar, Natacha Bruna. The chapter provides visions of alternative futures and the means to get there, as articulated by Mozambican scholars and activists as well as by people who have been working in Mozambique for many years. The eight individuals who speak in the final chapter have different political and scholarly orientations, but they all agree on one thing: that plantations need to go.

1. The Plantation Ideal

FLYING THE PORTUGUESE FLAG:
A POLITICAL ECONOMY OF DISCOVERY

On January 31, 1913, José Emílio Pinheiro de Azevedo of Lisbon wrote a letter to the head of the Companhia de Moçambique (the Mozambique Company), the private entity given control over a substantial area of Portuguese East Africa between 1891 and 1942 (de Azevedo 1913). José Emílio was looking for land. He had considered returning to Brazil, where he had worked previously, but now that Brazil was ever more independent of Portugal, he decided his efforts should help to advance his own nation. He wished to "dedicate his youth to the benefit of country and household. . . . Love for my country leads me to want to develop that which is ours, such that my sacrifices will not go to waste." In his short letter, José Emílio asked for information about the quality of the land and the possibilities for obtaining a concession in Mozambique. He included several specific questions, among them the following: (i) Does one rent or buy the land? (ii) What is the climate like? Can a person live there with a missus and two small children? (iii) What kind of crops will do best? (iv) What sort of profits could I make with an investment of six or seven *contos* [the Portuguese currency at the time]? (v) In the first year, will there be sufficient returns to pay for my subsistence? (vi) Is labor expensive or easy to get? (vii) Are the territories peaceful? and (viii) Is there sufficient water?

The letter he received in return was immediate, authoritative, and optimistic. A senior official in the Mozambique Company, A. Eduardo Villaça, responded directly (Villaça 1913).[1] He boasted of fertile land and seemingly endless water. The weather was very much like Europe's, he reported, so José Emílio should find it amenable, and there were areas along the coast that were particularly appropriate for women and small children. Among the cultivars the administrator recommended as most well-suited for the territory, given its situation and its climate, were sugarcane and corn. Neither sugar nor corn was native, but both had already shown themselves to be profitable, and the company was establishing teaching gardens to "give out useful and certain information to all who want to dedicate themselves to this." Other products that would be feasible were cotton, rubber, tobacco, coffee, and coconuts. All that was needed to make good on the discovery and exploration of this promising new land was dedication, "some few pecuniary resources, and a certain moral fortitude." In a similar letter to another aspiring colonist, Villaça wrote, "Whoever wants to go to the territory of the Mozambique Company has to have . . . good will and the desire to improve his fortune" (Villaça 1909). In return for a small fee, the company would outline the dimensions of the land to be conceded. In addition, although it was "not their responsibility," the company would help properly "engage" the necessary indigenous labor.[2] Villaça reassured José Emílio that the natives of Mozambique had been "pacified," in reference to the long struggle with indigenous groups that ended in 1897 with the defeat of the southern African Kingdom of Gaza (Serra 2000). Relations with local residents were still fairly hostile, though, and administrators warned would-be colonists that local labor was "unreliable" and prone to using unsustainable methods if one did not supervise workers closely. The Mozambique Company was primarily owned by British and French investors, but individual settlers were required to colonize in the name of Portugal. Anyone who wanted land would "have to fly the Portuguese flag" and no other (Companhia de Moçambique 1913b).

This exchange between a young man looking for land and fortune and the Mozambique Company sheds light on the relationships between land, labor, capital, and science in the former East African colony—relationships that endure today. When José Emílio wrote in 1913, he could not know what awaited him in Mozambique. Nor could he know that the enthusiastic response from A. Eduardo Villaça was more aspirational than accurate. Portuguese preeminence in acts of discovery—in navigation and conquest—was not matched by an ability to make the new lands or labor productive. This preeminence turned weakness propelled first a colonial strategy and then a political economy of discovery.

A *colonial strategy based on discovery* is one that privileges the initial moment of finding, rather than subsequent acts of settlement or development. As Patricia Seed (1995) argues, the Portuguese excelled at overseas exploration, or what they themselves were the first to call "discovery." In the 1500s this included discoveries of various kinds: new places, peoples, techniques, and knowledge (115). As "Lord of the Sea" (Newitt 1995: 17), Portuguese explorers adapted the Arabic astrolabe to navigate by both the stars and the sun, applying mathematical concepts of latitude and longitude to long-distance overseas exploration at a time when most European sea travel was coastal, closely connected to Mediterranean seaways (Seed 1995: 113–22). The characteristic Portuguese ship, the caravel that adorns countless paintings, sculptures, and lampposts in Portugal today, was an unlikely instrument of domination. A graceful ship with up to three sails and a capacious hold, which sat high in the water, the caravel could carry sufficient supplies, navigate shallow waters, and tack steadily through rapidly changing winds, going where Europeans had never before succeeded in going (Seed 1995: 113–22). Buoyed by their nautical success, the Portuguese asserted the right to "those regions inaccessible without their techniques" (Seed 1995: 128).[3] Portugal justified its claim based on having discovered a territory rather than on its subsequent development.[4] The pages of the archives from colonial Mozambique are filled with glorious invocations of the virtues of Portuguese discoveries as having "pushed back the limits of the habitable world for all nations" (Moçambique 1939: 18). And as one enthusiastic official wrote on the eve of the first visit by a Portuguese head of state to the territory, Mozambique was a brilliant "symbol of the Portuguese empire":

> We display our gratitude for what the motherland has done for this land,
> over the centuries, not abandoning it in its difficult hours, conceding
> to it the Progress of Civilization, investing it with the qualities that the
> Portuguese Race has given to the world, courage and the assimilation of
> the backwards races, conquering them, more by example, persuasion and
> teaching based in the Christian faith than by force. [Portugal] is a nation
> that dragged itself across the dark seas, fighting against the most terrible
> legends, the Portuguese of the 1500s, the first Europeans to arrive in this
> bay of Espírito Santo. (Moçambique 1939: 22)

To this day, the so-called Age of Discovery "endures as Portugal's national touchstone" (Penvenne 2005: 79).

Underlying and extending this colonial approach, a *political economy of discovery* is one in which territorial possession and utilization are defined by the initial moment of discovery rather than by subsequent activities of settlement, production, and development. To explain how discovery works in this context, we need to think about it in the abstract as well as in the context of the Portuguese colonization of Mozambique. In the abstract, a discovery is a claim to having uncovered something previously unknown, though it is often also applied to the "thing" (the place, the people, the process) that was discovered. As an act rather than an object, a discovery is the work of finding, uncovering, documenting, or making visible. Both usages describe only the objective characteristics of discoveries, however, as if the thing discovered were lying in wait in some sort of vacuum, a universal space wherein facts accumulate naturally, as if discovery were simply the act of coming upon new information. This leaves out the most important aspect of discovery: that in addition to being a noun and a verb, *discovery* is a *relationship*. It is a relationship between the discoverer and the discovered, the before and the after, the knowing and the not-knowing, the known and the not-known.

The success of a claim to having discovered something is shaped by the balance of forces in any given conjuncture, by who has the guns, the gold, the ships, and the ear of the king—or today, of the scientific funding agency, the aid organization, and the banker. The translation of a finding into a discovery depends, ironically, on who is able to make a virtue out of *not* having known something, a virtue out of ignorance. We don't celebrate the day Native Americans discovered Christopher Columbus, Pedro Alvarez de Cabral, or Francisco Pizarro—partly because the encounter was so devastating for native peoples, but also (relatedly) because indigenous peoples lacked the power to turn *their* new finding into a discovery. In the epistemological tradition of what Arturo Escobar (2007, 2010) calls coloniality/modernity, three elements are necessary for something to be considered a discovery: (1) the thing discovered has to be deemed of sufficient importance that it merits recognition and use by others; (2) the thing discovered must be successfully represented as not having been known before; and (3) the origin of the discovery must be attributable to a "discoverer," whether an individual or a specific collective—otherwise its presence and use will be understood to have been disseminated, not discovered. A political economy that runs on discoveries is a relationship of power, in which the ability to claim a discovery and enable extraction requires authority or control over those who labor to make the discovery bear fruit.[5] The Portuguese could only claim that they had discovered Mozambique, and were therefore entitled to its control, because they ignored the prior claims of local residents. Their search for profits in the new land initially resulted in the most extractive of activities: the enslavement and export of humans. In the 1900s, pushed to deepen its control over the territory, the political economy of discovery generated a plantation ideal characterized by a focus on the application of external ideas and research for the purpose of extraction rather than on production or development.

"THE MOST EXTREME MODALITY OF COLONIALISM": FROM DISCOVERY TO EXTRACTION

Portugal's colonial rule has been described as "ultra-colonialism" (Anderson 1962a), extreme extroversion (Harrison 1999: 545), extractive (Mosca 2005; Castel-Branco 2022), and, by one journalist in the *New York Times*, "absurd" (Kamm 1977). In this book, I focus on a specific period in Portuguese history: the late nineteenth and the twentieth centuries. This is the period when Portugal tightened its control over this East African territory. The link between discovery and profits, for the Portuguese, rested on the ability of external capital, force, and science to extract resources from local land and labor. This link was embedded in an older language of discovery: in Portuguese, the word *explorar* means both "to explore" and "to exploit."[6] Extraction was tied to the global market as motivation and means but was never fully or solely capitalist. At different moments, both capitalism and socialism were used as excuses to normalize or justify the brutality of extraction. From enslavement (Allina 2012; Cahen 2013) and labor outmigration during the colonial period (Macamo 2005; Newitt 1995) particularly to the South African mines (First 1977), to corporate extraction of coal, heavy sands, and other minerals (Chiziane 2015; Mosca 2005) and high expectations for natural gas exports (Cunguara and Hanlon 2012), the country's human and non-human resources have been exploited for decades (Isaacman and Isaacman 2013). The country's transportation network reflects the fact that extraction has persistently been prioritized: there are three railroad systems in the south, middle, and north of the country (Maputo, Beira, and Nacala, respectively), extending from extraction sites (mines) to ports along the eastern coast. These railroads carry more cargo than passengers, and they direct these goods outward rather than connecting people across the country.

My analysis of plantations contributes to this literature on extraction in Mozambique. Large-scale agriculture is not generally thought of in terms of extraction because agriculture is rooted in place and connected to local residents who farm for their own consumption, but crop production for the purposes of raw material exports and foreign exchange was the defining characteristic of twentieth-century Portuguese rule. After independence, the Mozambican government—ruled by one party since the end of colonial rule in 1975—continued to place Mozambique's land and people at the service of the global commodity market.

Part of the appeal of plantations is the possibility of gaining quick returns on a global market with a substantial appetite for tropical resources. First the Portuguese and then the independent and post-socialist Mozambican government saw commodity exports as the fastest and most reliable way to raise urgently needed foreign exchange, addressing national indebtedness and low levels of development. Today, in the context of global neoliberalism, a one-party state, reliance on external donors and creditors, and widespread absolute poverty, there is a consensus among state officials and development practitioners that large-scale industrialized agriculture for export, financed by foreign banks or investors, is the most effective way to bring development to Mozambique. But this predatory investment rarely leaves anything behind. What Castel-Branco (2014) calls "economic porosity" means that the profits don't trickle down, they trickle out; linkages between foreign and domestic capital are midwifed not for development, dependent or otherwise (Evans 1979), but for extraction by a rent-seeking state (see also Mosca 2019; Garcia and Kato 2016).

The cost of privileging extraction in Mozambique is clear today. It is evident in the combination of relatively high growth rates from 2005 to 2015 (averaging around 10 percent per annum if one includes foreign direct investment inflows) alongside persistently high rates of poverty, illiteracy, and ill health. Despite considerable natural resource wealth, Mozambique is one of the poorest countries in the world, ranking 185 out of 191 countries in terms of human development, with an estimated 60 percent of the population below the level of poverty. Of the thirty-three million people living in the country in 2022, roughly 70 percent lived in the rural areas, making a living from a combination of farming and petty retail or services. In 2024, the World Bank estimated that over 95 percent of those households lived in what the bank called "multidimensional poverty."[7]

According to recent documents presented by the Ministry of Agriculture and Rural Development, almost all farmers in rural Mozambique (99 percent) were family farmers: 98.7 percent of farms (3.9 million farms) in Mozambique were small (roughly 1.1 hectares), 1.03 percent (51,871 farms) were medium sized, and 0.27 percent (782 farms) were large. Only 4.3 percent of farmers had access to extension services, and only 4.6 percent had access to machinery or improved seeds, meaning that most farmers planted on their own with fairly rudimentary implements and techniques. A long history of privileging plantation production for export means that Mozambique imports basic food staples (rice, wheat, vegetable oils, fish, milk, corn) and exports market commodities (tobacco, sugar, banana, oil seeds, cotton, and cashews; see table 1). In early 2024, roughly 54 percent of Mozambicans could not afford sufficient food.[8]

TABLE 1. Top Agricultural Exports and Imports by Value, Mozambique, 2016

	Imports		Exports	
Rank	Product	Value (USD 1,000)	Product	Value (USD 1,000)
1	Wheat	141,000	Unmanufactured tobacco	233,573
2	Rice paddy	139,437	Raw cane or beet sugar	65,542
3	Rice milled	138,427	Sesame seed	45,381
4	Maize	53,107	Bananas	23,402
5	Palm oil	50,856	Beans, dry	17,756
6	Raw cane or beet sugar	43,199	Almonds, shelled	15,997
7	Chicken meat	32,518	Wine	15,996
8	Barley beer	24,511	Cashew nuts, in shell	15,781
9	Food preparations n.e.c.*	23,075	Cashew nuts, shelled	13,413
10	Soya bean oil	18,036	Cotton lint, ginned	13,213
11	Wine	17,560	Sunflower-seed oil, crude	12,353

SOURCE: FAOSTAT data, compiled by author on August 10, 2024.

*n.e.c = not elsewhere classified

In addition to absolute poverty, inequality levels in Mozambique are extremely high: the official calculation by the World Bank is an income GINI of .54, but this figure fails to capture the difficulty of life for people in the countryside, who, on top of low levels of income, do not have access to a functioning public system of health, education, insurance, infrastructure, or markets.[9] In spite of the overwhelming poverty, predictions for growth for Mozambique are always very optimistic. It is the thirty-fifth largest country in the world and seemingly "rich" in natural resources (minerals, natural gas, coal, and agricultural land), so the potential for extraction or development is high.

"THE PORTUGUESE WAY OF BEING IN THE WORLD": LABOR AND LUSOTROPICALISM

To say this another way, Mozambique is a rich country; it is the people who are poor (Castel-Branco 2014; Cunguara and Hanlon 2012). This is not an accident. From the late 1800s, Portuguese colonial leaders in Mozambique saw local residents not as individuals worthy of incorporation but as the labor that would enable them to profit from the land. The Portuguese argued that they were uniquely qualified to make this happen because their ability to understand and command local residents enabled them to extract the necessary labor. This was the essence of what has been called *Lusotropicalism*, an attitude said to characterize and connect Portuguese peoples and places across the globe.[10] In the 1950s Portugal's dictator, António Salazar, officially embraced the notion of Lusotropicalism. His foreign minister, Adriano Moreira, defined it as "the Portuguese way of being in the world" (Castelo 1999), produced through a long history of overseas exploration that generated multiculturalism, tolerance, flexibility, and "brotherliness." The African territories were thus a part of Portugal's "mythic identity" (Tomás 2016), one that suggested that the Portuguese were immune to racism, with a predisposition to live in harmony with other peoples and cultures, many of whom the Portuguese claimed to have "discovered" (Castelo 1999).

The academic father of Lusotropicalism, Brazilian sociologist Gilberto Freyre (1933, 1940), theorized that colonization in Brazil was distinct from all other colonial experiences (particularly those of the Spanish) because the Portuguese embraced (metaphorically, and for Freyre, literally) other races, particularly African descendants and indigenous peoples. For Freyre, this mixing was based in an ethic he labeled "adventurism" (*aventurismo*), or the love of brash and courageous adventure (see Ribeiro 2006). He argued that adaptability, mobility, and miscegenation were foundational to the Portuguese character (Freyre 1933: 9). Freyre was invited to visit Portugal's overseas possessions in the period immediately following the Second World War, and he accordingly extended this notion from Brazil to the wider territory, particularly Africa. As Cláudia Castelo (1999) writes, "Lusotropicalism penetrated the national Portuguese imaginary thanks to the propaganda of the Estado Novo (the New State, established in 1933) and to its acceptance by an overwhelming majority of the Portuguese elite (from the right and left). This process was facilitated because the image reproduced of the

Portuguese—flexible, tolerant, brotherly—had very old roots. Since at least the last quarter of the 19th century, in the media and in the political debate in Portugal, the idea circulated that the Portuguese had a special vocation to lead other people. Gilberto Freyre gave this conviction scientific authority" (28).[11]

The particular adaptability of the Portuguese, Freyre argued, stemmed from the fact that they were Christians before they were white or European. He defended the idea that language was a key element of connection of "brotherly love" of the Portuguese in the colonies. Local inhabitants who were not Christians and did not speak Portuguese could be governed but not included (1953). Lusotropicalism was a self-serving argument that drew on the experiences and ideologies of discovery to justify extraction. The Portuguese needed resources from the territories they had discovered, and they argued that their ability to get the native to work would generate those resources.

I elaborate on this argument in chapter 4 with a focus on manioc, a crop that played an outsized but under-appreciated role in the history of colonial and postcolonial Mozambique. In their search for tropical export commodities throughout the twentieth century, the Portuguese neglected manioc, seeing it as a "native" crop, one whose properties they argued mirrored the nature of local residents themselves: fast propagating with little technical sophistication, widespread, and lacking in (nutritional or economic) value. Manioc was problematic because it could be planted among the trees and left in the ground for months after ripening, making it difficult to count and facilitating itinerant livelihoods beyond the reach of the state, but it was also essential to providing sustenance for plantation workers. Ultimately, the history of manioc in Mozambique is a story of naturalizing and neglecting local crops and people in an attempt to bend both to the service of tropical commodities for the global market. The true nature of Portuguese rule was not in their lofty invocation of multi-racialism and tolerance, just as the true nature of the Mozambican state is not in its many proclamations, nor in the dizzying array of multi-year plans and programs. Rather, it is in the technologies, laborers, lands, markets, crops, and infrastructures built around plantation projects that one sees the true nature of twentieth-century colonial and postcolonial rule.

A POLITICAL ECONOMY OF DISCOVERY + EXTRACTION = THE PLANTATION IDEAL

The political economy of discovery was fueled in part by a need for the rapid extraction of resources—a need that plantations were designed to meet.

Plantations, defined here as monocrop natural resource entities producing at scale for an external market, are not meant to sustain local populations; rather, they take value from one place and send it to another. Although this book is situated in Mozambique and my own research is located primarily there and in Brazil, I think it is fair to say that where plantations dominate a landscape and economy, the land is degraded and the people are poor. In most countries, if there is a "plantation region," it is the poorest region, from Northeast Brazil (Schwartz 1986; Wolford 2010) to the US South (Woods 1998) and the oil palm fields of Indonesia (Li 2018; Li and Semedi 2021).

There is already a substantial literature on plantations (see in particular foundational pieces by James 1963; Beckford 1977; Stoler 1985; Schwartz 1986; Curtin 1990; Bernstein et al. 1993).[12] I contribute to this work by explaining how plantations operate as subjects of development and desire rather than simply or even primarily as productive entities with a clearly defined material footprint (Chao et al. 2023). Framing the plantation in this way allows me to go beyond any specific plantation as a case study to plantations as windows onto the broader landscape of international, multi-species extraction (Chao 2022b; Kenney-Lazar and Ishikawa 2019; Baird and Barney 2017). A focus on plantations highlights connections across time (through both colonial and postcolonial rule), through different economic systems (feudal, mercantilist, capitalist, and socialist) and space (a Portuguese sphere of influence and "South-South" connections between Brazil and Mozambique, centered around the plantation, patronage societies, and inequality). Part of the appeal of plantations for governments, landowners, and investors is their semi-permanence: they can be counted and held accountable, season after season. They are physically visible and formally legible entities that can be reliably assessed and taxed. If large enough or embedded in and productive of a plantation society (Beckford 1972), upstream and downstream markets can develop around them to both supply inputs and household goods for the workers and to process the raw materials and utilize them in the production of higher value goods.

From the 1500s, plantations were a mechanism of claiming land and accessing resources along a broad frontier within and between new territories and Europe, generating vast waves of dispossession, landlessness, ecological devastation, and migration.[13] Plantation production often involved the violent redirection of land away from smallholders, indigenous peoples, and those who would make a living from it through gathering, commoning, hunting, and more. Land meant much more to people than simply production, and the rise of the plantation accompanied a reduction in the variety of ways of living on the land (see Watts [1983] 2013; Hall 2013). Plantations served as "landscapes of empire, governed by processes of colonial consumption, production and expansion" (Besky 2014: 3; see also Behal 2014). They were a critical engine of primitive accumulation (see Perelman 2000; Schwartz 1986), providing resources that would fuel manufacturing in Europe and beyond. Plantations were a product of the desire for territorial expansion and accumulation, and in turn, they fed that desire (see Elden 2010).

In Brazil, where I have worked on former sugarcane plantations, landed estates were (and still are) status symbols, with the elegant Casa Grande (Big House) at the center of an elite social, economic, and cultural system.[14] Enslaved persons or workers were grouped into close-knit quarters to make supervision and discipline easier. As part of a plantation "community," workers (or their wives and children; see Stolcke 1988) might have access to small garden plots for their subsistence (Carney 2020) or job security, or to a house, as Sarah Besky (2017) illustrates for tea plantations in India. All of these resources served to tie labor to the plantation even when low wages or brutal working conditions might otherwise have motivated people to leave. Plantations often produced contingent "towns" or "communities"—placing labor and services nearby in settlements that were the seeds of today's towns and cities (Sigaud 1979).

The articulation between imperialism and plantations means that plantation economics and economies have always been racialized, with black and brown bodies tied to or ejected from the land through various mechanisms of compulsion or coercion (Cooper 1982). Plantations are "race-making" (Petitcorps et al. 2023; Bastos 2018; Aikens et al. 2019), place-making (Li 2023; McKittrick 2013), and nation-making (Marchesi 2016) projects. The effects of plantations "reverberate" (Navaro et al. 2021: 2; see also Desmond 2019), their "afterlives" (Thomas 2023) shaping the outlines of what is possible to imagine on the land and for laboring bodies. As Katherine McKittrick puts it, "The plantation spatializes early conceptions of urban life within the context of a racial economy" (2013: 8). Labor was fixed to plantations through enslavement, labor quotas, taxes, and debt arrangements; in many places, plantations "produced a new hierarchy of humanity" (Thomas 2016: 180), defining personhood (Allewaert 2013) as those who were "civilized" along racial and ethnic lines (Quijano 2000; McKittrick 2011; King 2016).

The spread of plantations from the 1500s onward benefited from and fueled an interconnected world market. Whole territories were connected to this market primarily as producers of raw materials. As Sylvia Wynter put it, "The plantation-societies of the Caribbean came into being as adjunct to the product, to the single crop commodity—the sugar cane—which they produce" (1971: 95). The commodification and long-distance trade in "sweetness" tied the Lusotropical world together through the supply of enslaved persons from East and West Africa to sugarcane plantations in Brazil (Paquette 2013). Because of their size, connection to the global market, strong-arm oversight, and deployment of modern production techniques, plantations are often seen as highly productive. Sidney Mintz (1986) argued that the first factories in industrial England were modeled after sugarcane plantations and mills in colonial Brazil. The development of the "industrial plantation' in the late 1800s and early 1900s represented a "worldwide shift towards agribusiness" (Stoler 1985: 17, cited in Brass and Bernstein 1992), organized and integrated into the global market (see Daniel et al. 1992). Today, new plantations are a critical mechanism of resource control on new commodity frontiers, from palm oil to eucalyptus and soybeans (Kröger 2012; Rasmussen and Lund 2018; Hetherington 2020).

But visions of plantations as efficient, rational entities or organizations are at odds with the reality: plantations are often not profitable, instead generating "persistent poverty" (Beckford 1972) and wreaking devastation on local ecologies and human life while ensuring their continued existence through political and cultural connections (Stein 1986; Grandin 2009; Li and Semedi 2021; Chao 2022a; Krupa 2022; Mitmann 2023). Under colonial rule around the world, the neatly ordered rows of plantation production could often only be maintained with strict labor control (Henriksen 1975); colonization was as much an attempt to provide that labor as it was to extend territorial control. Ann Stoler (1985) emphasized the violence of plantation life as governance over plantation areas in colonial Indonesia was contested, both within the planter class and against it. Plantation elites aspired to strict labor control, but even with a reliance on the legal apparatus of enslavement until the mid-1800s, they rarely accomplished this goal in full, and workers resisted plantation dominance by rebelling (James 1963), engaging in small acts of resistance (Isaacman 1996), organizing for greater access to land or other benefits (Medeiros 1989), and escaping (Bledsoe 2018).

Plantations have been so formative over the last five hundred years that I have elsewhere referred to the modern era as the *plantationocene* (Wolford 2021a; Chao et al. 2023). The concept of the plantationocene (Haraway 2015) emerged from conversations about the anthropocene (Haraway et al. 2016; Tsing et al. 2019; Stock 2023) and the capitalocene (Vergès 2017; Moore 2017, 2018), which locate the defining dynamic of the modern era— since the 1500s—in the human impact on the planet (Latour et al. 2018) and the development of capitalism, respectively. The plantationocene is a provocation: it is the argument that the dynamics decribed previously—from conquest to enslavement, commodification, and control—were fundamental to the contemporary global order. This argument has generated criticism, as scholars have argued that imposing a Eurocentric frame over "modernity" marginalizes alternative cosmologies and subordinated groups (Besky 2022; Curley and Smith 2023; Chari 2023), downplays race and racial violence in problematic ways (Davis et al. 2019; Aikens et al. 2019), and ignores previous Black feminist writing on plantations (Jegathesan 2021). These critiques all have merit, but the concept helps to explain what I saw in Mozambique: the "(il)logic of human mastery, discipline, and control in and through which particular plants and particular people are rendered productive, exploitable, or disposable under plantation regimes" (Chao 2022b: 167). Plantations look different in different time periods and places, and those differences are the point: what many scholars are calling "agrarian extractivism" (McKay and Veltmeyer 2021; Chagnon et al. 2022; Veltmeyer and Ezquerro-Cañete 2023) spans the history and geography of feudalism, capitalism, and socialism. Plantations have laid down the conditions for their own survival; the past "sculpts the future," as Mitchell (2021: 150, cited in Mason and Riding 2023) says, producing landscapes that come back over and over again because they have colonized the imagination (Mason and Riding 2023).

In recent years, plantations have made a resurgence around the world: "Plantations are back," says Tania Li (2018), referring to what has come to be called the global land grab (White et al. 2012; Borras et al. 2011). The zombie-like return (Thomas 2023; Kay et al. 2023) of large-scale land acquisitions (LSLAs; Deininger and Byerlee 2011) accompanied multiple crises in the 2000s, including the global recession and the world food crisis of 2007–2008 that prompted panicked declarations of the need to "double food production by 2050" (McMichael 2012, 2014).[15] Climate change and environmental degradation articulated with fears of growing global population, and investors—from hedge funds to national governments—sought access to land for "flex crops" that could satisfy food and fuel needs alike (Borras and Franco 2012; Sassen 2013; Borras et al. 2016). In the wake of these apparent market, demographic, and ecological crises, land became a coveted asset. With new financial tools providing greater access to land, brokers promised returns of 25 percent or more (Fairbairn 2021). Much of this new interest in land was initially believed to be in Africa, which multi-lateral agencies like the World Bank described as having idle land characterized by "high yield gaps," where significant returns could be made by introducing intensive techniques and technologies (Arezki et al. 2011; Deininger and Byerlee 2011; Cotula et al. 2011). Public and private investors rushed to acquire "unproductive," "idle," or "waste" land (where each is defined as not producing commodities or not using input-intensive techniques), organizing new ventures as large-scale entities or as aggregations of smaller-scale units through contracts, as in out-grower and sharecropping schemes (Chung 2019, 2023; Baka 2017; Feldman and Geisler 2012; Makki 2013).

Although LSLA numbers are difficult to determine with accuracy (Edelman 2013; Scoones et al. 2013), concentration in landownership increased after 2000 (Lowder et al. 2016; see also Lowder et al. 2021). Careful analysis of incomplete data suggests that the largest 1 percent of farms now operates roughly 70 percent of the world's farmland (Lowder et al. 2021: 4). As mentioned previously, activists named this increased investment in land a global land grab (GRAIN 2008; see Borras et al. 2011; Wolford et al. 2014), and local, national, and global coalitions of peasant groups organized to protest against the terms of their incorporation into the investment projects as well as the large-scale capture of their land (Hall et al. 2015). It wasn't always the investment they objected to; rather, it was that the investment was going where it always had—into the land and exports, rather than into people or places (Ali and Stevano 2022). Laura German quotes a representative of an eastern African farmers' association who spoke at the World Bank's Land and Poverty Conference in 2015: "We do not need people to invest in our land, we need them to invest in us" (2022: 1). Many ambitious projects that epitomized the land rush failed to generate returns, whether because of local protests, a miscalculation of local conditions, or land tenure disputes (see Gill 2016; Baird 2020; Chung 2023).

The global land grab demonstrates the resilience of what I call the plantation ideal; underpinning the rush for land and the warm embrace of investors is the belief in the promise of plantations. In Mozambique, the plantation ideal plays out like this (see figure 1): a given plantation proposal or mega-project begins with a fantastical analysis (optimistic, spectacular, urgent) of what is possible to achieve with the application of external science or funding to local land and labor with the goal of producing products of one kind or another for external interests/audiences (whether markets, research agencies, or donors).

These ambitious projects function as "showcases" that advertise Mozambique as open for foreign investment (Buur and Monjane 2016: 200). Politicians and allies (donors and multi-lateral agency officials) see these projects as attractive in part because they will provide fast results, "something to show within two or at most three years" (Smart and Hanlon 2014: 7), which they do not believe the local population is otherwise capable of. The desire for fast results means that those in elite positions privilege the extraction of raw, unprocessed materials for the external (global) market. As the economist

Ways of Seeing the World
Knowledge, Imagination, Aspirations

Feudal land/labor relations

Rule by elite minority

Relative resource poverty and backwardness

Demographic scarcity concerns

Territorial aspirations

Interests/opportunity of global market

New technologies for exploration and rule

Political economy of discovery → Extraction → Plantation ideal

Rule by elite minority

Foreign science and scientists

Tropical commodities

Global market

Ignore land management (separation between research and extension)

Forced labor

Fix people (labor) in place

Land open for investment

Ways of Organizing the World
Rules, Institutions, Incentives, Norms

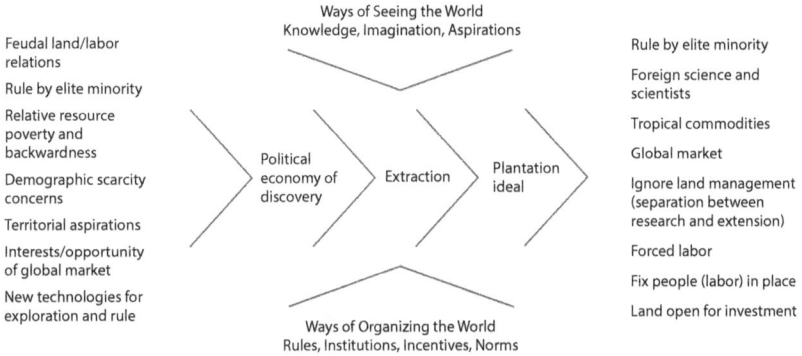

FIGURE 1.   Co-production of discovery, extraction, and the plantation ideal.
SOURCE: Created by author.

Castel-Branco (2022) writes, foreign direct investment in Mozambique is "concentrated in the extractive economy . . . minerals, energy and agricultural primary commodities for export, and the services and infrastructures that are directly associated with it, such as roads, pipelines, logistic systems, construction, engineering, financial, accounting, transport and communications" (19). Scientific research, investment, and aid flow into these projects and facilitate extraction by developing new varieties and management techniques for appropriate crops. Due to the particular history of forced labor under twentieth-century Portuguese colonization in Mozambique, plantations historically and today take two main but distinct forms: they are present as large-scale, mono-crop ventures run by corporations (or public-private ventures) and as aggregated production schemes in which smallholders are incorporated into large-scale corporate projects through forced crop and tax payments (under colonial rule) or into "block schemes" through contracts, credit, inputs and other incentives (under independent rule) (see Pérez Niño 2016). All plantation projects rely on both land and labor being available for production (extraction) and social reproduction (maintenance of the labor force).

Underneath the frenzy of boardroom meetings, spending money, clearing land, and experimenting with new crops, it is local communities and people who do the work. During colonial rule, an infrastructure of extraction (regulations, guards, taxes and tax collectors, local officials) tied local residents to plantations through force, although the appropriation of the best land for plantations and near-total failure to invest in other forms of rural development pushed many people to migrate to the mines in South

Africa or farming estates in Rhodesia. Today, scientific research is geared toward developing new varieties, the government is devising new land laws that privilege private investors, and community development projects provide subsistence resources to help rural inhabitants stay in place. Local residents engage in plantation projects willingly, for the most part, because they offer some potential for access to markets and social goods like education and running water. Participants need to be "animated" and "motivated" but not overly needy, because in the newly neoliberal context of twenty-first-century Mozambique, rural residents are expected to be self-reliant; asking for additional help is now framed as corruption or laziness, building on old, racialized tropes of native incapacity. High rates of rural poverty, small farm sizes, and the relative lack of farm machinery in use throughout the country are read as an opportunity—the possibility of plantations or projects like ProSavana to be transformational—rather than as an indictment of their historic and ongoing failure. And for as long as the people in power have plantations in their sights, longer-term and people-focused development goals—like schools, internal markets, health care, skill building, and the cultivation of vibrant small-scale farm communities—take a back seat. As with other forms of power, the plantation ideal is only sometimes directly asserted (as it was with the design of ProSavana). More often, it is the unspoken assumption about the best way to organize resources and rural production. In Mozambique, it is common to hear government officials, investors, and donors prioritize the plantation as a mechanism for achieving development goals or extractive profits quickly, but rural residents will also talk about the benefits of large-scale commodity production, in part because there are so few viable alternatives. This is how the plantation ideal "works" (or doesn't work, as Smart and Hanlon 2014 emphasize) in Mozambique.

TRUE IN EVERY COUNTRY: PLANTATION SCIENCE

Plantation production has been accompanied and facilitated by the development of agricultural science, research, and extension. For almost five hundred years, scientific experts have circulated alongside plantation commodities (Bray et al. 2023), finding new crops for the market as well as cures for the pests and diseases that originate in unnaturally crowded conditions (Paredes 2021; Boyd and Watts 1997; Mitmann 2017). Agricultural science came together in the 1900s with development policies that built on the assumption that concentrating land and intensifying agricultural production for internal and external markets would release underemployed labor from the countryside, lower industrial wages, and provide needed inputs for manufacturing

(Lewis 1954; Staatz and Eicher 1998; Latham 1984). Infrastructure from roads to railway networks would support the flow of commodities from field to factory and port (Li 2007). Water would be dammed (Sneddon 2015; Teisch 2011; Biggs 2008) and irrigation channels built (Pritchard 2012) to slake thirsty, input-intensive "factories in the field" (Fitzgerald 2005). Markets for basic resources such as land (Walker 2008) and water (Goldman 2005) were brought under the thumb of "rational" land governance, planning, and distribution (German 2022; Feldman and Geisler 2012), generating extractive socio-natural regimes from petrocapitalism (Watts 2004) and carbon democracy (Mitchell 2011) to hydroimperialism and hydrocapitalism (Pritchard 2012). The application of modern, Western science to the organization of life (land, nature, labor) generated significant advances in productivity, but the tools of Western science and technology and colonial and postcolonial experts have simplified, criminalized, and marginalized local ways of living on the land and with nature (Adas 1989). In recent years, corridors and export zone projects have created spaces of exception and sacrifice, providing assurances of "law and order," clear property rights, favorable trade rules, and more to interest global capital (Kirshner and Baptista 2023; Gonçalves 2020; Shankland and Gonçalves 2016).

In this book, I draw on and detail what I call *twentieth-century plantation science*: an assemblage of approaches, techniques, technologies, and ways of seeing the world that facilitate (and even necessitate) plantation production. The individual components of the assemblage may be used in other methods of production, but when combined they constitute a very particular relationship with the land, markets, labor, and ecological life. (In the same way that a skyscraper might be constructed with the same materials as a small, single-family house, but the two structures serve a fundamentally different purpose.) The concept of co-production is useful to clarify the contingent and highly context-specific ways in which "contemporary societies build agricultural systems through processes of knowledge making and material work" (Iles et al. 2016: 947; see Jasanoff 2004). Ultimately, the way we know the world is an active part of the construction of that world and the way we live in it.

Plantation science is both an effect and a manifestation of the political economy of discovery I described earlier. Plantation science is fundamentally an extractive business; land, labor, knowledge, and money are treated as commodified inputs utilized to maximize return. It is theoretically and historically of necessity an external science in Mozambique, because the approaches for coaxing such production and profit from the land all originated elsewhere, and so a side effect of plantation science in Mozambique is that valuable cropland is dedicated to commodities that are not native and not intended to enrich local economies or communities. Plantation science focuses on commodity improvement and varietals, making them conform to new places better and to resist the disease risk inherent in transplantation to different climates and to mono-crop production with the risk of wholesale wipeout from disease or natural disaster.

I situate plantation science within my analysis of the twentieth-century political economy of discovery, but here it is scientists who seek new discoveries, with prestige and profit accruing to the individual who can modify a variety in a way that expands productivity. Plantation science requires land consolidation because crops need to be grown at scale in order to be profitable. As the size of plantations has grown, science has narrowed its focus, moving from the farm scale to the nano scale. Such specialized research now starts primarily in the halls of industry and science rather than on farmers' fields. Innovations reach farmers through technology transfers, field days, company credit lines for input bundles and production specifications or requirements, and seed companies. New varieties arrive at the farmer's doorstep with a generic set of recommendations for cultivation, usually derived from relatively ideal laboratory or field station conditions. In chapter 2 I develop this analysis of plantation science, arguing that Portuguese colonialism in the twentieth century begat a specific set of scientific goals, geared toward developing plantations. The nature of colonial rule shifted over the course of the century, but throughout, the strategy was the same: foreigners would provide the scientific knowledge and capital that would make Mozambique's land flower, and the Portuguese would provide a disciplined local labor force. State-led scientific efforts were focused on tropical commodities deemed lucrative for export. This extractive logic was both grounded in and productive of broader global inequalities, market imperatives, and racial hierarchies. By the mid-twentieth century, one commodity—cotton—led agricultural production and dominated research efforts. In chapter 3 I show how agricultural research has been stymied by a persistent set of plantation-focused assumptions long after colonial rule ended. In the 2010s, when I was in the country, researchers competed internationally for funding, and so the political economy of international agricultural research shaped local methods, outputs, and audience. Funding was short term (three to five years), competitive, and prioritized scientific innovation over on-farm adoption. Research calls released by multi-lateral funding agencies were often hosted in one country and assumed that new technologies could be relatively easily applied across a set of others. All of this contributed to a body of agricultural research in Mozambique that

I argue represented the continuation of colonial plantation science: fragmented, opportunistic, extractive, and partial.

The dissemination and dominance of Western science in international agriculture efforts shaped the Green Revolution, in which Western scientists developed high yielding plant varieties (HYVs), particularly wheat and rice, for regions considered food insecure (Eddens 2024). Ostensibly motivated by concerns of famine in Mexico and India, the Green Revolution was also a geopolitical project in which science served as the handmaiden of the West in an increasingly heated Cold War (Perkins 1997). A rich literature documents the influence of Western training and assumptions in agricultural sciences and the marginalization of local knowledges (Gupta 2003), particularly with the development of new crop varieties that supplanted traditional ones (Bezner Kerr 2013). Plant breeding has often served as the linchpin of extraction, creating technoscientific organisms (Saraiva 2016b) that link land and labor to external markets, often generating inequality in societies where farmers have unequal access to seeds, labor, and inputs (Griffin 1979). As the "most fundamental agricultural input" (Kloppenburg 1988: 4), redesigning seeds is an inherently political project (Fischer et al. 2022; Scott 2017; Perkins 1997). The fear that Western plant breeding will push out local foods, customs, and relations is heated today, with the Doubly Green Revolution and the Alliance for a Green Revolution in Africa (AGRA) (Gengenbach et al. 2018; Schurman 2017). This concern is exacerbated by the relationship between breeding new varieties and bioprospecting for indigenous genes (Hayden 2003a, 2003b).

Because new varieties so often come from far away, introducing exogenous species into local production takes the form of what is referred to in agricultural economics as *technology transfers* (e.g., Ryan and Gross 1943; Ruttan 1960; Hayami and Ruttan 1971; Rogers 1983). The diffusion of technology from one region or group to another was and still is seen as key to unlocking the mysterious links between investment, labor, and profit (Hirschman 1958; Gerschenkron 1962; Schumacher 1973; Sachs 2005; for a critique, see Headrick 1988). Underlying the notion of technology transfer is a belief that knowledge can be produced in one place and applied to another because there are universal principles that are "true in every country" (Mitchell 2002: 54) regardless of local conditions or context (Anderson 2006). Western knowledge is seen as necessary to teach indigenous or local residents how to steward their environmental resources better. And yet, as the term *valley of death* (the airless region between innovation and adoption) suggests, transfer as a one-way process is both difficult and contested. There is often a performative element (Ramisch 2011) to the invocation of participation in the provision of scientific advice or education to rural communities (Welker 2012; Flachs and Richards 2018; Flachs 2017).

In Mozambique, discourses and practices of technology transfer dominate agricultural research because the science and the crops all originate elsewhere. Agricultural principles and technologies are produced in one place (foreign-owned laboratories, regional—e.g., pan-Africa—research agencies, government offices, multi-lateral boardrooms) and rolled out in rural communities or landscapes (Henke 2008). A key method of preparing the ground for such techno-fixes is fixing rural populations in place, which as Sarah Besky (2014) puts it, was a European "posture" toward land both inside and outside the plantation. I explore the relationship between technology transfer, rural development, and "fixity" in chapter 5, focusing on extension agents and community members in northeastern Mozambique. I argue that in the context of the plantation ideal, the support provided by hard-working extension agents and international NGOs largely succeeded in keeping rural residents in their places—both literally (ending swidden agriculture and tying them to plantation agriculture through contracts or outgrower schemes) and figuratively (enabling them to survive but not thrive).

WAYS OF SEEING THE WORLD: THE PLANTATION IDEAL AND THE IMAGINATION

Underlying these scientific principles and technologies are imaginaries (Drayton 2000; Brockway 1979) that legitimate and (re)produce particular land use practices (Robbins 2001a; Kull 2004; Carse 2012; Lu et al. 2013; Pritchard et al. 2016; Mason and Riding 2023). The plantation ideal rests on a handful of seemingly objective and scientific approaches that appear self-evident: large-scale farming is superior to small scale, and the global market for commodities is more reliable than local markets (see German 2022: 13). From Henry Ford's visions of orderly industrial rubber plantations in the Amazon (Grandin 2009) to concepts of biodiversity as pristine nature (Lowe 2006), imagination is key to the struggle over control of land (Slater 2001; Sundberg 2003). Pseudo-scientific concepts such as wilderness (Cronon 1996) and the "wild" (Whatmore 2002)—or their counterpart "invasives" (Robbins 2001b)—have worked similarly to imagine and organize entire landscapes. These ecological imaginaries (Peet and Watts 1996; Wolford 2004) are highly simplified representations of reality that draw on dualistic tropes of advanced and primitive (Ofstehage 2018; Bassett and Zuéli 2000; Fairhead and Leach 1996). They are also internalized in ways that become "common sense" (Crehan 2016; Wolford 2010) because they reflect the way people think about the distribution of resources—a moral economy of what is proper use established by plantation histories, norms, and requirements (see Thompson 1971; Curley 2019; Gorman 2014; Wolford 2005). Interrogating the plantation ideal is therefore to question the very foundations of knowledge and begets new ways of imagining life on the land and possibilities for rural development (see Quijano 2000).

In Mozambique, plantations have haunted as much as occupied the landscape, reappearing regularly as the solution to "underdevelopment" and poverty despite the ongoing failure of existing plantations to provide the returns envisioned. The ways in which government leaders and policymakers, investors, multi-lateral aid agencies, scientists, and donors have idealized plantations explain why ProSavana, the project discussed in the introduction, made sense. Imagining the territory of Mozambique as a blank slate to be fashioned by science and capital generated similarities in the agricultural research produced under the Portuguese and in ProSavana. Mozambican officials offered up the country's land and labor as they had done for over one hundred years. Politicians, scientists, investors, and aid workers imagined the possibilities for rural areas as tied to the ability to successfully introduce plantation production, orienting local residents, commodity markets, land leases, and rules around the as yet aspirational plantation.

Abstraction and equivalences populated the rhetoric around ProSavana.[16] The program architects justified the transfer of science and technology from Brazil to Mozambique by invoking universal principles of agronomic science and prehistoric geology. As the World Bank said, "Brazilian technology is easily adaptable to those parts of Africa that share similar geological and climatic conditions" (World Bank 2011: 47). Official proclamations from politicians in Brazil and Japan justified their collaboration in Mozambique on the grounds that the two countries had worked together to create the "miracle" of the Brazilian center west, turning unfavorable ecological and economic conditions into yellow gold (soybeans).[17] Vast areas of Mozambique were characterized as essentially equivalent to the center-west of Brazil, where large-scale soybean, sugar, and cotton production dominated (Shankland and Gonçalves 2016). For Japan, as Derek Hall (2020a, 2020b) argues, building grain production in Mozambique supported practical and ideological goals of ensuring Japanese grain sufficiency, but for Brazil, the goal was both more narrow and more ambitious: to develop new cultivars that could adapt to the ecology of Mozambique and propel an agricultural transformation. Thus, modernizing agricultural production in Mozambique would confer geopolitical legitimacy on Brazil as a global superpower and generate revenue through the sale of new technologies from tractors to seeds.

Discourses of expertise and universality served to make the partnership between Brazil and Mozambique seem "natural," ironically fostering a sort of intentional ignorance about actual specificities in Mozambique. As I show in chapter 6, Brazilian scientists thought they knew what Mozambique needed, bringing Brazilian plant varieties and farm management techniques with them. Not surprisingly, they were unsettled by what they found, and the World Bank identified "knowledge gaps" as the main challenge to a successful Brazilian presence in Africa: "Most Brazilian individuals and companies—including many small and medium enterprises—have limited and often outdated information on Africa" (World Bank 2011: 100). Embedding Embrapa scientists in Mozambique as part of ProSavana was intended to correct this ignorance, but Brazilians saw their immersion as a mandate to teach rather than an opportunity to learn. To understand the role of plantations as mechanisms of extraction, therefore, one needs to examine the production of the knowledge they depend on.

RESEARCHING AN IDEAL: METHODS FOR "A WAY OF SEEING THE WORLD"

The research in this book comes from a mixture of archival and qualitative methods, all required to understand the dynamics of the plantation ideal in Mozambique. The historical arc of the narrative is both substance and method—what Phil McMichael (2000) calls incorporated comparison. Understanding the differences across the twentieth-century colonial and postcolonial contexts sheds light on the similarities—namely, the importance of plantations in the two. Both the first decades of the twentieth century and the period in which ProSavana was implemented were characterized by global commodity crises and a need for raw materials that motivated first-world scrambles for land and resources in Africa. At the same time, both the Portuguese state of the early twentieth century and the Mozambican state of the early twenty-first can be described as institutionally weak and dependent on external funds to govern the territory (Pitcher 2002). In the face of global demand for raw materials, both governments viewed the land in Mozambique as one of the country's great, unused assets, whereby massive external investment could rapidly transform the land and country into a fertile producer of raw materials for the lucrative export market (Bowen 2000; Cunguara and Hanlon 2012).

The argument that history is important sits slightly uneasily in the context of a country that is relatively silent on its own colonial history, a reticence that has facilitated the persistence of plantation politics. Independent

Mozambique's first president, Samora Machel, referenced colonization and the war for independence regularly in his speeches. Since his death in 1986, though, national politics has been forward looking and dominated by calls for unity. In fact, most academic attention has focused on recent history in Mozambique (Pitcher 1998: 119), examining socialism (O'Laughlin 2000; Tarp et al. 2002; Young 1988; Wuyts 2001) and privatization (Pitcher 2002), rather than colonial history and its effects. Considerable work has also been done on the effects of the civil war (Hanlon 1984), which have continued to be felt long after the formal end of hostilities in 1992.

Among the development organizations involved in supporting agriculture, this historical foreshortening is even more pronounced. A scoping report written in the early 1990s to assess aid and agriculture during the 1980s acknowledges the role of the civil war in weakening agriculture, but it barely mentions the effects of the preceding century of colonization (Adam et al. 1991: 87). In my conversations with a highly knowledgeable colleague from one of the largest NGOs in the country, we argued over whether agricultural production in the Nacala Corridor (where ProSavana would take place) was influenced by the civil war, which officially ended in 1992. He believed that because the project beneficiaries had all been born after the war ended, it didn't have any impact on the way they farmed (Interview 54, December 13, 2016). In one sense, he was right. He had worked in the region for years and knew the demographics of the communities there very well. Many of those people farming in the region in the 2010s were not alive during the war. But this is a very literal view of history as a linear sequence of events that can be measured across objectively quantifiable units—people, years, births, deaths, and so on. It is a common but shortsighted view of the past. History isn't just lived; it lives on in the way people think and live, and the way landscapes—from individual fields to entire socio-ecological regions—are organized. These do not end or change just because a treaty is signed or a new party is in power.

The research in this book attempts to get at this living and lived history. I incorporated a combination of methods (less "mixed methods" than a mixture of methods dictated by what was required to continue answering the questions each new interview generated). My own introduction to Mozambique is relatively recent. I have studied land relations in Brazil for a long time, but my first trip to Mozambique was in 2013, when I followed the Brazilian scientists sent to the country to work on ProSavana. My work in Brazil has been largely ethnographic; going to Mozambique, where I spoke only the official language, the language of the old colonial power, I had to adapt my methods. I spent considerable time in the archives, conducted interviews in Portuguese, and worked with translators in rural areas where local languages dominated. I stood out quite visibly as not-Mozambican (as opposed to working in Brazil, where people often thought I was Brazilian, even after I opened my mouth), and that made it possible for me to access high-ranking government officials, aid workers, and research scientists, but also made it harder for me to see into the more intimate spaces of everyday life.

In 2014 I spent several weeks in Nampula province, in the northern region of the country, with two students, Amanda Hickey and Katherine Young. Together we designed and conducted interactive research in five rural communities. We held focus group interviews, mapped community resources, and interviewed seventy-nine rural producers. In addition to doing this work, I interviewed several high-ranking government, development, and scientific representatives and attended trainings and meetings related to agriculture and development.

In 2015 I returned to Mozambique to film a documentary with the videographer James Monahan.[18] We spent a week in the northern village of Colocoto, interviewing community residents, visiting the areas they thought should be in the film, and putting together a story based on a day in the life of a farmer and fisher couple. This experience was a new one for me and provided fascinating insight into the way community members wanted their lives curated for distribution. I also interviewed many people working in agriculture again and attended a weeklong training on conservation agriculture in Nampula. At the same time, one of my PhD students, Ryan Nehring, spent the summer as a research assistant in Maputo, conducting interviews and gathering information in the local archives.

In 2016 I returned to Mozambique on a Fulbright Research Scholar fellowship for six months with my family. Based in Maputo and affiliated with the Observatório do Meio Rural (OMR, or Rural Observatory), I attended research and extension events in Nampula and Maputo and interviewed forty-eight employees of Mozambique's public agricultural research institution (the Agricultural Research Institute of Mozambique, IIAM) as well as another twenty-five extension agents in the public and private sectors. I also interviewed a dozen development workers in the main agencies around the country. A highlight of this time in Mozambique was a trip back to the communities where we had worked in 2014 and filmed the documentary in 2015. One of my most valuable sources of information is their patient, repeated descriptions of everyday life. I went with my family (my husband and children; see figure 2), and we showed the documentary in different communities, with the screenings followed by a Q&A with community members and then a focus group interview with key spokespeople for the community.

FIGURE 2.   Author with community members in Nampula, August 2016. Photo by John Lynch.

In Maputo, I reviewed archival documents related to the construction of the agricultural services in the twentieth century in the Historical Archive of Mozambique. The staff in the Historical Archive were extremely professional, considerate, and skilled, but the archive itself was in bad shape. Many vital records were missing—something I only fully appreciated when I moved to Portugal and visited the official imperial archives, which are in much better condition (an unsurprising but unfortunate feature of imperialism). The most comprehensive and well-maintained archives belonged to the former Royal Charter Companies, particularly the Mozambique Company. This is why most historical studies of Mozambique focus on these companies. I spent six months in Lisbon, working in a handful of different archives.[19] I tried to use sources corresponding to Portuguese rule in the twentieth century rather than company rule, but the latter is definitely a richer set of resources. I was affiliated with the Center for Africa Development Studies (CeSA) at the University of Lisbon.[20]

The actors in this book are colonial and postcolonial government officials, foreign and domestic scientists, extension agents, international aid workers, NGOs, community members, and activists. Where I cite individuals I interviewed directly, I include the interview number and date. Where I am citing conversations that took place during events open to a broad audience, such as farmer field days, extension trainings, or large workshops, I include direct quotes from my fieldnotes but do not provide interview numbers. When I spoke with community members in northeastern Mozambique, I was almost always with a group and working through translators. In these cases, I include direct quotes as they were translated to me but do not provide attribution to a particular individual. In these interviews and discussions, I was always with a larger group, whether researchers from Cornell or translators from the local community, and so, as I suggested before, this information is qualitative but not ethnographic in its detail. I did not see very far off the public stage. I draw on interviews with activists in the conclusion of the book, in addition to the essays written by scholars and activists that Natacha and I approached. For all of these, we use their given names because they are public figures and wanted their visions for the future documented.

CONCLUSION: ALTERNATIVES TO DEVELOPMENT

The final chapter steps away from the plantation to imagine alternatives. This chapter is cowritten with a Mozambican scholar-activist, Dr. Natacha Bruna. Natacha has worked with OMR for years. In 2016 OMR was run by economist João Mosca and well-regarded for conducting rigorous, evidence-based research on rural programs, often critiquing the government's performance. Together, Natacha and I asked academics and activists in Mozambique what they thought the right path forward was for Mozambique in this post-colonial, post-ProSavana period. We present their ideas in their own words because, true to the argument in this book, alternatives to the plantation need to be imagined and articulated from within. Chapter 7 thus highlights the voices of peasant activists, farmers, researchers, and others who have worked in Mozambique for positive change for years.

A central takeaway from the final chapter is that not only has development as a twentieth-century, postwar, and postcolonial modernization effort (what Gillian Hart 2001, 2002 calls big D Development; Watts 2003) *not* produced positive outcomes in Mozambique, but the way it is defined—as a quantity of things, such as GDP per capita, literacy, and life expectancy, all captured by numerical indicators—promotes extraction as the answer to that absence. The focus on "objective" characteristics that belong to individuals lends itself to the idea that development is a personal choice between options presented as dualisms—between developed and un-developed, primitive and modern, agricultural versus industrial, communal versus individual, subject versus citizen. With its origins in colonial offices and economic departments in the West, the false dichotomies of modernization thinking represent and rely on processes of alienation, wresting people from the means of production (the land, water, common resources, self-employment) and means of community or social reproduction (family, social group, networks) and moving them to various forms of wage labor, whether on large farms or garment factories, in the name of improvement (Paprocki 2021; Li 2007). Extraction in the form of the plantation ideal is an extreme form of alienation.

Alternatives for a more just future in Mozambique and elsewhere require moving away from objective indicators about individuals to understanding and building stronger *relationships*—relationships to one another and to the land, the state, the community, the market, and so on. Alternatives to development might focus on building trust, community, social networks, wages (which are a relationship to the market), public safety nets, participatory governance, and so on. This would move us away from the present focus on growth, maximization, and profit and instead emphasize intergenerational resilience and repair. The final chapter points us more in that direction, but the ideas these scholars present will require better relationships inside Mozambique and with the rest of the world.

2. "Now Is the Time for New Innovations"

A Political Economy of Discovery in Twentieth-Century Portuguese East Africa

> There were two earlier phases of innovation—sea travel and the industrial revolution—and the effects of those still reverberate. Now is the time for new innovations.
>
> GOVERNOR-GENERAL ALMIRANTE MANUEL MARIA SARMENTO RODRIGUES, 1962

Portugal was, by all accounts except its own, a much-weakened imperial power by the end of the nineteenth century. Small by European standards, with an internal economy dominated by agriculture and a small number of feudal estates, Portugal had distinguished itself primarily on the seas, building a network of maritime trading bases along the East and West Coasts of Africa and into the Indian Ocean that it defended with military force.[1] In an economy oriented toward discovery, rich and poor alike were attracted by overseas exploration, leaving little investment or labor for the development of internal agriculture or industry. When early profits from the spice trade began to decline, enslaved persons from Africa and gold and sugar from Brazil took their place, "[saving] Portuguese prosperity and [preserving] its structure almost intact" (Anderson 1962a: 94). Portugal maintained its network of trading posts along the western and eastern coasts of southern Africa and supplied enslaved labor to its Brazilian colony. The production of sugar and discoveries of gold funded the import of basic goods, and without industry of its own, Portugal became increasingly indebted to its more productive next-door neighbor, England. In 1703 Portugal signed the Methuen Treaty, trading exports of wine for imports of English cloth and creating an unfavorable exchange that put Portugal in a position of "permanent economic dependence" (94).

Lacking in sufficient military strength, the Portuguese Crown was unable to adequately defend itself when Napoleon Bonaparte invaded the country in 1807. Escorted by English ships, the Portuguese monarchy fled to Brazil, where it set up a temporary court (1807–21). The embarrassment of flight was made worse when the king's son, Pedro II, declared himself the new ruler of an independent Brazil in 1822. Portugal hoped for strong ties with its former colony, but the new Brazilian regime rebuffed these advances, instead looking to traffic directly with Angola, leaving Portugal out (Paquette 2013).[2] The loss of the Brazilian colony in 1822 led Portuguese politicians and commentators to argue that a "new Brazil" (Newitt 1995: 332) was needed in Africa because "Portugal's sole chance of extricating itself from its post-Brazilian doldrums was through renewed colonization efforts" (Paquette 2013: 330). Gabriel Paquette (2013) describes Deputy José António Ferreira Braklami imploring his fellow lawmakers in an 1826 speech in the National Assembly, "But without capital what can we do? Where can Portugal obtain what it needs? . . . Where? In Africa. Yes, *senhores*, in our African dominions, we can find the means and resources necessary to pursue our ends" (cited in Paquette 2013: 33). Thus, historian Malyn Newitt (1995) suggests that unique among the European colonizing nations in the period, "Portuguese expansion was a direct byproduct of Portugal's poverty, not its wealth" (14; Isaacman and Isaacman 1983).

Engaging more concretely in Africa required a change in focus, however, as the Portuguese had until that time only maintained a presence in trading sites along the coast, even locating its capital in East Africa on an island just off the coast (the Island of Mozambique; see Penvenne and Sheldon 1999). Only a small number of Portuguese who traveled to Mozambique after 1500 had gone inland, bartering for land from indigenous groups. The Portuguese who did settle in East Africa gained access to land by negotiating with local indigenous leaders and petitioning the Portuguese monarchy for tenure. These landholdings were known as *prazos*, renewable for "three lives" (inheritable through three generations) with the right to all labor within the jurisdiction. The Portuguese who held prazos (called *prazeiros*) understood them to be land grants justified by Roman law, but local residents saw these land claims as part of traditional chieftaincies that were gradually taken over by Portuguese leaders who had "gone native" (Newitt 1995: 217). Prazeiros acted like "powerful warlords with private armies" (217), illustrating the worst of colonial excess in their exploitative treatment of local labor and unproductivity. It is estimated that in the mid-1600s there were roughly eighty prazos in the interior of the territory called Mozambique (Sheldon and Penvenne 2025).

The Berlin-Congo Conference, held in 1884–85, marked a turning point for Portuguese rule in East Africa. Portugal's presence in Mozambique at that time was so weak that its claim was not initially recognized at the conference: the "Great Powers decreed that pacification and effective control were prerequisites for recognition as the colonial power" (Isaacman and Isaacman 1983: 21). International pressure forced Portugal to defend its claim to possessions in Africa by demonstrating "effective occupation."[3] The regime laid out its ambitions to unite its holdings on the coasts of East and West Africa in the Mapa Cor-de-Rosa (Rose-Colored Map), created in 1880 and presented at the Berlin-Congo Conference in 1885 (Newitt 1995: 334). Although the Portuguese did not achieve this cross-continental ambition, losing significant pieces of the area to the British, the emphasis on "effective occupation" at the conference pushed them to tighten their rule over and in their African territories (Isaacman and Isaacman 1983).[4]

Despite the commitment to developing East Africa, it took Portugal a number of years before it was able to contain local resistance. The Kingdom of Gaza was only defeated in 1897, and even then, Portugal lacked the resources to directly colonize the territory. Unlike Germany, Britain, and France, which sought new markets for capital investment in the colonies, the Portuguese needed their colonies to produce a surplus for investment back in the metropole (Newitt 1995: 392). In order to develop Mozambique, Portugal attempted to attract international capital to its African territories. As Robert Nunez Lyne, the British agronomist who served as the territory's second director of agriculture from 1910 to 1912, said, "The Portuguese tell you that they can conquer but cannot colonize, so Portuguese East Africa is being developed mainly by British capital" (Lyne 1913: 221). Amilcar Cabral, the agricultural engineer and pan-African revolutionary, argued that twentieth-century Portugal was not so much an imperial power in Africa as it was an "intermediary of imperialists" (Amilcar Cabral, quoted in Serra 2000).[5]

Colonial administrators in Lisbon awarded huge tracts of land through royal charter to private investors on the grounds that they would be more successful than the government in extracting profit from the land. The royal charter companies, such as the Mozambique, Nyassa, and Zambezia Companies, dominated large-scale land governance from the late 1800s to the mid-1900s (see map 1).

The companies were controversial in Portugal, where the press denounced them for their extractive approach to colonization and inability to satisfy Portugal's need for raw materials (Saraiva 2009: 49–50), but Portugal lacked the funds to invest itself at this time (Direito 2013). The companies were consistently undercapitalized, relying heavily on British and French funds (Isaacman and Isaacman 1983; Vail 1976), even though the availability of capital was one of the most important requirements for winning a

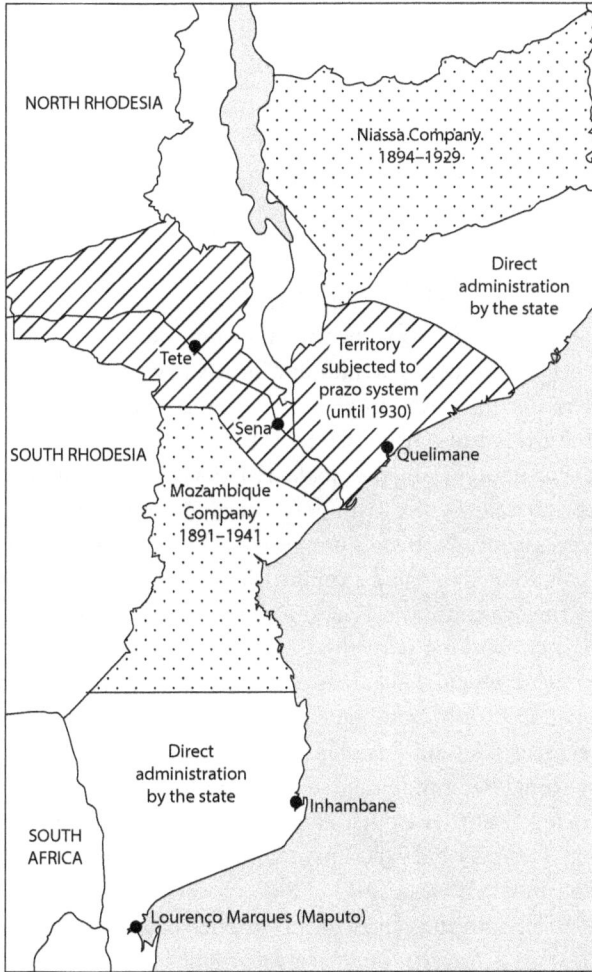

MAP 1. Territorial administration as of 1900.
SOURCE: Newitt (1995: 366), reprinted in Ribeiro Da Silva (2016: 119).

concession.[6] During discussions with the governor-general—in the territorial capital of Lourenço Marques, in the headquarters of the royal charter companies, or in Lisbon—one of the key considerations was to not "let land fall into the hands of people who don't have the necessary means to work it!"[7] In reality, however, decisions to award land often relied on social or political connections.[8] Because the Portuguese government lacked the resources to invest in the territory, much of the work was done by foreign capital and foreign scientists who, like the Portuguese themselves, were more interested in extraction than in investment, settlement, and internal development.

THE EARLY PROMISE OF PORTUGUESE RULE: A FOCUS ON DISCOVERY

Official agricultural policy in Portuguese Africa dates to the 1877 Regulamento de Agricultura (Regulation for agriculture). This dictum declared that agriculture would be the most important branch of the public services in Mozambique, as wealth and prosperity would flow from that sector back to Portugal. And in 1885 the national government created the Council of Agriculture (Grilo 1926: 247). This was reportedly "the first time that a [Portuguese] governor looked to this land with interest," but the council was originally staffed with only one agronomist. It would take several more years before Portugal's presence in Mozambique was established.[9] The royal governor nominated a commission to execute agricultural policy and further the agricultural services in the overseas colonies. He expected the commission, working with the Council of Agriculture, to appoint an agronomist who would have the responsibility of touring the "most important regions" of Mozambique to catalog the "flora, lands [terrenos], [natural] fertilizers, swamps, waters, crops and fauna" (Inso 1929: 6). The agronomist would determine the best location for an experimental station in which future scientists would plant the indigenous crops deemed most useful, breed livestock, and experiment with possible crops for development in the region (6–7). It wasn't until 1896, however—almost twenty years after the Regulamento and eleven years after the Council of Agriculture was established—that a forestry engineer was finally hired to travel through the colony and oversee the establishment of the agricultural services (Grilo 1926: 248). A new decree on November 9, 1899, emphasized the need for each district of the Overseas Provinces to have an agronomist, hired for two years, who would be tasked with determining the most profitable crops for each region and the methods necessary for their production. The agronomists were expected to provide supervision and advice for private farmers, both through consultation and by administering a demonstration garden and a nursery for new plants that farmers could use for experiments (253).

People who traveled to Mozambique in the early 1900s wrote official reports describing the crops that would do well in the territory. In 1901 the Portuguese agronomist Canto e Castro, who was employed on several different exploratory expeditions for the chartered private Mozambique

Company, wrote that agriculture had great potential in Mozambique but only if European farmers could be taught how to introduce non-native commodity crops in this new environment: "I have said before and I will say again that the only way to resolve the agricultural issues in this colony are to build experimental agriculture stations led by competent technicians who serve the company . . . which should have been done a long time ago, that is—to know the aptitude of this land." Colonists needed someone who would tell them what crops would do well and when to plant, particularly Portuguese farmers, who were often characterized as lacking in basic farming skills. As Canto e Castro said, "I stick my neck out to say that with Portuguese colonists . . . [building experiment stations] is not just advantageous but indispensable" (Canto e Castro 1901).

Another report for the Mozambique Company urged company leadership to do more to determine what crops would render the land profitable. Researchers were needed who could "scientifically study the plants that give many tropical colonies their riches." The unidentified author of the study warned that the limited research facilities already established in the territory were not capable of fostering real research, instead serving as little more than administrative outposts. "If you just create an agronomy department with bureaucratic purposes," the author of the report complained, "that will only add to the administrative work and not help production here one bit—I should know! I had to sit in such an office one day and they were not getting anything done that would help production" (Companhia de Moçambique 1902).

In 1902 the Mozambique Company established experimental stations in two different locations within its territory, Mambone and Chimoio (Newitt 1995: 402). That year, the agronomist F. Coulombier visited the experimental garden run by the Mozambique Company and provided the governor with an exhaustive accounting of the many "colonial crops" that were planted experimentally to see what might be suitable for "large-scale cultivation" (Coulombier 1903). Throughout the report, other colonies in South America and Asia were brought in as examples, both good and bad, of commodity producers that Mozambique should learn from. Coulombier, like other scientists at the time and in the present, used external examples as their referents, rather than local crops or conditions. Tropical commodities that did well in other countries all had one thing in common: the global market. Science would be called upon to smooth out local variations in soil, water, and weather. Brazil stood out as a model to be followed, particularly in its successful cultivation of sugarcane but also for interest in coffee and cotton. Cotton seeds from Brazil had already been tested in the territory, and it was an attractive crop for European farmers because it delivered a fast return. "The colonial farmers are generally very eager to make money and avoid cultures with a long wait," Coulombier wrote, concluding that "cotton meets the needs of farmers who have neither the time nor the means to wait" (21–22).

Even with early interest in establishing experimental gardens, research capacity in the colony was relatively primitive. Administrators with the Mozambique Company were concerned that colonists were not developing export agriculture production, instead using the small number of experimental gardens to produce corn for their subsistence and local markets (see Companhia de Moçambique 1902). Coulombier listed an array of possibilities for production but believed they would be hampered by the lack of research capacity and interest: "From the beginning, what we lack for the development of agriculture is examples. So and so may want to get into cultivation but doesn't have the slightest idea what to do to set up a farm, doesn't know where to get plows or animals. . . . It is the obligation of the company to create an installation that, on my advice, will be decisive for the attraction of capital" (37).

In order to better support Portuguese scientists who could advise on commodity crops in the African territories, the Portuguese government created the Colonial Garden of Lisbon in 1906. The mission of the Colonial Garden was to assist agriculture in the overseas territories by providing seeds, plants, and training. In connection with new courses on tropical agronomy at the Institute of Agronomy in Lisbon (which would become the Superior Institute of Agronomy in 1910), the colonial garden was expected to prepare an increasing number of agronomists and extension agents (técnicos) to work in the colonies, creating a link between the continental gardens, local experimental stations, and the global market, although this remained tenuous (Santos 1934).[10] After this promising start, retrospective analyses suggest that there weren't sufficient resources to fulfill the objectives of creating an effective link between the garden and the colonies, or for sending biological material either way.

That same year, 1906, the national government ordered the creation of the Department of Agriculture (referred to as Agricultural Services) in Mozambique. The decree creating the services echoed earlier proclamations of the primary importance of agriculture and its role in "exploiting new resources of flora and fauna, funding voyages and large estates [fazendas] that guarantee a full and enduring supply for our commerce, offering at the same time [opportunities for] emigration and investment . . . creating richness and sufficient activity to guarantee vast and profitable markets for the growing production of the continent."[11] Two years later, Governor-General Freire de Andrade (who held the role between October 1906 and November

1910) established the Department of Agriculture in Mozambique, which would consolidate all of the formerly independent government services related to agriculture and be staffed with a director, a subdirector, and a secretary.[12] The department divided its work into four districts that covered the full extent of Mozambique, from Sul do Save in the South to Niassa in the North. Most of the staff, however, resided in the southernmost district of Sul do Save, in the headquarters office in Lourenço Marques (the capital of the territory, now called Maputo). The South was the only area that Portugal effectively ruled at that time: the other subdepartments were highly aspirational, as were the two additional smaller posts created in Ribáuè and Mogovolas. The governor-general charged the new department with creating and overseeing four experimental stations, but these would also not be established for many years.[13] In the meantime, each district was expected to put on an annual exposition that would highlight new varieties and demonstrate the most effective technologies for planting.

To inaugurate the new department, Portuguese officials turned to foreign experts. The royal government provided the funds for a team of experts to tour the East African territory and make recommendations about its further development. Governor-General Freire de Andrade was tasked with organizing the scientific mission and "fostering agriculture in the province, understanding that its development would be too slow if undertaken only by Portuguese capital for this reason attracting foreigners to its agricultural areas."[14] The governor-general appointed three experts to evaluate the agricultural potential of Mozambique: Fred T. Nicholson, secretary of the Transvaal Agricultural Union; T. R. Sim, the widely respected forest inspector in the colony of Natal; and the American agronomist Otis Warren Barrett, formerly the head of the US Department of Agriculture. Peter Conacher, the head of the Veterinary Section for the new agricultural services in Mozambique, also accompanied the group.[15] Reports from the high-powered commission were originally published in English in the inaugural issue of the *Boletim da Repartição de Agricultura de Moçambique (Journal for the Agricultural Services in Mozambique).*[16] They were hastily reprinted in Portuguese in the second issue of the journal after receiving complaints that articles on a Portuguese colony commissioned by the Portuguese government could only be found in English. The English version of the reports were influential and published multiple times in journals in Lisbon (the *Bulletin of the Geographical Society of Lisbon*), South Africa, Natal, Lourenço Marques (*Futuro* and the *Lourenço Marques Guardian*, in English), and *National Geographic* in the United States. Barrett was subsequently named the inaugural director of Mozambique's new Agricultural Services.

The three experts who traveled the territory for this initial report marveled at the fertility of the land and declared Mozambique set to be a most profitable colony. Barrett's write-up bubbled over with optimism, claiming that Mozambique held "millions of acres of the finest alluvial soil fairly aching to show the farmer what big crops may be grown. . . . With careful management, large profits should be readily made in this promising region" (1910: 13). He urged all those who were interested to invest their time or capital in Mozambique: "With labor at $2 to $5 per month, good transportation, no more sickness than in any other country, perhaps, and good support from the government, colonists will come and then Mozambique will gloriously come into her own" (13). To make this happen, however, Barrett urged the government to invest in research stations. One of the major crops in the region explored—coconuts—was judged to be doing poorly compared to plantings in Trinidad and Puerto Rico, and in his estimation this was not due to the land or to the lack of eager, skilled labor, but rather to the lack of systematic experimentation (12). As he said of coconuts and of agriculture more generally, "Apparently many thousands of pounds have been lost by the syndicates [prazos] in experimenting with crops and methods—work which should have been carried out on a more technical basis by the government" (12). Barrett believed that Mozambique had a promising future as a producer and exporter of tropical commodity crops, and he oriented his descriptions and advice toward achieving that potential.

Nicholson's (1910) report, titled "Agriculture in Mozambique: Vast Agricultural and Pastoral Possibilities," was more subdued but equally optimistic about the potential for plantation crops. He drew from his experience "in the low veld of the Transvaal," which gave him confidence in proposing a suite of tropical commodities that would do well in Mozambique. Like Barrett, he was enthusiastic about the local residents and their ability to power successful plantations: "The natives here," he said, "are better than any I have seen in South Africa." All that Mozambique needed to catalyze production was the application of scientific research that could bring universal principles to bear on the local ecology. The report by Sim likewise emphasized the potential for commodity production in Mozambique with particular enthusiasm about the availability of indigenous labor power for large-scale production, especially compared to his experience farther south. "The following general features [in the neighborhood of Lourenço Marques and the coast from Limpopo to Inhambane] struck me: the happy, contented, loyal, industrious, agricultural native population—the Portuguese do much better with the natives than the British in the rest of South Africa. The Portuguese have a strong but gentle hand [which] is recognized as all powerful"

(Sim 1910: 31). To turn this labor power to use for plantation production, he presented a short list of requirements for the territory. Scientific research into new crop varieties and dissemination was once again at the top of the list, which also included "better transport everywhere, attractive land tenure on a fixed, easily understood and reasonable basis, suitable alike to the settler and to the concessionaire, [and] encouragement of native industries" (38). All of these things were required for Mozambique to be palatable to foreign investors who sought access to land and labor for the production and sale of global commodities.

Other observers who traveled through Mozambique at this time echoed the reports of the 1908 expert commission. They marveled at the potential richness of the land, believing that Mozambique could be one of the richest colonies in the world. José Daniel Cordeiro Dias, a Portuguese scientist who would go on to head the agricultural services in Mozambique, waxed as poetic as Barrett when he said in 1909, "The discovery of our colonies was and is immortal glory for us, from which we have already earned abundant riches, which I am fully convinced will be increased, taking us to broad horizons of prosperity when agriculture in the colonies is able to put itself on a level with the foreign colonies that have progressed the most [e.g., those of the UK, Holland, and Germany]" (Cordeiro Dias 1909: 299). And like Barrett, Nicholson, and Sim, Cordeiro Dias urged Portuguese administrators to invest in scientific study if they hoped to see a profit from agricultural production in the territory. As the "sick man of Europe" (cited in Isaacman and Isaacman 1983: 21), Portugal's possessions in Africa were "rich and enormous areas looked down upon by everyone," Cordeiro Dias said, because they were not yet planted productively. He bemoaned the lack of scientific education for farmers and demanded "the establishment of agricultural schools led by well-trained people" (1909: 299). He reminded the governor of Mozambique of highly profitable cultures that had been introduced in other colonies, like coffee, tea, and cacao in Java, and even offered his services to help build the plantation economy—"I think you should ask me to write a report about the conditions of the land, climate, and labor in this territory"—but the royal administration lacked the resources and never took him up on the offer (Cordeiro Dias 1909: 302).

Following Barrett's short tenure as director of agriculture in Mozambique (1908–10), another foreigner and agronomist, this time from England, Robert Nunez Lyne, assumed the position. There are few details available on what Lyne accomplished during his short time in office (1910–12), but he traveled the country widely and shortly after leaving office published a book describing the soils of Mozambique and the various crops that would be profitable with the right techniques. The book begins with an ode to plantations misattributed to seventeenth-century writer Thomas Fuller. Titled "Of Plantations," its epigraph, like the book that follows, imbues plantations with heroic, life-sustaining, nation-building qualities: "Plantations make mankind broader, as generation makes it thicker. Let the prime undertakers be men of no shallow heads, nor narrow fortunes. Let the planters be honest, skillful, and painful people. Nor must the planters be only honest, but industrious also" (Lyne 1913: 7). Of all the crops discussed, Lyne reserves his greatest praise for sugarcane, although he also urges greater investment in cotton, rubber, and coconuts (28).

To Lyne, the hoped-for transformation of the land depended on foreign capital and planters coming into the region: Mozambique had land that rivaled other colonial possessions, such as British-controlled Nyasaland and German East Africa, but Lyne was skeptical that the Portuguese could farm this land themselves—a skepticism that found frequent expression during the colonial period. Monteiro Grilo, the director of Agricultural Services many years later, complained that colonists from Portugal were inept farmers, more interested in quick profits than in working the land. As he said, "the farmer who attaches himself to the land, as if he wants to put down roots in it, and by his own hands takes forward the activity in spite of innumerable obstacles and difficulties, is the one who is the least represented in our mix of [Portuguese] agricultural forms." He lamented that "few people come to Mozambique with a passion to farm, as they do in neighboring territories and other regions of active colonization" (Grilo 1946: 222–23).

Indeed, the one handbook on farming published almost at the same time as Lyne's book was by a Portuguese colonist, who likened farming in Mozambique to fighting a military battle because so few resources were available to support colonists in their endeavors: farming was a constant ecological and political struggle. In a "Practical Guide for the Colonial Farmer," Miguel de Jesus Valladas Paes (1910) detailed what he had learned in order to "save others the suffering" he had endured.[17] Mozambique had enormous potential for successful plantation crops, particularly with coconuts, coffee, oilseed, and sugarcane (in that order), but the country had not yet realized this potential because, he maintained, the farmers themselves were not prepared to take on production in the tropics: they wanted the profits but not the work. "People say you cannot plant [the most valuable crops] because of the climate or because of the plant itself, but the truth is that it is due to lack of curiosity and usury. . . . [O]ut of a thirty or so individuals who call themselves farmers, only about half a dozen really are" (Valladas Paes 1910: 303). Among the Portuguese colonists and those who governed the province, he suggested that farming was "despised. . . . To be a farmer, for the majority of those who govern them, is synonymous with being an explorer [*explorador*], but in the most perverse sense of the word" (221).[18]

These reports were written by people with experience in tropical Africa, but they were short and impressionistic, without the benefit of long-term study of the soils, flora, or fauna. They were, however, the most comprehensive agroecological or farming studies available for Portuguese East Africa until the 1940s. Efforts to get more information from settlers or government employees in the territory had little success. At the end of 1911, the colonial minister sent the governor-general of Mozambique a survey, requesting answers to a set of questions about rubber and coffee. The survey was lengthy, including forty-one detailed questions about rubber and forty-two about coffee, along with requests for samples of all known varieties, maps of where they were grown, and photographs of the different varieties and the plants from which they came, as well as photographs of indigenous methods of cultivation and more. The governor-general sent the survey questions to the Department of Agriculture, expecting them to be answered in detail.[19] Then subdirector of the department, J. Oliveira Ferraz, wrote back when he received the questions. He was clearly appalled: "Most Excellent Secretary General, in our records there exist no such documents relative to the subject you have asked about. I don't think this is cause for surprise, given that the agricultural services have never been fully established, and they lack for absolutely everything with respect to agronomic and forestry knowledge. . . . I tried several times to answer the questions myself, but it was not even possible to get started" (Ferraz 1914: 90). Ferraz blamed his inability to undertake the survey on the lack of personnel in the department, which had been effectively reduced to one person, himself. He suggested that the secretary send the survey to the governors of each district and the administrators of the circumscriptions (areas set aside for indigenous peoples), which the governor-general did.

The responses to the survey from the districts, though, were not "what the General Leadership of the Colonies would have wanted" (Ferraz 1914: 91). As the article describing the responses says, "The truth is that, for Mozambique, they could not have hoped for anything else, because they know well the difficulties the Agricultural Department has in terms of technical people" (91). From the most populated administration of Maputo, the administrator, P. Viana Rodrigues, responded to the questions regarding coffee, saying simply, "I have the honor of informing Your Excellency that I do not have the technical competency to respond to [your] questions" (91). And to the questions on rubber, he wrote, somewhat peevishly: "I have the

honor of informing Your Excellency that the rubber present in this circum-
scription is, if I am not mistaken, the same as what one finds in the district as
a whole and whose samples you will find in your department of agriculture.
The methods employed by the natives are generally well known and can be
found in various relevant books" (92).

In the North, particularly in the areas of António Enes (present-day
Angoche) and Mossuril, where rubber was cultivated more intensively, the
answers were longer, although the information relayed was rudimentary.
On rubber, the responses all indicated (with the exception of the rubber
company, the Companhia do Boror) that contrary to widely accepted best
practices in other colonies, the cultivation of rubber in Mozambique was
done by indigenous peoples, who cut into the trunk of the tree or pulled
the trees out of the ground by their roots and pounded them to separate
the bark from the interior. In response to the questions of how to increase
production, the agreement was that increasing yields would require turning the industry over to Europeans. Those local residents who could overcome their "natural indifference" (response from the Military Command
of Matadane, *Boletim da Repartição* 1914: 105) and "indolent character"
(response from the town of Angoche, *Boletim da Repartição* 1914: 102)
should be encouraged to plant more and be forced to provide what they
gathered to the Portuguese (and be prohibited from trading with Indian
intermediaries). Out of all of the surveys sent out, only one was returned
with information on coffee, and that response contained only an apology
for its lack of answers.

In 1910, British Consul for Portuguese East Africa R. C. F. Maugham
summed up the situation succinctly in his damning review of the region,
attributing the colony's difficulties to a lack of scientific interest among Portuguese officials:

> Local company officials don't study the flora/fauna: The average
> commandant, as they are styled within their districts, does not as a
> rule occupy his spare time in the pursuit of information calculated
> to widen our knowledge of the obscurer pages of natural science, and
> this is a lamentable fact which inseparably connects itself with the
> unfortunate paucity of our information regarding African flora and
> fauna. (Maugham 1910: 100)

Maugham suggested that colonization in Mozambique still held promise, but that only modern methods and science would help to realize it.[20]
Farming would need to be on a large scale because, as Augusto Cardozo (a
member of the Board of Directors for Agriculture) wrote in 1915, "[T]he
soil loses its fertility quickly forcing farmers to either leave land fallow or

employ fertilizers and only the large farmer can use these techniques. Large farmers can deploy their labor more efficiently or get rid of [the need for] it by using machines." Cardozo further maintained that scientific surveys like the one sent to the governor-general in 1911 were needed so that Mozambique would one day realize its potential on an equal footing with South Africa and the Belgian Congo, both of which he admired greatly.

Unfortunately, the colonial Department of Agriculture never received sufficient funding to deepen its understanding of the local landscape. As an early report noted, the department was "almost always without capital. . . . Our difficulties come from the insufficient budget, people, and material" ("Relatórios e Informações" 1913: 7).[21] A review of the experimental station at Umbeluzi, successfully created in 1908 roughly forty kilometers from the capital city of Lourenço Marques, illustrated the difficulties of trying to undertake scientific research, which required time and resources for experiments and careful evaluation. The most (only) well-preserved records of the station in the first part of the twentieth century were two detailed reports penned by the interim director of the station, Francisco Meireles (1915).[22] The reports were full of complaints, primarily about the lack of funding and qualified agricultural scientists available to work in the territory. New hires from the mainland, he bemoaned, were ill-prepared for life in East Africa.[23] With limited staff, there was little they could accomplish, and "many good people and even some of the most illustrious" said that "the station doesn't do anything other than cultivate corn" (Meireles 1915: 4). The focus on corn was, in fact, a requirement from provincial leadership because corn was a staple food crop for Portuguese colonists as well as for local residents who worked at the station (4).[24]

In 1914 a new head, José de Almeida, was appointed to lead the Department of Agriculture. He immediately requested a significant increase in funds for the following year, to enable the department to do a thorough evaluation of the territory for agricultural production: "There has never been here a cataloguing of the land in Mozambique such that farming could be planned more 'securely'" (Almeida 1914). Almeida dreamed of establishing a "coherent" Department of Agriculture in the territory, one that could adequately plan production and coordinate the evaluation and monitoring of flora and fauna across regional borders. He compared Mozambique to other Portuguese colonies and noted that it was far behind in fulfilling its agricultural potential. He attributed this in part to the territory's inability to establish a functioning system of agricultural services when he wrote asking for more resources: "[T]he new budget project has at its base the definitive creation of a Department of Agriculture in this colony. Angola, India, Cabo

Verde have these services. . . . It isn't understandable why Mozambique doesn't take advantage of the same regalia" (80).

Calls for the government to provide more infrastructure for agricultural expansion were largely unsuccessful, even though the governor-general at the time, Álvaro de Castro, agreed that the problems were significant and issued a call for a survey of the "agricultural economy" of Lourenço Marques.[25] The director of the Agricultural Services at the time, José de Aleida, appointed J. Oliveira Ferraz to undertake the study. Ferraz did so willingly, perhaps motivated by the difficulties of filling out the information requested in 1911. As he said in his subsequent report, "If we do not seek to resolve the problem of large-scale agricultural production," he urged, "the agricultural future of the district of Lourenço Marques will never be more than a grand aspiration" (Ferraz 1918: 8). As the director of the experiment station in Umbeluzi at that time, Ferraz blamed the problem on the lack of a proper teaching facility where European colonists and indigenous farmers alike could see what sorts of crops and techniques would do well. He summed up his frustration with a description of the experimental capacities of the district less than one hundred kilometers from the colonial capital:

> The district of Manhiça doesn't have an educational plot. Instead, it has planted four hectares around the administrative headquarters where corn, manioc, and potato are planted for the natives and prisoners who work there. . . . This plot has no educational purpose—it doesn't work for the whites because it isn't worked [with techniques that are] any better than what they [already] do, and the natives never look at it because when they do all they see is forced labor, which is the thing they hate most. (Ferraz 1918: 11)

Ultimately, the conclusions from Ferraz's survey of agriculture in Lourenço Marques were brief. There were few successes among colonists, he wrote, save those who benefited from the natural environment and market access around Lourenço Marques. The Incomati Sugar Estates was the only productive agricultural enterprise in the district and would remain so, the author predicted, unless the government could "tie" the natives to agricultural labor for European agriculture and use the faculties in the experimental station to study the soil for the "continual improvement of farming methods" (Ferraz 1918: 13).

In spite of the widespread agreement that Umbeluzi should be developed into a working field experiment station, it gradually fell into disrepair. In 1922 the station was briefly converted into a school, having "never, for different reasons, matched the expectations by which it was created. . . . The station came to be in a state of complete abandonment, delivered to underage people, laboratory closed, its machinery arranged like junkyard trash [*sucata*], its orange orchards dying for lack of treatments, its lands without cultivation, its cattle dying of hunger."[26]

In 1928 Portugal was spending approximately 1 percent of its public services budget on agriculture, veterinary services, and forestry in Mozambique.[27] Local administrators fought to spread limited resources out more widely across the territory—"It's absolutely necessary to have an Agronomy Station in [Lourenço Marques] and an office [*posto*] in every district," one asserted—but they remained concentrated in the capital city of Lourenço Marques.[28] The desire for more specialized scientists was thwarted in part because it was so "difficult to find Portuguese botanists, chemists, entomologists, and mycologists."[29] Without dedicated resources and personnel, it was difficult to introduce and oversee the production of non-local crops in Mozambique, although this remained the goal for the agricultural services.

FROM DISCOVERY TO DISAPPOINTMENT: LATE 1920S–1940S

The 1920s ushered in significant change for Mozambique. The Great Depression decreased world prices for agricultural commodities and led to high inflation in Portugal and Mozambique. Growing levels of national debt contributed to political instability in Portugal, and in 1926 a domestic coup overthrew the national government. The creation of the Estado Novo following the coup marked the beginning of a long period of centralization and authoritarian control in Portugal. António Salazar became finance minister for the new government in 1928 and was given wide latitude in directing the Portuguese economy and colonial governance. Salazar saw the colonies as the vehicle for improving Portugal's position in the world economy. In 1932 he became prime minister and tightened control over the African territories, ushering in increased production for export through a "political regime of permanent violence" (Anderson 1962a: 88).[30]

The Colonial Act of 1930, written by Salazar, tied agricultural production even more closely than before to the benefit of industry in Portugal (see Caetano 1951). Building a plantation economy was a key pillar of the Colonial Act, which mandated the production of cash crops, primarily cotton and rice, and implemented forced labor laws to prop up small- and large-scale production. Local residents had to pay tributes (taxes) either in labor or in kind (crops). This labor tribute was extracted brutally, and Portugal would hold the distinction of having maintained forced labor long after most European countries retired such policies. I go into more detail on these forced labor policies in chapter 4.

The dual nature of the colonial tax (paid in labor or in kind) reflected a debate in the colony about whether indigenous peoples should support colonial agriculture by growing export crops on their land or by laboring on colonial plantations. Increasingly, the two became tied together: local residents could farm plantation crops on their own and deliver them to private or public distributors. Carlos de Melo Vieira, director of the Division of Agriculture in 1936, argued that natives should be allowed to hold heritable use rights to land and that the colonial government should focus on producing new varieties and distributing seeds as well as training native farmers. Vieira stood out as a strong proponent of greater incorporation of local residents into farming, arguing that supporting such farmers would benefit Portugal: "As we go forth attempting to study and improve indigenous agriculture . . . in the initial phase, this assistance must be limited to the distribution of good seed, controlling its use and providing advice geared towards improving the primitive methods used by the native" (Vieira 1936: 10).[31]

The more common opinion at the time, though, was that production would be improved not by supporting indigenous agriculture but by deepening scientific research into local viability for tropical commodities and better organizing the relationship between large-scale planters and their indigenous laborers. For Francisco Monteiro Grilo, the celebrated director of agriculture in the 1930s and 1940s, the Portuguese faced two problems in colonizing Mozambique effectively: the ecology was highly varied and still largely unknown, and the Portuguese settlers did not want to work, leaving most of the work of planting and building new infrastructure to indigenous residents. In "The Problem of Agriculture in Mozambique," Grilo concluded that "we're producing much less than our neighbors for two reasons: ecology and our colonial orientation" (1926: 4). On ecology, he was definitive: "[I]t is without doubt that the majority of our territory on this coast of Africa is not suitable for the settlement of the white race." Part of the problem with the ecology, pointed out by many observers, was that the territory had such a variety of environments and ecosystems that it complicated the task of building a scientific understanding of the landscape and ecology (10). "What we need to do is undertake an immediate survey of the very different regions, understanding their agricultural and silvicultural possibilities," Grilo declared (10). The Department of Agriculture had been created almost twenty years before, and there was still no recognized body of knowledge that described local flora and fauna. Grilo, echoing Barrett,

Lyne, and Sims twenty years earlier, called for surveys of the territory to develop better understanding of local conditions.

Building this knowledge would be difficult because the Department of Agriculture didn't have enough qualified researchers and technicians for the work. In Grilo's opinion, the Portuguese recruited in Lisbon for work in Mozambique were ill-equipped, poorly trained, and under-resourced: "The recruiting of people for the agricultural services in Mozambique takes place in Lisbon, through the competitive hiring system usually. The material conditions that are offered to functionaries do not constitute a sufficient incentive to combat the disinterest of the metropole for colonial life and bring the best [people] to the services" (Grilo 1926: 288). The people who did arrive in Mozambique often did not last in their positions because of the wide scope of the work required. They had to operate with very little formal knowledge about local conditions, and so they could not come to simply implement or supervise; they had to engage in scientific study and experimentation if the land was to be transformed into plantations. Preparing for such study meant consulting available sources of information, which at that time were largely produced by foreign scientists. As a result, the new agronomist "complains that they have to know English, they have to spend the first two years basically as interns, and they have to deal with conditions that only get worse if they go to the provinces" (288).

The reliance on foreigners was a source of embarrassment for local officials and researchers, whose requests for funding to undertake scientific studies were repeatedly rejected. In 1926 foreign scientists rarely stayed long enough to contribute to long-term development.[32] In 1929, Director of Agriculture Egídio Inso wrote mournfully, "What we know about the flora of Mozambique is due to the study of one German (Wilhelm C.H. Peters). . . . No Portuguese has yet taken the opportunity to travel the lands of Mozambique and study its flora."[33] The Portuguese themselves were too few, not appropriately trained, and often occupied with the bureaucratic work that became the hallmark of colonial institutions in the region. "It can be seen from the analysis of these lines," Inso continued, "the clear palpable fact that we had only two officials, the ones from the Agronomic Services Section, who are to be employed for merely bureaucratic work. That is why the forest guards and staff are busy with bureaucratic work. That is why agronomists and technicians are busy with bureaucratic work."[34] This problem of bureaucracy overshadowing more substantive work would continue to grow in subsequent decades.

In 1929 Portuguese officials tried again to conduct an agricultural survey of the territory. The survey was prompted—as happened on multiple

TABLE 2. Number of European Settlers
in Mozambique, 1900–1973

Year	White Population*
1900	2,064
1910	11,000
1928	17,842
1935	23,131
1940	27,438
1945	31,221
1950	48,213
1955	65,798
1960	97,245
1970	162,967
1973	190,000

SOURCE: Castelo (2007: 59, 97, 143).

*White population is generally used interchangeably
with European settlers.

occasions across the twentieth century in Mozambique—by the international community: it was part of a global effort undertaken by the International Institute of Agriculture (the predecessor to the Food and Agriculture Organization of the United Nations, FAO). The survey was supposed to follow one complete agricultural year, from November 1929 to October 1930. Indigenous agriculture was not included in this survey, even though local farmers far outweighed "civilized" ones. Indigenous agriculture was not defined by a set of practices; it was defined as that carried out by indigenous farmers in opposition to "civilized" agriculture, which was carried out by European or white farmers. By 1938 there were roughly 17,800 white residents in Mozambique and 8,350 Mestizos, in a total population of over 3,500,000 (Anderson 1962a). The number of settlers from Portugal only began to increase in the 1950s, when the Portuguese government made concerted efforts to promote emigration (see table 2).

There were high hopes for the 1929–30 survey, but in the end data collection was rushed, and little input was available from researchers or officials on the ground in Mozambique. Accordingly, the results were generally not seen as very useful in the territory. Looking back on this period after serving as director of agriculture for many years, the Portuguese agronomist tasked with leading the 1929 survey admitted that he was perhaps too early on in his career and lacked adequate preparation for a survey of territory-wide magnitude (Grilo 1946: 20).

Local scientists continued to argue that lack of knowledge of local flora and fauna was holding the colony back. The first ecologist in the colony, António de Figueiredo Gomes e Sousa, wrote with a frankness he became known for: [35]

> Knowledge of the physical environment—soil, climate, and flora—is the cornerstone of a good agricultural organization. Agrological studies in Mozambique are nonexistent [*nulos*] or almost, in spite of valiant attempts like those of Freire de Andrade and the recent Department of Mines [Repartição de Minas]. . . . The flora of this colony is considered in the centers of study as the least well-known [*a mais desconhecida*] of all of Africa. (Gomes e Sousa 1932: 7)

Even as local researchers experimented with foreign varieties, attempting to adapt them to the local context, they showed a lack of interest in and knowledge about local varieties. Well-funded and well-traveled foreign researchers were more interested in cataloging local species than were the scientists already in Mozambique. "That I know about, the USDA has asked us twice for plant species," Grilo reported, "and we can't help them because we don't know what we have" (1926: 4). In 1939 knowledge of the local ecology was largely unknown, and what little there was had been gathered by foreigners, "as sad as it is to confess this" (Gomes e Sousa 1939: 51).

One could see this lack of local knowledge on display at the Colonial Fairs and Expositions that were common in the first part of the twentieth century. While most European powers used these open displays to parade their findings, wealth, and control before a curious public, the pages of reports from Portuguese colonial expositions are filled with invocations of the potential wealth in Portuguese Africa—followed by expressions of disappointment at not achieving this potential. The First Colonial Exposition in Porto was dedicated to "the most important crops," which included cotton, rice, rubber, cacao, coffee, sugarcane, tea, beans, fruits, manioc, corn, oils, medicinal plants, textile plants, tobacco, and wheat.[36] The agronomist Paulo Cavique dos Santos argued that these crops were slow to develop in Mozambique because there was little connection between agronomic training in Portugal (through the Superior Institute of Agronomy or the Colonial Garden) and Mozambique. He and others urged Portugal to improve its own agricultural education, then at a fairly rudimentary level, so that people in the metropole could learn about agriculture in the colonies, while people in the colonies would be better trained in the methods of the metropole (Santos 1934).

One of the issues that made it more difficult for agricultural research to expand in colonial Mozambique was the "essentially bureaucratic" organization and orientation of colonial rule (Newitt 1995: 389). The New State established corporatist rule, extending state oversight into all areas of the economy and daily life. The bureaucracy was hierarchical, rule-bound, and conservative, "both excessive and inadequate, everywhere and nowhere" (Harrison 1999: 544). This extended to the agricultural services in Mozambique, which were organized throughout the twentieth century along regional lines, rather than in terms of scientific disciplines or specific crops, as was increasingly the case in the United States and elsewhere. Part of the issue was the general lack of state resources, which meant that staff employed in the agricultural services spent much of their time doing paperwork. The Conselho Superior de Agricultura Colonial reorganized agricultural services so that they mimicked the administrative or political divisions of the territory, "creating, in addition to the district delegations, some special services like hydraulics and botany, though their exact jobs were little specified." For the most part, however, the services were organized along administrative rather than academic lines. As Gomes e Sousa said, "The criteria of specialization were not taken into consideration [tido em grande conta], going so far as to create one position for a botanist and phytopathologist, as if these two specializations could be united in just a single person" (1932: 4).

This bureaucratic organization of the agricultural services, combined with insufficient trained personnel, made it easy for employees in the services to be pulled into administrative work, subordinate to the demands of infrastructure, taxation, property registration, and so on. According to Gomes e Sousa, "[T]he district delegations are just public agencies [repartições públicas], with their inevitable bureaucratic character [elenco], at the front of which, also bureaucratized, one finds the agronomist of the district" (1932: 9). This bureaucratic division complicated scientific evaluation, because "the administrative division does not correspond to the needs of agriculture, and there are not even agricultural regions, to be exact, because of the wide dispersion of properties and the state of transition that they are in" (4).[37] When he became director of Agricultural Services, Francisco Monteiro Grilo agreed, listing bureaucratic functions—including "planting food for the native workers and cattle, planting improved seed, demonstration fields and training the indigenous" (Grilo 1946: 169–70)—that took up more time than science-based research. He echoed the complaints of Francisco Meireles thirty years earlier: "Basically, the assistance we are providing [to farmers] consists principally of distributing seeds, plants and tools for the farmers to begin, restart, improve or enlarge their cultures" (252). The agricultural services spent a significant amount of their time on paperwork and incomplete surveys. Ultimately, Grilo said: "[I]n terms of specialized study missions, wholly recommended in poorly known territories like Mozambique, we accomplished little, and we could not have done more given that the scarce technical people we have were consumed by administrative and bureaucratic functions that always increase" (116).

In 1937 the colonial budget finally saw a significant increase. The central government created the Fundo de Fomento da Colonia de Moçambique (Development Fund for the Colony of Mozambique), increasing the budget for agriculture, which would be dedicated to commercial crops, particularly the territory's most profitable export crop, cotton. The increased budget, along with the creation of commodity boards that set price floors and supported purchasing, helped to increase the production of export crops, particularly cotton (see table 3). Other important crops at this time included sugarcane, tobacco (although it would really only amount to a substantial export crop after the Second World War), tea, sisal, coconuts, cashews, and tree plantations, particularly eucalyptus.[38]

Despite the increase in export production, in situ agricultural research lagged behind. In 1944 there were still only 160 people employed in the Department of Agriculture in the entire territory.[39] As director, Grilo lamented the lack of funding, dismissing indigenous agriculture but arguing for the importance of research in establishing a European system capable of reaching the global market. In the case of a country "without experience or any real agricultural tradition, like Mozambique" the research function was extremely important, he said (Grilo 1946: 20). One of the best indicators of the deficiencies in local production was the fact that the only seeds or seedlings available for purchase came from outside Mozambique. As Monteiro Grilo said in his review, "Until the end of 1944, no one sold seedlings (nursery plants) from a nursery established in the colony, nor were there garden seeds produced in the territory. Everything came from outside with the exception of what the agricultural establishments of the state cultivated and distributed" (41).

Experiments were generally confined to the agricultural stations, whose number and location varied between 1940 and 1945.[40] The level of experimentation in these stations was disappointing because of low staffing levels. The main cultures under study were "cotton, rice, banana, potato, sugarcane, 'improved cultures' meaning beans to use as fertilizer, mascate (cultivated by local residents for their food), various legumes (crotolarias, mungo, nhembas,

TABLE 3. Cotton Exports from Mozambique
to Portugal, 1926–1946

Year	Cotton Exported (kg)
1926	337,967
1927	291,654
1928	165,873
1929	249,558
1930	189,994
1931	159,251
1932	1,083,805
1933	1,057,214
1934	1,919,420
1935	1,829,277
1936	3,247,105
1937	8,226,107
1938	7,492,406
1939	6,576,288
1940	4,473,328
1941	5,012,612
1942	14,146,295
1943	13,245,704
1944	22,659,989
1945	17,256,570
1946	29,003,688

SOURCE: Arquivo do Instituto de Algodão, Junta de
Exportação de Algodão Colonial, Gaspar de Mello Furtado,
Chefe da Delegação, "Elementos para o século," June 15,
1954. Cited in Isaacman and Isaacman (1983: 45).

cutelinho, tremoco, derris, the last having been brought from Tanzania and
planted in the experimental station at Umbeluzi), fruits, horticultures, lin-
seed, corn and wheat." Manioc was mentioned and recognized as the greatest
food source for indigenous peoples, and Grilo (1946) suggested that resistance to the mosaic virus should be studied but, as I detail in chapter 4, little
research was invested in this wholly "native" crop.

The production of plantation commodities did increase significantly
through the efforts of the Colonial Act. There were successful plantation

enterprises in a handful of commodities, particularly cotton, sugarcane, tobacco, and coconuts. Cotton was the most important of these crops politically because the textile industry in Portugal depended on cheap imports from the colony. In 1943 Francisco Vieira Machado, a high-ranking figure in the Colonial Ministry and National Overseas Bank (Banco Nacional Ultramarino), created the Center for Scientific Cotton Research (Centro de Investigação Científica Algodoeira, CICA).[41] It would be in specialized institutes such as this that most of the original agricultural research in Mozambique would eventually take place. As Malyn Newitt (1995) writes, the institutes funded by specialty crop planning boards "built up cadres of crop experts, soil scientists, and even anthropologists who carried out some of the first serious studies of agriculture and problems of rural Mozambique" (456; see also Saraiva 2016a: 168–83).

A NEW APPROACH: DESENVOLVIMENTO TARDIO, 1940S TO INDEPENDENCE

In the second half of the twentieth century, the Portuguese government committed to intensification of a new form of development in Mozambique. In 1951 the colonies were renamed "overseas provinces" to suggest that they were not foreign possessions but rather extensions of the natural boundaries of the Portuguese nation. In an attempt to reap more from southern Africa and bring the region more fully under Portuguese control, this new approach mimicked the settler colonialism that had made the British colonies so successful. Calls for independence were increasing in the British colonies surrounding Mozambique; in 1962 revolutionary groups met in Tanzania and formed an alliance, but struggles would not begin in earnest in Mozambique until the late 1960s (Lunstrum 2011). Development was "late" (known as *desenvolvimento tardio* in Portuguese) compared to other colonies and relied primarily on increasing plantation crops and encouraging settlement from Portugal. Portuguese colonists had never gone to Mozambique in the numbers hoped for. In the *Gazeta do Agricultor* (Farmers gazette), a monthly journal inaugurated in 1949, the editors questioned the lack of Portuguese farmers in Mozambique:

> There is no justification for the inadaptability or impropriety of our European farmers. . . . These are the same mass of those who developed Brazil, our greatest work of colonization and whose economy was largely consolidated by agriculture, in various cycles of sugar, cotton, rubber, and coffee. We also have the example of Portuguese farmers in California and elsewhere in the United States, and even more in South

Africa where they enjoy the highest reputation for their contribution to the prosperity of agriculture. If the Portuguese can be a good farmer outside of the homeland, why should he not also be in our overseas territories?[42]

This quote illustrates the ideology behind the plantation ideal: that the qualities that produce success in any given place are universal (and adaptable) because the science behind the crops and the crops themselves are universal. Portuguese farmers should be able to produce in Mozambique as they did in Brazil even without knowledge of local conditions, because the plants, the knowledge, and the markets are the same. The relative lack of large-scale enterprises in Mozambique represented an opportunity for external science, investment, and farmers, rather than the manifestation of their failures.

From the 1950s to the 1970s the Portuguese government tried to encourage settlement in Mozambique by supporting emigration from continental Portugal and creating more incentives for indigenous households to settle in reserves or local villages. The First Development Plan, from 1953 to 1958, emphasized emigration from Portugal, in part to soak up unemployment from the Portuguese countryside. The Second Development Plan, from 1959 to 1964, displayed increasing sensitivity to calls for decolonization and emphasized local development (Newitt 1995: 462). In the second plan, the government hoped to build "a conservative landholding bulwark against Mozambican nationalism" (Lunstrum 2011: 248). Connected to this push for settlement, Salazar proposed the training of a new cadre of Portuguese scientists who would rationalize politics, society, and the economy (Saraiva 2009: 38). These plans fell far from the intended goal, however, with settlement from Portugal being particularly difficult to sustain. Portuguese looking to emigrate were much more likely to choose Brazil or western Europe as their new home (Penvenne 2005: 79). Once in the country, those settlers who did go to Mozambique displayed little knowledge of agriculture and had difficulty adapting to local conditions. The much-heralded Limpopo Colony began with ten Catholic families in 1954, opening to African indigenous people after 1959, but the colony never managed to become self-sustaining, instead relying on support from the central and colonial governments (Castelo 2012, 2016).

Without strong incentives to focus on local settlements or indigenous agriculture, scientific research maintained its focus on export crops. The first task for the newly created CICA was to find out what conditions existed in the province. Under the leadership of the Portuguese scientist Aurélio Quintanilha, ambitious studies were finally successfully conducted and eventually collected into two volumes with the title *Ecological-Agricultural*

Survey of Mozambique (EASM). Given the relative lack of information about agricultural conditions in the territory, these studies would be the most important in the history of colonial Mozambique.[43] A visiting agronomist from Brazil, Rui Paiva (1952), called the final survey "one of the most interesting works that we have seen in Africa" (164), although it has been largely overlooked in the literature on the territory (Saraiva 2016a).

In the introduction to the EASM, the authors noted that basic agroecological information about Mozambique was still needed: "[Cotton] is grown in places that are totally inappropriate and where the soils are poor. . . . It has become necessary, before anything else, to *know where cotton should be cultivated*" (CICA 1955: 7; emphasis in original). The authors developed technical recommendations for the newly established Cotton Institute of Mozambique (Instituto de Algodão de Moçambique, IAM; see Saraiva 2009: 52), but felt that their work should inform all of agriculture in the territory, not just cotton. The study was thus guided by three principles: (1) economic development in a country like Mozambique should be centrally planned, (2) such planning should be preceded by a general survey of the necessities on the one hand and of the resources and possibilities on the other, and (3) the execution of the plan should be implemented in the context of the broader planned economy (*economia dirigida*) (CICA 1955: 23). Underlying this emphasis on planning was the ongoing belief in the plantation ideal: cotton and other commodity crops could make Mozambique a rich territory, if large-scale tropical crop production was organized efficiently.

Prior to the study, the authors claimed, Mozambique had been "a region with more than 770,000 km^2 that was almost virgin with respect to soil and phytogeography studies." They ventured that "we should use this study to help plan our economy and put money into leading the economy in the appropriate directions" (CICA 1955: 17). The authors further suggested that such rational planning was already being carried out by the British in other (more successful) parts of southern Africa, as well as "in the Belgian Congo and in the French colonies" (17). Following suit, they suggested, would help Mozambique plan its commodity production more efficiently and effectively.

To complete the study, the small team of scientists worked in each of the territory's four districts in turn, taking six months at a time for field research and analyzing the data during the rainy seasons.[44] Fieldwork began in 1947 and ended two years later, in 1949. The study was widely praised, with the authors claiming that by the time the initial results were published in 1953, recommendations on where to locate production had been responsible for a nearly fourfold increase in yield per hectare (CICA 22).

Although the study contained six chapters, the sections on climate, soil, and vegetation were at the heart of the work. These were the chapters for which original research was conducted (although all of the chapters, particularly the climate study, relied heavily on published material). Maps were created to assist with the designation of agroecological zones. (Although the authors did not provide recommendations for zoning in the main document, they alluded to it, and recommendations were fleshed out in the provincial level reports.) The chapters on geology, physiography, and demography contained no new material, although the first two were detailed and well-supported with professional citations (for more discussion of the research on demography, see chapter 4).[45]

Research for the EASM was conducted almost fifteen years after the most well-known scientific study in colonial Africa, the African Survey, carried out in British Africa. The African Survey, conducted between 1933 and 1939 and detailed in Helen Tilley's (2011) excellent study, focused on deepening knowledge of the land and people of British Africa, reflecting scientists' increasing interest in and attention to the diversity of ecologies across the British colonies (Hodge 2007). The African Survey's executive committee described its developmentalist priorities: "History . . . looking back in retrospect on the part played by Imperial Powers in Africa, will be more concerned with the nature of the contribution which the European occupation will have made to the future of the African peoples, than with the profit or loss which the African connexion may have brought to Europe" (Tilley 2011: 73). The EASM in Mozambique took a very different approach, focusing on the development of large-scale agriculture for the purpose of benefitting the Portuguese. As Tiago Saraiva (2016a) writes, the two years of research conducted by the first Portuguese scientists to study Mozambique in depth focused only on the capacity of the land, water, and people to produce commodities for export; "the entire territory was now translated in function of the regional variations of the technological index of the cotton fiber" (176).

Unlike the increase in exports after 1937, the efforts that followed the EASM had variable success in increasing cotton exports from Mozambique (see table 4).

In the late 1950s, still dissatisfied with the performance of agriculture in Mozambique, the local administration debated whether or not to ask the general scientific institute of the region, the Scientific Research Institute of Mozambique (IICM), to expand its remit and take on agriculture. Governor-General Pedro Correia de Barros reached out to IICM administrators, asking them what they recommended as an institutional solution that could

TABLE 4. Cotton Production and Exports in Mozambique, 1961–1975

Year	Production (Tons)	Value of Exports (USD 1,000)
1961	36,884	24,010
1962	42,520	21,110
1963	28,680	18,200
1964	40,158	19,650
1965	28,500	19,260
1966	39,266	17,109
1967	44,166	22,210
1968	42,268	22,107
1969	45,213	27,636
1970	45,586	25,691
1971	34,852	23,250
1972	44,550	23,841
1973	35,308	45,425
1974	35,000	33,142
1975	39,000	17,232

SOURCE: FAOSTAT (2022). Data compiled by Andrew Ofstehage.

improve agriculture's performance. "Various factors," the governor-general wrote in his request, "have brought us, in 1958, to a delicate [*sensível*] situation of deficit in our balance of payments. The progress of our province, whose rhythm is ever more rapid, demands a growing number of machines and specialized products to be imported which has only been possible because of debt. So that we will not have to pause at all in our growth, certain changes will have to be made" (IICM report 1959: 1). To meet the need for raw materials and foreign exchange, the government needed agricultural production to increase dramatically. To do this, the provincial government hoped the IICM would help rationalize agricultural assistance, in exchange promising to increase the budgets for agriculture and forestry and veterinary services and to "provide assistance and the utmost consideration for the producer" (3).

On July 31, 1959, IICM Director José Emílio dos Santos Pinto-Lopes responded to the governor-general, returning an ambitious proposal for reorganizing the agricultural services in Mozambique (IICM 1959). He put his energy into imagining what "a balanced and progressive agriculture" could look like. The report sought "to balance the need to advance production and productivity with the need to keep expenditures down and improve the overall balance of payments." Pinto-Lopes's report divided the proposed measures into technical ones (rational use of the soil and of plants and human effort); economic ones (assuring that markets and prices will earn farmers money and when possible will be stable); social ones (working toward the elevation and the education of the farmers); and organizational ones (related to the cooperation of the different services and coordination of their respective activities, with the goal of maximizing efficiency).

Like the agronomists and department officials who had come before him, Pinto-Lopes believed that Mozambican agriculture would only be improved with more funding for research, training, and education: "[A]griculture techniques have evolved and improved like any other field. [But] we need to introduce more experiments quickly." More planning and rational use of the soil was also needed, but Pinto-Lopes was practical: he did not believe that agronomists in the country (whether in the institute's own ranks or in the already existing agriculture-oriented services) knew the ecology of Mozambique well enough, so he suggested that even a revamped scientific institute would need to rely heavily on research undertaken by the specialty institutes, particularly the Cotton Institute of Mozambique. This would help produce results quickly, even if the understanding of the local landscape in Mozambique would be shaped by knowledge produced at the service of a small number of commodity crops (see table 5).

The response to Pinto-Lopes's plan was quick and dismissive. The governor-general maintained the official position held for the past half century: the Portuguese needed plantation agriculture in the territory to succeed in order to improve their economic position, but they were unwilling or unable to provide the resources needed for local research or education. In the end, even with increasing urgency to expand production, the administration decided against extending the IICM's reach into agriculture, which would have required significant resources, and instead brought together various pieces of the existing Agricultural Services, including the IAM, the Cereals Institute, and the Junta Provincial de Povoamento de Moçambique, into a unified entity, the Agronomic Research Institute of Mozambique (IIAM; created through Ministerial Legislative Diploma no. 15 on December 18, 1965, cited in Esteves 1967: 3). With its headquarters in the capital, the goal was to promote research and experiments in agronomy, forestry, and livestock through the "application and dissemination of knowledges, having in sight the general economic and social progress of the nation."[46] The

TABLE 5. Mozambique's Principal Agricultural Exports by Value (1961) and Percentage of Total Exports (1960)

Export	Value in 1961 (USD 1,000)	Percent of Total Annual Exports in 1960
Cashew nuts	10,899	11.12*
Cashew kernels	856	
Cotton	24,083	32.47
Sugar	11,242	13.25
Tea	8,157	8.40
Copra	9,234	9.26
Sisal	5,609	8.47
Vegetable oils	2,194	2.43
Total agricultural exports	74,219	—
Total exports	88,170	—

SOURCES: *For value of exports in 1961:* Anuário Estatístico and Boletim Mensal, Lourenço Marques, Mozambique, cited in Missiaen (1969: 9). *For percentage of total exports in 1960:* Isaacman and Isaacman (1983: 44, table 3.2).

* Cashew nuts and cashew kernels combined as percent of total annual exports.

new organization included provincial juntas in the hopes that this would strengthen the connection between the government, researchers, and the farmers, as the latter generally had very little contact with "official establishments" (Barros 1965: 173).

It was increasingly clear that the colonial government would not dedicate new resources to local agricultural development. As a former director of IICM, Manuel Gomes Guerreiro wrote, "Even though we helped lead the Renaissance, we have fallen behind Europe in the sciences since. We are very behind in understanding the physical processes and characteristics behind the products we produce, whether it is in agriculture or forestry. Perhaps this is because our environment here on the Mediterranean is so different than that of the rest of Europe, but we ought to know about things like coffee in more scientific ways so that we profit from them better" (Guerreiro 1965). As the struggle for independence heated up, Portuguese officials worried about the ability to effectively secure their claim to Mozambique. In 1962 the closing speech at the First Agrarian Conference in Mozambique was titled "We Need to Produce More, Better and Faster, Increasing Profits," and was given by the provincial secretary, Engineer Ruy Ribeiro

(Ribeiro 1962: 169–70). Scientific research was the means to connect commodity crops with local conditions, enabling the sought-after returns.

The first director of IIAM, Baião Esteves, was appointed on August 18, 1966, although the institute itself was not operative until the end of that year. The IIAM was meant to be a single unit that would be decentralized and operate flexibly. It was divided into four departments: agrarian knowledge, research, experimentation, and planning. These four departments, Esteves believed, corresponded to the four fundamental phases of scientific investigation: observation, formulation of hypotheses, experimentation, and induction (Esteves 1967: 4). Under these departments, the twelve units that focused on applied life sciences (soils, bioclimatology, botany, plant breeding, vegetable sanitation, livestock, and agroindustry) were staffed, while the units for basic sciences and agricultural engineering and four other units that would have dealt primarily with people (agriculture and silviculture, economy and society, statistics, and environmental design) had no staff. The mandate of the new institute was to "produce inventions and recommend innovations required for economic development." Well into the 1970s, though, the only active departments were agrarian knowledge and experimentation (Esteves 1967).

The journal *Agronomia Moçambicana* presented research results from IIAM (and some independent agencies) from 1967 to 1973, and its output reflects the continued emphasis on plantation agriculture. Very few original field trial studies were conducted; rather, most of the work is based on meta-studies and laboratory experiments. There is a significant focus on cotton, particularly in the articles that present results from field experiments: in the first five years, forty-one field-based study reports were conducted, twenty of which focused on cotton, mostly on new varieties and various insecticides and herbicides. Later on, more studies of particular varieties and of a wider variety of crops appeared, but most of the later studies on non-cotton crops were scoping papers assessing the landscape and potential for increasing production and commercialization, while the papers on cotton presented new experimental results.

Much like his predecessors in the Department of Agriculture, the new director of IIAM bemoaned the lack of materials and resources, especially in terms of laboratories and experimental units (Esteves and da Silva 1967). The department had originally planned for thirty-eight experimental units, but by the early 1970s only sixteen were in operation.[47] There were also plans for twenty-two scientific laboratories, only nine of which were functioning in 1967. The problem was less the availability of space than the scarcity of trained personnel. In 1967 there were only 24 university-trained professionals working in research in IIAM while the other 85 employees were in education, administration, and extension. This number was lower than any Organisation for Economic Co-operation and Development country, lower than the other Portuguese territorial possessions, and lower than Portugal itself. Out of these 109 people, only 9.1 percent were younger than age thirty-five. This concerned Esteves, who saw it as an indicator that the staff "did not constitute, as a whole, a specialized body in the modern sense of the term" (Esteves and da Silva 1967: 59). The staff in IIAM was insufficient to produce the knowledge needed for the territory, and the budget equaled less than 0.5 percent of the gross product of Mozambican agriculture in 1968 (IIAM 1968: 5).

In 1973, on the eve of independence, J. A. L. Martins Santareno, the new head of the Department of Agriculture, who would remain in the position until the Portuguese left, praised the network of extension and technical assistance that was being fortified throughout the country: "This coverage is thickening in the context of our financial and human limitations, but the latter deserves particular emphasis [*relevo*], given that the financial problems are being resolved and the issue of human resources—known as the scarcity in qualified personnel—has caused greater difficulties" (1973: 18).[48] As the Portuguese fought to retain their control over the territory, agricultural agronomists worked to encourage indigenous peoples to leave their itinerant practices behind and take up settlement. Martins Santareno wrote optimistically of the Portuguese government's plans to replace swidden agriculture with new poles of development:

> In Mozambique, as it is in the greater part of the African continent, the rural populations, in accordance with their ancestral customs and habits, live in a way that is somewhat spread out. This form of living creates a big number of difficulties for economic and social uplifting and for the integration with a more evolved civilization, in the sense that it is not viable, no matter how much good will and means exist, to create a technical and social infrastructure, namely in terms of schools, sanitation and agricultural assistance for dozens, if not hundreds of thousands of population centers. . . . And so, in Mozambique, as in other pieces of the Portuguese overseas territory, we are taking forward a whole campaign of "rethinking" [*mentalização*], associated with many experiences . . . which we call rural reordering, rural villages, neighborhood, community storage sites, all with the goal of bringing the benefits of civilization to the rural population. (23–24)

At the close of colonial rule, Portuguese officials like Martins Santareno were committed to a vision of villagization that would deliver the supposed moral benefits of "civilization" as well as reorganizing labor for the benefit of large-scale plantation agriculture. Yet this official turn to embedding the indigenous farmer with Portuguese values and nationalism would be too little too late, not least because it was carried out in a self-serving way to prop up the failing colonial rule. Countering the practice of mobility with inducements of civilization proved to be difficult work for a colonial power that had only ever mistreated the local population: "This work is naturally delicate and complex," Martins Santareno conceded, "because of the natural resistance that one encounters in populations with millennia-old habits of dispersion. Thus, this whole scheme is naturally slow to take hold" (1973: 24).

EXPLORATION, EXTRACTION, EXIT: THE END OF COLONIAL RULE

When the rule of the Portuguese ended in 1975, they left the new state with little knowledge about the local flora and fauna. In 1989 one of the most respected agronomists to work in postwar Mozambique, Mário de Carvalho, admitted that he wasn't sure what the Portuguese had accomplished in Mozambique with respect to agriculture. He had led both the Cotton Institute and the Agricultural Services and directed one of the research missions that conducted the EASM. He was proud of the EASM, saying, "this is, without doubt, the most important scientific work that the Portuguese agrarian technicians carried out in Mozambique, and it was the first carried out in Portuguese territory and one of the first in all of Africa" (De Carvalho 1989: 108). But he lamented its inability to effect significant change: "Unfortunately, it is also an example of the imposition of private interests on the true interests of the state. . . . After a fair bit [*bastante*] of reflection . . . I must apologize for this incapacity. . . . We produced a lot of knowledge, but that knowledge was not well used" (110). This ignorance, a product of the focus on discovery, would shape rural development in Mozambique for the next fifty years.

This chapter highlights the way that Portuguese colonial rule shaped the landscape in Mozambique, with the concentration of government resources and effort channeled toward the bureaucratic aspects of rule, mostly focused on parceling land, commissioning international investors, engaging international scientists with their knowledge of and access to foreign species, and ensuring the supervision and control of labor for the purposes of both governance and production. This focus flowed from the belief that Mozambique would only profit the Portuguese if it were planted in tropical commodities for export. Unable to realize their vision of large-scale commodity production, the Portuguese left Mozambique with little practical knowledge of local ecological conditions, plants, and animals for agricultural practices. In the next chapter I show how many of these dynamics persist today, in part because the ideas and institutions that support them are so deeply entrenched, and those who have access to resources, knowledge, and power fight to hold onto them.

3. "A Question of Habit"

The Contemporary Dynamics
of Plantation Science in Mozambique

FIELD DAY AT UMBELUZI: WHERE ARE THE FARMERS?

The morning of September 19, 2016, was clear but cold. After living in Mozambique for almost three months, a 60-degree day felt chilly, even with the sun shining brightly. I left the capital city of Maputo early, around 7:00 a.m., to avoid traffic, which was always bad going in and out of the city but particularly so in the morning. The crisp morning air seemed full of excitement because I was headed out to a much-anticipated farmer field day at the Umbeluzi Experiment Station in the Umbeluzi Valley, about an hour outside of Maputo.

As I wrote in chapter 2, Umbeluzi is the oldest, and for a long time was the only, functioning agricultural experiment station in Mozambique. I had visited the station two weeks earlier in the hopes of finding more archival records on its history (which I never found). When I talked with the director, he mentioned that they would be holding a field day to disseminate new varieties to the local farmers. I was excited to join, and he promised to call when the details were set. A week later, they had determined that they would hold the field day the following week, and that it would focus on orange-fleshed sweet potatoes, a project headed by Cape Verdean scientist Maria Andrade, who had just been awarded the 2016 World Food Prize for creating a nutritious alternative to a local staple.

Once outside the heart of the capital city, the well-maintained road passes mile after mile of small-scale gardens planted with lettuce, peppers, and tomatoes. This is the "green belt," a success story of contemporary Mozambican agriculture. Many of the country's "emerging" market-oriented farmers are found here, supported by projects funded and staffed by external agencies from Brazil (through Embrapa) and the United States (through

USAID), with production geared toward Maputo, the largest urban market in Mozambique. This work started in the fields of the Umbeluzi Experiment Station.

At 8:15 a.m., the station director welcomed us outside the main administrative office building. Built in the early 1900s, this once-grand colonial building stood at the station's entrance, large mango trees in the front yard and experimental fields on all sides, planted mostly with garden vegetables, corn, and potatoes. It had rained hard the day before, but the dirt road and paths that snaked throughout the property were dusty, having quickly absorbed the moisture after an unusually dry September. Nevertheless, the trees were green and baby mangoes the size of golf balls were visible between the leaves. There were about twenty-five people at the gathering that morning, bundled up against the slight chill. The majority of the crowd was from IIAM and, unexpectedly, the director of the institute herself was in attendance, along with the heads of the two largest departments, the Department of Agronomy and Natural Resources (DARN) and the Department of Training, Documentation, and Technology Transfer (DFDTT). The appearance of the institute's top leadership suggested that the field day was a special event. A woman with a large camera from the Communications Department was also there.[1] In addition to the people from IIAM, three or four extension agents from the nearby districts were present. Noticeably absent was anyone who looked like a farmer.

We milled around, waiting expectantly for the farmers to show up. I did not often see farmers at the IIAM compound in Maputo or at other IIAM events or locations, but this particular invitation was for a farmer field day, and I was interested to see the interaction between IIAM researchers, extension agents, and farmers. Eventually the station director came out and apologized. He said the farmers were not coming because they had been pulled into a "parallel" event regarding vaccination that the Ministry of Agriculture had organized at the last minute. The IIAM director said that she regretted the "absence of beneficiaries." An extension leader from a nearby town stepped forward and echoed both of them, thanking IIAM for inviting the extension services to the field day and apologizing for the lack of farmers, saying they really couldn't come. There were other farmers from nearby associations who were supposed to attend the field day, but they didn't show up because of the recent rain; they were going to stay home and plant. He was calling around to find some other farmers who could attend, but it wasn't clear if any would come.

The absence of farmers at a field day ostensibly intended for them illustrated a central dynamic of agricultural research in Mozambique: it took place without the farmers. Research in the country was done primarily to advance scientific goals supported by external funders and audiences, not to improve the lives of farmers, although many researchers believed that the former would lead to the latter. Researchers in contemporary Mozambique continued the earlier focus on new varieties that could be developed in laboratories and experimented on in research stations and on a handful of farms before being "liberated" to an uncertain fate. This work relied on an array of international research agencies and connections. It was justified by humanitarian concerns about local development and reducing hunger in the country, but the structure and dynamics of knowledge production made it difficult for scientists to answer the only question farmers had when they finally showed up at the farmer field day: How can we get some? The coproduction of scientific research, a political economy of extraction, the influence of donors, and a persistent belief that local residents did not know and could not learn advanced farming techniques generated agricultural research that fed and was fed by external actors (donor audiences, scientists, and commodity markets) rather than local residents or ecologies.

BACK TO THE BEGINNING?
INDEPENDENCE AND SOCIALIST EXPERIMENTS

Defeating the Portuguese was an astonishing victory for a small army of liberation fighters, but independence in 1975 confronted the new leaders of Mozambique with perhaps even greater difficulties than mobilizing resistance. In a country terrorized by colonial rule, divided by region and ethnicity, and with a small fraction able to read or write, the challenges of unifying the nation and providing for the inhabitants were enormous. The Portuguese colonists in the territory, many of whom were recent arrivals (see table 2 in chapter 2), were given "twenty-four hours and 20 kilograms," or twenty-four hours to leave with 20 kilograms of luggage. As they left, many destroyed whatever they couldn't take with them, setting fire to their establishments, pulling up crops, and freeing cattle from their enclosures out of spite (Isaacman and Isaacman 1983). As a later report on the problems of the countryside recounted, "Cattle abandoned by Portuguese colonists were said to be wandering around in the bush" (Adam et al. 1991: 1). One year after independence, the white population in Mozambique was 10 percent of what it had been, going from two hundred thousand to twenty thousand almost overnight. Almost all of the roughly six thousand private traders (predominantly from Portugal but also from South Asia) in Mozambique on the eve of independence also left, taking or destroying their vehicles on their way out (62).

What the Portuguese left behind was a population, institutional structure, and body of knowledge organized around extraction and militarized coercion. A new independent government came together under the leadership of the resistance, organized into a party named the Mozambican Liberation Front (Frente de Libertação de Moçambique, known as Frelimo). Mozambique's first indigenous PhD, Eduardo Mondlane, was elected the inaugural president of Frelimo during the resistance in 1962. He led the party until 1969, when he was assassinated, likely by another member of Frelimo. Internal disputes had emerged over whether to organize the resistance along class lines or tribal ones. The next year, Mondlane's close friend and ideological ally, Samora Machel, was elected president, but factionalism would haunt Frelimo.

Under Machel, Frelimo developed an organic, class-based, "optimistic" (Harrison 1999) approach to socialist governance based on historical experiences in Mozambique and on pan-African regional conversations. The need to secure food supplies, however, meant a continued focus on large-scale agriculture. Frelimo's initial economic plan "fundamentally rested on agriculture . . . to liberate people in rural areas" (Isaacman and Isaacman 1983: 23). Frelimo created collective farms and encouraged rural inhabitants to move into settlements, a policy referred to as "villagization" (Mahoney 2003: 180–81). The hope was to build solidarity among smallholders while accelerating agricultural productivity and development: "According to the party, the official objective of the policy of 'socialisation of the countryside' was to 'organise the people' who lived in an isolated and dispersed manner, and to create a 'New Man': Portuguese-speaking, not superstitious, not religious, not alcoholic, not polygamous, and inhabiting a communal village" (Chichava 2013: 112). In the north of the country, villagization was intended to counteract the potential for subversion or "contamination" by opposition forces (Garcia 2003: 130, cited in Monjane and Bruna 2019).

By the late 1970s, losses in food supplies and production due to the war and the subsequent departure of Portuguese farmers and traders made the need to increase rural production urgent, and the national strategy came to rely even more heavily on the infrastructure left behind by the Portuguese, which meant a focus on collectivization and mechanization. Several official campaigns were announced to this end, including most prominently the Production Offensive in 1976 and the Year of Production in 1983. After the latter's implementation at the Fourth Party Congress in 1983, unemployed urban youth were rounded up and forcibly deported to rural areas (Newitt 1995: 567).

Frelimo turned the large Portuguese estates into "unmanageably large" state farms and privileged these areas for attention (Bowen et al. 2003). Smallholders who fought for independence were hoping for access to land under Frelimo, but the Land Law passed in 1979 gave the state the legal right to expropriate land—whether abandoned by the Portuguese or occupied by peasant farmers—for state farms (Mosca 2005). The majority of farming households in Mozambique after independence were family farmers, particularly in the center and north of the country, but they "received very little assistance from the government because family farmers were understood to be—by definition—self-supporting" (Wuyts 2001: 2). Collective and state farms received over 90 percent of all agricultural investment during the first five years after independence (Newitt 1995: 555). A post hoc review of farming during the socialist period suggested that the problems encountered had colonial roots: namely, the racialized segmentation of agricultural production and support into hierarchical, mutually exclusive categories of native and European (or subsistence and market-oriented agriculture), as well as the weakness of Portuguese agricultural efforts during colonization (Adam et al. 1991: 41). In spite of the new orientation toward socialism, collective farms continued to rely on seasonal wage labor and "preserved the social relations of colonialism" (Newitt 1995: 555; see also Cahen 1987). Frelimo also continued a longer European tradition of attempting to entice men into agriculture, despite the fact that farming was predominantly women's work.[2] The government assumed that labor was "almost infinitely available from the subsistence sector" (O'Laughlin 1996: 21), even though under colonialism, labor was always considered difficult to "fix," whether in place or in productive capacity.

Independence gave birth to an internal power struggle that was exploited by outside powers, resulting in the creation of the armed opposition movement Renamo.[3] White-only governments in Rhodesia and South Africa were nervous about an independent Black socialist nation on their border and carried out a "ruthless" and "savage" assault on the newly independent country (Saul 1985). The formation of Renamo proved to be a powerful disruption. Mozambique was mired in civil war for the first twenty years of its independent existence, one of the effects of which was nearly permanent dislocation for a significant portion of the population. In all, it is estimated that fully half of Mozambique's population in 1992 (sixteen million people) had been dispossessed of the means of production during the war, whether through dislocation, inadequate subsistence (food, water, health care, housing), or fighting and death (Isaacman and Isaacman 1983). Not until the Peace Accord was signed in 1992 did the approximately six million displaced Mozambicans begin to return "home." This dislocation is part of the reason for the lack of attachment to place I found in many community histories, as discussed in chapter 5.

The socialist organization of agricultural production dominated official policy from 1975 (Frelimo's Third Party Congress) to 1983 (the Fourth Party Congress). The Third Congress tried to abolish large private companies, thus reducing the weight of both traditional authorities and the family sector (Pitcher 1998: 124). Yet perhaps the most consequential component of socialist transition was villagization. To foster collective settlement, the Ministry of Agriculture created nine state farms intended to be "poles of development" that would channel resources toward the villages and cooperatives and foster export production (41). Family farmers were assumed to be tied to or supported in some way by the cooperatives. As Anne Pitcher says, "in continuing to work with the rural sectors and groups that had been favored under colonial rule, Frelimo 'disrupted, reshaped and unsettled' social and economic relations without 'transforming, replacing or reconfiguring' them" (119; see also Matusse 2023). Instead of supporting smallholders or providing them with more access to land, Frelimo created *aldeias comunais* (villages) as a mechanism for organizing and retaining power in the countryside (Mosca 2005). Villagization was supposed to ensure the smooth delivery of government services and was originally voluntary, but smallholders were increasingly forced to join, particularly in the northern areas (Bowen et al. 2003: 229).

Christian Geffray (1990) has documented the initial support from rural areas for Frelimo, an enthusiasm and pride that slowly turned into a feeling of betrayal (see Brito 2019). They rebelled when Frelimo implemented policies that treated them as a relatively homogenous group, a "blank slate" (Geffray 1990: 16) that could be transformed by removing traditional authorities and creating new communal villages. All of the people Geffray interviewed for his 1991 classic on the conflict between Frelimo and Renamo gave "villagization" as one of their reasons for siding with Renamo (23). Frelimo replaced traditional rulers with party secretaries, but these party-loyal administrators were widely disliked because one of their tasks, especially in the north of the country, was to oversee villagization, a process that "brutally re-organized [local life], often in their own favor" 51–52). Rural residents did not exist as individuals who could exercise their own agency in this new historical moment; rather, "the agents and development specialists of the state see the rural populations only as an 'arithmetic series' of socialized individuals . . . as if peasants exist isolated from each other and waited, curiously, for Frelimo to give them a social organization" (53).

Frelimo's struggle against the legacies of colonialism, as well as the country's attempt to implement a new form of African socialism, received considerable support from Scandinavian countries. The Mozambique–Nordic Agriculture Program (MONAP) provided approximately 1,200 million SEK (US$192 million in 1992) over thirteen continuous years, 1977–1990.[4] Each of the countries that supported MONAP (Sweden, Finland, Norway, Denmark, and Iceland) was engaged in other development activities throughout the country, but agriculture was considered particularly important because it was the primary activity for the majority of residents and had been catastrophically undermined during the struggle for independence. These donors provided material support, and the FAO provided technical assistance, as it was considered more adept in tropical agriculture than the Nordic countries.

Between 1979 and 1984, MONAP provided approximately 80 percent of the budget for the Ministry of Agriculture in Mozambique. Funding was relatively flexible, allowing ministry officials to use it to build up ambitious and far-ranging new programs. A summary report written by independent consultants (Adam et al. 1991) assessing the aid program concluded that "the finance available for MONAP has generally exceeded the capacity of Mozambican agencies to effectively use that money" (24), but (as is often the case with international donor funding) there was significant pressure to spend all available funds. A review of the literature on this period suggests that Frelimo's focus was on achieving results quickly, in part through large-scale agriculture with a desire for mechanized commodity farms and little in-depth understanding of the diverse nature of rural inhabitants in the country. Agricultural research focused on a small number of commodity crops and a desire for overly advanced technologies, generating "large over-capacity in the equipment supplied" (24). Reliance on external funding contributed to these problems, especially in the context of growing tensions and violence; more money was spent propping up the administrative structure than on building the capacity of the local people, whether scientists, extension agents, or farmers.

MONAP encountered significant difficulties in its efforts to support the family sector. The program supported Frelimo's policy of bringing all peasant farmers into the cooperative sector, but the government's ability to provide good agricultural training was hampered by a number of factors, including the fact that "unfortunate views about the 'backwardness' and inevitable historical redundancy of peasant systems of production have been confirmed or not sufficiently questioned" (Adam et al. 1991: 103–4). In addition, the government saw rural producers as a relatively homogenous group, echoing colonial perspectives (Bowen 2000; O'Laughlin 1995). Reviews of MONAP suggested that "a better policy will require recognition of how diversified and heterogeneous the family sector is."[5]

Staff working under MONAP adapted to these difficult circumstances by focusing on getting things done quickly, an attitude that still shaped agricultural aid in Mozambique thirty years later. Ministry officials diverted funds on an "emergency basis" from sectors that had been compromised by violence or security concerns (much of the north of the country), putting these resources into sectors with a "substantial absorptive capacity" (Adam et al. 1991: 57): namely, seeds, machinery, and livestock. Generous funding allowed government officials to indulge their desire for advanced machinery and to adopt more than was necessary. For example, there was widespread enthusiasm for the tropicultor, a two-wheeled carrier for various agricultural field implements. The tropicultor was intended to be carried by oxen and had become popular among European aid organizations and agricultural research agencies in the 1970s. Though heavy, it could be used for plowing, planting, and fertilization. Under the MONAP programs, approximately four hundred tropicultors were imported and distributed around the country, but in 1990, Aid Under Fire consultants were "unable to find evidence that any were still in use." The problem was that they "had been introduced without taking into consideration the regions where tsetse flies would prohibit the use of oxen." Even worse, "traditional implements had been abandoned prematurely in favour of the tropicultor, resulting in difficulties getting fieldwork completed" (80–81). This preference for the tropicultor by MONAP aid workers and local officials had many analogs in Mozambique when I was there. Indeed, this paragraph from the Aid Under Fire report describes well what I saw: "[There was a] determined resistance on the part of some national staff and cooperants to the idea of intermediate technology, to the use of local materials, and to the notion that the peasantry had the capacity to resolve their own problems. Conversely, there was a strong commitment to mechanization, fertilisers and large-scale production" (81).

Under MONAP, varietal research focused on rice and corn, with researchers lamenting that "some of the major family sector food crops, notably manioc and millets, will not benefit from [the development of new varieties] for a long time to come" (Adam et al. 1991: 35). The review of MONAP in the end deemed the program's focus on the seed industry to have neglected upstream analyses of land management with local practices of selection and exchange. In general, agricultural work under the Ministry of Agriculture suffered heavily from "projectification," defined as "the tying of most of its financial and personnel resources to a very large number of individual foreign aid projects" (24). The authors further concluded that insufficient funding had gone into capacity building for Ministry or research staff: "A notable omission . . . is formal training" (31). Part of the problem was that most MONAP interventions were rooted in very little baseline data (63) and demonstrated very little concern with the impact the projects had on the beneficiaries (85). The MONAP projects, the report found, were inappropriate, too capital intensive, and dependent on foreign aid. Even with all of the attention that agriculture received in the years following independence, production and productivity dropped precipitously after 1980. Falling commodity prices, global economic stagnation, mismanagement, and the difficulties with armed conflict exacerbated the difficulties of early postcolonial agricultural management. I cite the Aid Under Fire report (Adam et al. 1991) for the postwar period extensively because it so closely matches my own observations of agricultural research and rural development in the 2010s.

In 1986 the first president of independent Mozambique, Samora Machel, died tragically and suspiciously in a plane crash. A year later, the socialist experiment was modified significantly. In 1987 Frelimo embraced a new policy labeled the Programa de Reabilitação Econômica (PRE; Economic Rehabilitation Program) that introduced reforms to liberalize the market. Collective farms were largely dismantled in the 1980s as part of the civil war, and land tenure issues were one of the most pressing questions as the country ended hostilities in 1992 (Tanner 2010). With the PRE in place, the government reached a deal with the International Monetary Fund (IMF) on a funding package (Newitt 1995: 567), and structural adjustment policies were adopted (Wuyts 2001: 1). This opened the door to greater funding from Western nations that had previously turned their backs on Frelimo— particularly the United States, which tied its funding to programs that would privilege the private sector and the market. Increased funds from external aid, the privatization of roughly fifteen hundred state enterprises (Castel-Branco 2022: 18), and the associated sale of national and natural resources (particularly aluminum, natural gas, and coal) provided resources that were increasingly accumulated by a small elite affiliated with Frelimo (Brito 2009). There was a "tacit assumption" that Frelimo elites were able to extract rents from privatization and large-scale, "market" projects (Buur and Monjane 2016: 211; also see Matusse 2023; Adalima 2022b; Hanlon 2002, 2004; Pitcher 2002; Sumich 2010). Notwithstanding an official emphasis on smallholders (Pitcher 1998: 131), agricultural spending in practice would replicate many of the structural priorities of previous eras, with a focus on commodity agriculture at scale and a reliance on external funds and external knowledge.

PROAGRI: COORDINATING INTERNATIONAL AID FOR FARMING, 1998–2011

In the late 1990s a newly expanded group of donors came together to try to coordinate aid in agriculture for Mozambique. Ten years earlier, in 1977, MONAP had been the only significant source of funding for the Ministry of Agriculture, but by the late 1980s, the Nordic countries were just one of many donors. There was a common perception that the Ministry of Agriculture and Livestock (MAP) had more money from external sources than it could spend, in part because the money was located across many different "programs supported through a confusing and uncoordinated array of donor initiatives" (Rivera and Alex 2004: 3). The Program for Agriculture (PROAGRI) was an attempt to bring all of the donors together, pool their funding, and coordinate activities: "PROAGRI would reform MAP's structures around a rationalized set of core activities and would coordinate donor support to these programs" (Cabral 2009: 34). In 1997 the total budget for the Ministry of Agriculture was US$48 million, roughly 90 percent of which was provided by external donors (34).[6]

The World Bank and the FAO led the coordination effort, building support for PROAGRI among donors. The Danish aid agency, DANIDA, hosted a meeting of donors in Copenhagen to bring everyone together in the new program. The technical group for PROAGRI consisted of the World Bank, DANIDA, the Swedish International Development Cooperation Agency (SIDA), the United Nations Development Programme (UNDP), the United States Agency for International Development (USAID), and the FAO. "PROAGRI would replace fragmented donor-driven projects," the World Bank maintained, "with a comprehensive program consistent with MAP's role in a market-based economy" (1999: 5). Echoing the Washington Consensus of the 1990s, the market was the centerpiece of the programming: "While responding to the needs of the sector as a whole, PROAGRI will focus on overcoming failures in markets and regulations which hold back the development of the 3 million smallholder subsistence farmers" (8).

PROAGRI provided US$216 million to Mozambique for the first five years, with the World Bank providing $39.7 million, other donors providing $154.8 million, and the government of Mozambique contributing $22 million. In the end, PROAGRI's efforts to decentralize agricultural infrastructure and rationalize aid would last from 1998 to 2011. The final report for the first phase PROAGRI in 2005 listed many of the same problems that had characterized the colonial and socialist period. One of the key issues noted in the final report was that although creating a connection between research and extension had been a key focus, little or no improved linkage was achieved. Research and extension had their own agendas, the report stated, and did not collaborate well. Both needed to work harder to get to farmers. Researchers were urged to "diversify their activities away from [new plant] varieties towards subjects such as pests" that involved land management and local farmers. In most provinces, the report authors said, "researchers had very little knowledge of the needs in the field and the extensionists did not convey relevant information to any research institutions" (PROAGRI Final Evaluation 2007: 27). Part of the difficulty in coordinating service delivery was that "farmers were so heterogeneous," but the main issue was the separation between the activities of research and extension: "From our interviews, most of the researchers feel that their role terminates once they produce a report on their research findings and the rest is the responsibility of the extension agents and producers" (70).

Complaints about PROAGRI were ultimately similar to the complaints about MONAP, and more energy might have been expended to understand the reasons for this similarity. The final evaluation of PROAGRI documented its "biggest failing" as the inadequate "record on capacity building" (PROAGRI Final Evaluation 2007: 14). One researcher I interviewed in 2016 seconded this, saying that both MONAP and PROAGRI focused too little on developing production or people and too much on developing bureaucratic systems (see also Cabral 2009). A retired senior administrator from the Ministry of Agriculture (Interview 51, December 20, 2016) remembered, in bemusement, how many cars had been paid for, and how they all lined up every day at the Ministry of Agriculture headquarters in Maputo. That long line of new cars symbolized the difficulties in coordinating PROAGRI. The program, he said, focused too much attention on building the institutional framework for the ministry and not enough on educating researchers, extensionists, or farmers themselves.[7]

SUPPORTING AGRICULTURAL RESEARCH IN MOZAMBIQUE: IIAM

Under the auspices of PROAGRI, the IIAM transitioned in 2004 from an "agronomy" research institute to an "agrarian" research institute because the latter was seen as broader and more interdisciplinary. A new agricultural research institute was formed, the Mozambican Institute for Agrarian

Research (Instituto de Investigação Agrária de Moçambique, IIAM).[8] This revitalized and reorganized IIAM was a technical research institute and concentrated on adapting universal principles of plant and soil science to the Mozambican context. The interpretive social sciences (such as economics, sociology, and anthropology), with their focus on understanding local histories and contexts, were largely left out, although when IIAM was formed it contained departments such as the Training Center (Centro de Formação) that developed an interdisciplinary farming systems pedagogy. The disappearance of the training center and the near-total lack of social sciences in IIAM reflected the priority placed on scientific principles. It also highlighted the difficulty the researchers had in going beyond the technical aspects of agricultural science to connect with farmers and communities.

In 2016 IIAM was organized into four departments: Administration and Finances; Training and Technology Transfer (DFDTT—this was the old Centro de Formação that in 2016 was considered the communications department); Animals; and Agronomy and Natural Resources. DARN was the largest of the four in 2016, with forty-five "superior technicians" who had postgraduate credentials.

In December 2016 I talked with a man I call Fernando who worked in IIAM's senior administration for ten years, from 2004 to 2014 (Interview 20, December 5, 2016). We met in a noisy café in downtown Maputo to talk about the early years of the institute. He was nostalgic but regretful. Working in research in Mozambique was hard, he said multiple times. So many people were committed to seeing real progress, but there was so much to be done and limited resources: "The idea was that this reorganization would bring about a real transformation [an integrated approach to research], but that didn't happen." Fernando said that the donors, particularly the World Bank "influenced the conversation," although the process was relatively participatory, and people from the government and former research agency in Mozambique were included. Another agronomist, who had been the director of the national extension agency for many years, remembered that Mozambicans in the government hadn't wanted to create IIAM, but the donors insisted. Over many years, "some changes happened," Fernando said, "but unfortunately I can't say they were the changes we imagined."

One of the important goals the funding agencies and government representatives had when IIAM was created was to address the long-standing problem of having the research services located predominantly in the capital city of Maputo. Fernando talked about this at length: "We wanted the headquarters to become a very small thing and to guarantee that most of the research would happen in the regional offices," he told me. "But this was a very big challenge." IIAM lacked sufficient infrastructure to adequately support the regional staff and activities, but the biggest problem may have been a cultural one. Maputo—long considered the "pearl of southern Africa," as one high-ranking USAID official said (others called it the "pearl of the Indian Ocean")—was an island of relative colonial grandeur, modern amenities, paved roads, and political relevance. The elite from government agencies to NGOs and private sector companies wanted to be there (Kleibl and Munck 2016) because once outside Maputo, basic necessities like electricity, cell connection, paved roads, and clean drinking water were scarce and unreliable. It is not surprising that as late as 1997, only 21 percent of the agricultural staff in the original IIAM with academic training worked outside of Maputo (World Bank 1997: 7).

This preference for the capital was cited in the final report on PROAGRI, which echoed the earlier "serious concern about what seems to be a lack of balance between headquarters and zonal centers" (World Bank 1997: 7).[9] For Fernando, changing this culture would have required changing the political and cultural economy that shaped access to government work in Mozambique: "We inherited a situation in which most of the people who worked [at IIAM] lived in the city of Maputo. We couldn't force people to move. . . . How could I take a woman who was married and had children here . . ." He trailed off. "People already had their lives established here—and their husbands. . . . We had a lot of women working for us as agronomists and their husbands couldn't be asked to move. Their husbands were often in political leadership. We wanted to build capacity in the regional centers, but we didn't really have the people power." As a next-best strategy, Fernando hoped to train new agronomists who would work in the regional offices, but while "there was pressure from the partners [donors] to change things," there were "no real resources." USAID financed a dozen masters' students, and these researchers went to the regional offices, but they were not enough to pull the focus away from Maputo. As a result, "research hasn't been decentralized." People traveled from Maputo to the regions periodically, but that was not optimal because (as research directors throughout the twentieth century had noted) "agronomy is very local."

New projects were often located in or near Maputo even if another location might have made more sense. One example was More Food (Mais Alimentos), a highly successful horticulture project funded by USAID and the Brazilian government that focused on improving vegetable production in the green belt around Maputo. I talked with the lead agronomist for this project in the experimental garden plot at Umbeluzi as he proudly loaded up a wheelbarrow with project vegetables for me (Interview 11, July 29,

2016). He directed field assistants this way and that while answering my questions:

> When [the Brazilians] came here, it still hadn't been decided where IIAM would locate the project. We knew that it would focus on horticultures, but we didn't know where to host the project, which unit would be the unit of reference. We went around and around until we came to the conclusion that it had to be the experiment station at Umbeluzi. It's 27 kilometers from the city of Maputo, which would facilitate the whole process [of communication] with the headquarters.

In this way, the centrality of the capital city to agricultural research reinforced itself over time.

FOLLOWING THE MONEY: PAYING ATTENTION TO DONORS

Given the lack of resources in the Mozambican state, donors played a dominant role in the early days of IIAM. The importance of donors and diversity of opinions and funding streams made coordinating agricultural research difficult. As Fernando said, "[R]unning IIAM and depending on donors [in the early days of the institute was] not easy." As with MONAP in the late 1980s, in the 1990s and 2000s donors were providing more funding than IIAM was able to productively use: "IIAM can't spend all of the money it receives," another long-time IIAM researcher said, "because it doesn't have capacity" (Interview 6, July 20, 2016). With so much money coming in, there was an enormous amount of bureaucracy: "IIAM had to keep good records and be accountable to the funders in the end" (Interview 20, December 5, 2016). At the same time, IIAM found it difficult to assert any real control over what the donors funded or what projects the external research organizations took on. The main building on the Maputo IIAM campus had a "collaboration floor" that held offices for its most prominent international partners. The Consultative Group for International Agricultural Research (CGIAR) was well represented, particularly IFPRI, the International Rice Research Institute (IRRI), and the International Livestock Research Institute (ILRI), as was USAID, Michigan State, and Embrapa. There were attempts to get these organizations to work together, but they all came with their own funding and generally, as Fernando said, "worked in isolation." In many cases, they even "acted as if they were in competition with researchers from IIAM when there were competitive calls for external funding" (Interview 20, December 5, 2016).

One researcher who worked at the Umbeluzi Experiment Station said that IIAM generated its own research plan, but final decisions depended on funding. "We did a priority setting exercise—I think it was 2006," she said. "We recommended the type of technologies, types of crops to focus on, and so on. But, sometimes, you know, we rely on funding, external funding and sometimes we, how can I say, we adjust things according to what is available, you know, what will be funded" (Interview 41, November 10, 2016). This pragmatic approach made sense given how dependent Mozambique was on external funding for agricultural research, but it undermined IIAM's ability to produce research tailored to the country's needs, particularly given that the donors all had their own interests based on national interests, agency focus, and the suite of projects already in their portfolio. As another agronomist from Mozambique who worked for the FAO put it:

> The donors have areas of preference. For example, I am not going to talk about gender with the Japanese embassy, they don't have any interest in this! Or about human rights with the Japanese, they don't have any interest in this! But if I discuss the issue of fishing, I can do that with the Italian embassy; if I talk about wildlife and forests, I can do that with the Germans; and if I discuss the topic of gender, I can do that with the Norwegians. If I want to talk about emergency questions, some rural poverty, I can do that with the British. But if I want irrigation, I can talk to the Japanese. If I want statistics, I can talk to the Swedes. (Interview 9, July 27, 2016)

These preferences were well known, and researchers targeted their project proposals with the intention of capturing specific interests. It was a challenge, however, to keep in sight any overarching goal, such as improving well-being in rural Mozambique, with such distinct interests by each foreign donor or entity.

For reasons to do with their own funding sources and metrics of success, donors prioritized projects that could be carried out "at scale," addressing problems seen as similar across multiple countries. Researchers in Mozambique often scrambled to fit national or local priorities into these more easily generalizable studies. Even within Mozambique, distinct ecologies across the country provided a challenge to programs designed in the capital city. This approach meant that local priorities were sometimes neglected, and post-project analysis of impact was more difficult. As one researcher admitted when I asked him how he assessed the impact of research in IIAM, "[I]t's hard to do an evaluation of impact because when you do, you have to do it for/in the various counties who are partnering on that project so you design the study to assess adoption, but the big problem is that this has to be endorsed by at least two countries, of the three that took part. So this is complicated sometimes, because the thing that interests me might not interest the guy from Zambia, or the guy from Malawi, and what interests that person might not interest me" (Interview 14, September 15, 2016).

The sweet potato project was a good example—it was clearly intended for farmers, but it originated with the International Potato Center based in South Africa. The work on the sweet potato had begun in the late 1990s. They first received a handful of varieties from other countries, but because those varieties weren't from Mozambique, they didn't do well in the country, being particularly susceptible to drought. In 2005 the project received funding from the Alliance for a Green Revolution in Africa (AGRA, primarily funded by the Gates Foundation), and it developed new varieties based on local potatoes. These were more tolerant to local conditions. The orange flesh, of course, came from outside Mozambique and was crossed with local varieties to improve yield, nutrition, and resistance to stressful conditions. This wasn't a project that farmers in Mozambique had asked for, and farmers had to be convinced to try the new varieties because they were different from the traditional ones. The scientist who led us around for the farmer field day at Umbeluzi blamed the lack of adoption on extension agents, saying said that if the orange-fleshed sweet potatoes were better promoted, farmers would adopt them, knowing that they could feed their families and sell them: "[W]e are seeing more and more sweet potato in the market," he said enthusiastically, "and this is a good thing."

The focus on the market had been a key element of donor engagement in Mozambique since the liberalization of the 1980s, and it was perhaps most evident in the bilateral aid relationship between the United States and Mozambique. Various projects funded by USAID brought together a focus on cash crops, seed companies, input sellers, and machinery rentals. The Mozambican director for USAID described its efforts to foster trust in markets (from both farmers and commercial actors): "USAID is also pushing seed companies to work on branding and developing systems for traceability. [If this is in place], it will encourage extension agents to promote the crops. Seed companies need better technological capacity. They need to build trust such that clients know they can rely on them for quality. Extension agents should know the agro-dealers in their areas, and so on" (Interview 17, September 20, 2016). An agronomist with IRRI echoed his predecessors throughout the twentieth century when he divided crops into "market crops" and "food crops." He said, "There is a Big Division [*grande divisão*] in this country between market commodities [*culturas de rendimento*] and food crops [*culturas alimentares*]" (Interview 16, September 19, 2016). He recognized that this was "an artificial division" but maintained that it was one that existed both in discourse and in practice: "The market crops are cashew, cotton, tobacco, et cetera, and the food crops are manioc, corn—and rice. The former crops have a complete value chain, all of the elements of the value chain are working. The latter have a value chain that isn't closed. Producers here hold back much of their production to eat or seed the next crops and they only sell the surplus. The market here simply doesn't exist."

Markets were fickle creatures, though, and local farmers did not always trust them. There was a history of state or other actors such as local merchants encouraging farmers to produce a crop, only to have the market disappear. The public declaration of the existence of a market was often a way to bring it into being. The story of chickpeas (*feijão boer*) in 2016 was indicative. Extension agents and local traders were promoting the crop aggressively that fall, telling local farmers that the Mozambican government had signed an agreement with the Indian government, with the latter promising to buy a sizable amount of the harvest. Farmers I talked to were nervous, but many planted in the hopes that they would have a sellable crop. In the end, the Indian farmers produced a better crop in-country than expected, and the buyers never materialized. An agronomist from the northeastern city of Nampula indicated that producers were starting to get fed up: "Sometimes there's a case, I think the government was promoting one specific crop and they recommended farmers produce it, but in the end the farmers couldn't sell it, so they just took all the production to the government and said, 'Ok, we produced it, where can we sell that?'" Therefore, as another researcher put it, "to say 'there is no market' is not totally accurate. Sometimes 'there is no market' because the government promoted a market for a product . . . but when it came time to sell, the buyers weren't there. So, for that crop it was true that there was no market, but it wasn't necessarily an indication of supply and demand" (Interview 13a [first interview], July 22, 2015).

One researcher at the Center for Socio-Economic Studies (CESE) at IIAM summed up this point in a story that centered on corn agriculture in the early 2000s:

> I don't know if you've heard of Global 2000 [a market promotion project in Mozambique from the early 2000s]. That program had technology—improved varieties—inputs tripled or quadrupled, and yields quintupled, but then in the end the farmer couldn't sell what they planted. He ended up poorer than he when he started, because that fertilizer, the new seed, all of it was on credit, with the idea that after he sold it, he would pay back the loan. He ended up in debt because he couldn't sell that surplus. This for me is the big problem, it's not worth just looking at the technology alone, without looking at the whole chain. (Interview 14, September 15, 2016; see also Howard et al. 2003)

USAID maintained its focus on the market even if doing so went against the interests of the Mozambican state and against the advice of researchers at IIAM, who thought there were more immediate needs in technology development. As the USAID director quoted earlier said, "[W]e [USAID] have our own country strategy—they [the Mozambican government] can't just tell us what to do" (Interview 17, September 20, 2016).

In the end, there was a lot of synergy between the external research and donor agencies and the Mozambican state because donors influenced the national agenda. The Mozambican government had a surplus of strategic statements, issuing them regularly as guides for external engagement. When I was in Mozambique in 2016, there were several different national-level plans and strategies that were relevant for the organization of agricultural research. They were ambitious but long on vision and short on strategies (or funds) for execution. These plans had all been co-designed with external donors, who therefore directly influenced the programs they then aligned with.

RESEARCH AND TECHNOLOGY: A FOCUS ON NEW VARIETIES

In part because of the influence of these external donors, IIAM's focus in its early years (one that continues today) was on developing new technologies. Echoing the report on MONAP, Fernando said that these research groups came to Mozambique "to develop technologies but they should have come here to develop capacity in research. They only talked about this. . . . Their role was to develop technologies, not to develop people. They were not impressed with the local talent" (Interview 20, December 5, 2016). In 2011 IIAM published its first strategic plan (2011–2015) and emphasized its commitment to technical solutions for agriculture: "Many of the problems confronted by consumers, like costs, regularity, and quality of food are of a technological nature and can be treated by the agricultural-livestock research institution" (IIAM 2011: 7). The goal for the first five years was to develop fifty technological innovations, and so the focus on discoveries that had characterized Portuguese colonization continued. Work on subsistence crops was generally funneled through aid organizations and NGOs (not research organizations) that focused on land management alternatives, such as conservation agriculture and farmer field schools (see chapter 5). One IIAM scientist dismissed such land management alternatives as "a thing of the university," meaning that he thought it was theoretical work, rather than applied, practical research. A grant maker from the FAO office in Maputo agreed, saying that conservation agriculture was just for "poor people," whereas what Mozambique really needed was research that would help it to develop (Interview 10, July 27, 2016).

The emphasis on varieties was the key feature of the farmer field day at Umbeluzi. IIAM had released more varieties of sweet potato than any other research program in Africa. It was helping researchers in other countries in Africa and Asia adopt the varieties it produced. Sweet potato varieties had been researched in the laboratory and then developed through field experiments; the vagaries of land management were not part of the experimental process.

At about 9:00 on the morning of the farmer field day in Umbeluzi, the farmers finally showed up. As the scientist continued his discussion of the difference between the pink- and orange-fleshed sweet potatoes, a group of five farmers—three women and two men—rushed into the station and were ushered to the front of the group with great flourish. The extension agent, at the station director's behest, had gone to a nearby producer association and rounded up as many farmers he could find there.[10]

Oblivious to the excitement, the scientist continued talking, explaining that they were looking for varieties with more iron. Following an awkward pause and some brief discussion, another man was brought to the front of the group to translate the discussion into the local language for the farmers.[11] Everyone laughed cheerily at the difficulty of translating technical words into the local language. "How do you say 'iron'?" someone asked.

"We mostly did the sweet potatoes for kids under five and for pregnant women," the scientist continued. The director of IIAM intervened excitedly: "Tell them about anti-oxidants and how sweet potatoes are good against cancer."

Urging the farmers to try the sweet potato, the scientist admitted that they might not like the new varieties at first: "Maybe we think this new potato doesn't taste as good [as our traditional varieties]," he said, "but this is a question of habit." If it was a habit not to eat sweet potatoes, it was a bad one and one that needed to change. The variety's off-putting smell, he added, came from the beta carotene, and "we have to get used to it. If you want better health, we have to use this potato and promote it in our communities." The director of IIAM said, helpfully, "[I]f you roast the potato, it's tastier than if you boil it." Everyone nodded, and the farmers laughed quietly, clearly unsure of what to make of being told how to cook their food by the head of the country's agricultural research institute. People like the director were figures of high status in the rural areas, and cooking was considered "women's work" and fairly intimate. To be lectured on family diets in a public setting by a "doctor" was likely off-putting for the men and embarrassing for the women.[12]

The scientist continued in a similar vein: if you harvest the sweet potato and let it sit a few days, he recommended, it will be tastier. "We learned many things [during the research]," he said, "like the juice [is good]! We're going to try some later [back at the station headquarters]." At this point, the head of another local extension office arrived and apologized for being late. He had only found out about the field day yesterday. He joined the conversation to say that "the leaves [of these new sweet potatoes] are good. . . . We have to substitute [potato] for bread, our famous bread!" "Yeah, they're tasty!" the director of IIAM jumped in again. "Tell [the farmers] how we should switch from bread."

But for farmers to adopt the seed, they had to be able to produce according to recommendations established under experimental conditions. The difference between good yield and bad was clearly not just a function of the seed, although IIAM researchers tended to focus on the seed itself rather than land management, and blamed farmers if they could not get the same results when they planted the new varieties. But land management should also have been considered, as well as the diversity of agroecological conditions. An agronomist with IRRI highlighted this point: "[W]hat we need is better land management, not varieties. . . . We have lots of good land that could be utilized—if we managed to do three things: good preparation of the soil, level out the land, and banding for irrigation, then you would increase production from 1 ton/ha to 3 ton/ha. Production methods are our biggest problem. If you go to the producer and give him better seed, you also have to level the land and help with water" (Interview 16, September 19, 2016). This seemed clear with corn seeds, for example, as there were pamphlets (published in 2015) for six different varieties at the 2016 field day in Umbeluzi. Each variety had a wide range of potential yield, suggesting that while new varieties might have the capacity to produce a certain amount, much still depended on farm conditions, weather, and management.[13]

After this discussion of how the new sweet potatoes tasted, the group began walking out to the fields. We circled the first variety, named Irene, which had been dug up, cleaned, and laid out on a small tarp. The scientists pitched the potato enthusiastically, as if in marketing, selling us on how good the variety was. "Irene, she adapts to any area locally, the variety is in almost every little farm [around here]; it is used to very little water and people like the thinner leaves . . . beyond the food source, the leaves help with 'headache.'" People laughed again as the speaker mimed a headache, his gestures insinuating that such a headache might come from a night of excessive drinking. One of the farmers asked how the variety should be planted.

The scientist said, "This new variety does well in drought conditions so the kids will always have sweet potato in the schools. But just because it's tolerant doesn't mean it doesn't need any water—we do need to put some in in the first few days." He continued, "If it rains regularly for one month the potato will do well. It produces 10 ton/ha. Here in the station [the potato] produces 20 tons/ha and if you used (commercial) fertilizer you'd get 30 tons/ha. The cycle takes four or five months. Colleagues—sweet potato right now is money—25 meticais per kilo. You do the math!" Following the scientist's enthusiastic pitch, someone from IIAM asked if any of the farmers had this new variety in their fields. There was some confusion at the question, but the conversation trailed off after one person said that maybe they had it and had harvested it already.

The Erica variety was named after the breeder's daughter. All of the varieties except for three were named after women. Someone said this was "because women do more." Another variety was named Tio Joe after the representative from AGRA who had brought them some of the first plants.

A farmer asked a question about irrigation, to which the scientist responded that it depended on the rain and air temperature. "Where is your farm?" he asked; after the farmer's answer, he declared, "[Y]our soil is like ours, irrigate once per week." Irrigation was a continual source of concern for smallholders, as few could afford motors to draw water to their fields from nearby rivers or creeks. They watered by hand, relying on children and women to fill buckets and carry them to the fields on their heads.[14] The director of IIAM asked the communications person to take a picture of the farmer who asked about irrigation. Another person asked about fertilizer, whether they should use urea or compost. Answer: if you're doing it for seed, urea, if you're doing it for the tuber, compost. The IIAM director waved us all on impatiently; these questions were too much in the weeds! But we had to wait because the women farmers were all in the experimental plot collecting sweet potatoes as quickly as they could to take home with them. One woman complained loudly because she had run out of the house so quickly when they were called to attend the field day that she left in a dress that didn't have any pockets. She took off one of her *capulanas* (her cloth wrap traditional dress) and rolled sweet potatoes up in it, still complaining.

Eventually we stopped in front of a corn plot and a new breeder took over. He said he would speak in Portuguese and just translate the important things for the farmers, but the director of IIAM was getting impatient. "Only say important things," she admonished, "and translate all of it." There was another pause as we looked again for someone who could translate.

Some of the ears of corn in this plot had white and yellow kernels mixed together, which wasn't intentional. A female farmer commented on the frequency of such unintended outcomes: "Sometimes you have beautiful clean seed," she said, "and you plant it but the ears come out small and yellow." A male farmer agreed, suggesting that maybe there was something wrong with the seed: "[S]ometimes just the male plant grows nice and tall, but alone." The breeder denied that the issue was the seed, arguing that the cause was likely bad planting practices: "Yes," he replied, "there's something you can buy; you buy it at the same time as the seed from the same place, mix it in." "But," the same farmer insisted, "it often happens that you buy seed from elsewhere and it's not the same thing." Another farmer suggested that the station should have a window of time in which they sold the seed to local farmers (presumably after releasing the variety but before liberating it to private companies that would sell only small quantities and often in stores far away). The scientist objected, saying that the seed had to be certified and multiplied and IIAM did not control that process: "We produce basic seed in IIAM—it's not our fault if it isn't good! Why don't we deliver seed directly to you? It's because the seed we deliver is genetic seed."[15] There was some nervous laughter and discussion about how to translate the word "genetic" into the local language. The farmers were not in on the joke, and it wasn't clear how the word got translated. The scientist attempted to explain why the farmers might get lower yields on their land and then think that they were getting inferior seed: "These plants are produced under perfect conditions, so if we get 20 tons per hectare you won't get that because here it's very well controlled. Maybe you'll get 10 tons per hectare and that would be really good. Our quantity of seed is quite low. We have perfect conditions, fertilizer, water, et cetera, because we have to know how much water it needs."

The varieties being introduced to us that day in Umbeluzi, like most of the varieties produced in IIAM, were bred to be productive (high yielding) under optimal conditions. They were not bred with resource-poor farmers in. mind. All of the farmers I met cared about yield, but maximizing productivity was secondary to getting a harvest at all without technical assistance or inputs. The same IRRI scientist quoted previously explained:

> We spend a lot of time on varieties but we're always promoting productivity at the expense of resilience, ironically. . . . The problem here is not varieties! We have great varieties, but the producers don't have good management. The varieties that they have are not bred for

resistance; they are bred for productivity. There was a breeder who created a kind of super rice, and this is what all the breeders want; the super rice is one that can yield 15 tons/ha. The characteristics for productivity are all vertical ones, and so if you mess with the [horizontal] characteristics for resistance . . . then your rice won't be as spectacular. You need to balance these two demands. (Interview 16, September 19, 2016)[16]

The longtime lead for USAID's work in Mozambique made a similar point, but in her experience the push for more productive varieties came from the government: "The government really just focuses on production. . . . The government's relationship more generally to the market is very unclear—the government is still very much focused on production and productivity" (Interview 17, September 20, 2016).

THE AFTERTHOUGHT? ADOPTION

The focus on producing new varieties in accordance with external demands meant that farmers often did not know how to enter into the research process. This was clear when the farmers finally got to ask the key question about the new sweet potato varieties.

"Any questions?" the scientist asked. Everyone looked at the farmers expectantly. There was only one question. It was clearly the most important question and the one that no one in attendance could answer. A male farmer asked if there would be credit available from the government to help people purchase the sweet potato and plant it. At this, there was an awkward pause, then laughter. "We're IIAM," the scientist replied, as if that was the end of the discussion. When the silence continued, though, he went on: "We're looking into how to multiply the stalks—for a while we multiplied new varieties and distributed them for free. But now there is no money, it has disappeared, so we have to find a private seed seller to multiply the seed. But just for this year, because of the drought, some people will benefit from a project funded by the IPC [International Potato Center] here in the South of the country. Also, we work with Producer Associations and if you have a very well-organized association, we can give you one plant that will multiply in your association."

Another farmer, a woman, asked, "Where can we get this seed?" The breeder was hesitant: "Ah, well, there's a whole chain of seed production . . ." He looked around, and another person filled in, "you can get this seed in Chokwe, a company there sells it." Chokwe is a small town in Gaza province about 250 kilometers (at least a three-hour drive) from the station. "How are we going to get out of here to get that seed?" another farmer asked. The answer was that IIAM was not involved in dissemination. "We release the seed and there is a supply chain that has to do this work."

One of the farmers said, stubbornly, gesturing around him, "[W]ell, given that we live close to [the experiment station where it was produced], we should be able to get seed easily." Another farmer agreed, suggesting that IIAM should actively build the supply network. He was sorry to insist, he said, but they lived here in the neighborhood, and it was difficult for them to get to Chokwe. He politely requested that IIAM release the seeds "directly to the farmer." The scientist, seemingly surprised by this reaction, said defensively, "[T]he station has already done its work." He echoed others I had spoken with in IIAM when he said that the research institute couldn't address adoption because once the seed was produced, it no longer belonged to research. "The seed goes from here—in kernels. It goes to processing . . . and then is reproduced. . . . At that point it belongs to the company, not to IIAM, and the firm has to produce certified seed."

None of the researchers I spoke to factored adoption into their work, whether prior to breeding or afterward. As a scientist with a large international research organization put it, "Scientists say, 'I am not a politician.' They—we—are worried about technical problems. We are worried about the number of varieties we liberate. This is a serious problem. The focus is still on new varieties and technologies" (Interview 16, September 19, 2016). Although this scientist suggested that the focus on varieties—to the exclusion of a more holistic focus on the farm or farmer—was problematic, he insisted that his job ended at the research gate: "I don't know how the varieties we release are received, we usually don't [know]" (Interview 16, September 19, 2016). Researchers just have a sense that "people like this or that variety." Adoption does not enter into decisions about which varieties to develop because adoption is not considered science: "People—farmers—do their own seed selection on the farm and it's not science: they just decide here and there what they like—leaves, taste, et cetera" (Interview 16, September 19, 2016). There was a recognition that adoption was important, but this was for social scientists, and they weren't consulted at the beginning of the research process. As a scientist with the International Fertilizer Development Center (IFDC) told me, "They say that we should have this socio-economic component but some of the projects start just thinking about the technology, so this integration is hard to do in practice" (Interview 33, November, 28 2016).

An agronomist from IRRI described the new varieties that it had liberated and was clear that concerns about adoption did not factor into the process for approval (Interview 16, September 19, 2016). IRRI Mozambique liberated one new variety in both 2012 and 2013 and three in 2015. IRRI and IIAM researched the varieties and together applied for approval from the Subcommittee for Registration of Varieties (Subcomité de Registro de Variedades, SRV), which is made up of representatives from extension, the National Institute of Normalization and Quality (Instituto Nacional de Normalização e Qualidade, INNOQ), the private sector, and so on. If the SRV approves the seed, then IIAM goes through the multiplication process to create the pre-basic and basic seed, which it sends to the Unit for Basic Seed (Unidade de Semente Básica, USEBA). At that point, the new seed joins the list of official varieties. With every variety they produce, the agronomists issue a *carta tecnológica* (technological card), which contains a generic set of guidelines (when to plant, how much water, etc.), even though every farmer is different and has different resources. IRRI researchers generally do not know how the varieties they produced and liberated are received. An agronomist located at Umbeluzi agreed: "We are generating a lot of technologies, but they are not being used, because there are problems along the chain. For instance, seeds. We have a lot of new varieties released but if you go to the market, you will not find them" (Interview 41, November 10, 2016).[17]

At the farmer field day in Umbeluzi, one of the team leaders from IIAM then said that adoption was an important issue and maybe the association should talk with extension to see if the association could help to multiply seed. This did not stop the conversation, though, which continued heatedly: small groups of farmers, extension agents, and scientists formed, arguing about whether and how a farmer could get access to seeds and whose responsibility this was.

Finally, the director of IIAM sought to broker a peace: "Our friends from Extension, they're bringing up an important issue. IIAM says 'it isn't our problem' [*não cabe a nós*], but that isn't enough to say." One of the IIAM researchers objected loudly: "But it's the company [that disseminates], not us!" This reignited the discussion, which continued for quite a while, until one of the IIAM scientists said that it was time to close the conversation and go through more of the corn plots to see which varieties people liked. This seemed like a dangerous suggestion to me, as it was clear that the farmers liked a lot of the varieties and would only want to know how to get new ones they were shown. But we continued with the plan.

As a gesture of goodwill, an agreement was made that IIAM breeders would go with the extension agents to a couple of associations and see whether conditions existed to plant some varieties, with the idea that the associations could multiply the plants and distribute them locally. A date was set for the following Monday, and an uneasy peace ensued.

At the closing of the day, after we had eaten several sweet potatoes each and seen a brief demonstration of a new mini tractor (with people riding happily around the demonstration area and others cheering them on), the director of IIAM said that three people should volunteer to say how they felt the field day had gone. The director waited expectantly, but even after a long pause no one volunteered. The director repeated that she wanted to hear from "a mamã," at which one of the women said, formally but quietly, "[T]hank you for everything we saw, we say thank you, and we would like to have the material to reproduce Irene." Another man stepped forward, speaking on behalf of his fellow farmers. "We also would like to say thank you. As an association, we need research, so we ask for more occasions like this."

The representative from the extension office in Matola also took the floor: "Thank you—there should always be a tie between research and extension because this is what is important. Extension always needs to go to research because this relationship will help extension to do its work. Next time we will really try to have farmers here."

"We all need to tell others," one of the team leaders from IIAM agreed, "to share the value of these plants. We shouldn't talk about extension, research, and farmers separately. Everyone should be proactive and go to the struggle together."

The director of IIAM wrapped up the proceedings: "Today was excellent," she declared, "because we heard from the farmers."

At that, a pickup truck backed up the dirt road to where we all stood. The director of IIAM was beaming; it was clear she had arranged this. Several of the scientists jumped into the back of the pickup and handed out sweet potato and corn plants to the farmers, who took them eagerly. I think I was the only person in the group that day who was surprised. The station and IIAM weren't required to distribute resources to farmers, and in fact many layers of bureaucracy and a long-standing division between research and extension worked against them having the opportunity, but doing so as a handout in the context of a field day fit within a local moral economy shaped by scarcity, inequality, and patronage. Without this encounter, it was extremely unlikely that these farmers—or, indeed, most farmers in Mozambique, as this chapter suggests—would have been able to access the new varieties. Watching the farmers stack their plants on the side of the dirt road, the director said happily, "[T]he farmers who came to the field day can multiply these plants in their fields and distribute them to their neighbors."

As I watched, one of the men selling the mini tractors that people had been riding around on (a man of Indian descent born in New Jersey, who didn't speak Portuguese well) came up next to me and said quietly, "[T]his is corruption, right?" And as I watched the excitement, I said "no," thinking that that was much too facile a description for something so complicated. Under colonial rule, rural inhabitants had received some minimum assistance from the chartered companies. In the 1980s when the economy liberalized, such dependence was recast as small acts of corruption or even begging (Adalima 2022a; Matusse 2023), but looking for every possible resource was a survival strategy in the context of conditions that often fell below the level of social reproduction. I tried to convey this to the tractor salesman even as he shook his head. I said, "It's just the station trying to help out in a difficult situation." The farmers wanted these new varieties not because they were dying to plant sweet potatoes but because they wanted and needed every advantage that they could get their hands on. They were living precarious lives: access to a handout could mean the difference between life and death. And the scientists and the director of IIAM were desperate to hand out these plants because the field day was intended to be triumphant—a chance to show that their work could benefit Mozambique and make life better for its poorest residents, even if this was rarely their focus.

CONCLUSION: GROUNDING THE PLANTATION IDEAL

In the late 2010s, the impoverished Mozambican government looked to export agriculture for foreign exchange, much as the Portuguese did. Perpetually underfunded, agricultural research was still focused on a search for new varieties of tropical commodities that could be planted at scale for export. As was the case under the Portuguese, this concern for new varieties trumped research into local varieties or land management; the selection of new varieties became the end point of the research process. Technical guides for new varieties of sweet potato, cotton, soy, manioc, pigeon pea, corn, and more littered the small tables in the IIAM waiting room, but it was estimated that less than 5 percent of these varieties were ever adopted by farmers in the country. Research efforts across IIAM were divided—sometimes formally, sometimes informally—into projects for "emerging" entrepreneurial farmers and projects for poor, subsistence farmers, thus echoing the colonial categories of "civilized" (European) and native farmers. Most of the research projects in IIAM were intended to benefit the former—entrepreneurial farmers—while most of the country's farmers fell into the latter category: they lacked the resources to purchase new seeds, fertilizer, or machinery and were rightly cautious about entering into new markets, given their considerable experience with rapid market booms and busts.

In 2016 researchers depended entirely on foreign funding for research (only their base salaries were covered by the Ministry of Agriculture), and research dynamics were shaped by the political economy of international agricultural funding. Most competitive funding was short term (three to five years) and prioritized technical innovation over adoption or implementation. Research calls released by multi-lateral funding agencies were often hosted in one country and assumed that new technologies could be relatively easily applied in another. When research was based in Mozambique, agencies tended to have their headquarters and even their field offices in the capital city of Maputo, echoing the reluctance of their colonial counterparts to travel to "the districts." All of these factors—the legacy of colonization, the influence of the global market, the nature of the state, and the pull of foreign funding—contributed to a body of knowledge on agriculture in Mozambique that was fragmented, opportunistic, and partial, focused on discovery rather than development. The farmers themselves were largely absent.

4. "Incompatible with a Progressive Agriculture"

The "Problem of Labor" in Colonial and Postcolonial Mozambique

At 7:00 a.m. on Friday, December 2, 2016, Teo picked me up outside my hotel in Nampula, the dusty capital of the province by the same name in northern Mozambique. The day was already hot—full sun and no wind. It would rain later that afternoon, but unless someone told you it was raining, you wouldn't know. You could hear the drops, but you couldn't see or feel them, and the moisture made no difference to the temperature. The road from Nampula to the much smaller town of Ribáuè was one of the few paved roads in good condition in the province. We drove fast and made it to the DADTCO collection site early.

DADTCO is a Dutch company that was moderately famous in Mozambique for having developed a mobile manioc processing unit (MPU). The unit consisted of a conveyer belt that loaded freshly dug and cleaned manioc roots into a machine that pulped, milled, and cleaned the manioc before expressing the water to create small blocks of pure starch. These blocks had multiple uses but were primarily destined for distillation into a beer called Impala. DADTCO partnered with the International Fertilizer Development Center (IFDC), a somewhat oddly named research NGO (given that it does much more than fertilizer) funded primarily by USAID and allied with IIAM in its work assisting farmers in two different regions of Mozambique. Given that farmers here had been planting manioc for centuries, the researchers and DADTCO weren't really teaching them how to plant so much as teaching them how to plant manioc in ways that matched the rhythm and needs of the market.

The DADTCO collection site in Ribáuè sat right off the main road, surrounded by fields of manioc: the head-high, telltale knobby stalks standing silently, their sparse green leaves providing little shade for the soil. When we pulled in, several men in a pickup truck were loading manioc roots onto the conveyer belt (see figures 3–6). A small, covered area with two tables and plastic chairs sat off to the side; two young women were waiting with a small cash box, ledger, and laptop to make note of any manioc deliveries. No one took much note of me, and I wandered around the machine and eventually plopped down into an empty chair under the tent. As I sat there, writing field notes and taking pictures, activity began to pick up. Teo brought news that a government minister would be visiting shortly (people thought it was the minister of agriculture, but it turned out to be the minister of transportation and commerce). The workers at the DADTCO mobile MPU were given blue hairnets, and a few were given brand new red gloves still clipped in the middle with plastic ties. People looked at the equipment oddly, as if at a loss, but upon Teo's urging, they gamely put the nets on their heads and gloves on their hands.

At 9:30 a.m., the minister pulled up in a convoy of trucks and an SUV. Surrounded by a group of bodyguards with dark sunglasses on, as well as by reporters and others, he looked the machine over, asked Teo if any Mozambicans had a share in the company (the answer was no), and then went over to the tented area. A farmer sat in front of one of the tables and looked startled when the minister clapped him on the shoulder with a hearty greeting and asked how much land the farmer had planted in manioc that season. The farmer blinked but eventually answered, to which the minister replied, still heartily, "Well, you're going to plant more next time, right? You have to expand!" The farmer responded that he would plant more "if he had the *força* [strength]." At that moment, as he sat somewhat limply on his chair, it seemed very unlikely that he would indeed have the strength, but the minister declared, "Of course you have the *força*!" Facing the audience, the minister said that what the farmer had planted this season he had done with one arm, and he held up one of the farmer's arms in demonstration, but now the farmer would have to plant with the other arm too! Everyone, including the farmer, nodded in agreement with this nonsensical statement, and the minister and his incredible retinue marched off, getting back into their cars and driving away in less time than it had taken for people to get their new gloves on.

The ministerial visit to the MPU was probably just one of a dozen meetings he had planned for that day, but it represented a century-long attitude toward rural inhabitants in Mozambique. The minister never paused to ask the farmer whether he had eaten that day or if he had access to basic services or even the tools he needed to plant the manioc. In fact, he was likely only there because the new market for manioc beer and the international partnerships that supported it had received so much attention. Unconcerned

FIGURE 3. DADTCO mobile production unit, December 2016. Photo by author.

FIGURE 4. Loading up manioc for DADTCO, December 2016. Photo by author.

FIGURE 5. Documenting deliveries and assigning due dates, December 2016. Photo by author.

FIGURE 6. Planting manioc for DADTCO, December 2016. Photo by author.

with the specifics of the farmer's life on the land, the minister told him he needed to work harder and produce more to make this market profitable, for the good of the country.

In the context of this book's larger argument about the plantation ideal, this chapter examines how the prioritization of plantation agriculture has shaped labor relations in Mozambique. Colonial and postcolonial periods alike have been characterized by an extractive approach that sees local farmers as an inconvenient but necessary labor supply rather than as constituting a distinct agricultural sector with its own practices. This perspective has reduced the possibilities for developing local markets and communities.

This chapter picks up the history from chapter 2, focusing on colonial and postcolonial perspectives on Africans as farmers. The Portuguese believed that the success of colonization in Mozambique depended on recruiting local residents to do the work: first as forced labor on plantations and in urban areas, and then increasingly as contract farmers growing commodity crops for the benefit of the metropole. Committed to plantations for export, they dismissed local techniques and crops, investing very little time in understanding either. A perspective grounded in Portuguese racial superiority vis-à-vis both the local population and other colonial powers—or Lusotropicalism—lay underneath both the ignorance and the harsh methods of this period.

In the second half of this chapter, I illustrate this argument with an elaboration of the way in which local officials and scientists treated manioc—both the tuber itself and its production. Manioc, the most widely planted and consumed indigenous foodstuff, was discussed regularly in colonial handbooks and discourse but never received any research or support, instead being seen as "naturally abundant," appealing to local residents because it required little technique to plant and grew easily with seemingly no effort. Moreover, the neglect of manioc would continue during the transition to independence. From the 1970s to the 1990s, there was little research into how to make this tuber more productive or nutritious—or even just less poisonous (as discussed later, some varieties are toxic if not cooked or dried correctly). Only in the 1990s, as drought and plant disease combined to threaten mass starvation, did international agencies fund a series of programs to develop new disease-resistant manioc varieties. As this new program developed, plans emerged for turning the tuber into a commodity crop by changing the way people planted and harvested it. Although well intentioned, the project would eventually falter because local farmers were once again expected to adapt their labor in service of the spatial and temporal logics of a distant market.

"ONLY THE BLACK CAN FERTILIZE AFRICA":
COLONIAL LABOR POLICY AND PERSPECTIVE

There is excellent and growing scholarship that details the legal and political infrastructure created to extract and govern labor in Mozambique, referred to as the *Indigenato*, as well as the myriad ways in which local residents evaded or challenged their circumstances.[1] Mozambican history was marked by the brutal treatment of indigenous residents under Portuguese colonization. This was not settler colonialism, with its logic of elimination (Elkins and Pedersen 2005); rather, Portuguese colonization was predicated on the logic of extraction, in which labor remained on the land in order to be deployed more effectively (Castel-Branco 2014; Penvenne 2005). Although conditions differed throughout the period of Portuguese rule and across the territory, colonization alienated local inhabitants from their land; deprived them of equal rights in the face of the law or colonial society; and regularly subjected men, women, and children to inhumane, degrading, and abusive treatment with the ultimate goal of extracting their labor and other services. When Portugal deepened colonial rule in Mozambique in the early 1900s, it quickly became clear that there would not be a sufficient supply of colonists from Portugal to make Mozambique profitable (Macamo 2005: 69). White settlers were regarded as not only too few in number but also hardly able to withstand the rigors of the tropics. As Governor-General of Mozambique Mousinho de Albuquerque wrote in 1898, Portuguese colonization depended on securing indigenous labor, because "the climatic conditions of the province of Mozambique . . . make it impossible to use the European immigrant, not just as an agricultural worker, but in many violent jobs, because they will not last in that climate" (Albuquerque 1898: 99).

Labor was difficult to secure, however, particularly for plantation work. Other opportunities for work were available in southern Africa, particularly out-migration to South African mines and work in neighboring Rhodesia and Nyasaland (Macamo 2005: 76; First 1977; Harris 1959). Alternative methods of enticement would be needed to generate sufficient labor to make colonial plantations productive. In 1899 Portuguese High Commissioner Antonio Ennes established the Regulamento de Trabalho Indígena or the Labor Law of 1899, which stated definitively that "the black and only the black can fertilize Africa" (cited in Newitt 1995: 384). This legislation formally abolished the prior system of forced labor (enslavement), instituting the concept of "tutelage" under which local residents had "moral and legal" obligations to work a certain number of days per year, a system referred to as the *chibalo* or *xibalo* (Newitt 1995: 363–84). Slavery in Portugal had been abolished in 1869, and the local residents of Mozambique were "free," the Portuguese were at pains to point out, to at least choose where they worked. The law also codified the legal difference between Europeans (civilized) and indigenous (natives, or non-civilized), requiring all adult indigenous males to voluntarily engage in work. The bridge between this stated commitment to freedom and the more than seventy years of forced labor was the piecemeal set of rules known as the Indigenato.

The Indigenato subordinated the indigenous to *régulos*, local chiefs who governed everyday life in rural *regadorias* (O'Laughlin 2000).[2] Régulos collected hut taxes and had wide authority to take and use land as long as they supplied labor for official and commercial purposes. Under the chibalo, indigenous men over the age of eighteen were required to perform six months of service each year, usually for the plantations or settler farms. Women were incorporated into the labor system as primary providers for their families and communities, allowing the Portuguese to benefit from labor while women provided the means of social reproduction. In return for providing labor from local residents, régulos were given higher prices for cashews, bonuses, and the right to use forced labor for their own purposes (Isaacman and Isaacman 1983). Local residents identified as police (*sipaios*) were enlisted to enforce labor and production regulations. If they fulfilled these obligations fully (although "fully" was not clearly defined), they would be granted "assimilated" status. Very few ever achieved this status; at independence, fewer than 1 percent of all indigenous peoples occupied this legal category (Isaacman and Isaacman 1983).

This was arguably the harshest labor regime of any colonial power in the twentieth century. In his compelling in-depth treatment of labor in the Mozambique Company territory, Eric Allina referred to it as "slavery by any other name" (2012). The regime's harshness was embedded in deep prejudice toward local residents. Mousinho de Albuquerque captured the sentiment at the time: "One of the most difficult problems and at the same time the one whose resolution is most insistently imposed on Africa is, without doubt, that which results from the necessity of using indigenous labor and the difficulties that their habits of indolence common to all wild things [*selvagens*] present" (Albuquerque 1898: 99). The Portuguese felt they had no choice but to rely on indigenous labor, and at the same time they resented being captive to what they saw as the whims of a population that felt little allegiance to the Portuguese or affinity for plantation agriculture.

The Portuguese perspective on indigenous farming and farmers was simple and repeated often in the archives.[3] Local officials and scientists alike believed that local residents were "inclined to indolence" and thus maintained primitive farming techniques that relied on long fallow periods and regular movement (swidden agriculture).[4] Only patient education, the incentive of a wage, and the requirement of tax payments would educate or "civilize" the indigenous person, teaching them the value of regular labor (Vilhena 1910: 150–51). In his presentation to an international audience, the colonial administrator Ernesto Jardim de Vilhena emphasized the supposedly educational aspects of forced labor,[5] arguing that more force would be required initially, as indigenous peoples were introduced to the benefits of work:

> [T]here is proof that for natives in their primitive state, who are wild and not affected by the presence of white people, a regime of compulsion is needed to teach them the habit of work, guaranteeing, at the same time, labor for the white colonist that he cannot do without. In relation to the more civilized [native] people, it is appropriate to adopt the principle of the legal and moral obligation to work, in his own business or that of others, so that the indigenous laborer will present himself in his place of work on a regular basis, without long periods of scarcity or intermittence. (150–51)

The proper cultivation of local labor, Vilhena insisted, would bear spectacular fruit, guaranteeing "a brilliant future of intensive agricultural and industrial exploitation" for the colony.

In 1930 the Colonial Act—written by António Salazar—laid out new regulations to extract more labor for plantation production. Indigenous "reserves" had been authorized in 1909, but with the Colonial Act, the checkerboard organization of land, in which local residents planted commodity crops on small plots of land in reserves alongside Europeans living in separate areas, gained more official support (Direito 2013). In 1936, at the First Economic Conference, Director of Agriculture Carlos de Melo Vieira argued that while "European agriculture" was paramount, indigenous agriculture should be developed alongside it: "It is necessary to protect [European agriculture] because this is what truly secures the continuity of sovereignty, and it is what most collaborates with the State in the work of civilizing the native and in taking advantage of and developing native agriculture. The coexistence of the two activities (European and native agriculture) is therefore indispensable, at least until the native reaches a higher degree of civilization; the progress of each and the development of the country depends on their harmonious operation" (1936: n.p.). What is clear from this quote is that Portuguese officials like Carlos de Melo Vieira felt that their success in Mozambique depended on the extraction of labor and other services from local residents.

The demand for cotton production to supply Portugal's textile industry increased in the 1930s, resulting in the establishment of the Cotton Export Committee in 1938 and requirements for export provisions. In 1939 Francisco José Vieira Machado presented his work on creating indigenous villages (*aldeamento indígena*) that would allow local residents security in tenure, thereby creating a love of property and an end to their "vagabond habits" (Direito 2013: 782). In 1940 the Estatuto do Agricultor Africano outlined the rights of indigenous farmers producing subsistence and cash crops on the land.[6] By the mid-1940s roughly one million Mozambican peasants were producing cotton for Portugal (Isaacman and Isaacman 1983: 45), particularly in the north of the country. These farmers were required to sell cotton to private companies, which then sent the material on to Portugal.

Even as Portuguese officials turned land over to local residents, they worried that production would be hampered by what they saw as poor agricultural methods. The perception that local residents were incompetent farmers turned in part on their use of swidden agriculture. This manner of cultivation, with long fallow periods and regular movement to new fields, struck the Europeans as extraordinarily wasteful. As Lyne (1913: 48) summarized, "Generally the African method of cultivating is to till the ground in patches, so that while a lot of land is occupied a little of it is used. This wasteful system, or want of system, is, at bottom, the reason why Europe has appropriated Africa in accordance with the maxim, 'The tools to him that can use them.'" While some scientists recognized the value of swidden agriculture, they were a minority, and even if it could be proven to be a productive strategy for managing soil fertility, it was still antithetical to plantation production.[7] Swidden farming frustrated so-called development because it occupied excessive land with little return and made it difficult to distribute assistance and public services (Grilo 1946). One of the foremost agricultural officials in the territory, for example, maintained that "everyone knows that native agriculture is backwards in our colonies as well as in other colonies in Africa"; as far as swidden agriculture (*culturas móveis* or *agricultura itinerante*) was concerned, he believed that "the state needs to intervene, not just to distribute improved seeds, or things like that, but above all to teach the native to build his property as the basis of his permanence [*fixação*] and, therefore, his civilization" (Gomes e Sousa 1932: 5). Several decades later, the survey of agricultural practices conducted by the reigning scientific institute in the territory similarly concluded that fallows needed to be "eliminated because they're not economical and they are incompatible with a progressive agriculture, and they will not aid us in our goal" (IICM 1959: 30).

The Portuguese established a limited number of teaching facilities to train local residents in "modern" or high agriculture—plantation agriculture—that would discourage swidden practices. The royal government ordered "regional farms" to be established throughout the territory to help educate would-be farmers in the colony. The highly influential commissioner António Ennes encouraged the creation of teaching plots within each farm. These regional farms were intended to aggregate "large numbers of blacks" who would plant their native crops and provide for their own subsistence, while the teaching plots would serve as "agricultural propaganda, educating the native and facilitating practical experiences." They should be expanded, Governor-General Albuquerque wrote as early as 1898, because they could fulfill subsistence needs, provide hay for the governor's cattle, and accelerate "the slow transformation of the character of the natives. . . . They are centers of teaching and propaganda."[8] In 1914 the colonial administration created a school at the Agronomic Station of Umbeluzi to "propagate the love of agriculture among natives."[9] On March 4, 1922, High Commissioner Brito Camacho expanded the school in the hopes of dedicating Umbeluzi's infrastructure in a more purposeful manner, but one year later (on April 5, 1923) Moreira da Fonseca, acting governor-general between 1919 and 1921 and between 1923 and 1924, shut down the school.

In 1942, when Portugal took over the land formerly leased out to the charter companies, national analyses of agriculture reflected dismay over local farming practices. Director of Agriculture Grilo described in blunt terms what he saw as the primitive nature of "native agriculture" in his two-volume report in 1944–1945:

> [O]ne can say that there is not any real agricultural professionalism among them, which is evidenced by their little farm [*machamba*] with such a small amount of land, without garden or orchard, almost always without cattle, just a forlorn chicken coop, practically without tools, in the hands solely of the woman, and with the desolate air of an individual who prepares to move and abandon the land. (Grilo 1946: 14)

For the Agricultural Services, the main issue for Mozambique was to secure a more compliant and hardworking indigenous labor force: "The biggest problem for organized agriculture in Mozambique is, without doubt, that of indigenous workers" (Grilo 1946: 154–59). The Agricultural Services also relied on indigenous workers, and Grilo saw firsthand the negative effects of compulsion:

> Whenever we can, we [in the Agriculture Department] try to get voluntary workers—meaning workers who are not forcibly recruited.

Prison labor is pretty good because the prisoners prefer working on the experimental stations to being in prison. We had to take natives who were brought in for light crimes or for not paying their taxes; these worked at Umbeluzi or in the government forests because those places couldn't afford to pay higher salaries. But this is the worst sort of labor because it's ill-fitting and undisciplined. (154–59)

General disdain for indigenous farming practices was based on very little actual knowledge of those practices. Lyne, the director of Agricultural Services from 1910 to 1912, noted his regret that so little effort had gone into understanding the local residents of the region. This ignorance, which he compared to a hunter not taking the time to acquaint himself with the characteristics of his prey, would hamper efficient growth in Mozambique:

When we go big-game shooting in Africa we prepare ourselves by studying . . . the habits and behaviour of the game we are going to hunt, but we do not take the same pains with the labour we are going to employ. Under the modern system of high cultivation, involving the elaborate study of the plant, the soil and the climate, we have overlooked the fact that in the Tropics there is another element to study of which the laboratory can tell us nothing. Hence the intending planter has few facilities for acquainting himself with the characteristics of the people whom he will be compelled to employ. . . . The African is what he is and what Nature has made him; and it is as much our duty to study him as to study the soil and climate. (Lyne 1913: 208–9)

Only in 1925 was the first relatively detailed study of local inhabitants, titled *Raças, Usos e Costumes*, published. The author, António Augusto Pereira Cabral, came from a family of local elites; his brother was the governor of the province. He described the various commissions charged with cataloging the indigenous populations of Mozambique, none of which had produced published reports: in 1916, the secretary of indigenous affairs had distributed an ethnographic questionnaire in the provinces "but with very little success." Cabral's review was intended to serve as the basis for a Civil Code to regulate indigenous affairs, because "European law is totally inapplicable" to local residents (1925: 6). Cabral echoed the belief, popular at the time, that colonial rule in Portuguese territories differed from that in other European colonies both because "their" indigenous people were different and because the Portuguese understood better how to govern in the tropics. The British had adapted their own laws into a set of "Native Laws," but "our natives," Cabral argued, "are not competent to govern themselves, as they do in British colonies" (8). Moreover, Portuguese law would favor labor time as punishment for infractions of the law because "[the Portuguese] recognize the need to obligate the native to work" (8).

Cabral's text was as detailed and informative as it was Eurocentric and discriminatory. The observations he cataloged, for example, included opining that the indigenous peoples of southern Mozambique were "better looking," taller, and more astute than their Macua brethren in the North, whom he described as ugly, short, and cowardly. All indigenous peoples, however, were "lazy by nature" (Cabral 1925: 26) and resembled "big children." He argued with scientific authority that they learned quickly as children, but their intellectual capacity stagnated and then declined upon reaching puberty (26). They had to be shown how to work the land because they were not farmers themselves. What yield they did take from the land was only the result of the labor of nature itself, not from any conscious intention by the indigenous person. Cabral summarized his short section on agriculture thus: "[T]hey have absolutely no notion of agriculture: what they do they do with simple intuition. They don't have the slightest idea about fertilizing plants, breeding, grafting, etc., and no irrigation by any system exists" (57). Cabral's overview of the indigenous peoples of Mozambique was largely designed to help Europeans understand what needed to be done to make local residents work in settled plantation agriculture.

Cabral's study bore many similarities to the ecological-agricultural survey conducted twenty-five years later, discussed in chapter 2. The chapter on demography in the EASM stood out for its extreme superficiality: the authors of this chapter stated that demography—"the human element"—was a "primordial factor of agricultural production" and so it could not be left out, even though the research team did not include a specialist qualified to take on questions related to the topic (CICA 1955: 231). The chapter authors described their information as being based on other works as well as on "data collected by the team," which must have consisted entirely of observations made while collecting field data for other chapters. The short chapter (only the section on geology has as few pages) represented the population in terms of available census numbers (inhabitants in the country) and drew heavily on categories such as "civilized" and "indigenous" that were not scientific but were "common-sense" for Portuguese or European colonists at the time. Indigenous peoples merited attention primarily in their capacity as laborers on so-called civilized farms, rather than as farmers in their own right.

The first and largest section of the demography chapter is "Population of Mozambique." The population is divided into two groups—non-indigenous

(1.6%) and indigenous (98.4%)—whom the authors describe tautologically: "The non-indigenous population is made up of civilized individuals and the indigenous population is made up of fairly backwards elements in terms of their degree of civilization" (CICA 1955: 232). The handful of people in the country (roughly four thousand) who had achieved the ambiguous status of "assimilated" were described thus: "The assimilated indigene belongs to the black race and is more evolved and acts as a transition between the European civilization and the civilization of the aborigine, that is a phase not far from nomadism" (233).

Information beyond these census numbers was very superficial, employing qualifiers such as "almost" and "commonly" without citations or evidence to support the claims: "Almost all the men in the non-indigenous group work in specialized professions, only a small group being in agriculture. . . . The male 'mixed' population can be . . . commonly found working as mechanics, truck drivers, etc." (CICA 1955: 234). The authors of the chapter lamented the lack of more refined census data: "[W]e wanted to collect information on the population in such a way that we could divide into age groups to better evaluate the labor capacity of this population. That wasn't possible because of lack of data" (236).

The conclusions garnered from the small amount of census data presented were simplistic and self-serving. The chapter did little more than count the people living in the territory, and it was only as laborers that the indigenous people counted, whether they were working as wage laborers or providing raw materials from their small plots of land: "From an economic point of view and as a factor of production, the indigenous population has the greatest weight in the economy, as this is the group that provides almost all of the labor" (CICA 1955: 236). The authors of this short chapter suggested that more work was needed to evaluate the growth rate of this valuable population as well as to gain some understanding of traditional practices and food, clothing, and other needs. The authors also presented a crude ethnic breakdown and a brief overview of the different economic activities undertaken by various ethnic groups.

In a version of the report written specifically with material collected in the southern province of Mozambique, the authors included a list of recommendations for indigenous agriculture. Despite their lack of familiarity with indigenous farmers, these recommendations once again focused on moving them away from traditional practices, crops, and norms and toward "easy" market-oriented products such as fruit trees and honey. Again without data, the authors insisted that indigenous farmers be taught—or forced—to stop practicing swidden agriculture. Even though many local scientists recognized the value of mobility for maximizing soil fertility, the recommendations in the report advocated a heavy hand to get indigenous farmers to abandon traditional methods: "Avoid, through advice but, in the last resort, though fines or penalties, the use of itinerant farming and burning, and demonstrate practically the utility of taking advantage of the land of old crops." The goals for working with local residents emphasized unidirectional directives such as elaborate, distribute, classify, introduce, improve, and guide and never learn, listen, observe, help, or build: ultimately, the research should "guide the native farmer in the sense of helping him to abandon the rudimentary techniques and to manage his property in harmony with the norms of village life, followed by the administrative authorities and by the Portuguese religious missions." These recommendations were intended to promote cash crops, specifically cotton production, although the commercial value of all their production was to be assessed. Efforts to fortify indigenous food and farming were likewise geared toward reaching the market.

Despite the difficulties they encountered in Mozambique, Portuguese rulers believed that they were uniquely adept at colonization because they had a special skill for ruling over local peoples, a skill that could unlock the productive potential of Mozambique. As I explained in chapter 1, the discourse of Portuguese exceptionalism was captured and elevated in the writing and philosophy of Gilberto Freyre, the Brazilian sociologist whose work on plantation society in Northeastern Brazil articulated the belief that the Latin American giant was a "racial democracy" borne of "multi-cultural" miscegenation, or intermarrying between white Portuguese settlers, Blacks, and indigenous peoples. This theory was politically useful to authoritarian governments in Brazil and Portugal but often appeared in quotidian and scholarly material. Perhaps the best illustration of this set of beliefs in Mozambique was written by a contemporary of Gilberto Freyre, the agronomist Rui Paiva, who was sent from his home state of São Paulo in 1951 to assess the competitiveness of African agriculture. Paiva was an agricultural economist and is now widely considered the father of agricultural economics in Brazil. Just one year before Freyre himself traveled to Europe, Paiva was sent to the colonies of sub-Saharan Africa (and later to India) to determine whether agricultural production from those regions could threaten Brazil's competitiveness, particularly in relation to coffee production.[10]

On his journey, Paiva visited each of the four major colonizing countries (Britain, Belgium, France, and Portugal) to investigate the plans they had for colonial rule.[11] He was very impressed by the elaborate plans laid out by Britain, Belgium, and France. Portugal, on the other hand, had no plans. Paiva wrote: "Portugal does not have a plan formulated for the development of its colonies. . . . The measures taken for its colonies are dictated by the necessities of the moment: they do not obey a general, previously delineated program. . . . The Portuguese say, jovially [*em tom de graça*], boasting of their accomplishments, that a plan isn't needed to make its colonies produce. . . . Planning, they add, is very easy on paper, but making the native work is what counts, and no one does this better than they" (1952: 43). For Paiva, this relationship with the indigenous was the principal difference between Portugal and the other colonizing countries. He argued that the reason the Portuguese colonies were not suffering the same rebellions as the other colonies was that "they treat [the native] with more kindness and they do not look to develop in him the more complicated sentiments of civilized man, such as a sense of responsibility, political conscience and a civic spirit or some other such thing" (43). Paiva echoed Cabral's 1925 study, arguing that the Portuguese had succeeded in ruling in Mozambique because they treated the indigenous person as fundamentally different than themselves but also as part of the "family": "Someone confirmed for us," he wrote, "that the native remains a friend and likes the Portuguese because the Portuguese treats him like a child: he gives him work and demands that he does it, punishing him if necessary but also giving him human attention and caring" (43–44). Paiva reported that he heard often that "armed force is not necessary because the natives have a lot of respect for the Portuguese and it's very rare to have a case of rebelliousness" (157).

Nevertheless, it was difficult for Paiva to understand why the indigenous peoples seemed to like the Portuguese so much, given that the Portuguese were so often cruel: "[W]hen you meet a native outside the colony, they say proudly 'I am Portuguese too'" (1952: 159). Paiva concluded that the explanation for this relatively harmonious relationship "comes from the fact that the Portuguese has taken the place of the 'chief' in the native hierarchy—he yells, punishes, and also helps the native and above all he is never afraid of them and does whatever they won't do just to show them" (159). To Paiva, this approach contrasted with that of the British, who closed themselves in and didn't mix informally with local peoples in their colonies:

> There is a huge difference between the Englishman, who builds a nucleus of comfort around himself and makes an effort to maintain all of the habits, customs, and attitudes of a highly civilized person, and the Portuguese, who shows himself to be daring [*ousado*], adventurous in his work of colonization and who makes an effort to show that in terms of courage and energy no one raises a hand to him [*lhe leva a palma*]. (159)

Paiva characterized the Portuguese as governing through the figure of a *Grande chefe* (chief), while the Englishman cultivated authority through the figure of Senhor, the civilized "master."[12]

In spite of the ease with "the natives" that he observed, Paiva was ambivalent about Portuguese colonization in Africa. On the one hand, he opined that "the Portuguese colony [of Mozambique] is one of the best that we visited in Africa" (1952: 149). On the other hand, he also observed that Portugal colonized not for the colony's sake but for Portugal's. The organization of agricultural production into plantations negatively affected the indigenous peoples upon whom the plantations depended as well as other smallholders: "[T]he large plantations," he commented, "work against the interests of the small farmers because they employ machines and so keep down the demand for and cost of labor" (165). Further, the concessionary companies and the commodity boards were authorized to take a surprisingly wide profit margin when purchasing crops from local producers and reselling them in Portugal: "[T]he prices that are set for these crops always favor the metropole (the purchaser) to the detriment of the colonial producers," and so "one can conclude that Portugal, of all the colonizing countries, is the one that least protects its colonies" (48).

This extractive and protectionist approach to the territories was also evident to Paiva in the very different approach to the agricultural sciences in Portuguese colonies relative to those of other countries. Paiva admired the extension and research services provided by the British in Tanzania, Kenya, and Uganda, saying that they not only showed the best new methods and crops but "also took time to demonstrate the validity of methods or crops the extension agents were already convinced were good but other farmers in the area were not." The researchers in these British colonial endeavors, he further noted, took a "very practical" approach, avoiding the pitfalls of a focus on "academic problems." In Mozambique, Paiva admired the Cotton Board and the work of the concessionary companies, but he singled out technical extension as an area that was not working well: "Used to seeing the functioning of the technical services of the English, who achieved great dissemination of the measures for combating erosion and crop rotation among the natives, what was being done in Mozambique seemed deficient to us" (1952: 162). This lack of attention to technique was evident throughout the colony: "We were surprised that the companies that owned the tea plantations hadn't adopted any measures to combat erosion, which is fairly visible in certain areas" (152–53). This lack of research into agricultural crops and production, as discussed in chapter 2, was a product of the belief that technique mattered less than the successful application of labor.

As calls for independence among the local population intensified, there were new efforts to target agricultural research and outreach directly to local residents. The 1959 report by IICM Director José Emílio dos Santos Pinto-Lopes (introduced in chapter 2) contained more detailed suggestions for planning indigenous agriculture, arguing once again that indigenous farmers should be moved away from swidden agriculture and that improving agricultural practices for all farmers was necessary for "evolving the nation" (IICM 1959: 16). The recommendations given for indigenous agriculture in the report were highly prescriptive, much as they were in the EASM, and focused on helping local farmers produce crops for the market, rather than producing primarily for their subsistence and marketing the surplus: "Indigenous agriculture is a way of farming not specifically or solely attributed to a particular group. It is family, subsistence, without well-defined properties or even erratic, with the habit of establishing new plots and abandoning the old ones. . . . With planning, we can end soil degradation, transform a more or less nomadic agriculture into an 'organized activity.' Proper planning [ordenamento] will do a lot! It will help to assimilate the native and to free people from agriculture for other activities" (20). Recommendations in the IICM report for agricultural areas of the "European type" were much less prescriptive and centered on the need for providing increased technical assistance and machinery (32).

In 1964 two distinguished agronomists, Camilo M. Silveira da Costa and Homero Martins Ferrinho, laid out the various elements of production in their handbook *Agricultura, silvicultura, piscicultura, apicultura* (Agriculture, silviculture, aquaculture, and apiculture). They urged the Portuguese regime to do a better job helping the Portuguese to settle Mozambique rather than relying on foreign capital, "which just extracts value," and emphasized the importance of addressing the colony's "lack of technical assistance and, not less, moral assistance" (Costa and Ferrinho 1964: preface). The authors believed that moral assistance was needed in part because there were so few Portuguese women in Mozambique, which had fostered too great a reliance on (and mixing with) the local population. What was needed was technical assistance and white women. Then, happily married Europeans would produce the technically demanding crops (like tea, coffee, and fruit trees) and indigenous peoples would produce subsistence and simple crops like papayas, mangoes, cashews, and bananas. Steeped in prejudice, the handbook instructed the reader on how best to extract value from the land and local residents of Mozambique.

That same year, prodded once again by the FAO, Portugal undertook a general agricultural survey of Mozambique. It created the Missions for the Agricultural Survey (Missões de Inquérito Agrícola) in January 1961 and started survey work in April. The survey divided farmers into two groups, following very different methodologies for gathering data for each of them. The first group included the "more evolved" farmers who were using modern (mechanized) techniques and producing for the market. The second group was the "large mass" (*grande massa*) of farmers who cultivated small areas with traditional methods, mostly producing for subsistence. To survey the first group, the team relied on questionnaires distributed by the extension agents and agronomists who serviced those farmers. Accessing the second group—which had never been done before, in any general agricultural survey—was more difficult, as this group had little connection to government assistance. The survey team therefore had to camp out in their study areas and visit the farms in their sample in person, marking off ten meters by ten meters and counting and weighing the produce at each site. Manioc—the most common food crop produced throughout the country—presented a particular challenge because it was not generally harvested all at once, so the team had to devise a method for estimating production based on rough calculations of the age of the manioc plants in any given field. Throughout 1961 the mission had only a handful of technical and administrative staff, but they conducted their work with a rigor that made this survey the most complete survey of indigenous agriculture during Portuguese rule.[13]

The study gave birth to a report on "traditional agriculture" (De Carvalho 1969). Using the survey figures, Mario de Carvalho, the head of the Mission for the Agricultural Survey, described the "agricultural regions" throughout Mozambique and the practices by which indigenous peoples had been adapting their farming practices to their local environment over the years, particularly to climatic features (rather than to soil, which he believed the Europeans concerned themselves with more). His analysis was more sympathetic than those that had come previously. Native crops, de Carvalho wrote, "are the crops, done with a minimum of outside interference, that translate the empirical knowledge, accumulated over generations that shows the degree of balance that the autochthonous farmer has managed to establish between the crops and the environment" (9). De Carvalho praised indigenous agriculture for adapting so well to climatic factors, rather than, as some suggested, to "superstitions, habits, races or even dietary necessities"—although, as he recognized, he had little knowledge of the specific practices of indigenous agriculture. The only way in which he (as well as the ethno-biologists before him) knew "the native" was in terms of broad ethnic classification and population density.

Years later, however, reflecting back on his time as an agronomist and lead researcher in Mozambique, de Carvalho concluded that what scientific research had been done had neglected indigenous farmers, almost exclusively focusing on colonial settlers and large-scale commercial crops:

> [W]e did not work very much in relation to the traditional food crops; one notes that we did not have any improved material in corn, manioc, or peanuts but the debt goes beyond that because we didn't take forward any work that was improved by our research, not only in regards to crops and techniques but, and principally, in terms of valid systems capable of substituting traditional ways, which the growing pressure on the land was making incapable of maintaining the fertility of the soil. (1989: 113)

The fifteen years since independence had given de Carvalho a newfound perspective on the exploitative nature of colonial rule: "[S]ometimes," he added "we lacked the humility and wisdom to try to understand the reasons, many times very logical, of certain practices of traditional agriculture" (113).

"YOU CAN ALSO FEED IT TO YOUR PIGS": MANIOC UNDER COLONIALISM

A crop that epitomizes this lack of humility and wisdom both during colonial rule and after is manioc.[14] Despite being a staple throughout the country, there was little to no research on the tuber, which was seen as embodying all of the traits of the local Mozambican that the Portuguese disliked: the tuber was easy to plant and, to the outsider, required few skills or tools or even technique to cultivate. The plant was hardy and hard to see or count, growing underground and interspersed with the natural vegetation. In the European plantations that the Portuguese forced indigenous Mozambicans to work on, cotton was the dominant crop, but it was manioc, as the food crop for local laborers, that made cotton possible. Thus, one could argue, manioc enabled the colony. Manioc is in many ways a miracle crop: high yielding in difficult conditions, a good source of carbohydrates, drought resistant, and easy to grow. But it is a miracle crop for keeping people alive, not for enabling them to live well. It is less filling than corn or potatoes and it is not nutritious, particularly given that the bitter varieties favored in northern Mozambique have levels of cyanide that are poisonous without proper preparation. Manioc is life, but not living, and not a livelihood for most of those who plant it. Manioc is thus the foundation for Portuguese colonization as well as a metaphor for it: the crop that kept people and colony just healthy enough to serve their function as laborers for the metropole.

Manioc (also known as cassava, yuca, or Brazilian arrowroot, as well as the plant that gives us tapioca) is a perennial woody shrub that grows anywhere from five to twelve feet tall. The many (thousands of) varieties are classified as sweet or bitter, depending not on the taste of the tuber (which can be quite misleading) but on the level of hydrocyanic acid (HCN). Bitter varieties contain cyanogenic glycosides that are toxic if not cooked or dried correctly. Although the sweet varieties have the advantage of a slightly shorter growing season, in addition to not being poisonous, the bitter varieties tend to yield larger roots and can be left in the ground longer (Karasch 2000). The manioc plant yields well in soils that are low in fertility, particularly in the acidic soils of northeastern Mozambique. Manioc propagates vegetatively and grows well in wet or dry conditions. It requires relatively little work, can be left in the ground for up to three months after reaching maturity, and grows below ground so has natural protection from many pests (including locusts, monkeys, and representatives of the state). "Even in poor land," one Portuguese scholar wrote in 1960, "it's enough to stick the stalks in the ground at convenient intervals to get a reasonable harvest" (Rodrigues 1960: 76). The peel is the richest in proteins, fats, and HCN, but most people peel the tuber because the skin is quite tough, difficult to clean, and tastes like bark.

As numerous as the advantages of manioc are, the crop does not appear to have dominated local diets in Mozambique until well into the twentieth century. The exact date and route by which manioc was introduced into East Africa is not well known.[15] It was originally incorporated into a local diet rich in diversified grains, legumes, and meat. Early accounts of the region from European travelers describe the seemingly bountiful indigenous gardens, filled with sorghum, millet, groundnuts, and squashes (Jones 1959). R. C. F. Maugham's account, written in the early 1900s, provides one such example:

> In the neighbourhood of the older established villages one finds
> planted, in addition to the food-producing cereals, ground nuts (Arachis
> hypogeia), the castor-oil plant (Ricinus comunis), melons, pumpkins,
> cucumbers, gourds, of which serviceable household and other utensils
> are fashioned, sweet potatoes, manioc (cassava), tobacco, tomatoes,
> red pepper, and kidney beans. In addition to the foregoing, pineapples,
> pawpaws, bananas of various kinds, and, more rarely, lemons, limes,
> and sugarcane. Numerous other wild fruits are gathered and eaten
> in their season, but their native names would convey but little to the
> reader at home. (1906: 288–89)

In 1913 Robert Lyne described the plants cultivated by "indigenous" farmers in his guide for "the intending settler and investor" as including "manioc, pigeon peas, groundnuts, sweet potato, yams of enormous size, citrus, cashew, bananas, tobacco, turmeric, tonniers, castor oil and sesame" (36).

Manioc seems to have been planted widely, but as a famine or reserve crop for periods of low harvest. As early as the late eighteenth century, Francisco José de Lacerda e Almeida, who traveled across Mozambique on behalf of the colonial administration, provided a detailed description of manioc agriculture, noting in particular how it was eaten when other food sources were less available:

> The soil of this land is fertile, and would produce all that the people want; there are many kinds of food, but the principal is manioc. They eat it in dough, toasted and boiled and even raw; and they drink it in pombe with a little mixture of millet. Manioc flour for dough is easily made in the following way: after gathering the root, they peel it, and soak it in a stream for three days; on the fourth, when it is almost rotten, they dry it in the summer sun, or in winter over a fire which they light under the cots used for this purpose; and, finally, they pound it in a tree-trunk mortar. We may say that they are collecting and sowing this root all the year round, but the harvest is when provision is wholly wanting. At such times they dig up a small quantity to last for a few days, and in its stead they bury a few bits of stalk which act as seed. (1889: 129)

Increasingly, however, manioc became more significant in local diets. The full extent of manioc production is difficult to estimate definitively, given that, as I have shown, little official investigation was ever done of indigenous farm production, but by 1970, "manioc, cultivated throughout the province, can be considered the food crop that occupies the greatest area" (Mota 1970: 23).[16] Despite the earlier evidence of diversified farm production, European observers concluded that indigenous peoples "naturally" relied on manioc because of the plant's ecological characteristics and the indigenous propensity to laziness and disorganization in their farming methods. As one agronomist wrote, echoing the general sentiment in the archives, manioc's "expansion is primarily due to the easy method of production [à fácil cultura] and good productivity in varied climatic conditions and in almost all soils" (23). A compendium of best agricultural practices likewise stated authoritatively, "The popularity of this plant, among the indigenous in all of Africa, is due to its vigorous growth, to its certain and good yield, to its resistance to drought or dryness, to the limited and easy work that it requires as well as the ease with which it can be kept in the soil which, together with its long harvest season, allowed the roots to be collected according to necessity" (Costa and Ferrinho 1964: 88). Manioc was widely considered suitable for people who had no concept of fixed property rights, migrated from one plot to another, and harvested the plant opportunistically when it was time to move on.[17]

Manioc may be the ultimate "famine reserve" crop (Jones 1959), but it has serious deficiencies: it is low in necessary nutrients as well as potentially toxic. In the early 1960s, Salvador Nunes conducted one of the few studies of manioc during the colonial period. He focused on the nutritional content of different varieties in order to assess the potential for expansion (Nunes 1964). He found corn and sorghum to be significantly better for calories, protein, and iron, as well as considerably less toxic. "Effectively," Nunes concluded, "the low or trace percentages of protein and fat put manioc in the category of 'unhealthy food' [*alimentos desequilibrados*]. Although the native (autochthon) is interested in manioc for its carbohydrates, its easy cultivation and low cost of production, and this brings him to consider manioc a basic subsistence good" (137). Manioc is best if it is one of many elements of a diet, providing starch while other goods like peanuts, squash, fruit, and vegetables provide the balance.

In contrast to popular belief at the time, manioc production did not expand because its agronomic characteristics mirrored the natural desires of the indigenous population; rather, manioc production grew because it was the food colonial rulers used to prop up the labor force. Manioc was the crop chosen by government officials, plantation owners, police officers, and military commanders to feed those under their control, from African slaves in the sugar mills of Brazil, to plantation laborers across Africa, to prisoners captured by opposition forces in Mozambique (Karasch 2000: 183; Geffray 1990: 66).

Providing cheap food was important in colonial Mozambique because cheap labor was so important for the colonial enterprise, as I have argued, but it was subject to a delicate balance: too little food and the laborers could not perform, too much and they would refuse to work on the plantations. Survival, rather than starvation or thriving, was ideal for the colonial administration. As the agronomist Ernesto Jardim de Vilhena (1910: 11) wrote, "[T]he irregularity of the rains in season and quantity hurt the natives' agriculture a little, and directly influences the solution of the labor problem because it frequently causes scarcity of subsistence production, which, at least in theory, is intimately tied to a greater demand for work [by local residents]."[18] In other words, Vilhena suggested that a bad harvest would benefit the Portuguese, because the lack of food required local residents to seek paid work.

In these circumstances, manioc was not considered a viable plantation crop (most writers at the time believed that Europeans would find no profit in food crops in general, because those crops required more indigenous labor than was available to the colonists), but it came to be seen as the key to unlocking the potential of indigenous plantation labor. The commodity with which manioc was probably most closely associated was cotton. This relationship went back as far as the eighteenth century: "From 1765 to 1799," Maugham recounted, "the destinies of the country were in the hands of one Balthazar Manuel Pereira do Lago. . . . The cultivation of cotton and manioc became obligatory, and many feiras [places of exchange and barter] were founded throughout the colony" (1906: 24).[19] Under harsh conditions on the cotton plantations—which Allen Isaacman describes as the "Mother of Poverty"—manioc became an important staple for cotton growers (Isaacman et al. 1980: 594; see also Bowen 2000: 36; O'Laughlin 2002: 518). Isaacman and colleagues note that "many peasants supplemented their meagre diets by eating roots and tubers and planting manioc which, though of lower nutritional value than other food crops, required only a minimal amount of labor" (1980: 594). The historian Merle Bowen asserts that "in most parts of the country, forced crop production led peasants to change from the cultivation of grains such as sorghum, a labor-intensive subsistence crop, to cassava, a less labor-absorbing and less nutritious crop. Cassava also interfered less than sorghum or millet with the agricultural calendar of commodity crops like cotton or rice" (2000: 36). Bridget O'Laughlin similarly documents the way that "the development of plantations created a demand for cheap staple foods—principally maize and dried cassava—which was not satisfied by settler farms" (2002: 518). Miguel de Jesus Valladas Paes, who penned the practical guide to agriculture described in chapter 2, said of manioc that fellow colonists should plant the tuber because it "provides an assured source of food for your indigenous personnel. In case of necessity, you will have something to eat instead of bread, because manioc roasted or boiled is very edible." In addition, he noted, "you can also feed it to your pigs" (1910: 236).

Manioc production increased further when government control over cotton production intensified with the abolition of the private royal companies in the mid-1940s (Saraiva 2009, 2016a). Once the forced labor regime that António Ennes had instituted (the chibalo) was outlawed, Mozambican farmers were supposed to pay taxes with the surplus from their individual plots. Forced migration to plantations was replaced with production quotas, whereby residents planted in place for the colonial administration (see Saraiva 2009: 50). "Soon, the diet basis of the local population was based on manioc, a less demanding crop but also a less nutritive one. Famines started to show up in the cotton regions and in 1951 in the Mogovolas some two to three thousand people died from starvation" (Saraiva 2009: 54). In his 1944 report, the head of the Agricultural Services, Monteiro Grilo, described manioc's increasing dominance: "[M]anioc is the culture that occupies the greatest area in the territory. When produced within 'organized agriculture,' manioc is for food rations for the workers. When produced on native lands, we have no accounting of it because it goes right into consumption—so all figures of manioc production do not include native farms [*machambas*]" (Grilo 1946: 176–78).

Land area planted in manioc on non-native farms (what were referred to as "civilized" agriculture) tripled between 1941–42 and 1951–52 (from 1,178 hectares to 3,614 hectares; see Esteves 1957: 11). By the 1960s, planting manioc and cotton together was the official recommendation. The government-*produced Introductory Manual for Economic, Agricultural, Forestry, and Livestock Knowledge in Mozambique*, which outlined the various crops that would do well in different regions, suggested that "if one is going to set up locally an industry of cotton textiles, it will be necessary to increase concomitantly the industry of manioc, to make use of the sub-products" ("Manual de iniciação" 1962: 108). On the eve of independence, manioc production was estimated at 2,400,000 tons per year in fresh roots, whereas corn was registered at 450,000 tons per year, principally produced in higher-elevation regions and Sul do Save (Martins Santareno 1973: 16).

In spite of the expansion of manioc consumption, little scientific work was done on it in Mozambique. In 1962 the official handbook on farming in Mozambique reported that "the study of varieties existing in Mozambique has still not been done although we are already working on introducing varieties from other countries" ("Manual de iniciação" 1962: 182). As a result, the "technical" recommendations for production were simplistic. In 1961 the *Farmer's Gazette* (13, no. 144) provided very basic advice on how to plant in sandy soil: essentially, dig a hole. "The harvest," the *Gazette* continued, "is very easy, especially in sandy soil. Just pull the stem up and to the sides, shaking it each time, until all of the roots are pulled out. If, by chance, some roots are left in the ground, use a hoe to take them out" (138).

In 1970, however, the Technical Planning and Economic Integration Commission of the Province of Mozambique recommended that manioc yields be improved through improved varieties and planting techniques. J. A. L. Martins Santareno (then provincial secretary of lands and settlement) collected information from experimental stations across the country. The twenty-three-page report highlighted the weakness of agronomic research in Mozambique—it was research that "doesn't have logical planning or security that [experiments undertaken] will be continued" (Leitão 1971). Studies had been undertaken in 1943 (in the station at Mocuba) and in 1957 (at the experimental station of Mahalamba), but the results were unreliable because of "the lack of continuity and of method" (3). Many of the experiments were wasted or useless without additional work. Overall, the author of the study concluded that more work needed to be done, and that it was important to outline from the beginning whether a study was geared toward traditional agriculture or business-oriented agriculture (*agricultura patronal*), as these would likely require different approaches. That same year, IIAM made an initial attempt (*um primeiro passo*) to understand manioc production and practices in the country (Mota 1970: 23). IIAM researchers brought together the best varieties from a collection of eighty in the Agronomic Station of Nhacoongo, selecting for resistance to mosaic disease, productivity, and attractiveness to consumers. They sent these to the Namapa Agronomic Station to see how well they could do in that environment. But the focus of this attention was not to improve the diets or livelihoods of the indigenous farmers who were primarily responsible for the crop's cultivation; rather, it was to assess manioc's export potential, connecting the widespread cultivation with demand for cellulose: "With a little interest and some effort to improve the manioc crop in Mozambique, one could entertain the hypothesis of reaching international markets" (Mota 1970: 28). This focus hinted at a recurrent theme with manioc production: if the state took an interest in this critical food crop, it was almost always to turn it into a crop for export.

"DO YOU HAVE THE FORÇA?" POSTCOLONIAL MANIOC AND THE MAKING OF A NEW MARKET

The persistent lack of interest in smallholder agriculture—and in manioc in particular—that characterized the colonial period was also evident in the postcolonial record of work done on manioc. Mozambique has occasionally pushed for research on manioc, but such endeavors have generally not been considered feasible for cross-regional projects. In the Agricultural Productivity Programme for Southern Africa (APPSA), for example—the multicountry program funded by the World Bank across Zambia, Malawi and Mozambique—Mozambique was classified as a center of excellence for rice, even though researchers in Mozambique had initially suggested that it be a center for excellence for manioc. The other countries, however, weren't interested in manioc, which was considered much more relevant to former Portuguese colonies (Interview 12, September 15 and 16, 2016).

Research scientists I interviewed in Mozambique explained that the lack of research into manioc was due to the continued division of projects into those focusing on market crops versus those focusing on subsistence crops, or between projects for rich farmers and for poor farmers (mirroring the division between "civilized" and "native" farmers under the Portuguese). Manioc research fell into the subsistence category and therefore warranted very little research, despite being the largest single source of calories in the country. The director of the International Institute of Tropical Agriculture said that he wished IITA could focus more on manioc, but it was difficult to find donor support—and without donor support, government support was even more difficult to find. "Some of the donors," he explained "changed their strategies and priority countries. For example, Gates changed their priority countries, and Mozambique is not a priority anymore. Mozambique, Malawi, Zimbabwe, Kenya fell out. I think they based their decision on some of the priorities they have. . . . Because their strategies change too" (Interview 47, December 8, 2016).

The largest single funder of agricultural research, USAID, was emblematic: in 2016, USAID would not fund manioc research, as its crops of interest in Mozambique were soy, cowpeas, pigeon peas, groundnuts, beans, and sesame. Researchers, policymakers, and farmers alike were sold on the idea of the Green Revolution coming to Mozambique, and the government saw this as the solution to the very serious problem of smallholder poverty. Rhetorically, then, the government was focused on reducing hunger and improving nutrition, but as I have suggested in previous chapters, donors were clear that the government was following strategies that focused on production and productivity (Interview 17, September 20, 2016).

In the 1990s, manioc began to receive more attention because of an outbreak of cassava brown stripe disease (CBSD) that affected production, greatly endangering people across sub-Saharan Africa. International organizations like IITA began the research effort to tackle "Brown Stripe," starting in Nigeria and expanding outward. There were two options for treating CBSD, according to the IIAM/Save the Children/USAID document outlining the success of the manioc breeding program begun in the mid-2000s. One was to work with clean material (in situ selection by farmers, getting rid of the infected material, and replanting clean stalks), and the other was plant breeding. There was good evidence of the former succeeding in other countries, such as Tanzania (Hillocks 2004), and the 1962 handbook cited earlier reported that "taking stalks from healthy plants is the best means of preventing disease that we have available now, given that we do not have resistant varieties" ("Manual de iniciação" 183). But it was decided that a program focusing on land management would not work in Mozambique because, according to researchers assessing the CBSD collaboration, "clean seed programs for vegetatively propagated crops are typically not successful in developing countries especially those as poor as Mozambique. Success usually depends on having a well-defined commercial seed sector operating in an institutionally developed economic environment" (McSween et al. 2006: 8). This is a surprising statement given that new varieties and clean versions of existing varieties both depend on a functioning seed sector for distribution. In the context of Mozambique's externally funded and results-dependent research system, the underlying argument against "clean seed" approaches was that teaching smallholders how to maintain virus-free seed would have required working directly with smallholders, building on connections, familiarity, and trust that did not exist. Developing new varieties was the more customary and easier path.

A senior research scientist in IITA suggested further that the focus on breeding was a result of the international network in which manioc research had started. In an interview conducted in IITA's Nampula compound, I asked the director whether there had been a conversation about better management as opposed to better varieties, and he responded, "no." He attributed the decision to the structural conditions that determine which research projects receive funding: "[M]ost projects," he told me, start by "identify[ing] where the problems are, and the country offices write the proposal, and then we look for funding." For manioc, the process was no different: the network consisted of "seven African countries, Nigeria, Mozambique and others" that shared similar problems, "so they came in here and the breeders did the breeding and got new materials—and the new varieties [come] with management [guidelines] and then also capacity building of the research system" (Interview 47, December 8, 2016).

From interviews across IIAM, it was clear that an international emphasis on breeding dominated the agenda. Breeding might well have been the best option in the case of CBSD, but it was often done without attention to the demands of the farmers themselves, instead focusing on the genetics and pathology of the plant. One of the scientific leads of the manioc program in the early 2000s said that they had lost time because they tested varieties that were not what the producers said they wanted and ignored local varieties that had some clear advantages:

> An example I give is one I saw with the producers in Mongicoal [a small town in the province of Nampula]. We were working with cassava and, at the end of the season, at the end of the study, you know, as researchers we said "that," "that," "that" . . . but the producers didn't always choose

what we recommended! . . . They did their thing, but when we looked at the varieties [they wanted], they were not always the resistant ones, and we said, "but there's disease, there's this, there's that." And as time went on, we released new varieties, more of the researchers' but some of the producers'. Over time we have seen that the producers' variety had a very desirable architecture for production, although every now and then they discover the disease on the root or some such. . . . That is, the new variety is not fully resistant, but it tolerates the disease [well]. Maybe we would have saved a lot of time . . . if we had given the producer directly what he wanted. And on the other hand, the researchers' variety has been developing as a very woody plant, and it has . . . certain architectural problems, while the producers' does not. Today, I give my hand [to the producer]. (Interview 19, September 23, 2016)

Another researcher who had briefly headed the national extension agency blamed this lack of information on a theme I have mentioned and discuss in greater detail in the next chapter: the near-total separation between research and extension in Mozambique. In the 2000s, when the new national research institute, IIAM, was created, the original idea was for everyone to work in teams, following a farm systems approach. Such a method might have helped with the breeding programs for manioc, he suggested, because the early varieties were not popular: "The adults could [bring themselves to] eat it, but the children didn't like the color of the manioc meal [*xima*] it made." He emphasized the importance of social context, concluding that the research team's shortcomings ran deep: issues like food color, he noted "are some of the things it is necessary to look at first. . . . The breeder has to have a sociologist also at his side probably. If he cannot be both then he needs to have someone [with him]. It's partly because of the way we were trained . . . the very way . . . that our extension and research [services] formed" (Interview 18, September 22, 2016).

As this story suggests, while research on manioc was finally set in motion by CBSD across southeastern Africa, the focus was on breeding new varieties with better disease resistance rather than on the farmers themselves or on land management techniques that might have enabled the farmers to plant more fields with a healthier distribution of crops. The extraction of manioc from the farm system and research scientists' focus on breeding continued a long-standing emphasis on breeding new varieties in Mozambique rather than focusing on the context in which those plants were used. The new varieties were being produced and slowly disseminated when I was in Mozambique between 2014 and 2017. The arrival of these new varieties prompted an effort to develop new markets for distribution and consumption, taking advantage of more robust manioc supply.

The most well-known initiative was a mass-marketed beer made from manioc roots, called Impala after the small African antelope and distilled by Cervejas de Moçambique, SA (CdM), a subsidiary of the largest beer conglomerate in the world, Anheuser-Busch InBev. The initiative was organized by IFDC and DADTCO first in Nampula (where this chapter opened) and then in the province of Inhambane. These two began working together in 2004 in Nigeria, and in 2011 DADTCO came to Nampula. The biggest problem the three organizations ran into with the project in Mozambique was not the market for the beer (which was very popular even though the taste is, to put it charitably, unexpected) but the supply of manioc. That supply would be the problem was perhaps surprising in a country where manioc still occupied the largest number of hectares of any single crop, but IFDC, DADTCO, and CdM required that the supply conform to certain characteristics; namely, the manioc had to be delivered in specified quantities (not too much or too little) at specified times. This meant a different approach to production than the farmers were familiar with; manioc, after all, had primarily served as a reserve crop, valued for its capacity to sit in the ground until needed.

IFDC and DADTCO therefore selected farmers carefully. They promoted the project over the radio, through field days at the local agricultural experiment station and through "awareness-building sessions" (sensibilizações), or quick informational meetings. Farmers were required to sign statements that they would plant as they were told to, using new varieties and methods provided by IFDC. They were given orientations around creating a nursery, selecting good stalks, planting, timing, spacing, and harvesting. IFDC cultivated key "mobilizers" (also called "facilitators" or "animators"): community members who had a little more land and who were selected for their higher capacity for both production and leadership. Their role was to mobilize the rest of the community to use proper methods and to provide their harvest on the right day and in the right manner. The emphasis on timing was critical, as manioc begins to ferment roughly twenty-four hours after the roots are pulled from the ground. If fermentation began before the manioc was processed, it could not be used, so DADTCO invented a ticket system, handing out tickets stamped with a date to every farmer, providing them with a three-day window in which to deliver their manioc to the MPU. Once the starch (massa) was processed into blocks, the blocks could sit around for months, so the crucial time period was the first twenty-four hours after harvest.

Soon after the DADTCO/IFDC project got started, difficulties emerged. Based on interviews with two different manioc grower associations in Nampula, DADTCO representatives and IFDC scientists (I never got access inside

CdM, although I did interview the director of sales for Impala in Nampula), three observations became clear: first, IFDC and DADTCO worked hard to distinguish the manioc they wanted for the market from subsistence manioc; second, this meant that they applied these new techniques to the former, but the farmers struggled because these techniques differed so dramatically from the way they traditionally planted (and thought of) manioc; and third, the farmers rebelled against DADTCO because the company took the market logic too far, failing to provide subsidiary benefits such as schools or wells to which the communities were accustomed, per most development efforts in the region, and pricing the product according to the demand from CdM. As such, it makes sense to understand the challenges faced by the project as symptomatic of the persistence of the plantation ideal, with its emphasis on large-scale production for the global market and its tendency to see indigenous farmers as a generic labor supply rather than as agricultural producers with their own established practices and values.

IFDC and DADTCO favored bitter manioc varieties, and they encouraged the farmers to plant sweet varieties for their own consumption and bitter varieties for the market. There was a brief media scandal when it was widely reported that the new initiative was stealing manioc from impoverished households, pushing farmers to sell their crop instead of eating it. Both IFDC and DADTCO asserted publicly that this was inaccurate and doubled down on their insistence that farmers separate their land into easily distinguishable plots: one for the market and one for subsistence. The organizations favored the bitter varieties because those produced more per plant and the cyanide was easily removed during processing, but the bifurcated approach also meant that unless households could expand the area under production, increased manioc production largely benefited the market, not household consumption.

The new methods that IFDC promoted were disseminated through small workshops. One association I spoke with on December 7, 2016, had attended a three-day workshop at a local hotel, which they liked because it was "focused on manioc" and really got the information across "without any distractions." The president of the association suggested that although the farmers had heard the same advice before the workshop, the repetition in a formal setting helped it to stick. For IFDC technicians, these new methods were challenging to teach because they represented a "transformation," in large part because "people here never used to see manioc as a commercial crop, it was just a subsistence crop."

At the workshop and in other one-day trainings at nearby experimental stations and experimental fields, the farmers learned how to plant in lines (*alinhamento*) and how to space them more closely together. They used rope to help measure out straight lines, and so planting had to be done with more than one person, to lay out the rope lines. Farmers were asked to measure the distance between the lines of manioc, which was supposed to be exactly one meter, according to the IFDC technician I interviewed. This spaced the manioc out sufficiently and provided room for planting other crops such as beans or even corn in between the rows of manioc. These practices of intercropping and live mulch were core practices of conservation agriculture and were intended, in part, to keep farmers from moving around from plot to plot each year. In interviews with farmers involved in this project as well as in the projects I elaborate on in chapter 5, one of the main benefits listed was always, "I have learned that these methods allow me to stay in one place rather than always moving around."

IFDC spent a lot of time working on alinhamento and tended to focus these efforts on the men because, as the men in the association I interviewed said laughingly, the women didn't like to plant in rows because it was "too difficult." One of the older women in the group laughed and said she planted half of her field in lines and then "gave up and planted the rest randomly." IFDC also taught the farmers to cut short stalks for seed so that they could plant a larger field with fewer stalks. In addition, the farmers learned to mulch, but IFDC didn't recommend mulching manioc fields because the plants "don't really need it, so they're not likely to waste [the mulch]." (Association Interview, Ribáuè, December 7, 2016).

In general, these new techniques were not difficult; they were just different. As Heidi Gengenbach (2020) writes about attempts to promote manioc production for cassava beer in Inhambane, the project failed due to its "ahistorical vision of rural economies, its monolithic caricature of rural women and its blindness to the ecological, cultural and social logics of women' farming decisions" (226). Gengenbach argues that women in the project region saw manioc as a life-sustaining "cradle" that could not be easily adapted to the neoliberal notion of a value chain (226; see also Heckler 2004 and Heckler and Zent 2008). Importantly, planting manioc according to IFDC specifications required considerably more labor than planting for subsistence. This was likely the reason why women—who were juggling many jobs—didn't take to planting in lines. In order to satisfy the higher labor demand, the associations and the farmers who had more land or who had managed to secure more manioc plants (whether because they were better connected, had leadership positions, or became familiar with IFDC or DADTCO early on) hired the labor to clean their land, plant, weed, and harvest.

Although the relationship between the farmers and IFDC/DADTCO was very promising during the first year, by the second year the market price for manioc had dropped by half, and there were strenuous complaints from the farmers. DADTCO established a floor price, but at 2.5 meticais per kilo (roughly 4 cents today, minus transportation costs from field to MPU, if required), it was considered too low to warrant the sale. DADTCO insisted that it could pay better only if it could be guaranteed getting sufficient supply at preset times. Otherwise, the beer company would not increase its beer production, and there were few other market possibilities.

The farmers I spoke with conveyed their bitterness at DADTCO for not delivering what they considered to be a fair price, but they were also upset at not receiving what they saw as appropriate "help" from the company. DADTCO representatives shook their head in disgust at this request for help, arguing that people were trained to ask for things instead of working. But asking for help is part of the history; it is the way people do business, as the president of the association I spoke with said: "We are asking for any project to help, any visitor that appears, we ask for help." He complained that "the company asks me for everything, and they don't do anything for us, we just think they should help us" (Association Interview, Ribáuè, December 7, 2016).

When I asked one of the DADTCO representatives about the things that the company had supposedly promised, he became agitated and said the company was doing social responsibility just by operating its mobile processing units. "We never promised anything," he protested. The representative framed the farmers' demands for wells and medical facilities as irrational: "You can get water right on the DADTCO site—they have tons of water and the community already had four or five wells, why would they want another water source? And they ask for a hospital but there's a hospital right there—it's less than 500 meters away!" He concluded that "they just want things just for the association. It's not the company's responsibility to do something about social responsibility" (Interview 34, November 29, 2016).

That sentiment illustrated the problem with the new initiative for manioc production. Manioc was the crop the colonial government and landowners had used to maintain a labor force for their plantations. As such, manioc was the glue that allowed communities to survive harsh labor conditions. Under the new system, however, manioc was stripped of its social meanings and recast as a new market crop for which the farmers were to provide labor. That this labor was separated from social reproduction was evident in the fact that none of the farmers I interviewed had ever tasted Impala beer: it sold for 50 meticais per bottle (roughly 75 U.S. cents at the time) in the local bars. One beer would have cost them their earnings on 20 kilos of manioc.

Ultimately, although the players had changed and the targets were different, an analysis of manioc production suggests that the broader dynamics have remained the same: rural producers in Mozambique were expected to assume responsibility for both their own survival and the survival of the market, with no one caring for the needs of the community. Local residents wanted to engage with the market, but they wanted the market to work for them; instead, they ended up working for the market.

Manioc is a plant that is both sweet and bitter: it is a miracle crop that provides relief in times of famine and drought but does not nourish those who labor in its fields. Far from the diversified fields in which manioc once grew, the very nature of the plant has been manipulated to serve the needs of empire and market.

5. "It's a Shame It's So Difficult"

Life in the Shadow of the Plantation Ideal

The first time I drove out to the community of Colocoto in Moma District along the northeastern coast of Nampula province, a good half hour off the main road on sandy trails through low-growing bush, fourteen members of the community association were assembled in greeting. My colleagues and I were interviewing community members for a documentary on life in northeastern Mozambique. As the pickup pulled to a stop near the meeting tree, the assembled community group sang in greeting. The song had a tongue-in-cheek, almost droll quality that ran through many of the conversations I had with local community members in the area. They sang about the practices they were "supposed" to adopt according to the principles of conservation agriculture that the extension agents and NGOs in the area were trying to teach. The song's lyrics poked fun at the idea of spending so much time learning how to mulch and plant in rows when there was so much suffering and life was so hard. These were people well used to foreign visitors. They were welcoming and warm even though they knew they were on display for an outsider. They were proud to show off how well organized they were and hopeful that my visit might portend the arrival of new resources. At the very least, it was a visit by their extension agent, whom they all seemed to like.

THE WELCOME SONG FROM COLOCOTO
To weed is very good
It's a shame it's so difficult (repeats)
Not burning the fields is very good
It's a shame that it's difficult (repeats)
Minimal disturbance [no till] is very good
It's a shame it's so difficult (repeats)
Colocoto is a very good place to live

It's a shame it's so difficult to live here (repeats)
Moma district is very beautiful
It's a shame it's so hard to live here (repeats)
Viva Conservation Agriculture! (repeats)
Down with Swidden Agriculture! (repeats)
Down with disturbing the soil! (repeats)

One of the women in the community association sat with me and talked about her life, which was occupied with securing subsistence, survival, and social reproduction:

When the sun comes, I wake up at 4:00. I go to the mosque to pray and when I get back, I wake the kids up. I say, "it's time to get up" and I tell the girl to go to the well and wash dishes at 5:00. She goes with her friends. Then, with the boy who studies in Mecan, I wake him up when I go to the mosque and I tell him to sweep the yard, afterwards he gets ready and gets his books. At 6:00 he goes to school, and I go to the field.

On her small plot of land, she and her husband planted manioc, peas, sweet potatoes, bananas, sugarcane, rice, jugo beans (groundnut), sesame, mango, coconuts, and cashews. Her diet and day were dominated by subsistence activities:

I'm the first one to come back. I come home, sweep, and usually cook manioc. When I arrive in the field, I weed. If I don't have wood at home, I get wood. I put the manioc in the basket and the wood on top and then I go back. After I get home, I peel the manioc and the boy comes back from school, then I send each child to wash plates, one grinds the manioc, one looks for water to drink. At times, I go to the madrasa. There are twenty women [in the madrasa]. I go every day except Friday, Saturday, and Sunday. When I come back, we're all together. After I come home, I grind manioc. After that, night is coming, and we start to cook. We eat dinner at 7:00.

I asked her what she hoped the future would bring. It was difficult not to compare her aspirations to the aspirations embedded in the ambitious mega-projects driven by the plantation ideal:

I would like to put a proper roof on my house. And given that there is no electricity, I would like one of those solar panels. I would like a good chair and I would like it if there was a mill in the community. I think one of the things that I want is that if the children finish their studies while I am still alive, that they can help me out. But I doubt that all of this will happen.

Two extension agents standing nearby heard her describe what she hoped for. One shook his head ruefully and said, "They're not going to become rich with a short-handled hoe." The short-handled hoe was an expression meaning very simple handheld rather than mechanized tools.[1]

The work these extension agents were doing, promoting conservation agriculture, was intended to support the rural poor. In the context of the plantation ideal, however, conservation agriculture was valuable because it enabled (required) the rural poor to stay in one place rather than practicing swidden agriculture. As I wrote in chapter 3, the search for profitable plantation crops that kept scientists focused on new varieties meant that they paid little attention to land management, and so they had little interaction with the main group of people tasked with improving local land management: extension agents. Living in the shadow of the plantation ideal constrained the opportunities available to those who worked primarily with local communities, whether extension agents, state planners, or aid practitioners funded by external development agencies. The extension services, both public and private, operated without scientific support, promoting basic principles of conservation agriculture in order to increase production enough to keep people alive and stop them from deploying traditional techniques of swidden agriculture. This fixity supported plantation agriculture because it provided laborers for large-scale operations and opened up more land for such investments. In the chapter that follows, I describe extension services in Mozambique and analyze this relationship between extension, communities, and place.

A BRIEF HISTORY OF EXTENSION IN INDEPENDENT MOZAMBIQUE

In 2016, a history of the extension services in Mozambique was, as one of the former heads of the department said wryly, "brief." It was brief because extension was only created as an independent department within the Ministry of Agriculture in 1987.[2] Before that time, public interaction with farmers was done in an informal way by researchers, who answered questions in written format in one of the journals published by the Agricultural Services during the colonial period. In part because funding was limited during the socialist period and in part because the focus at the time was on large-scale mechanization of agriculture, the first national plan for the extension services was not completed until 1999, a full twenty-four years after independence. The number of extension agents in the National Directorate of Agrarian Extension (Direcção Nacional de Extensão Agrária, DNEA) then grew steadily, from five hundred in 1999 to almost two thousand in 2019 (Marassiro et al. 2020: 430), but coverage was still thin, particularly outside of the urban areas and urban peripheries. One review estimated that if the extension agents hired by the government as of 2018 had to provide full national coverage (which would mean covering the 80% of Mozambique's roughly sixteen million people who lived outside of urban areas), they would have been responsible for three thousand households each (Cunguara and Thompson 2018: 22). Figures from the Ministry of Agriculture showed that coverage by public extension agents declined significantly (from already low levels) between 2002 and 2015, with 13.5 percent of all farmers receiving at least one visit in 2002 and only 4.3 percent of farmers receiving a visit in 2015 (23). The authors of the review, which was funded by USAID, attributed the decline from 2002 to 2015 to three factors, each of which came up repeatedly in my own interviews with extension agents: the prevalence of short-term contracts making it difficult to imagine a longer career in the department (with many of the best extension agents picked off by private firms), poor working conditions (including lack of good housing, wages, or gasoline for motorcycles), and government budget cuts (23).

In addition to government extension agents, there were extension specialists who were trained and employed by the commodity sector (particularly cotton and rice) and NGOs, but data on these groups was not widely available, and government officials did not have a good sense of who was carrying out extension-like activities in the countryside.[3] A former DNEA director confirmed that there was very little coordination of NGO efforts in extension in rural Mozambique, because "NGOs can all participate in extension, this was in the master plan" (Interview 23, December 16, 2016). Without coordination, some districts had multiple NGOs providing support of various kinds, including extension, while others had no support services. "And then the NGO leaves suddenly," the former director continued, "and those populations go back to being the government's responsibility." DNEA would regularly get reports from the Ministry of Foreign Relations with long lists of NGOs that had registered with the government and indicated that they were working in the countryside, many of whom DNEA had never heard of (Interview 23, December 16, 2016). In 2016 the government was trying to change this lack of coordination, but it had little real control and did not want to police NGOs too severely, given that these organizations were critical to the provision of public goods in rural areas.

DNEA had a hard time attracting qualified extension agents because prior to 2019 the department had only been able to hire "general technicians" (*técnicos gerais*) as opposed to more highly trained specialists. DNEA hired agents on one-year contracts through the General Ministry of MASA (as opposed to IIAM, which hired researchers through the Ministry of Science and Technology). This meant that the private sector or the research division provided more security than DNEA.[4]

Without secure funding from the Ministry of Agriculture, DNEA was forced to rely on collaboration with NGO partners and local government officials. Similar to the experience of IIAM, this generated a willingness to entertain new ideas from external donors: "We're trying out new things," the former DNEA director quoted earlier said. "We learn from the Japanese, the Brazilians—we try out new ideas to see what works!" (Interview 23, December 16, 2016). This reliance on external funding led provincial and district directors to be opportunistic in organizing staff time. Extension agents were often rerouted quickly to respond to a donor-driven opportunity. For example, in 2016, 31,065 farmers participated in short workshops offered by DNEA, but over half of these farmers (roughly 16,000 of them) were in the populated areas around Maputo, because representatives from a South Korean NGO flew in and offered to provide a training on organic fertilizer, and participants had to be mobilized very quickly.

RESEARCH AND EXTENSION: DISCONNECTIONS

The ongoing lack of extension services was amplified by the divide between research and extension, and in particular the divide between the national institutions representing both.[5] In the twenty years prior to my fieldwork, there had been multiple attempts to try to bridge this divide, including a high-level effort funded by USAID and the Brazilian government called PLATAFORMA I and II that ran from 2011 to 2016. PLATAFORMA was a forum created to bring together all of the domestic and international stakeholders funding and working in rural Mozambique to openly discuss their objectives in an attempt to coordinate activities better. This project ended abruptly just before I arrived back in Mozambique in 2016. Although most participants I spoke to argued that PLATAFORMA had been necessary and that it could have succeeded, the project seemed to fail because multiple participants tried to claim leadership over what they saw as one more donor-funded project, when it was intended to be a horizontal partnership. According to the lead from USAID, "IIAM saw PLATAFORMA as a project that USAID was funding and they were implementing, but USAID saw themselves as equal *partners* in this and were hoping to foster a dialogue" (Interview 7, July 25, 2016; emphasis added).

On November 2, 2016, I went to a national meeting of research scientists and extension agents in the hopes that I would learn more about the way they interacted. The meeting was known by its acronym REPETE (Revisão Periódica de Tecnologias, or Periodic Review of Technologies). Led by DNEA, the meetings were supposed to happen every two years. They began in the late 1980s, originally supported by funding from the World Bank. In the 1990s, REPETE was held at the local, regional, provincial, and national levels, but once World Bank funding ended, REPETE was only held at the national level and moved to a roughly biannual schedule, held in 2011, 2013, and 2016. DNEA leadership decided on the agenda and invited participants from the state-level extension offices, IIAM, and donor organizations and NGOs involved in research and extension. Usually the meeting focused on one crop, but in 2016 the director of DNEA decided to highlight four crops because there had been no meeting in 2015 and there was a lot of information to disseminate.

A few weeks after the 2016 REPETE, a top leader in DNEA clarified why the meeting was so necessary. "You have to understand, our farmers are mostly illiterate. They don't understand [the science], and there is no infrastructure," he explained. "In normal conditions, the tie between research and extension should be like this." He drew a Venn diagram in my notebook: "[There are] separate circles for research and for farmers, with extension as the overlap." He described the hypothetical process: "When research [IIAM] has a new technology, they teach the extension agents how to use it, whether it's a new variety or whatever. They teach the leadership, then those people go to the provincial level, then they will train the extension agents and they train the farmers." This was a very traditional view of the relationship between research, extension, and farmers—a one-way flow of information—but even this was rarely possible in Mozambique. My interviewee attributed this to two things: first, both research and extension lacked the infrastructure needed for collaboration, from personnel, to supplies, to access to farmers; second—and this was at the top of his mind and came up multiple times during our conversations between 2013 and 2016—IIAM's reliance on external (foreign) funding made it difficult to ensure a regular flow of information. As he put it:

> With research partners, they don't have the capacity to train extension agents. In normal conditions, [what should happen is that] when a researcher does a project, they have to do an on-farm study and the farm is selected by the extension agent. And so the farmer and researcher and extension agent all work on the experiment together— when they decide it's good, the extension agent does demonstrations. The researcher goes back to IIAM, or Japan, or wherever, while the extension agent does the on-farm work. The agent organizes farmer

field days, where they invite the researcher—they show the process of dissemination, and they invite back the researcher.

Ultimately, however, this rarely happened. "The problem," the director said, "is that all of this is very difficult and . . . there are certain financial and attitudinal challenges." Those challenges were evident at the REPETE meeting in 2016.

The weather was sunny and mild on November 2, 2016, and there was an energetic buzz in the meeting hall the first morning of REPETE. More than seventy people had traveled to the site near the Maputo International Fairgrounds (Feira Internacional de Maputo, FACIM) in Marracuene. This was not an easy feat when they were coming from across Mozambique, and the conference setting was "the hotel run by the nuns," said to be about a half hour outside of Maputo. It took me over an hour to get there from downtown Maputo, getting lost at first in the sandy, unmarked villages around the conference center. Luckily, as I got closer, everyone I asked knew where "the nuns' place" was, and I arrived just before the meeting started. The provincial heads of extension (*chefes dos* Serviços Provinciais de Extensão Rural, SPER) and some of the district heads (Serviço Distrital de Actividades Económicas, SDAE) attended the meeting. Approximately 80 percent of the participants were men, a gender imbalance characteristic of extension services in Mozambique more generally.[6] This imbalance was problematic, as women did the bulk of the farming in the country, and women often had difficulty speaking to men or being heard by those in official positions. A small number of research scientists were in the room, and it was increasingly clear that although REPETE was supposed to include both research and extension, the only research scientists in attendance were the ones who had presentations to deliver. The small group of foreigners present included me, as well as Brazilian and Japanese representatives of various extension efforts linked to ProSavana. On the second day of the meeting, we were joined by a group of NGO leaders from the US-based National Cooperative Business Association Cooperative Leagues of the United States of America (CLUSA), the IFDC, and the FAO, all of whom were doing work on conservation agriculture around the country.

A senior official from DNEA kicked off the meeting. He noted that the day had started with rain, which meant our meeting would be blessed.[7] That blessing would be needed, I thought, as the official reminded the audience that the central government had committed to increasing agricultural productivity by a whopping 70 percent over five years, in line with the pan-African Comprehensive Africa Agriculture Development Programme

(CAADP), signed in Maputo in 2003. To try to streamline services and increase efficiency, the Ministry of Agriculture and Food Security (MASA) had decided that every province should choose three products in which to specialize. Research and extension efforts would be geared toward those products.

After introductions around the room, research scientists from IIAM presented their work on the three agricultural products and one animal chosen for the meeting: rice, tomato, potato, and chicken. The presentations were detailed and scientific, with very small text on each slide, which the presenters read aloud with their backs to the audience. The presenters for tomatoes and chicken stood behind the wide column to the side of the projector, so they were largely hidden from the audience, and their voices seemed to come out of the column itself. Each of the presenters expounded on the value of their product: "Rice is strategic," one declared. "It's an important food for a majority of people. [Mozambique] has a good area in which to produce, and consumption will likely double." Another presenter said that "demand for potato is always increasing and it's a very important product," while a third exclaimed, "tomatoes are a source of employment and income, and they are nutritious." Only chicken, already much loved and a coveted source of protein in Mozambique, needed no introduction.

The presentations focused on new varieties for these products (with the exception of chicken, where the presenter focused on processing and the lack of sanitary processing facilities in Maputo, ruining everyone's lunch). The scientist presenting on rice mentioned four new varieties: Simão, Flimbeta, Nene, and Huwa. He had a slide that showed an IIAM scientist generating useful technologies. The image showed new seeds (representing new technologies) next to an extension agent reading the *carta tecnológica* (the technological memo that accompanied every new variety, providing the researchers' guidance on planting, tending, and harvesting). The extension agent was handing out the seeds while pointing back toward IIAM, and a farmer was depicted grabbing for the seeds. The slide mirrored the DNEA director's description of the ideal connection between research, extension, and farmers.

When the presentations ended, the reaction from the audience was immediate and angry.

One provincial head channeled what was clearly the emerging consensus among the extension agents, saying he was "very annoyed. I felt like I was back in a classroom. In the presentations, I was hoping you could discuss recommendations that we could actually take to the producer. For example, with rice, [you could say] 'what we've found is X and you could take this technology to the producers, and they would spend X, and this is how you produce in these different regions; and if the producer has X or X yield, they will have X profit.'" He and other speakers who followed him pointed out that rural producers could not reproduce the conditions that IIAM tested their varieties in, so they needed to know what would happen with each variety if they planted it in less than ideal conditions without fertilizer or with little water.

The room got heated as the questions continued, and the scientists sat back in their chairs, arms crossed. The rice scientist looked particularly angry. Before things could get too out of hand, the director of DNEA took back the microphone and urged everyone to be reasonable: "If you were paying attention, I said we haven't done the REPETE in a long time because of resources . . . so we decided to do four products on one day. We will deepen these [initial] presentations in focus group meetings now."

Accordingly, we split up into four groups. I joined the rice group, which was supposed to be moderated by the IIAM scientist, but he was too angry to participate at first. Our charge, given to us by the DNEA director, was to talk about the rice commodity chain, from inputs to post-harvest and consumption issues. But we started in silence. No one wanted to be the first to speak. And then, all at once, everyone jumped in:

> "In fifteen years, we've taken seven or eight varieties to the producer— do we know how they've done? Now when you go to Chokwe, no one wants to talk about Ida, everyone wants Macaça and soon it will be Simão . . ."

> "Do we have Simão seeds? In Gaza, everyone wants Simão."

> "We need to look for companies and find out about the quality [of their seeds]! People have to finish out what's already available and we have to know if the companies are putting out good seed!"

> "We need a credit program for farmers to buy seed. If not we will be here talking about this problem next year."

> "It's not just availability that is the problem, it's supply—we have to do a mapping, we don't know what the real demand is in this country."

> "The producers decide they like something and research [IIAM] is already making another variety! So the company puts out that new one, but it's not what the farmers know or want."

> "The time we spend demonstrating technologies is not enough. Just showing them once isn't enough! They need to see it over two or three years."

> "The job of the researcher should not end with the liberation of the seed. Our researchers just hand us the carta tecnológica and say go produce!"

After several minutes of these complaints, someone announced that "the problem is the lack of connection between research and extension." This incited a furious back and forth. "This thing of connection is so old!" one person said. "We've been talking about this for forty years!" But another insisted, "The problem is that the results of research stay with the researchers. The problem is the connection."

At this, the IIAM scientist who had presented on rice and who had been sitting quietly, stewing, exploded. "You always say this!" he said. "What do I have to do, deliver a pamphlet to you every month? What is it you want? I presented the results of the research here today!"

The researcher's anger illustrated the problem. Researchers were funded to develop new varieties or to develop other technologies. That was the scientifically valid work; including extension agents or farmers in the process was extra, something that happened after the technology or knowledge was generated, if they had the time and patience. Eventually, everyone calmed down enough to agree that it wasn't the researcher's fault, it was the system's fault. The structure of both research and extension was problematic. The group agreed that, really, it was the funders' fault: "We should include in every project a period during which the researcher follows the technology—follows it in a particular community. This period should be included in the responsibilities of the research project. Many researchers go to England or Tanzania to talk about their work, but we don't know about it here [in Mozambique]. Research has so much money, make them pay for dissemination." In a later interview, a director in DNEA agreed with this sentiment but insisted that the money would have to come directly from donors, not from IIAM: "[IIAM] has difficulties too—they have no budget. So, often the researchers work according to the priorities of the donors. They should ask what are our priorities, but MASA doesn't have any resources so . . . they can't dictate [the priorities]."

In the face of these challenges, the Integrated Program for Transfer of Technology (Programa Integrado de Transferência de Tecnologias Agrárias, PITTA) sought to literally ground the connection between research and extension. Under this program, also known as "one extension officer, one hectare" (Cunguara and Thompson 2018: 32), small plots of land—referred to as PITTAs—were supposed to be given to public extension agents. The agent would grow crops and raise livestock on that plot, using scientifically informed best practices from research scientists and supplementing their own subsistence from the harvest. DNEA started to develop PITTAs in 2011, and they were the source of considerable irritation in 2016 when I was in Mozambique. Research scientists for the most part had never seen one, and extension agents complained that they didn't get access to land or to the technologies or resources they would have needed to develop the plots.[8] Although the objective of the program was to improve technology transfer and "teach by doing," when PITTAs came up at REPETE, the reaction was skeptical. "There is all this talk about PITTAs," one person said, "but where are these PITTAs?" Even if they did have the resources to create them, one extension agent from the north of Mozambique argued, most of them wouldn't know how to manage something so complex: "A well-done PITTA is not less than 39,000 *meticais* and a well-done demonstration plot is not less than 4,000. So, an extension agent who makes 8,000 meticais per year is supposed to supervise a project [valued at] 45,000 meticais?"

When the four groups came back together to report on our discussions, every commodity group mentioned the problem of the link between research and extension. No one had solutions for how to address the problem; it was clear that despite being blessed by the rain, the meeting hadn't solved the issue, even temporarily. Instead, our discussions had only highlighted the difficulties of working together when the systems for research and extension were structured around separate arenas, principles, methodologies, and incentives. On the second day of REPETE, the director of IIAM started the proceedings with an apology. She acknowledged that the extension agents had made valid arguments the day before; she echoed the DNEA director, laying the blame on the system and saying that it really wasn't IIAM's fault: "We can only do research with the support of a [donor-funded] project." Everyone had to focus on their specific projects, and in a country where ambitious mega-projects were designed to extract specific commodities within a short timeframe, no one could imagine re-structuring research or extension. Dismantling the divide between the two would have required starting with the farmers, focusing on land management, and prioritizing the creation of a sustainable farm economy.

A colleague I had interviewed earlier argued that such a holistic approach should have been possible at REPETE. The issue with REPETE, he said, was that the researchers just did presentations of new varieties rather than taking one crop and looking at it from multiple angles and along the whole chain, from research to market:

> So, if it's corn, ok, call everyone together, then there are researchers, there is an extension worker, there is a guy who provides inputs, there is a trader. . . . [E]veryone is there, we are going to discuss what the problems are! Is it seeds? Ok, maybe it's seeds, maybe someone might be interested in producing the seed. . . . Ok, someone there will produce the seed, they will take care of seed supply, everything. What is the

[next] problem? The problem is the fertilizer, ok, that's fine, if it's the fertilizer, ok, someone will buy the fertilizer. What quantity do you want? Just say what the quantity is, the person will go buy it, have it delivered, and have it done, from the moment he has a guarantee that someone will buy it; everything and anyone will do that, but buy just to stay in the warehouse, in the store, without having gone out, nobody will do that because they're tying up the money, isn't it. If it's the market problem, ok, what are the issues with the market? (Interview 14, September 15, 2016)

This description of a "farm systems approach" was notable for not having farmers in it, but it also highlighted the sense among researchers that reaching the farmers wasn't that difficult; it was just a matter of dissemination, delivering the information. For researchers, the real work was the science; dissemination could be done by anyone—or anything. In October 2016, researchers from across IIAM assembled in the auditorium of the headquarter campus in Maputo to hear the results of a master's thesis one of the researchers had just completed. The thesis had been funded by USAID and was part of that agency's emphasis on promoting information and communications technologies (ICTs) in research and extension. Accordingly, the title of the talk was "Can Animated Videos Replace Extension Agents?" The presentation was upbeat. Yes, the speaker argued, videos created for display on smartphones could replace extension agents. In his experiment, a group of farmers were taught how to properly store beans by watching short videos sent to them by a local extension agent. Feedback suggested that the extensionist could narrate the technical specifics in an audio recording and depict the proper way of storing beans in a clear and comprehensive video. The video had the advantage of being accessible forever so farmers could watch it repeatedly in the comfort of their own homes. In the experiment being presented, farmers were able to demonstrate successful storage practices after watching the video.

The audience was appreciative. The speaker was well known and well liked, and his message resonated with the widely held opinion that extension agents were primarily communicators, tasked with transmitting (not producing or developing) information generated by the researchers to the farmers. You could therefore replace them with cell phones with little negative effect. I had pushed my way into the seminar and hesitated to ask any questions, so I was relieved when someone else asked what seemed like the obvious question, Would small farmers in Mozambique have smartphones? The answer was, no, probably not, but the research was hypothetical, and now they had a rigorous answer to a question that could be asked in the future.[9] People seemed to accept this logic, and the conversation continued. As the discussion continued, I finally asked a question that seemed essential to me: Was the person who recorded the audio on the video an extension agent who was known to the test community? The answer was yes. So, I asked, wouldn't that have made a difference? If one of extension's key jobs is to create trust with the community, then the success of that video probably depended on the extension agent already having built up trust with community members. It might be difficult to scale this method up given the need for a locally embedded narrator. The researcher took this in stride and agreed, but argued that it would be easy enough in the future for videos to be narrated by people the community knew and trusted, whether the extension agent or someone else.[10]

Trust, he seemed to suggest, was in generous supply; it would not get in the way of scaling up information dissemination. And yet I knew that the extension agents and administrators I had talked to across Mozambique would say (and had said, pounding the table for emphasis in conversations) that trust was the most important component for success working with farmers. Trust was necessary to get rural residents to participate in new projects, to try new techniques, and to plant new crops. These same extension agents insisted that trust was even harder to come by than smartphones. The ease with which the IIAM researcher argued that extension could be replaced by online videos reflected a popular perception that research could produce new technologies, and all extension agents had to do was deliver them into people's hands. Questions such as whether those technologies were appropriate or how people would manage their land and safeguard their subsistence with the new varieties were rarely contemplated.

After the IIAM director's apology, the second day of REPETE was reserved for extension agents and affiliated organizations. These projects seemed even more divorced from local conditions than the research presented on new technologies by IIAM the day before and highlighted the fact that many of the difficulties extensionists experienced in reaching local farmers were a product of relying on external funders who brought highly experimental new ideas more grounded in their home countries' context than in Mozambican reality.

One example of this was a project that was unfolding at that time in thirteen countries in Africa, funded by AGRA with support from organizations like IIAM, National Association of Rural Extension (Associação Nacional de Extensão Rural, AENA), and CARE (Cooperative for American Remittances to Europe). The objective was to improve the efficiency and profitability of agriculture by optimizing fertilizer use—deploying the fertilizer optimization tool (FOT). At a workshop in August 2016 for extension agents promoting conservation agriculture, a young extensionist hired to work on the project demonstrated an interactive worksheet into which a farmer could input how many hectares he was working on and other information about his soil, geomorphology, and crops planted. The system would make calculations based on best practices for fertilizer use and tell the farmer how much fertilizer to apply for optimal yield. "You do this for each crop [on the farm]," the extensionist said. "The extension agent has to fill this out. When IIAM comes, they do research, and the recommendations are scientifically supported. Then the program helps you to optimize, and a new table appears that tells you how much fertilizer you should add with how much sand per hectare for each crop. Then you print up a sheet with tables for the producers that show how much to put in and how much the farmers will spend/ earn." This presentation was at a workshop for extension agents working with small-scale, resource-limited farmers, so the FOT, with its far-fetched assumptions about farmers' ability to access technology and the cash needed to purchase fertilizer, provoked some funny looks. The presenter forged on. "The producer says, 'ok, I want to earn more,' and so you say, 'okay, let's use this tool and put in first how much you want to earn, then we will have the number of how much you have to invest to earn that much.'"

The FOT was clearly aimed at farmers who had more land and capital than the vast majority of the rural poor in Mozambique, most of whom would never refer to their land in multiples of hectares. As one of the other extension agents in attendance said in disgust, "We work [with] family farmers in this country who are planting for their subsistence. Exactly where will these farmers get the money to buy the fertilizer? We really shouldn't get their hopes up, promising things that they can't achieve." The workshop continued, but the presenter was upset with his colleagues' negative reactions. He realized that the tool went against the principles of conservation agriculture but argued that it would be useful to think ahead because farmers were not going to grow with conservation agriculture alone. "Basically, it hasn't been and won't be adopted here [in Mozambique] because the farmers here are all subsistence farmers. But it's still interesting," he said to me later, "to see what is out there and to think about how it might be used by the farmers here." This spirit of experimentation—prompted in part by the dynamics of dependence on foreign funding—echoed the DNEA leader's earlier comments: experiments were necessary because no one knew the answer, not because the experiments would necessarily lead to an answer. He argued, "People criticize us because they have never worked with farmers. If you have never worked with farmers, then it all looks easy. People can only criticize you if you're doing something. . . . [T]he observation that there are problems [is] just an indication that we are working!" (Interview 23, December 16, 2016)

A final example of the mismatch between foreign funders and local needs was the training promoted by the Chinese who were in Mozambique to share best practices from China's agricultural experiences.[11] The week after REPETE, I attended a two-day training for extension agents at the China Friendship, Agronomy and Technology Transfer Center (as it was called in 2016) out on the grounds of the Umbeluzi Research Station. The building was imposing, with a large, formal metal gate at the entrance and two guards standing loosely at attention. Wide marble stairs led into a grand entrance hall with high ceilings that featured an enormous painting of the Great Wall of China. The training that week was organized by a small group of visiting Chinese agronomists. The first day included a handful of research scientists from China and IIAM, as well as twenty-two extension agents (eighteen men and four women) from Mozambique who had been invited to learn how they produced salt licks and animal forage in China.[12] In accordance with informal protocol, the first day of the workshop IIAM presented on salt licks, and the second day the Chinese agronomists presented on forage. At different moments during the two days, the conversation between IIAM and the extension agents in attendance was acrimonious, which didn't surprise me after REPETE. The Chinese were nevertheless very eager to present their technologies to the audience and very anxious to please. They enthusiastically served us Chinese bao for our snack on the first day. "So delicious," I noted in my field notes. One woman said loudly that she couldn't eat it, though, because it seemed like the bread wasn't done and she was afraid she would get sick and go into convulsions in the street. Everyone laughed, but most people ate the bao.

Over the course of two days, we learned the technical proportions of ingredients for a good salt lick, and we got lessons from both IIAM and the Chinese agronomists on making forage. The IIAM scientists used a chipper to cut up corn stalks for forage, while the Chinese showed us a video with roughly fifty Chinese farmers working with two tractors to fill an enormous pit with hay, then tamping it down collectively. The extension agents listened along but were not enthusiastic about either method. The first required a machine that very few farmers in Mozambique had access to ("in the whole metropolitan region of Boane/Maputo, there is only one farmer who has this chipping machine," one complained), and the second required not only two large tractors but also fifty people working together in producing forage, something that China's high population density and collaborative work practices made possible but that was difficult to imagine or implement in much of Mozambique.

After the two-day training, I sent a survey to the extension agents in attendance and asked them which were the most important technologies they had taught farmers to use and why. I also asked where one could go to find assistance with these technologies.[13]

Reading the responses to the survey made it clear that many of the extension agents already knew how to make forage, and that their experiences could have been (but weren't) solicited or incorporated into the training. It was also clear from the responses and from the discussions in between workshop sessions that the extension agents wanted to share the knowledge they learned with farmers, so it might have been valuable to spend time on pedagogical techniques for knowledge transfer. At the same time, many of the extension agents argued that what farmers needed were simple, agroecological techniques stemming from conservation agriculture, and they wanted information from IIAM that would help them extend these practices to local farmers. This was not, however, part of the technological package with which IIAM researchers worked. This one-way transfer of information and the lack of training in the pedagogy of incorporating new technologies at the farm and household level were two of the central dynamics of rural extension practices in Mozambique.

These three examples—REPETE, the FOT sponsored by AGRA, and the Chinese workshop on forage—illustrated fundamental and widespread dynamics of agricultural extension in Mozambique. They highlighted the separation between extension and research, of course, and also the influence of and dependence on foreign funding, which resulted in often inappropriate technologies and short-term projects and an emphasis on donor-funded experimentation to make up for not knowing what would work or what people wanted. More than that, though, and the subject of the rest of the chapter, most of the proposals and programs directly engaged with rural farmers were focused on fixing them in place, either by aggregating them in new versions of colonial villages or by teaching them principles of conservation that would allow them to farm the same plot of land year after year.

FIXING FARMERS I: AGGREGATION

Outside the main cities and meetings such as REPETE, the national state is largely a political presence, embodied by a local party secretary. There are rural schools and clinics, but they are insufficient and underfunded. The lack of funds and focus of the state on election politics help to explain its effective absence in the countryside. In an interview in 2014, the director of the provincial office of the Ministry of Agriculture in Nampula likened his department to a "toothless lion" because it made a lot of noise (created the rules) but had very little money to implement new programs or develop effective policies. Although government officials usually occupy the grandest and most ostentatious buildings in any town, dependency on aid and NGO labor has led to a "degree of surrogacy and substitution of the government's role" (Thomas 1992: 43). When we noted during an interview with a government official that interventions into farming would be more effective if they were supported by functioning schools, a local health system, markets, and infrastructure such as roads and potable water, he shot back, "But [that is not what governments do], that's what NGOs do." NGO workers spent time "in the field" working on particular projects and then in capital city offices, overseeing finances; attending countless meetings; and developing new frameworks, approaches, and strategies—from sustainable livelihoods to capacity building to resilience—for understanding development (see Mosse 2005). The NGOs I saw in action in Mozambique, such as CARE and CLUSA, all demonstrated long-standing dedication to grassroots pedagogies of participatory development, farmer to farmer training, and self-help associations, but they operated in a context where the needs were great and there was little coordination or infrastructure from the government. These NGOs came with outside funding, deliverables they needed to produce, and deadlines. The programs NGOs provided were often limited in scope and short-lived, and they were a poor substitution for long-term, coordinated development, but local residents took what they could get. Community members sometimes participated in NGO-led projects because they believed in a program's goals, but just as often they participated because doing so might provide access to much-needed resources.

The state made up for having very few resources by promoting public-private ventures that sought to tie local communities to public or private farms as producers who received inputs and advice from the farming corporations, which then purchased surplus from the farmers. These plans were reminiscent of colonial-era plantation enterprises. One government official said in 2016 that those enterprises had been so productive that Mozambique should emulate them today. A popular approach when I was in Mozambique was government projects to build "centers" or "blocks," with multiple producers who would focus on a single commodity crop and tied to companies (agrodealers) who would provide credit, inputs, and output markets. A longtime political official (who served at a high level in three different ministries between 2013 and 2016) said when I interviewed him in 2016 that his plan for progress in the countryside was based on the colonization patterns of the Portuguese, which he thought had worked well and should be copied. He argued that the problem with Mozambican agriculture was that people farmed "a little plot of land here, a little plot there," and they would never achieve anything that way. He proposed bringing farmers together into a single plot of land so that they could work together and rent or purchase mechanized tools (such as tractors) (Interview 15b [second interview], September 16, 2016).

"Collectives?" I asked in response. He quickly demurred, saying that the farmers would all work individually and on their own land, but the government would give them contiguous plots if they agreed to plant the same crop. This would allow them to partner with a commercial input provider and utilize large-scale technologies. The state would plow the land and provide incentives for private firms to sell inputs and purchase the harvest: the Mozambican government, he argued, had to stop providing so many resources directly to people; rather, it should create an environment in which businesses could operate successfully, and people could respond to market signals and incentives. Then, when the producers were all gathered together (into villages near their aggregated plots), the government or the company or (more likely, given the lion's missing teeth) an NGO could easily provide services such as health care and schools.

In a subsequent interview, a different official in the Ministry of Agriculture sketched out the rationale for this sort of center. He described the "old way" of living in isolated individual fields (on the left in figure 7) compared to the more "modern and developed" way of living in gridded communities (bottom right in figure 7).

These projects—alternately called centers, blocks, and green blocks—were classic out-grower or contract farming schemes. They had become increasingly common in conjunction with the large-scale land acquisitions that multiplied across Africa in the 2000s and beyond.[14] An extensive literature on contract farming (see Little and Watts 1994 and Meemken and Bellemare 2019 for overviews) suggests that such vertical integration can be an efficient way to capture economies of scale and increase production, but it also results in greater risk for producers, as they are responsible if the product does not meet specified standards. Contract farmers bear the costs of establishing their production sites, and even if the company or government offers resources, these usually have to be paid for with the first harvest or sale.

A widely distributed poster advertising the benefits of ProSavana for rural communities presented a vision of aggregation in colorful cartoons.[15] The first panel showed "Agriculture in the Nacala Corridor Today," with

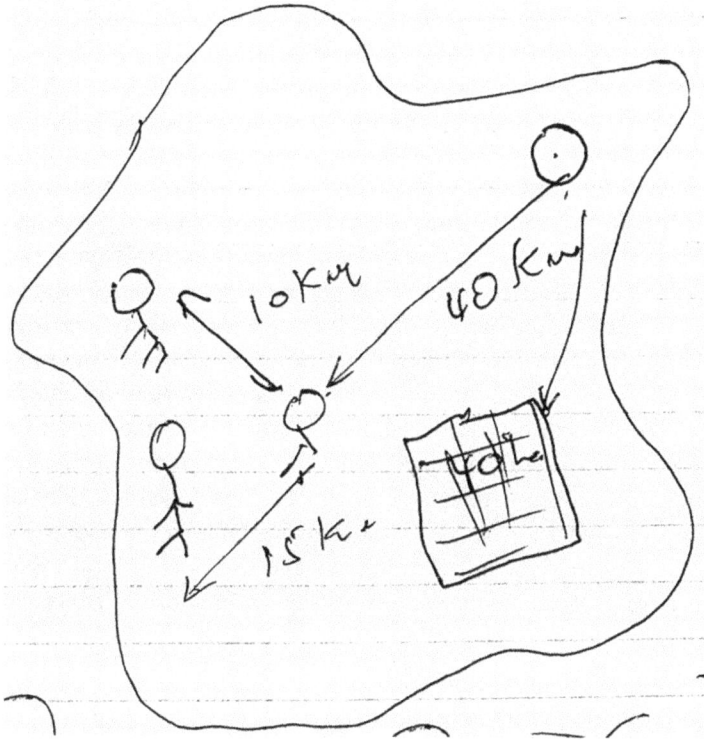

FIGURE 7.   Notes on the "old way" (on the left) and the "modern and developed way" (on the right). SOURCE: Interview 29, November 21, 2016.

what looked like a married couple bent double over short-handled hoes working a single field of manioc. A man on a bicycle passes by on the first road, and a woman buys supplies at a roadside shack with just three products visible for sale. The transformation begins with scientists developing new varieties in test fields. In the next panel, labeled "Transfer of Agricultural Technologies," an extension agent is explaining how to plant the new varieties. A subsequent panel shows the beginnings of improvement: a town has grown up with shops for supplies and tractors. This is followed by a picture of a huge field of corn, rows leading off into the distance with no end in sight, and several adults harvesting the "Increase in Production and Productivity." The final panel shows the family plot again, side by side with other families with houses, a motorcycle, and small tractor, all next to a road that is now paved, with a truck stopping by to collect what look like grain sacks. This is the "Vision of ProSavana for the Development of Agriculture in

Nacala Corridor," and it fundamentally turns on the aggregation of small-holders who will work together on commodities grown at scale.

Moving rural residents into settlements was expected to help the Mozambican state in many of the same ways the colonial and socialist states expected it would help them. It would promote the production of single commodity crops oriented toward the larger domestic or export market. It would make it easier for the government to know where people were—and where they weren't. More land could be created by aggregating small-holders and then leasing the newly liberated area to investors, who would bring advanced technologies to more intensive production in agriculture. This made economic and political sense for a resource-poor state focused on promoting plantation agriculture, but it meant that rural residents were treated like chess pieces: disrupted, moved around, and then told to adopt new production practices that would keep them from moving again. The government's tendency to compare these projects directly to colonial-era projects of forced labor and villagization suggested that the state was completely out of touch with the memories and concerns of local residents. People in rural Mozambique were very skeptical of efforts to relocate them (Chichava 2013).

FIXING FARMERS II: CONSERVATION AGRICULTURE

In 2016 conservation agriculture had become very popular in Mozambique as a way to counteract the historic tendency toward inappropriate, top-down technological models and to provide immediate relief with subsistence production of staple crops like manioc and beans. Many public extension agents had initially been trained to work with commercial crops like cotton and cashews, and they had to re-learn new techniques. One of the original directors of extension expounded on this mismatch:

> A mindset change has had to occur (and still has to occur) viz the "classic" models. Extension used to be restricted mostly to market crops of interest to the colonial government, and the preparation of técnicos [extension agents] was both very basic . . . and all oriented toward commercial agriculture. . . . And it's this extension agent, who then has to go work with a farmer who works with a short-handled hoe. . . . [S]o, here we have to talk a little about politics, right . . . like how are things organized. . . . [W]e enter into that cycle where there is a lack of information about appropriate technologies to deliver to the small farmer who is not going to use a tractor or a seeder and [who] won't use other more sophisticated means of production. (Interview 18, September 22, 2016)

From 2014 to 2016 I observed and worked with one project, called Primeiras e Segundas (P&S) after the set of islands by the same name that ran along the northeastern coast, where the project was implemented. The program was financed and designed by CARE Mozambique and the World Wildlife Fund in 2008; the partnership between the two organizations was called "the Alliance" by community members and practitioners alike. The Alliance's work was divided such that WWF was responsible for training community members on community based resource management, with the goal of conserving and protecting the local estuaries, while CARE took responsibility for training extension agents and implementing farmer field schools (FFS) and farmer associations and introducing conservation agriculture, partly to offset any losses in subsistence or income from the conservation of the local estuaries.[16]

Communities in that region relied on fishing and subsistence agriculture, planting rice, manioc, sorghum, peanuts, and many different kinds of beans. The Alliance program promoted a suite of farming methods, including the cessation of burning to prepare fields, reduced tillage, mulching, crop rotations, and intercropping. Although program leaders insisted that participation was open to all, many community members believed they had to promise not to burn their land anymore (refrain from engaging in swidden agricultural practices) to join. Program organizers supported the methods they were promoting, saying that solutions to the deepest issues of rural poverty did not always require "high fashion" solutions; rather, they could be addressed with small-scale participatory programs based on simple technologies and collaborative work with farmers. When the Alliance started in 2008, it focused on food security and the multiplication of improved varieties. Extension agents trained by CARE provided improved manioc varieties to coastal communities and built nurseries to propagate and distribute more cultivars, focusing on staples such as manioc and cowpea as well as nutrient-rich fruits. These resources were targeted toward the so-called hungry season when families could not provide for themselves with agricultural production. The Alliance also formed a savings group, bringing families together to deposit their money in a community fund, a format made popular by the Grameen Bank in Bangladesh.

CARE introduced FFS to the program in 2011 as a way of promoting new techniques of conservation agriculture that were seen as critical to improving livelihood security in farming, while at the same time requiring less land than swidden agricultural practices. The FFS methodology had been around for decades, especially in Asia, and it became popular in Africa in the 2000s, along with conservation agriculture. The FAO was instrumental in popularizing the methodology.[17] CARE developed trainings in both con-servation agriculture and FFS methodology for extension agents from a pri-vate, nonprofit extension agency it helped to establish in 2007, the AENA.

As of 2010, the program had eight agricultural technicians and thirty-two community "demonstrators" who were jointly selected by program leaders and the community. Demonstrators were supported by particularly tal-ented or well-regarded individuals designated as "facilitators," who worked directly with the FFS, or by "animators," who worked to raise interest in creating associations. The animators, demonstrators, and facilitators were "focal points"; the Alliance expected them to spread information about the projects and to motivate the communities to organize and participate. The extension agents had high expectations for these focal points. They were expected to be able to read and write; accurately spread information; work with all different kinds of people; show up on time for meetings; and be responsible, dynamic, dedicated, influential, honest, believable, exemplary, organized, and hardworking.

These focal points were not paid but were invited to attend semi-regular trainings in agricultural topics and techniques. Most animators and facilita-tors were male—due, we were told, to the requirement that they travel to trainings and/or to communities, something a woman would not normally do without her family in rural northeastern Mozambique. Facilitators and extension agents updated their knowledge in two-week trainings on con-servation agriculture principles and on the pedagogy that was utilized by the schools. This pedagogy was intended to be field based, hands on, and participatory. "The producer has to see the changes," one extension agent explained. "If we begin turning the soil, after it rains, we have to take them to see the two different plots with soil—where we have mulched and where we haven't—and do some exercises, like filtration tests where you show them the difference in how the water goes through [the soil]."

Conservation agriculture practices are a standard part of agronomics education in Mozambique, even if many extensionists argued that they have been overshadowed by more input-intensive agricultural techniques. Most of the extension agents hired for the project were well versed in the basic principles of conservation agriculture and had been teaching them before beginning the FFS curriculum, although such projects were not coordinated across the country, and various groups (NGOs, FAO, the government) used different principles or pedagogies. The lead FFS agent, who was affiliated with IIAM, expanded on the consequences of this inconsistency:[18]

For these FFS, the extension agents who put the schools together, some are from World Vision, and CARE, others are from the State, and there is overlap, sometimes in the same community, right! But those organizations don't put the schools together like they should. . . . [T]hey don't carry out the work the way they should. [It should be that] the state, the landowners, say: this project can operate in Angoche, this project has to be in Maputo, this project in Inhambane, in a very clear way. Because from experience, with all the projects that have taken place here, there are few that have any visible impact. (Interview 38, December 1, 2016)

None of these different visions for conservation agriculture were coordinated by the state. When I asked the head of CLUSA (one of the most active NGOs creating new farmer associations in Mozambique) if the organization was participating in the government working group on conservation agriculture, she replied, "Yeah, we participate in that but save for the conversations nothing is going on. Even though the government is also pushing CA as a policy." "What does 'pushing [CA] as a policy' look like?" I asked. "Well, the implementation is a bit weak," she admitted. "The government is setting up service provision centers, with tractors, but none of the tractors are set up for conservation agriculture. We were with DNEA in June, and we raised that to them, and I don't know if they hadn't thought about it; I mean, the policy is in place, but I don't know if people have really absorbed what the implications are" (Interview 49, December 15, 2016). Given that conservation agriculture represented a key rhetorical focus of the state's strategy to promote smallholder well-being, the lack of a vision and coordination was both unfortunate and telling.

The Alliance worked with roughly twenty-eight communities in Nampula. Katherine Young, Amanda Hickey, and I met and worked with a small subset of these in 2014. Some of the elders spoke in Macua or Coti, and so we worked with local translators, but many also spoke Portuguese, especially those who had held skilled or supervisory positions in colonial factories or plantations. All of these communities were ethnically Macua, the group that dominates northeastern Mozambique. With a small team from the university and translators, we asked community leaders how they would describe their communities. They answered with descriptions of community that were grounded in place and time, rather than in any particular group of people.[19] This grounded but disembodied notion of community was shaped by the conditions of colonial rule, the war for independence, and ensuing civil conflict in Mozambique. People in rural Mozambique had moved around a lot for a variety of reasons, whether seeking work in the South African mines, practicing swidden agriculture, hiding from the Portuguese, or fleeing from internal violence (or all four). Community members often had little history together or openly mistrusted one another, having been thrown together by virtue of proximity or the opportunity of a project. When asked to describe the history of "the community," people tended to describe the people who had lived in that place rather than the various places a set group of people had lived.

Many of the elders divided their histories into eras. The first era was before colonial rule, which they labeled simply "the first generation." One participant in an oral history group said that the community at this time belonged to his uncle, which meant that his uncle was a local king or the *régulo* (small chief), though he mentioned that when his uncle arrived in the community, there were already people living there. Another community was led by a queen (*rainha*) for some time, and she had only recently passed away. People fished and planted. The second era was during colonization, when many people were taken from their communities to work on roads or in the fields owned by the Portuguese and European settlers. This was the time of the régulos: people had small fields of their own but were forced to work collectively by and for the régulos. They lived in straw houses that "weren't worth anything," and planted cotton, peanuts, corn, and rice. They couldn't have significant material possessions and were not allowed to marry "a pretty woman," and "if you walked on the street without shoes, you would be put in jail, just to keep control over people."[20] People were taken to sisal and sugarcane plantations in Beira as slaves and never came back. This was a time of the *força de sipaios* and *cabos da terra* (when the local population was coerced into policing communities for the Portuguese). The Portuguese created indirect rule through the regulado. Portuguese rule introduced a system of taxation in kind: *impostos grandes* (big taxes) were paid with products such as eggs, sorghum, and fish. The chiefs were given authority over the land, but people were allowed to work, and after paying taxes in kind, they were allowed to sell the surplus. Then in the 1930s, the rise of António Salazar in Portugal resulted in a transition to more direct colonial rule. Taxes had to be paid in money, and community members had to earn that money by working on plantations such as the new coconut plantation, Boror, owned by the Portuguese.[21] Community members were forced to pull up existing vegetation and plant coconut trees. People in the community remembered that as a difficult time. One community member who was a guard recalled, "You just had to keep walking all around and find anyone doing anything abnormal, then you had to grab them and put them in jail." Another community member's father was a cabo da terra and tasked with disciplining people for the Portuguese. They were allowed to plant small, individual fields, although one community member said that if you worked for the plantation, having an individual field was possible only if you had a wife who could work the land; in all cases, one had to ask permission from the chiefs to break ground. You couldn't "get out from under the chiefs unless it was to go to the factory." People planted on the factory land for themselves but also for the administrator, the prisoners of the Portuguese, and "the Indian traders."

The third era was the time of "the government" of Frelimo, which was introduced by the War of Independence, during which many people died. For the most part, these were post-independence communities. Frelimo was the "mother of the community," people said. Songs about resistance began to come across the radio (performed by the singer João Júlio; see Vail and White 1978), and people began to organize in the region. The chiefs were already fairly powerless, people said, and they accepted this struggle. In 1975, freedom and independence came; Frelimo instituted many controls on the districts (to go from one district to another, you had to pass through various control points), but it was still a time of liberation. People embraced their individual plots because "it was your own will [*vontade*]; you got to choose for yourself where, how much, and what you were going to produce and when you would sell." At harvest time, "no one comes and forces you to sell your products." The civil war came after Frelimo was established. Boror closed down, and a new administrative system was established that centered around Frelimo and community secretaries. One local resident was elected district secretary in 1975 and had remained in that position since then. With independence, people began to move around from community to community. They saw movement as a privilege after having been kept in place by the Portuguese. They worked in their individual small farms (*machambas*) and came to realize that they would not be rounded up and put into prison or "captured" for doing so. Frelimo saw the dispersed nature of rural settlements as a hindrance to administration, however, and began a campaign to consolidate the settlements. This angered community members, who also noted the disappearance of stores and commerce during the Frelimo era, most likely due to the civil war. As one community member put it, "Frelimo is like a child, one who has been learning and maturing all this time." With independence, community members planted many different crops—manioc, sorghum, corn, millet, sesame, and different kinds of beans and peanuts— but most did not have a tradition of agriculture passed down from their parents. This was, however, still a time of war, of civil war. During the war, the soldiers burned houses and killed or captured many people. The population of the community grew smaller. The chiefs all supported Renamo (they "were friends of Renamo because Frelimo wanted to get rid of the régulos"), and so the fighting was fierce.

The fourth era (from about ten years ago to the present) was the time of democracy and "diverse parties," and of *desenvolvimento* (development). When the civil war ended with the *casamento* (marriage) of the two parties, Frelimo and Renamo, they said, the communities began to grow. More people came to the community. Many of the elders who narrated their community histories arrived around this time. They came after working in factories, or to marry, or to get out of the city. They came to the community to work in agriculture—there was nothing else to do and nowhere else to go. Now there was "real democracy," and people planted rice, manioc, sorghum, peanuts, and many different kinds of beans. They were learning how to plant in a more systematic way in the conservation agriculture program brought by this external organization. When the CARE project came, the communities created associations and dedicated small plots of land near the *zona da machamba* (small farm zone) to association activities.

These histories described community as individuals who had lived in a particular place and the leaders who oversaw the place. Community members did not generally move together, and so the notion of community was more an administrative relationship than a social bond. Community was a term of convenience and a somewhat contentious word, especially in rural areas where it had so often been mobilized in essentialized and problematic ways. Local residents in colonial Mozambique were assigned to "native circumscriptions" that were ruled by leaders the Portuguese characterized as traditional, although the ethnic or tribal connections were often invented or manipulated to facilitate governance (see Berry 1992). In 2016 the communities we met had been formed when NGOs like CARE appeared and said that projects would require a community association.[22] In order to initiate work in any one of these communities, the NGO had to sign an agreement with a community leader confirming the group's commitment. In the case of P&S, an extension agent with AENA described the NGO's approach. They would tell the community, "We are from AENA. We are trained in the area of agriculture, but we are not here to teach. We are here to augment your knowledge. . . . You talk and we will partner with you. You are your own master [*dono de você mesmo*]" (Interview AENA, June 12, 2014). Having formal approval from "the community" was required in order to begin a project, and any new FFS had to have at least twelve to fourteen families sign on as an association before an extension agent could formally bring them into the program. This reliance on communities is a staple of both government and NGO practice, but it is well known that the availability of a project often calls the community into being, rather than the other way around.

One of the program directors for the FAO in Mozambique elaborated on this opportunistic dynamic in 2016:

> [The presence of projects] has created a syndrome, a sickness; namely that getting a grant requires having a [community] group. If you don't have a grant, there is no group. Just to tell you one story: one time this mission came from Rome. They said, "hey [program director], let's go visit the group in Gondola." But what group is this? I know almost all the groups, that one isn't a group anymore, are you sure you mean Gondola? Yes, I know Gondola. And so I discovered that it was a group of thirty men, and I said: 'no, this is a group of drunks! It isn't possible to have a group of thirty men! If it was thirty women, ok, but thirty men! Something is wrong here, this is a group of drunks, they are the ones who asked for a grant, they get a grant, and they go drink, the history is a big lie! Now, because men are always like this, you know, they want to do something where there is cash immediately. (Interview 9, July 27, 2016)

Although it was true that many community groups were opportunistic, donors nevertheless relied on them. The result was a "process where we call the groups right from the beginning, they have to have their own seeds, their own land, their own hoes. We bring technology, but we don't make any promises, because anything can happen!" (Interview 9, July 27, 2016).

In our 2014 review of FFS projects (Hickey et al. 2015), we found that while community members originally formed associations and started FFS as a way to access resources, they learned new practices and increased their harvests as a result. They were used to engaging in diversified activities, with the farm being just one means of sustenance, but they believed the new techniques would help them to stay in one place for several years. One association member said, "We learned a lot about the humidity, that the humidity in the soil is sufficient to grow our products. Before we used to plant in our plot of land and then leave it to plant somewhere else, but now we can plant two or three years and not move, and when the rain comes it stays in the field and waters it." On their individual plots, most had adopted techniques of minimum soil disturbance and planting in lines. Women who formed an association said it was not difficult to convince their husbands to let them join: "They liked it and they all supported and adopted [the practices]." The various associations were working together two to three days a week, planting manioc, beans, peanuts, sesame, and vegetables (*hortíco-las*) on roughly 3 hectares of land; they sold products from their FFS plots and put some of what they earned into an association fund (for both future investment and social support if needed). They divided the other portion of their earnings among group members.

In 2014 the associations had many plans for the future. They did not want to remain simple subsistence producers dependent on their small farms (see Ruth Castel Branco's 2022 excellent study); they wanted "development" and a market for their products. To that end, they were looking for a way to combine their products, store them, and negotiate better terms with the buyers. They also planned to ask the government for a loan so they could hire people to work on the farm and open up more land. One association had submitted all of the necessary documents for a loan, although they had yet to hear back. With the help of CARE and AENA extension agents, members were stockpiling their products in a new storage facility in a neighboring community, though there had been some issues with lack of proper storage and low prices for raw products. Members received improved cassava culti-vars, which they planted and sold to neighboring towns. The women in one association said that many people outside the association had also adopted these practices. They wanted to learn about additional practices because they "have already decided to learn, and now we want more."

In August 2016, after the FFS project had been running for several years, I attended a weeklong training of extension agents who were responsible for the Alliance in Nampula. The organizers also invited representatives from the district extension office (SDAE). This was the third such training I participated in between 2014 and 2016, and the workshop was animated and participatory, intended to teach new extension agents the philosophy of both conservation agriculture and FFS. It took place at the time when exist-ing extension agents had to calculate and submit their requests for materi-als (seeds, tools, funding, etc.) for the upcoming season. These calculations happened at the end of the long workshop days, with people sitting around communal tables and experienced extension agents teaching the new ones how to estimate the need for seed, stalks, signs, gas, and more.

The extensionists had all been working with the communities I described earlier as well as with many other communities along the coast. They were enthusiastic about the FFS pedagogy but also expressed serious concerns about the inflexibility of the approach. For example, planting in raised beds was commonplace in the region but not allowed in the FFS areas because doing so disturbed the soil. And there were regular complaints about the rigidity of the intercropping associations. Communities in particular did not appreciate the introduction of jack bean (*canavalia ensiformis*), which was supposed to be intercropped with manioc. People in the communities disliked the crop because they didn't eat it, but there was pushback from the leadership of the project, who argued that jack bean had to be planted because it was so valuable for soil melioration: "We need to have the will to incentivize the planting of jack bean," one of the project leads insisted. The problem, the extension agents said, was with the consultation process. There needed to be more discussion about which crops to include. "We should be more open to the producers who can decide what to plant." During the training, one relatively new extension agent asked, "Are we authorized to add things to the FFS?" Not really, was the answer. "If we make them all different," the leader of the training explained, "we won't be able to compare [the results] across communities." Extension agents also pushed back on what felt like the constant need to create new schools. "This is an obligation the donor has imposed," one said, and others agreed. They wanted to develop a new approach that would "train the trainers" and allow extensionists to be more involved in training and less involved in the development of new schools per se.

The donor was also responsible for introducing a complicated form that required community members to carefully document the changes they had witnessed in the different sections of the FFS. The need to rethink this form (the Agro-Eco-System Analysis, or the AESA) became one of the main subjects of the training. The new AESA would incorporate more observations about climate change than the previous form, and those filling out the form were supposed to write—or draw if they couldn't write—a description of their traditional practices as compared to the conservation agriculture practices being employed, including plots and crop use, plants and plant size, soil erosion, weeding, pests, and cover crops. There was an evaluation of the project at the end of the form. Questions arose during the presentation about the illustrations used in each section and how to translate the questions and categories into different languages. "The AESA is inappropriate and doesn't work," one participant concluded. "There is often only one person [in the community] who can write, and the AESA has to be completed in writing. Sometimes it ends up just being the extension agent who does the work."

The biggest disagreement at the meeting, though, was over whether the FFS and conservation agriculture should also include attention to markets and marketing. In trainings in both 2015 and 2016, the agents were specifically asked not to delve too deeply into matters of commercialization or the market more generally, as their task was to focus on conservation agriculture and soil management, not markets. "We can't do everything," was the rationale. This exclusion of the market would be one of the primary challenges of the project, and the conversation returned to this topic repeatedly. One extensionist who was widely respected by the others insisted that market access was one of the most important issues they had to deal with in the communities. Another agreed, summarizing the problem: "If we want to reduce vulnerability, we need to help them increase their production. But if we help them to increase their production without helping them to sell the surplus, then they will produce a surplus and it will just sit there."

The organizer of the workshop, however, objected:

> If we expand and add a lot more materials, like commercialization, will we overload the curriculum? Another thing, peasants are intelligent people, and they can look for ways to sell their products on their own. What we need to do is to help them increase their production. If we say that they will produce more and have surplus and then say we are afraid that it will rot in their houses, then we are underestimating them. . . . Both conservation agriculture and markets are essential, but they're complementary and shouldn't be mixed.

In addition to the argument against extension agents addressing markets, there was concern that the priorities of conservation agriculture— particularly soil fertility—were at odds with the requirements of the fickle rural market: "Right now, pigeon pea is in great demand; but there are other cultures that are very good for the soil, like black bean, that have very low market value." Another extension agent agreed: "We are not really well equipped to talk about commercialization. In the first few years of an FFS, we have to focus on soil fertility and can't mix in [or confuse] a whole bunch of things. If they sell some of their product, it might be surplus or it might be because they are going hungry." But those who supported adding commercialization to the FFS curriculum countered, "We could avoid talking about selling with the farmers and they would still sell! What we need to do is to help them sell at a good price. We want to teach them where and how to access a just market or a just price."

By the end of the discussion, everyone except the director of the program seemed to agree that the FFS needed to be more flexible and to take opportunities where possible to help the farmers with commercialization, "because if not, they will lose that surplus. The thing that motivates the producer is money. We will have real impact on these communities when we help them to sell their products." In the end, though, the topic of commercialization was deemed to be too far from the goals of the project. Extension agents could talk about commercialization, but it couldn't be formally introduced into the curriculum. Another extension agent explained the reasoning behind the decision:

> We can't forget the objective of our project. When it comes to the evaluation [of the project], we will be evaluating vulnerability particularly in relation to women. So even if we take on a new approach, we will still have the same indicators to achieve. We have to have our indicators in mind. So 50 percent of our participants will need to be women. If we don't do this, then we will be racing to accomplish our targets in the last year of the project. Given that we can't commercialize the stuff we produce on our own demonstration fields, this component of commercialization really has to be complementary, not fundamental.

This refusal to expand the Alliance programs to include commercialization reflected a key challenge of relying on short-term donor funding and projects that were not integrated into broader plans for economic or social development. The extension agents wanted to include commercialization because they saw this desire in their communities. And communities wanted this to be their next step, to market the produce they had accumulated during the conservation agriculture project. But the donor-led projects, with their scope of work, predefined indicators, and timelines, made addressing these urgent needs impossible.

The conservation agriculture project needed to be embedded in a more inclusive, state-led, rural development approach, but for the state, the conservation agriculture project *was* rural development, not a means to an end. After this training, I visited two other communities that had implemented FFS as part of the CARE project. They were happy with the project but wanted more—they wanted tractors and market access. If they had a tractor, they could "clear a big area and really do well," they argued. Without one, they didn't have enough labor to clear the land effectively. A small group of participants I met with one evening argued that it would look good for the project to be able to say that it had secured a tractor, and then all of the communities affiliated with the project could use it. The machine could stay in the project area and be rented out on a regular basis. There was a tractor nearby that they could hypothetically rent, but it was never available to them because the local party secretary had control over access.

The community members had many ideas; there were so many things they wanted. They wanted extension agents who would stay with them for more than a few weeks or one harvest. They wanted an electric motor for irrigation. They had a bicycle pump, they explained, but they were all old, and it hurt too much to sit there and pedal it—and their kids didn't help (and even if they did, they argued that it would be too much for them, too).

Finally, they talked about needing pesticides to be able to deal with the pests that infected the garden crops, particularly—that year—the onions. They already used repellent plants, but these lost their effectiveness after a few years. "If we had more income, we would attract more members [into the association]. A mill would be a good idea, then we would have money." To make money, they needed credit: "We would pay it back! The association savings isn't enough. The government does have money, but we can't get it. It's not easy." And so, the community relied on the NGO to find them more resources: "We don't want to speak badly about the government, but it doesn't really help us, it just helps itself. So, we depend on projects." I left the conversation that evening with a sense of hopelessness, even though the community members were so hopeful. Their relationship with CARE had helped them realize a basic level of food security, and they were starting to accumulate surpluses. But without government support and economic infrastructure geared toward smallholders, the primary achievement of CARE's decade-long project would be to enable community members to abandon swidden farming and stay in one place for multiple years. That this suited government and investment plans for large-scale agriculture was an unintended effect of the plantation ideal.

CONCLUSION: COMMUNITY DEVELOPMENT IN RURAL MOZAMBIQUE

This chapter highlights how extension agents and local community members navigated the landscape created by the plantation ideal in rural Mozambique. The brief history of the public extension services illustrates the structural challenges of underfunding and reliance on short-term projects. The separation between research and extension meant that the latter had the difficult job of bringing new technologies to people who were not consulted and did not get to dictate the terms of their own inclusion. The foreignization of funding meant that extension agents were tasked with creating models that would reach significant numbers of people, making sure they hit their yearly targets, all while attempting to remain true to the participatory and people-centered philosophy of extension. Satisfying the need for scale without sufficient extension agents meant that there wasn't enough money to provide basic necessities for each one, like motorbikes and fuel to get to the farmers' houses.

Without a functioning public system in rural Mozambique, the roads, markets, and public services were all unreliable. There were schools, but they were overfull and incapable of teaching much beyond reading and writing for the majority of rural residents. The lack of a public system meant that even when a project like the conservation agriculture project described earlier achieved some success, there wasn't capacity for turning that success into something more. The donors stopped at the end of their projects, circumscribed by the demands of their own funders. And so, community members worked with NGOs for as long as they were able, hoping that something else would turn up that would provide more resources, even if it wasn't connected to the project they had agreed to join.

If you asked rural residents what they wanted, they would tell you: a chance. They would engage in new projects and take on new practices if it helped to get them a home with doors and a chair for sitting up off the ground. They wanted some security and the ability to plan for the future. What they got were short-term projects that focused on problems they didn't know they had—like moving around in search of land—and on solutions they didn't know they needed—like new plant varieties. And they engaged in these projects knowing that the projects would end soon, but that if they played their cards right, they might get access to future projects, or a well, or a pump—something they could hold onto. These were the politics of agricultural life in Mozambique. Everyone was invested in discovery, whether of new projects, of new techniques, or of new sources of funding. And everyone was a little bit disappointed that they hadn't accomplished more, hadn't gotten more—before they had to move on to the next thing.

6. Awakening the Sleeping Giant
ProSavana, the Devil, and the Details

In 2009, almost one hundred years after José Emílio Pinheiro de Azevedo of Lisbon wrote to the Mozambique Company asking for information about the territory, it was the Brazilians who were exploring the possibility of relocating to Mozambique. A headline published by Reuters trumpeted, "Mozambique Offers Brazilians Land to Plant" (Ewing 2011). The article read like Eduardo Villaça's letter to José Emílio, unconsciously mimicking the Portuguese politicians who sought a "new Brazil" in Africa for their colonial ambitions: "Mozambique invites Brazilian soy, corn and cotton growers to plant on its savanna and introduce their farming know-how to sub-Saharan Africa." The reporter suggested that Brazilians had the right "know-how" because Brazil had been "successfully growing crops on its center-west plains since a breakthrough in tropical soybeans in the 1908s unlocked the productive potential of the expansive region by breeding soy to grow closer to equatorial regions." The assessment of Mozambique's land was an update on the reports logged by Barrett (1910), Nicholson (1910), and Sim (1910): "While Mozambique possesses similar climatic and soil characteristics. . . . [S]ome areas in the country on the southeast coast of Africa even had more fertile soils than Brazil. . . . 'The price of land there is too good to ignore' said Augustin [the head of Brazil's largest state cotton producers association AMPA]." The government would make it easy for Brazilians to settle, in the hopes that they would bring advanced techniques and modernize agricultural production in Mozambique: "Producers who are granted concessions to plant would be required only to pay a tax of 21 reais per hectare and would receive an exemption from import tariffs on farm equipment" (Ewing 2011).

A year after the Reuter's article was published, representatives from Brazil, Mozambique, and Japan announced their plans for a new agricultural mega-project. ProSavana would create a new frontier for Brazil, one in Africa; or, as one Brazilian businessman put it, describing an extractive frontier, ProSavana would create "a Mato Grosso in the middle of Africa, with free land, with fewer environmental impediments and much cheaper shipping to China" (cited in Perin 2020: 7). Grounded in the extractive nature of agriculture, science, and rural development in Mozambique, ProSavana unfolded as concerns over global food and fuel supplies combined with high commodity prices to generate a rush of new investments in land around the world (Li 2014).

ProSavana was located in the Nacala Corridor, amid what USAID called the "vast, untapped agricultural potential" (2011: 4) of northern Mozambique, characterized by perhaps the highest "high yield gap" in the world, where recorded yields were far below those achieved in other countries with highly mechanized and input-intensive systems. Scientific research for ProSavana was coordinated by the Brazilian agricultural research agency Embrapa, which framed the project as a way for Brazil to "[pay] its agricultural success forward"; "what Embrapa sows," the agency suggested, "the world reaps" (Embrapa n.d.). Officially, the logic behind Brazil's South-South assistance to Mozambican agriculture turned on the notion of similarity—or what the Brazilians called "parallels" (Embrapa 2010; Wolford and Nehring 2015). The concept of parallels is a legacy of Cartesian logic: it groups together countries that share latitudinal space in categories such as the tropics, the subtropics, and the temperate regions. The Brazilians invoked parallels because the region of their own country's greatest agricultural success (the cerrado grasslands of the Center West) sat at roughly the same latitude as the northern part of Mozambique. The World Bank, without any apparent irony, went even further, tracing the similarity between Brazil and Mozambique back to Pangaea—roughly two hundred to three hundred million years earlier—when "Brazil and African landmasses were connected" (World Bank 2011: 2). In this century, the World Bank suggested, the two countries still shared ecological characteristics such as their warm weather and acidic soils—and "Brazilian technology is easily adaptable to those parts of Africa that share similar geological and climatic conditions" (2; see figure 8).

Parallels between Brazil and Mozambique framed the invocation of South-South development (Abreu 2013), a new approach to development between developing countries predicated on similarity and solidarity rather than on inequality and difference, as in former colonial relations. Unlike Hobson ([1902] 1978), who cautioned the British to avoid colonizing in Africa because the indigenous peoples were so regrettably foreign, and Lugard (1926), who emphasized the contrast between the "communal life

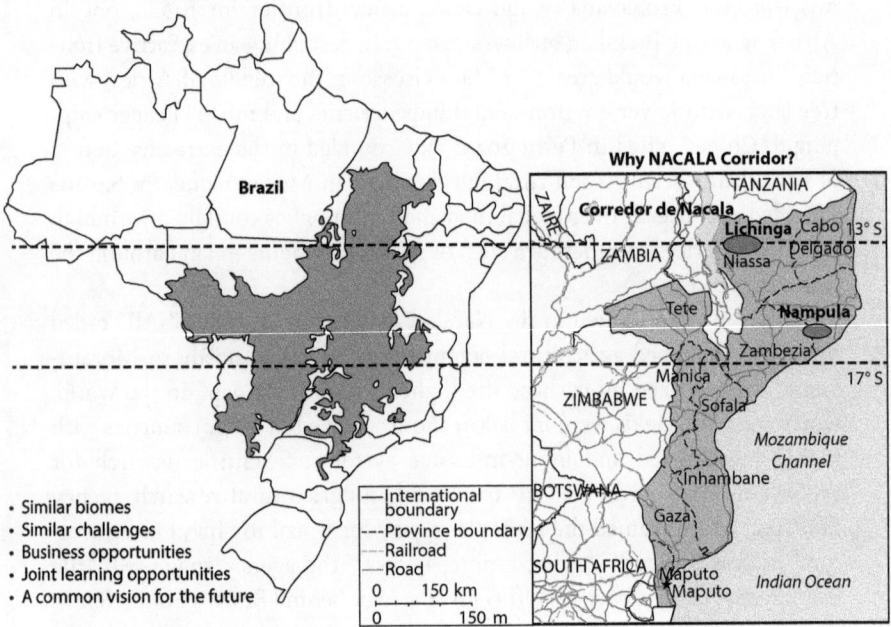

FIGURE 8. Parallels between the Brazilian cerrado and Nacala Corridor. SOURCE: EMBRAPA, used in many PowerPoint presentations, cited in World Bank (2011: 55).

of the primitive tribe" and modern Europe, the new approach to African development was based on a partnership between emerging economies—the BRICS (Brazil, Russia, India, China, and South Africa) and developing nations (Scoones et al. 2013). There was a long connection between Brazil and Mozambique, primarily through the slave trade, and there had long been diplomatic connections between them (Dávila 2010), but Brazil had not been part of a coordinated plan for development in Africa until the 2000s, when Luiz Inácio Lula da Silva was in office. The World Bank called this shift a "pendulum swinging from North to South" (2011: 33). The Brazilian development office put things in similarly rosy terms, arguing that South-South development offered an alternative to official development aid (ODA) by not officially imposing conditions or obligations and by respecting the rhetoric, values, and sovereignty of its counterparts (ABC 2010, 2012). Brazil's development approach was described as "demand driven" and noninterventionist (Cabral and Shankland 2012; Captain 2010), based on bringing the "Brazilian miracle" of rapid growth, particularly agricultural growth, to Africa ("Miracle" 2010). In both Japan and Brazil, collaboration over the earlier project, PRODECER, was seen as legitimating a new round of partnership, in spite of the increasing concerns over the ecological damage of unbridled crop production (sugarcane, soy, cotton, and rice) in the Center West of Brazil (Lopes et al. 2021; Calmon 2020). The rise of South-South development evoked an older history of solidarity between "nonaligned" or former colonial nations even as it deemphasized obvious differences between a handful of emerging economies and the developing world as a whole (Abreu 2013).

The 2009 World Bank report *Awakening Africa's Sleeping Giant: Prospects for Commercial Agriculture in the Guinea Savannah Region and Beyond* described sub-Saharan Africa as the "largest non-used agricultural area in the world" (3; see also Camana and Almeida 2019). ProSavana would extend the earlier collaboration between Japan and Brazil to Mozambique, where the "exploitation rate of arable areas is approximately 4 percent" (World Bank 2009). In May 2009 a delegation from the Ministry of Agriculture visited the Brazilian Center West and "confirmed that there are several points of similarity between the Brazilian Cerrado and the Mozambican tropical savannah, as well as many examples of agricultural techniques used for development of the Cerrado that can be transferred to Mozambique." Of particular note were the soil correction techniques and use of proper varieties. Various reports cited the potential for agricultural productivity increases but also the country's long-standing political stability, which was expected to help ensure the project's success. The northern Nacala region (including the three provinces of Niassa, Nampula, and Zambezia) was selected based on its perceived similarity to Brazil's cerrado, reliable rainfall, and availability of agricultural land (the state of infrastructure and Mozambican laws and regulations were also listed as reasons for choosing the Nacala corridor, but those elements were never explained in more detail).

Much of the new technical knowledge the project required was to come from Embrapa, whose scientists would travel to Mozambique over the next several years (Cabral 2015). Embrapa was interested in the project for scientific reasons—to recreate the scientific victories of the 1970s in Mozambique—and also for economic reasons, as changes in public resources required them to find roughly one-third of their budget from external sources (Nehring 2016; Cruz 2012). Embrapa leaders said in media interviews that they hoped to expand their revenue from seed royalties from 2 percent of their budget to 10 percent (quoted in Wolford and Nehring 2015: 218; see also De Carli and Wehrmann 2007). Project leaders acknowledged the differences between the Brazilian and Mozambican savannah (Interview 20, December 5, 2016) but believed that agricultural research—

a cornerstone of the project—would help in selecting the technologies that could be easily adapted and adopted.

The division of responsibility under ProSavana echoed the division of agricultural services in Mozambique more generally, where research (Brazil's responsibility) was separated from extension (Japan's responsibility) and from the political authority to acquire land or assure a steady labor supply (Mozambique's responsibility). Drawing on its experience in the cerrado, Brazil committed to providing technology and expertise—genetic materials, scientific orientation, and organizational experience—while Japan was responsible for providing significant funding as well as developing the models by which research results and development funds would be disseminated to local communities. The Mozambican government, for their part, committed to making land available to external investors who commanded sufficient financial resources to make the land turn a profit. The total budget for the project was estimated at US$13,483,840, with Japan providing the most funding (approximately 54 percent), Brazil providing 37 percent, and the Mozambican government providing the rest, mostly in counterpart personnel and land.

As outlined in project documents, agricultural research under ProSavana had five key objectives: (1) strengthening the institutional capacity of IIAM, (2) evaluating natural resources (primarily soil, vegetation, and water) and socio-economic conditions in the corridor in order to develop a land use plan, (3) improving soil technologies and conservation, (4) improving cultivation technology by selecting appropriate crops and varieties and helping to develop seed production systems, and (5) validating the technology on pilot farms and training extension workers through demonstration units (ProSavana 2009: 3–5). All five goals were predicated on assistance from Embrapa scientists and leaders who would provide the "knowledge accumulated during the development projects [in] the Brazilian Cerrado and semi-arid [region]" to Mozambican research staff, who were designated as the "direct beneficiaries" (farmers in the Nacala Corridor were listed as the "indirect beneficiaries") (3–5).

Six years after the unveiling of this ambitious agricultural development project in sub-Saharan Africa, I had an appointment to talk with the official project spokesperson, Américo Uaciquete (I include his name here because he was designated the official spokesperson). In November 2016, it was difficult to find government people willing to talk about the project. Américo was the agreed-on point person for the partnership, so I chased him down, ignoring his repeated suggestions that we simply communicate by email. We met in the old cashew industry headquarters in the dusty provincial capital of Nampula. Before I could start talking, however, Américo told me that despite being the spokesperson for ProSavana, he was not really able to speak. ProSavana had been unfairly "vested with bad intentions," so if all of my questions were about the project, I should send them to him in an email (Américo, personal communication with author, November 2016). He said firmly that he would "evaluate the questions" and respond within ninety days. Somewhat dismayed at not being able to have a conversation in person, I emailed him a set of the most basic questions I could think of: What is ProSavana doing, where, and with whom? What is the role of agricultural research, and what has been accomplished?

Américo responded immediately with a polite thank you and promised a quick response. Two months later, I wrote to remind him of my questions. He responded politely again with assurances that they were working on the answers and would respond the following week. Ninety days later, I emailed again. He responded less happily and forwarded me a PowerPoint presentation that the team had presented publicly earlier that year.[1] Six years into the largest trilateral agricultural development project in sub-Saharan Africa, the public window had essentially closed. Or, as the Mozambican activist I quoted in the introduction said during a high-level meeting in Brasília with activists and political leaders from Brazil and Mozambique, by 2016 ProSavana had gone "into hibernation."[2]

PROBLEMS WITH THE PARALLELS

From the very start of the project, the supposed parallels between Brazil and Mozambique were undercut by power differences between the two countries. There were complaints that Embrapa scientists were developing new cultivars but not training Mozambican researchers, with the budget providing little funding for the latter. The Brazilian government viewed ProSavana as a technical cooperation project rather than as traditional development assistance and therefore expected the Mozambican government to fund the participation of Mozambican researchers. This expectation was unrealistic, however, given that the Mozambican government relied on development aid to fund agricultural research.

The idea that Brazilian scientists could bring technologies developed elsewhere to Mozambique was justified, in the project's vision, both by the notion that Brazil's environment was similar (parallel) to Mozambique's (Wolford and Nehring 2015; Shankland and Gonçalves 2016) and by the singular focus on the selection and introduction of new cultivars as politically neutral technologies that could be adapted to the Mozambican context via universally recognized scientific techniques. Brazilian scientists were confident that agricultural development would flow once the right varieties had been selected, as Felix Paulo, director of ProSavana, said in a meeting in Brasília on May 31, 2016: "[ProSavana] starts with the assumption that improved varieties will increase agricultural income, transforming subsistence agriculture into modern intensive agriculture mechanized by the promotion of initiatives oriented towards the market, increasing employment and processing and conservation of agroindustrial productions."[3] These new varieties were assumed to be Brazilian, given the country's experience with and research on relevant crops, particularly cotton, corn, and soy (Shankland and Gonçalves 2016). In 2014, when I asked a lead scientist for ProSavana if they were interested in crossing Brazilian varieties with local varieties, he expressed impatience with the idea (Interview 4a, Nampula, July 7, 2014). Brazilian genetic material was far superior, he insisted, because Brazilian scientists had been experimenting for decades. He was confident that these varieties would transfer easily to Mozambique, and using Brazilian material would facilitate investments by Brazilian farmers, who were originally seen as some of the most likely investors. From 2009 to 2013, Brazil was the largest source of foreign direct investment in Mozambique (Nogueira et al. 2017: 2).

The transfer of varieties ran into problems because of "disappointing" agroecological conditions in Mozambique. In 2015 the lead scientist for the project said that returns were not what the scientific team had hoped for because the weather "was not good. There was a year when it didn't rain like last year, this year it didn't rain at all either" (Interview 4b [second interview], Nampula, August 14, 2015). Uncertain precipitation is to be expected in agriculture, but the Brazilians were surprised by the lack of irrigation capacity in Mozambique, and low rainfall completely disrupted the project, "so the technical team decided not to work with those conditions anymore. This year [2015] we didn't do any activities in the field." Part of the issue with the uncertain climatic conditions was that the team brought all of their varieties from Brazil, to see how they would do in the Mozambican environment. "Did that go well?" I asked the scientist. "No," he admitted. "Only cowpea [did well], because cowpea has a very short cycle of three months. Rice that requires four months has not produced well. It was very beautiful, but the grains did not fill out. There were many flowers . . . and it seemed like there was a lot of production, but then there was no water for the grain to fill out, and only seeds were left, only the husks." The Brazilian varieties also suffered from diseases. The Brazilian scientist acknowledged ruefully, "We didn't do any disease control studies, and you have to do it from the beginning." He insisted that the Brazilians brought "good varieties, one variety has a better fiber than the Mozambican ones and they produce a little more than the Mozambican ones, but they . . . have more disease problems." In the end, he did not blame the foreign varieties or the Brazilians' mistake in overlooking local conditions. Instead, he blamed the Mozambicans and their inability to manage intensive agriculture. "In Mozambique, adequate disease control is not used. . . . [T]here is only one insecticide on the market, a pyrethroid that kills everything, so we were not able to establish disease control with adequate insecticides, and then we preferred not to continue with the studies. Basically, that is how things are."

Local scientists were disappointed that relations with the Brazilians weren't easier. Fernando, the IIAM administrator I cited earlier, described the problems:

> Embrapa was seen as having had, in quotes, [Fernando mimes air quotes] "some successes in Brazil." [And we wanted to] take advantage of their experiences, as an institution, so we specifically developed a relationship with Embrapa. But . . . afterwards we began to understand that Embrapa has a culture, a way of being. We thought our researchers would get better training through Embrapa, but Embrapa wasn't a very good collaborator. . . . At times, communication was very difficult. Embrapa is very big, very big; we had to go through the Cooperation Sector [of the Brazilian state.] . . . That doesn't mean that nothing happened, but it wasn't what we desired because of this administrative-bureaucratic system. (Interview 20, December 5, 2016)

Technical projects established by Embrapa in Mozambique operated under strict bureaucratic guidelines. The imposition of these guidelines together with the unequal standing of Embrapa and IIAM meant that power differences ran through and often undercut parallels and the vision of equal-terms South-South collaboration.

Although Mozambican government officials would later insist that Pro-Savana was intended to help develop the small farmers who constituted over 99 percent of farmers in the country, project documents and leaders focused from the beginning on research efforts that would help to build agroindustrial export capacity.[4] They believed that the proposed large-scale plantations would have multiplier effects, creating "development poles" that would build on local technology to support the still incipient Mozambican private sector and a handful of larger farmers, while incorporating the bulk of the very poor rural population as contract growers and laborers (see also Perin 2020).

For the Brazilians, the goal was clear: they were to create the conditions necessary for large-scale "modernized" agriculture. The lead scientist for the project summarized this approach when I interviewed him in 2015:

From the first we had the idea of developing large-scale agriculture. The project was designed as part of the development of the Nacala corridor, and so [our] expectation was that we would work with advanced agriculture; we would work with machinery, with experiments on large plots of land, with the development of commodities like soy and corn, and other crops too—with what they call market crops and subsistence crops, like rice and beans. (Interview 4b [second interview], Nampula, August 14, 2015)

The first project the Brazilians implemented, called Paralelos, was Embrapa's initial attempt to map the country's soils and find the best places for new crop cultivation. In many ways, the study mirrored the ecological-agricultural study from the early 1950s discussed in chapter 2. The introductory research document for the effort, seventy-four pages and supported by many images, provided a roadmap of sorts for Brazil's efforts in Mozambique (Batistella and Bolfe 2010). What is noteworthy is that the sections titled "Agriculture" and "Women's Role in Agriculture" were the only places where people appeared. These two sections covered a total of four pages, most of which was taken up by images of people farming. The rest of the document focused on climate, soils, land use, and land cover, both in Mozambique as a whole and in the Nacala Corridor, where ProSavana was located. A Mozambican technician who worked on the project argued that he didn't need to talk to people to do his work or include them in his document. He only needed to see them in order to "ground truth" his satellite images because people were not the priority. Everyone in the project understood the goal to be large-scale agriculture.

When asked how the researchers in Paralelos decided the scale at which to present their information, the same technician replied, "Well, I want to produce information to get an idea of where people are, for example, and what land can be used for agriculture." Another person present during the interview interjected, "But why would you need such detailed mapping when the population [in the region] was high enough that you would know where there was good land just by knowing where people lived?" The technician's response once again exemplified the project's prioritization of plantations over people: "But this mapping was specifically to find land that was good [and available] for large-scale agriculture" (Interview 13a, July 22, 2015).

But it didn't go well from the beginning because Embrapa sent expertise but no money, and the government had no funds to allow IIAM researchers to accompany the Brazilians as they worked. There was little familiarity between the two groups, as the technician said: "ABC and Embrapa, yeah, I don't know exactly, for me they were things that sort of fell out of the sky." Because they didn't have the resources and IIAM's personnel were limited, they decided to focus on just a few regions in the country. Mozambique didn't have the resources to pay for the satellite images, so those were downloaded in Brazil. "They were the ones who came with the images, they had the ability to download the satellite images, and we did the interpretation, to say . . . for example this unit here has these 'X' soils and a unit of the terrain has other types of soils. It was more a description of soils. And to evaluate these soils, what is the usability in terms of which crops are suitable for this particular type of soils." Even then, the analysis of the samples was done primarily in Brazil instead of partly in Mozambique and partly in Brazil: "We did the work and then they went back to Brazil. All the data processing happened there, and we even sent some samples, and they analyzed them there."

The key focus of Embrapa's research, then, was not to help Mozambican farmers. Much like the EASM decades earlier, the initial research was to find the "right" location for cultivation of the "right" cultivars. Crops targeted included subsistence crops (although several crops were included in this category that were not historically or currently subsistence crops in Mozambique, such as soy, rice, and wheat), commercial crops (tobacco, sugar, cotton, and cashew), and an array of new crops (including fruits, vegetables, and biofuels). Most of these crops were plantation crops in Mozambique, and there was only a small handful of commercial or "emerging" farmers in the country who were in a position to adopt the new varieties at scale. So the project initially hoped to interest Brazilian farmers to buy land in Mozambique and establish production. Two groups of Brazilian farmers did visit Mozambique to evaluate investment possibilities early on in the project, but they were discouraged by the density of the population they saw in the Nacala corridor, which contrasted with the official presentation of the region as "empty" (Shankland and Gonçalves 2016; Camana and Almeida 2019).

"THEY DON'T EVEN KNOW WHAT SOY IS!"
THE MISMATCH BETWEEN CROPS AND LOCAL REALITIES

With the withdrawal of Brazilian farmers, Embrapa researchers were forced to work more closely with Mozambican producers. One of the frustrations for ProSavana's lead scientist came from the unexpected difficulty he and others were having in disseminating soybean production in Mozambique. In 2014, when I first interviewed him, he was optimistic that he could get people to plant soybeans, which he called a miracle crop (and indeed it was the crop behind the "miracle" of the Brazilian cerrado). Soybean production had been growing in Mozambique since the early 2000s but was still concentrated in just two provinces (Smart and Hanlon 2014: 25–28). Many people were reluctant to plant soy because it wasn't a subsistence crop in Mozambique, and people didn't traditionally eat it. "They don't know the potential of soy," the scientist said in 2014 (see Wolford 2015). "But they should! Soya fixes nitrogen and produces oil and meal for people, and that improves their livelihoods; and then if people start eating more meat [as it is assumed they will do if their livelihoods improve] they will need feed!" By 2015, though, the scientist was discouraged, acknowledging that before soybean technologies could be disseminated, people would have to be "taught to eat soy, not just feed it to their chickens" (Interview 4b [second interview], Nampula, August 14, 2015). A scientist with the Paralelos group I spoke to defended Embrapa's decision to focus on crops that Mozambique didn't consume. He insisted that it was the extension agents' job to convince people to plant new varieties: "They're the ones who work directly with the peasantry. The purview of researchers is to 'produce technologies'" (Interview 5a, Maputo, July 1, 2015).

Researchers focused on discovering new cultivars and new land for cultivation because that was what they were trained to do. It was also because ProSavana was designed to produce technologies for modernized farmers, who would most likely come from outside Mozambique. In the project's vision, the research process did not need to be tethered to existing conditions, preferences, or practices because the project was imagined as a transformative one, not a development one. It would work its magic on a territory seen as relatively unknown.

This focus on modernized farmers, to the exclusion of actually existing local residents, was highly racialized. The top-ranking Brazilian technician I quoted earlier insisted that the project did not fail because of the Brazilians or because of inappropriate technology: for this foreign scientist, the problem was that Mozambicans themselves didn't have the skills to keep up or the drive to work out difficult problems. "Macuas [as he called the Mozambicans, referring to the largest ethnic group in the North] are very lazy; they don't want to work hard. They have basic technological skills but they need better management and they need to stop burning and moving around" (Interview 4a, Nampula, July 7, 2014). For this scientist, the success of agriculture in the Brazilian cerrado had been due to the superiority and variety of the labor force. In Brazil, he maintained, the workers had

> skills and the capacity to learn that doesn't exist in Mozambique. For
> example, we had German immigrants in Brazil who knew how to
> work with machines, they knew how to work with large-scale crops;
> and we had Italian immigrants who knew how to work with fruits and

machines, they had a very old agricultural tradition. We had Japanese immigrants who worked on small farms and knew how to work with irrigation and horticulture. (Interview 4b [second interview], Nampula, August 14, 2015)

This racialized frustration was echoed by a high-ranking official from the Brazilian Cooperation Agency (Agência Brasileira de Cooperação, ABC) who said that he didn't believe that ProSavana could work in Mozambique because modern agriculture was a technology of the "highest sort, one that requires education and private property." The combination of a lack of knowledge about local farmers along with a racialized sense of superiority suggested that the only real role local residents would play was as laborers or out-growers affiliated with large farms (Mosca and Bruna 2015; Wise 2014).

THE BRAZILIANS AND THEIR "ALTA MODA" (HIGH FASHION) IDEAS

A set of presentations by Brazilian researchers highlighted the very experimental nature of their work in Mozambique. On day two of the REPETE event (introduced at the beginning of chapter 5), the Brazilians involved on the extension side of ProSavana (ProSavana PEM) presented an ambitious vision for an electronic platform, the Plataforma de Extensão Rural (the Rural Extension Platform), which would allow extension agents to access and build a comprehensive geo-located database containing information on all of the farmers they visited. The agents would fill out questionnaires when they visited a farm and upload the form when they had access to the internet. The resulting resource would serve as a database of production and activities for the farmers, for the extensionist, and presumably for the supervisor, as one extensionist pointed out, who would have a way of checking on what the extensionists were doing each day. The Brazilians were very excited about their plans for spatial monitoring software, but the presentation prompted many questions. People were leery of having one more form to fill out; new software programs were constantly being developed—much like the new plant varieties—and as soon as they had mastered one program, it was dropped for the next thing. They wanted to know if the coverage the Brazilians were developing in the context of ProSavana would overlap with coverage from other private programs. No one in the room knew the answer to that, though the Brazilian presenting on the geolocation software pushed back against the doubts, arguing that the key to modernizing land use would be in cataloging it: "If I don't map the area, I don't know how to develop it. If you know where people are, interventions can be much more efficient. You can do all sorts of spatial mapping with this software."

Later, the highest ranking official from Brazil in attendance, a mid-level bureaucrat from the ABC, told me it didn't matter if people liked the software anyway, because most of the things the Brazilians brought were too advanced for Mozambique (see also Cesarino 2017a, 2017b). With a smile, he said that the Brazilians were "implementing a technology of the 'highest fashion' [alta moda] that would require education and private property." He was skeptical that any of the Brazilian research or extension proposals would ever really be useful in Mozambique, but he and his team had been asked to attend the meeting to present examples from Brazil, and so they did.

FINDING LAND FOR PROSAVANA

In addition to the racialized resentment toward Mozambican farmers, ProSavana also faced obstacles in the form of ambiguous land tenure arrangements that risked turning off large-scale farmers and investors. The ongoing desire for large-scale export agriculture meant that there were great ambitions for available land in Mozambique. But first, according to a growing "land governance orthodoxy" (German 2022), land rights would have to be titled in order to "protect" smallholder use of the land and to free up "unclaimed" land for investment. In Mozambique, all land became state land with independence in 1975. The Land Policy of 1995 and Land Law of 1997 strengthened the rights of customary users and systems (traditional management systems, either communities or individuals; see Chiziane 2015, Negrão 2002, Norfolk and Tanner 2007, and Trindade and Salomão 2016), giving Mozambique one of the most progressive land laws in the world on paper, but the state still oversaw all land transactions, whether for community use rights or foreign investors. A project to title land in Mozambique was put into place by the US-based Millennium Challenge Corporation (MCC), the organization created in 2004 to "advance American values and interests" by aggressively pushing aid recipients to institute good governance (accountability, transparency) and economic freedom (free markets) (MCC n.d.-a). The MCC provided loans to competitively selected recipients, structuring its work around rigorously designed and continuously evaluated projects that were preidentified as guaranteeing a high economic rate of return (nonironically referred to as the EROR indicator). The MCC intervened regularly in the projects it selected in order to assess progress, with the threat of delaying or cutting off funding as it saw fit.

The MCC and government of Mozambique signed a "compact" (as the MCC's agreements are called) in 2007 that focused on four projects in four northern states, including water and sanitation (funded at approximately US$200 million over five years), roads ($175 million), agriculture (particularly coconut sales; $17 million), and land administration ($39 million). The goal of the land administration project was to help "beneficiaries meet their immediate needs for registered land rights and better access to land for investment." In other words, the project sought to assist local residents in registering their land use claims, creating a tenure system in which access and ownership would be clear, excludable, and exchangeable. The project framed itself as benefiting communities and smallholders first, even though the reality was that the large commercial investors stood to benefit much more.

The project of providing clear title developed alongside the search for large-scale land acquisitions that became known as the global land grab. Multi-lateral organizations argued that "good land governance"—in the form of clear legal markets for land rights—was essential for protecting rural residents and investors alike (German 2022). Yet the idea that land titles are politically neutral and protect rich and poor alike is a fantasy of Western property law (Craib 2004). In fact, property is about access and entitlements (Peluso and Ribot 2009), and titles can be manipulated in the interests of those who have more power, whether external investors, local chiefs, or state leaders (Boone 2014). Concerns about land tenure security in Mozambique have to be situated within the country's particular history of land use, state ownership of land, and strong support for community rights (O'Laughlin 1995, 1996). In this context, the MCC's investment in land administration was somewhat mysterious. If all land in the country was legally owned by the state, and the state was already empowered to transact leases of up to fifty years (renewable for another forty-nine) on unoccupied land, how could providing land use certificates be profitable or generate a high economic rate of return? It was clear that tenure security could have many collateral benefits for individuals and communities, but land would still not be freely exchanged or divisible; how would higher returns be realized? In other words, without a market for land, how was profit to be made from land titling (as required for an MCC compact), and to whom would it accrue? I asked this question of the head of the MCC program in Mozambique in March 2013. We sat in his high-rise office in the port of Maputo, six floors up from the intense press of people and cars on the street below. I had to go through an ominous security process on the first floor, sliding in on short notice with an introduction from a USAID program officer even though visitors were supposed to be cleared twenty-four hours in advance.

The head of the MCC projects in Mozambique explained how the organization determined which projects it would take on and how this process had led the agency to fund land administration in Mozambique. I interrupted him not long into our conversation to ask how land certification and overall land governance could possibly generate high returns when there was no legal or official land market in Mozambique. He answered, with a polite smile, that it was true that there were no sanctioned land markets, but that the model the MCC used could include a variable for an "informal land market." When one made the assumption (in the model) that landholders would be able to lease their land to others and profit from doing so, then certification generated incentives for exchange and high returns (again, in the model). Officially recognized certificates would allow outside investors sufficient confidence to do business, either with the certificate holders or with the representatives of communities or districts, who could now assure such investors that they did indeed control the land (Tanner 2010). Given that, in accordance with the 1997 Land Law, investors could already negotiate leases with government officials for unoccupied land, the real difference expected as a result of the MCC's program (and model) was that it would enable smallholders to transfer the rights to land they were currently using.[5]

This way of viewing, allocating, and exchanging land through the lens of business and economics sat uncomfortably with the understanding of land use and authority in local communities. Many people have written about the multiple, overlapping traditional, customary, and bureaucratic authorities in rural Mozambique who have some influence or recognized right to allocate land use rights (Carilho 1994; Fairbairn 2013; Negrão 2002; O'Laughlin 1996; Tanner 2010). In my research, I came across three different systems for adjudicating access to land (or controlling it; see Peluso and Lund 2011), all of which were mediated by a variety of factors including market access, capital and labor resources, political affiliations, authority (Lund and Boone 2013), and social identity (Fairbairn 2013). In an agricultural system that had long relied on swidden (slash-and-burn) methods of regularly clearing new land, some people said they consulted the local community members in order to locate fallow land that was not too close to other fields. Others said that they consulted with local rulers (the régulo) and asked for permission to plant. A third avenue for negotiating land access was through the state administrative system, overseen at the local levels by secretaries appointed by Frelimo. As a result of the ongoing struggles between local communities and political parties, different systems of land administration and authority overlap in rural areas, making it difficult to know how to access land securely (Hall and Paradza 2012).[6]

In one community, the régulo approached our research team after we had been interviewing in the area for several days. He was unassuming and even diffident, although one of our team members, a local extension agent, told us we should have contacted him before beginning our interviews, given that the chief had traditional jurisdiction over land and political affairs in the community. There was some disagreement over how relevant the régulo still was, but we arranged a conversation for the next day (Interview 29, June 7, 2014).

I arrived at the régulo's compound the next day. It was relatively spacious, with two well-built houses, one cob and the other adobe, and a smaller, separate building that appeared to be for storage. Neat fields of corn and sugarcane, intercropped with pigeon pea and beans, surrounded the house, and the courtyard was swept clean. I sat on a mat with a translator and the régulo; his two wives and three children sat on another mat laid out ten feet behind him. He explained to us in a very matter-of-fact tone that he had authority over land use in the entire region. People who wished to break ground for planting were required by traditional rule to seek his permission.

The régulo's soft-spoken words in the courtyard that day reminded me of the hush in the MCC office, hundreds of miles away. In the end, though, land in a model defined in Maputo is largely incommensurable (Kuhn 1962) with land in a kingdom in rural Nampula—even if the land itself looked the same on the ground. Overlapping and often contradictory visions of what land is and how land should be accessed, used, or exchanged animated these two very different imaginaries. Who would win the struggle for authority over land rights would depend on who was able to marshal the resources to defend what they knew. While the MCC had the power to rally considerable support for its form of knowledge—knowledge produced through the framework of business and market economics—as applied to land, other ways of knowing worked to gain the upper hand or to undermine official land titling projects. This struggle was much more than symbolic. As the plantation ideal suggests, the land itself—the fertility of its soil, the products produced, the livelihoods cultivated—is fundamentally shaped by who gets to set the rules that govern access to the land.

Securing sufficient land in Mozambique therefore depended on overcoming a number of obstacles, from alternative frameworks of landownership to convincing the rural poor to stop moving around and to accept the idea of land titling as part of a "dream of universal fixity" (Craib 2004: 12) that appealed to the modern state and the market alike. This helped to explain why government officials in 2016 were arguing that there was not enough land for farmers to "do as they please," and that rural Mozambicans needed to be grouped more efficiently in villages. As one of the leaders of the Extension Directorate declared, people needed to stay where they were and produce: "There is no space for the farmer to go anywhere he wants—he can't just move around!" (Interview 23, December 16, 2016).

In IIAM, many people believed that there really wasn't land available because of the growing population. According to one of the scientists who worked on the Paralelos study,

> My parents said they used to have a lot of land, but they had a lot of land because they moved regularly to good parcels that hadn't been used in years. But the population grew and now we can't do that anymore. . . . I was born at a time when . . . my parents produced for one year, two in one place, when they see that it's not doing that well. So, they would leave that plot and go to farm in another. Afterwards they left that one and went on to produce [elsewhere]. . . . After ten years here it's already ok to go back on that one to plant. But now, the population, the size of the population increased, there are a lot of people. This way of leaving here for there, the time in between planting [in any given place] is becoming very, very short. (Interview 5a, Maputo, July 1, 2015)

But this lack of land was relative—because there was land for investment. "There is virgin land, and a lot of good land," a former director of the extension agency affirmed. "What we need for real is to invest to get out of this problem [of underdevelopment]; we need to invest with seriousness, meaning invest in irrigation, in mechanization in general, you know. And we also have to create conditions to fertilize our soils, to increase production and productivity; if not, if we don't fertilize, we are not going to reach what we want to in any crop" (Interview 23, December 16, 2016).

According to this director, the problem was one of competing visions of land use: "There is actually a lot of land available, but someone is there saying 'it's mine.'" He was involved in a mapping project to try to determine where land was available, so the government could bring investors in for large-scale commodity projects. "We shouldn't reject these investments," he said. "I want agriculture to be organized, but we have no food security in this country—they keep coming back to the government [for handouts] because there is no food security. We did a mapping project, we looked for areas of more than 100 hectares that had no one using it and no owner. [. . .] We will bring investors—from Brazil or South Africa—to those places. They will have experience and buy tractors; they will bring inputs and will work with other farmers through contracts" (Interview 23, December 16, 2016).

PROSAVANA'S STUDY OF LOCAL CONDITIONS: ECHOES OF THE 1951 ECOLOGICAL-AGRICULTURAL SURVEY

The confusion over land rights was exacerbated in ProSavana by the fact that the people responsible for executing the project were not very familiar with conditions on the ground. Like the Paralelos study, the investigation into local conditions for the ProSavana Master Plan was eerily similar to the soil, climate, and topography studies done by the Portuguese decades earlier, with notable lack of attention to local inhabitants, customs, politics, or markets. Prepared by three consulting firms hired by the Japanese team in the project area and published in 2012, the study was highly detailed (Interim Report 2012).[7] It contained considerable information on agricultural markets, infrastructure, agroecological conditions (water, soils, topography, climate), legal dispositions, and aid organizations. The section on land title rights (which are referred to as the direito de uso e aproveitamento da terra, DUATs) is particularly impressive for the amount of detail it contains, as the process of acquiring a DUAT is quite lengthy, and understanding the entire legal chain likely required multiple conversations with relevant government officials. The sections on infrastructure and markets were also remarkably detailed: it is clear when reading the report that secondhand data was scrupulously gathered and that many government officials were interviewed. Just as with the Paralelos document, however, it does not appear that the consultants ever talked with people in the region. This study of "socio-economic conditions" in the Nacala Corridor contained little information on or from the people living and farming in the region.

The head of the Japanese team in Nampula confirmed this lack of information in an interview in 2016. He said that no baseline studies in the communities were used to guide the work that the Japanese International Cooperation Agency (JICA) had carried out. He remembered that an outside consultant had been contracted to do community studies at one point, but they weren't good quality and were never used. He regretted the degree to which JICA had "trusted the Mozambican government"—but it didn't occur to them not to, because they believed that the government represented its people truthfully, and so this was the data presented in the report (Interview 37, Nampula, November 29, 2016). According to Funada-Classen (2013a and b), the study was based on interviews with a total of twenty farmers, and the Japanese consultants lacked the necessary experience "to really understand the local context" (Funada-Classen 2013b: 4n12).

What came through clearly in the report's discussion of agricultural practices was the authors' identification of swidden agricultural practices as the key problem in the study region and as one of the main obstacles to the development of modern agriculture.[8] "Farmland use in the Study Area still obeys traditional practices," the authors recounted, "which are characterized by low use of technology and inputs. These traditional practices consist of non-systematic mixed cropping, slash and burning farming and shifting cultivation" (Interim Report 2012: 3–33). In this statement, the report's authors echoed themes emphasized throughout the colonial period. They argued that agricultural backwardness and swidden farming practices—rather than land grabbing or state-led land expropriation—were the cause of land conflicts in the study area, and that Mozambicans should be trained properly to adopt new sedentary practices:

> In some area[s] in the Study Area, population pressure on land has started to appear, and it causes land conflicts between people, especially in the area[s] where [land] is fertile and easy to access from main roads. Farmers in the area are at a crucial point to change their familiar farming practice for surviving. Even though most of the farmers don't recognize the present situation well, their existing farming practice may trigger . . . serious environmental destruction as we have experienced in . . . other part[s] of the world. They should understand that there is no remain[ing] vast land for farming in the Study Area, if they continue the present extensive farming practice. (Interim Report 2012: 4-2)

Bowen and colleagues (2003) illustrated a similar example in Nampula, where government and donors in Nampula blamed smallholders for lack of land and environmental degradation instead of examining the more input-intensive practices of cotton production. Echoing the land titling initiatives taken up by the MCC discussed earlier, the study's authors suggested that in order to address land disputes and ensure that sufficient land was available for improved farming methods, the government should register farmers' land (provide a legal certificate of occupation), but only after the farmers had shifted to settled farming: "This also might be a good incentive for farmers to cease their shifting cultivation" (Interim Report 2012: 4-9).

The perspective provided in this study was important both because it formed the basis of one of the most ambitious and potentially transformative trilateral development projects in sub-Saharan Africa and because it represented the latest official information available on the Mozambican agricultural sector. The study's authors had considerable resources at their disposal (US$8 million), and yet government representatives were allowed to stand in for—to speak for—"local people." Ultimately, local inhabitants of rural areas came to be seen as, quite simply, limitations: people whose ways had to be changed if progress (large-scale agriculture) was to happen. Without real knowledge of people in Mozambique, the study presented mere assumptions about how they lived and what would have to change if the innovations promoted by the researchers were to have their desired effect.

When the Japanese first got involved in extension in Mozambique through ProSavana, the lead for the program in the northern province of Nampula said, they went straight to the government and asked what they should work on in agriculture. But when they began, they realized that the government did not have the support of the people, and there were significant protests against the project. This shocked the Japanese, according to a JICA official: "JICA always goes through the government—but here, this is not effective. With US or EU projects, they go right to the local leaders, to the farmers; but the Japanese government never goes directly to the farmers. . . . So ProSavana became very politicized. It was a scandal. It was JICA's fault too. Just five years ago, the Japanese government looked at the land and thought Official Development Assistance [ODA] meant helping locals to cultivate large land areas to import to Japan, but this idea is changing" (Interview 37, Nampula, November 29, 2016). The JICA official said this change had taken place because of the political outrage ProSavana engendered, but also "because there is no potential here [for large-scale production]. So, policy has changed. [We realize] that people need to diversify production." Despite this apparent revelation, the staff working with the Japanese on ProSavana hired consultants to conduct their community studies for them: even after the scandal, they were basing their community extension projects on a hastily done report that included interviews with just a handful of community members.

By 2016 the Brazilians were packing up. The lead scientist said that ProSavana's scientific plan was sound, but politics got in the way. He was disappointed by this in the same way he was disappointed by the lack of rain and limited use of pesticides. He said:

> The project apparently never had the support of the Mozambican society as it should. . . . It always had the support of the Government, but this did not necessarily translate into a need for society. So, in a way, we were always working on the razor's edge, we didn't know if it would go this way or that way, or if it was going to cut down the middle. So, it's very difficult. We did our part, the technical work, but always without knowing [about the politics]. Today, Brazil apparently

doesn't want to move resources here anymore in this form of work, but of course there is a commitment between countries. The Mozambican government still insists on the project, [but] I don't know how to translate that. I know that technically there are no more conditions to execute the project as it was originally planned. (Interview 4b [second interview], Nampula, August 14, 2015)

CONCLUSION: FROM PROSAVANA TO PROTEST

When the global land rush began in the mid-2000s, there was an outpouring of research into the causes—and to a lesser extent, the consequences—of the global rush to acquire land. As outrage mounted, however, research began to uncover more and more stories of large-scale proposals and projects that had gone wrong. In some cases, the investors encountered environments they didn't understand, local customs they couldn't explain or get around, and rural residents who either didn't believe the promises of employment and social support or who exploded in protest once they realized these wouldn't be forthcoming. The scholarship on these failed projects is important, but each case raises the questions I began this book with: Why did people think they were a good idea in the first place? Why assume technology can be adapted from one place to another just because the landmasses were connected in a previous geologic age? Why assume that varieties bred in one agroecological and cultural milieu would translate to another? Why imagine that the best way to feed the world is to grow more crops for export? These are questions I would have liked to pose to the agronomists who traveled across Mozambique in the early 1900s, but when I did ask the research scientists and government officials and activists a hundred years later, the answer was that peopled worked with what they knew, and that knowledge was the product of at least a hundred years of favoring a small set of tropical commodity crops grown at scale for an export market. The coup de grâce of scientific discovery is finding a new variety that can turn empty land into fields of gold. This was what the Portuguese envisioned when they colonized Mozambique in the early 1900s, and they brought the weight of their empire with them to build a colonial economy around the ideal of plantation extraction.

Within months of the news getting out about ProSavana, the ambitious plans were hotly contested. Mozambicans, from local government officials to farmers and farmer organizations, were outraged that they had not been consulted regarding the project. They had no say in how it was designed or in formulating the overall goals, and most of the people I spoke with in Mozambique from 2013 to 2016 said that they had first heard about ProSavana from newspaper articles. In September 2013 the Civil Society Platform of Nampula released a statement denouncing ProSavana. Japanese civil society groups collaborated on the statement (see Funada-Classen 2013a, 2013b), and in 2014 the No to ProSavana campaign was announced. In February 2016 the largest Mozambican farmer organization, the União Nacional de Camponeses (UNAC) and the No to ProSavana campaign published another letter saying that the government's repeated promise of dialogue was a means of co-opting the resistance. The two strongest voices against ProSavana were UNAC and Justiça Ambiental (JA); the latter was against ProSavana from the beginning because of the danger that ProSavana would both increase deforestation and promote industrial tree plantations (see chapter 7 and the contribution by Anabela Lemos). By 2016 there were three distinct civil society positions: No to ProSavana from UNAC, and JA, though it was not clear that the rank and file supported the strict "no" anymore; Yes to ProSavana; and Yes to co-creating something new from the outlines of ProSavana. UNAC continued to receive the most attention because, according to one observer, it was the "drum that beats the loudest," but this group also did the most to keep national and international attention on the project. Part of the fragmentation of the response to ProSavana came from a regional division between the South and North, as there was a feeling in the North that UNAC was a southern organization. They had little presence on the ground in the Nacala Corridor, and one extension agent said that when UNAC representatives came north, they "hang out with the leaders. It's difficult to find them in the communities" (Interview 55, June 18, 2014). One member of the newly created Mechanism for Dialogue of the Civil Society Organizations for the Corredor de Nacala said, "We diverged from UNAC because they had no vision of an alternative" (Interview 32, November 28, 2016). Some people also argued that Brazilian social movements viewed ProSavana through their own domestic lens and misinterpreted Mozambican resistance as "a landless struggle." A long history of mobility, community access to land, and the nationalization of the entire territory after independence complicated this comparison with Brazil.

In October 2012, UNAC distributed a statement arguing that ProSavana was a thinly disguised land grab, a second Scramble for Africa in which foreigners would once again benefit from illegitimate occupation. In March 2013, UNAC and twenty-three other organizations published an open letter denouncing ProSavana.[9] The scale of the protest seemed to take government officials on all sides by surprise. Indeed, the protests were a key difference between the colonial and the contemporary period. The leaders of ProSavana were particularly surprised that Mozambicans came together in defense of their land. Government officials and scientists alike had castigated the local population for their mobile farming traditions but had counted on their being eminently movable (that is, easily dispossessed) when it came time to allocate land for investment.

In its defense, the government of Mozambique insisted (increasingly defensively as protests heated up) that the program was not primarily a plan for large-scale agriculture and was instead intended to alleviate poverty and help develop small farmers in the region. It described the courting of investment as a way to harness the power of the private sector for economic development in the region. Government representatives lamented the international and domestic outcry over the project. "It wasn't what the protestors made it out to be," one of the founding members complained. "It was just a group of us at a meeting," he said, pointing to a photograph pinned to his corkboard of several men around a table; "we were just going to try out some ideas" (Interview 22, November 28, 2016, paraphrased). One of the key Mozambican signatories of several of the early documents for IIAM expressed similar bafflement: "I was disappointed when we held a seminar in Nampula to promote interest in ProSavana. The social organizations didn't understand the plan and they don't understand the process" (Interview 20, December 5, 2016). A high-ranking member of the national extension office agreed, summing up his irritation with the protests against ProSavana this way:

> People criticize us because they have never worked with farmers—if you have never worked with farmers, then it all looks easy. . . . You can't look at the way people are living now and say they should continue to do the same thing they've been doing and that is how they will develop—people aren't going to develop doing what they've been doing. So we're trying out new things. . . . [W]e learn from the Japanese, the Brazilians, and we try out new ideas to see what works. (Interview 23, December 16, 2016)

The lead scientist for ProSavana also registered his surprise over the protests:

> I personally didn't know that there would be so much resistance to the project itself, and this caused the project to break away from its original objective. . . . (Interview 4b [second interview], Nampula, August 14, 2015)

This surprise over the scale of the protests is rooted in a long history of erasure, wherein the local landscape and people have been largely ignored or rendered meaningless in order to present the territory as a blank canvas that can be easily manipulated or transformed by capital and science. Local people have served political plans primarily as laborers who can be allocated as necessary, with little consultation or consideration as farmers who might carry out development themselves. In both the colonial and postcolonial periods, modernization has been predicated on adapting external knowledge to the local context in order to promote large-scale plantation production for export. In both cases, local people represented obstacles that had to be disciplined in order for the technologies envisioned for development to be able to succeed. And from the Portuguese administrators to ProSavana, government officials were surprised when their plans met with resistance.

7. Afterward

Beyond Discovery, Extraction,
and the Plantation Ideal

Coauthored with
Natacha Bruna

Featuring contributions from
Uacitissa Mandamule, Teresa Cunha, Bernhard Weimer,
Anabela Lemos, Jan de Moor, Bernardo Mançano
Fernandes, Máriam Abbas, and Boaventura Monjane

INTRODUCTION: AFTER PROSAVANA

In August 2016 news broke of a scandal. An estimated US$2 billion in shaky loans secretly awarded to three companies in Mozambique had been uncovered even as it became clear that much of the money was gone. Mozambique rarely garnered international press, but the story of what became known as the "missing" or "hidden" debt made headlines in major newspapers across Europe and the United States ("Tuna and Gunships" 2016; "State Loans" 2017; "Mozambican Accused" 2023). It was reported that Credit Suisse and the majority-state-owned Russian VTB Bank had executed the loans back in 2013 and 2014 with state guarantees that were not authorized by parliament as required by Mozambican law. As news of the unpayable debt ricocheted across the globe, international donors reacted, saying they would withhold financial and technical support until the funds were accounted for.

For those who work in or study international development, media reports on the debt story sounded familiar. The stories highlighted the weak or "failed" Mozambican state, the rule of corruption over law, and the diversion of resources from the entrepreneurs and emerging sectors that would have been Mozambique's hope for sustained development. The discovery of missing debt also highlighted the incentives of the international development and banking industry, in which loans could be made in secret and a small group of government officials could make life-and-death decisions for a whole country, taking money intended for productive purposes and diverting it for personal use.

The stories were familiar in part because they drew on long-standing stereotypes about African states and societies. They relied on and affirmed superficial analyses of poor countries as poor because they were incompetent or corrupt. They—in this case a small number of individuals from the highest offices in Mozambican politics as well as the international banking sector—had made bad choices that kept the country from working its way out of poverty, and they were thus responsible for the situation the country was in. This analysis—while largely accurate in its individual pieces—left out the long shadow of twentieth-century colonial rule and the deliberate organization of a landscape around extraction.

A more accurate understanding of how US$2 billion could be offered, be accepted, and go missing requires the deeper historical analysis that this book provides, centering the extractive orientation and infrastructure set into motion under colonial rule in the early twentieth century and explaining why it is so hard to get out from under the spell of fast profits, generous aid, inappropriate technology, external science, and global markets. Mozambique's extractive politics were built on the backs of the plantation ideal—a vision of the region's land and people that suggested profit would be made from large-scale commodity crop production for export. The land would be leased to those who could realize such a vision, with local residents offered up as the labor. The *plantation ideal*, as Wendy calls it in this book, shaped the production of knowledge about both land and labor and the boundaries of the possible for governance, markets, and community development. After independence, a small group of people established political prerogatives, namely party membership, that allowed them to benefit from the available resources, whether from mining, agriculture, or foreign loans and investment. Most of those who benefited did so in their capacity as political leaders, and almost all of the capital was external, from investors, governments, and private donors. Reliance on foreign capital and knowledge meant that catering to foreign markets and ideas was what paid. People were seen as factors of production, and loans were seen as private funds; both were profit, not an end in and of themselves.

The research for this book started with ProSavana, the trilateral project intended to modernize agriculture in Mozambique's central corridor. ProSavana had such obvious problems and generated so much protest that the book shifted from being a study of that program to a study of the underlying factors that initially made it seem like a good solution to poverty and hunger. When ProSavana came to an end around 2016, tapering off without producing the anticipated results, new initiatives were put in place to replace it. Instead of incorporating lessons from ProSavana, these new initiatives suffered from many of the same problems. They operated according to the same fundamental logic. One example is a program officially called Sustenta but widely known early on as "the new ProSavana." The World Bank and Mozambican government worked together to create the program in the hopes of correcting many of the problems associated with earlier projects. The goal of the nationwide program was to create integrated value chains connecting roughly one million smallholders to commercial farmers whose holdings were at least 50 hectares in size. Both of these producer groups, small and commercial, would be integrated with agroindustry and consumers through seven program components: technology transfer, credit, markets, planning (village-like associations), infrastructure development, environmental maintenance, and subsidies. The government funded a series of pilot projects from 2017 to 2019 to test out the approach, and in 2020, researchers from the Rural Observatory (Observatório do Meio Rural, OMR) analyzed the results of the pilots, gathering both the available quantitative data and conducting participant and key stakeholder interviews (see Mosca et al. 2023 for much more detail than is provided here).

The OMR researchers found that although Sustenta looked very different than ProSavana from the outside, it suffered from a set of issues very similar to the ones described in this book. Sustenta pilot projects benefited commercial farmers in the form of mechanization and incentives while leaving smallholders largely out of the program. The "kit" that program farmers received contained inputs and subsidies that were often inappropriate in the local ecologies and economies and fostered mechanization on very small farms and in environments where heavy machinery was unsustainable. The focus of the project was overwhelmingly on commodity production for urban and export economies, and the resources were distributed disproportionately to those who had some sort of political affiliation with Frelimo. The report also found that there was little coordination between the central offices in Maputo or other capital cities and provincial ones, and the performance of extension agents was disappointing. There were few ties between Sustenta and public and private extension networks. The program ultimately reduced food security because participants replaced subsistence food production with production for the market but were not guaranteed sustainable selling prices. In sum, as Wendy found in the archives and her contemporary research, Sustenta maintained a focus on large-scale producers, inappropriate technology, private support staff (extension), and nonlocal market production, with the result that local, small farmers were more insecure than before the program was implemented.[1] This is the landscape of extraction—one that perpetuates itself in part because government officials, aid workers, and multi-lateral professionals look out their windows and see rural poverty as justification for yet more ambitious plantation projects to make both land and people productive and profitable.

Pressure to attract outside investment explains the ongoing interest in re-working the rules for accessing land in Mozambique (Chiziane 2015; Tanner 2010; Wolford and Nehring 2015). Negotiating the rules for accessing land in Mozambique has been a heated source of contention since independence. The new Land Law in 1995 and the Land Policy in 1997 helped to establish ground rules on paper, but these remained unclear in practice. Considered one of the most progressive tenure systems in the world, the new legislation introduced legal recognition of customary rights, occupation in good faith, mandatory community consultation, and many other issues intended to safeguard inclusive land access and management in the country. The origi-nal idea was that individuals and communities would register their claims to land and receive formalized direitos de uso e aproveitamento de terra (DUATs, rights of land use and benefit of the land). Individuals and com-munities have the right to a DUAT on the basis of historical occupation even if not legally registered, although they may find an unregistered DUAT to be harder to protect if a local official cedes part or even all of their land. The vast majority of communities have chosen not to register their land claims, however, because the process is cumbersome, bureaucratic, and expensive: between 1997 when the Land Law was finalized and 2016, only 387 of 5,000 rural communities had completed the process of registering their DUATs.[2] The lack of registration, along with the unwillingness of government actors to defend customary rights, makes land claims illegible to public and private investors alike. There has been constant pressure to register land use and claims in order to make land available for outside investment. In 2022 the Mozambican government introduced a country-wide effort to revise the statutory basis for land claims.

The revision of the Land Policy and Land Law was (and still is, as of this writing) of major concern to civil society organizations such as the OMR, Centro Terra Viva (CTV), Justiça Ambiental (JA!), and the Rural Mutual Aid Association (Associação Rural de Ajuda Mútua, ORAM), and many others working with community land rights and rural development. Numerous studies have shown that the main source of land conflicts across the country from 1997 to 2020 was the lack of implementation of exist-ing legislation rather than a problem with the legislation itself (Chiziane 2015; Bruna et al. 2022). Despite this, the multi-lateral institutions fund-ing the revision process (including the World Bank, USAID, FAO, Swiss Development Cooperation, Millennium Challenge Corporation of the US, and others) and the government commission conducting the legal process are focused on creating a more flexible land market, with the goal of providing a better business environment for investors.

Although the revised Land Policy did not go through a rigorous consultation process with local communities, and in fact faced significant protest from civil society organizations, activists, and academics, it was approved at the end of 2022. Three major changes in the land legislation built on and have the potential to expand plantation projects in Mozambique: the promotion of land title sales at market price; the state-led creation of reserves that threaten the land rights and autonomy of the rural poor; and the development of new ways to extract profit from the land, including payments for ecosystem services and carbon credit schemes, that seem likely to favor those with the cultural and financial capital needed to navigate such markets. These priorities are evident in the proposed new Land Law as well, which has been under public discussion since 2023.

Creating clear rules for accessing land is not in itself a bad thing. It is the fact that the government and outside actors are leading the effort, with little room for or interest in hearing contrary voices from local residents. The argument is that moving toward a market in land will be fair because markets are fair—they provide clear incentives and signals of supply and demand. And this may be true in theory, but the playing field in Mozambique has been shaped by over one hundred years of extraction; the rural poor will have a hard time benefiting from a new market for land (they already have land rights, and they won't use their land as collateral; see Negrão 2002). They will once again participate in these ventures as laborers with little power to demand better wages or the infrastructure to take their products to market. External investors are not coming to Mozambique to help out; they're hoping to profit, and there is no infrastructure or will to capture any of that profit and invest it back into local people or places.

ADVOCATING FOR DEVELOPMENT: MOZAMBIQUE FOR MOZAMBICANS

So, what sort of alternatives might work in Mozambique? In what follows, we present a series of ideas based on conversations with well-known activists and scholars who have worked in Mozambique for many years. These individuals are intimately familiar with everyday life in Mozambique as well as the nature of local markets and political institutions. To imagine alternatives, they have to un-see plantations, to look beyond the infrastructure that supports the imperative for extraction. They have to put plantations in their place, instead of people. Most of the passages that follow are taken directly from responses to our question, "If you could say what Mozambique needed to prosper in the future, what would it be?" In contrast to the ambitious mega-projects that characterize the plantation ideal, these suggestions for the future are simple; they do not require new technologies or substantial external funding or global markets. They start from the belief that the greatest resource Mozambique has is the people who live there.

One key aspect of building these alternative landscapes is taking the plantation out of politics and agricultural research—moving away from a focus on global markets, commodity crops geared toward export, and large-scale investments that may or may not materialize. Removing the plantation as a priority or the primary objective would mean working with projects situated in the local context and with local communities. It would mean recognizing that productive investments won't go far unless they are embedded in and then foster better relationships between people, the land, local ecologies, regional markets, and democratic political representation. Asking people what they want probably means spending money and time on clean water, better schools, health care, chairs for everyone in the family, and distributed and reliable energy, and then thinking about what sort of land management works best in each agroecological area and how to build local opportunities for market expansion. Multi-dimensional, coordinated, and sustained projects would take longer to bear fruit, and attribution would be harder to prove: Did the community improve their diet because of new varieties, or new land management practices, or learning how to express themselves in public settings? But they have more chance of succeeding in making life better for everyday Mozambicans.

There are many debates going on in Mozambique related to development and poverty reduction by academics, activists, former and current government officials, social movements, civil society organizations, and many other societal actors, but these debates tend to be scattered, often opportunistic, and/or motivated by external stimulus. The lack of a joint and cohesive agenda among civil society organizations, activists' and academics' calls for more dialogue, and an extended conversation about what "alternatives" mean for Mozambique and what changes can be realistically implemented.

A Perspective from Mozambique's National Union of Peasants

In 2016, Wendy spoke with one of the leaders of UNAC, the peasant union headquartered in Maputo. This longtime activist had been part of the movement for almost two decades, since it formed in the late 1980s to push back against the abrupt introduction of neoliberal reforms. He was born in the city but was the son of peasants and spent time in his mother's fields (his father was a worker). He had rural roots, he said, as almost all Mozambicans did. While still in high school, he took an administrative position with UNAC and then moved into advocacy when he became passionate about the organization and then the cause. Connections between UNAC and the the Landless Movement (Movimento Sem Terra, MST) in Brazil date back to the late 1990s and picked up in the 2000s; they exchanged ideas about organizing and about defending peasant rights. He said, "We learned a lot from how Brazil was dealing with neoliberalism and then [in Mozambique] we were dealing with Vale do Rio Doce, a Brazilian coal company, and the MST experience was instructive." He thought UNAC might not have been so aware of what ProSavana presaged if it hadn't been for Brazil's experience in the *cerrado* decades earlier. He first heard about ProSavana from a newspaper article in the Folha de São Paulo in 2010. "And we all said, what is this?" UNAC started to ask questions, and MST sent activists to Mozambique, arriving at the same time that Brazilian investors themselves were first arriving in the country. UNAC, in return, sent delegates to Brazil to study the "cerrado model" that was being proposed. As a result, since the 1990s the two movements had supported each other, despite the differences between the two countries and the differences in landownership and control (Wolford and Nehring 2015). In Mozambique, as this activist put it, peasants had access to land in Mozambique, unlike the landless in Brazil, but they were not able to use it effectively to prosper.

After seeing the landscape in Brazil, UNAC came out as one of the principal organizations against ProSavana in Mozambique. "People can get confused. They say we're against investment, that we're trying to hold Mozambique back." But, the activist countered, "this [ProSavana] is a perspective of development that is not situated in the reality of Mozambique." UNAC wanted a different plan that would take into account local desires and demands, discussions that people had been having in UNAC and other civil society organizations and communities. "We had all of these discussions, but they weren't part of the [official] process. Instead, [the government] called consultants from Brazil and Japan, and *they* told us what we needed. Mozambicans were marginalized in this process." UNAC wasn't opposed to new projects. This activist disagreed with those who said that the peasant movement was closed or provincial. He welcomed input and outsiders, and he met regularly with organizers from other movements and with researchers from around the world. But UNAC wanted a program that began with Mozambicans, for Mozambicans:

This was one more document from outside, designed by foreigners who have finance capital and will come here for investments. And so this is why we say no. . . . That is why we keep on pounding the table! Pounding with our feet on the ground, you understand! Demanding that ProSavana should be an inclusive program, a program in which the peasants should accompany the whole thing, so that they also feel like they are owners of the program. It cannot be a program imposed from outside without counting on the participation of the people who live in that area, because this will not succeed, it will only generate conflict.

When he put it like that, it didn't seem as though he was asking for much—to be heard and have a say in the development process. And yet everything he said went against the infrastructure of knowledge that had supported extraction in Mozambique for over a century. Continued requests to engage with ProSavana's Master Plan were stonewalled, with documents being released at the last minute, so that there was no time to read them properly or to consult the movement's base. For UNAC, this was an effort to use participation to legitimate the process, without actually engaging on the ground. "We need a different model of extension, one based in popular education, in the pedagogy of Paulo Freire. And this approach to extension is how we need to organize our conversation with the government—interactive, participatory, starting with someone who is based in the community." If you started with the community, the UNAC activist argued, you came up with proposals for an alternative form of extension based in smallholder agroecology. UNAC had developed this alternative proposal for ProSavana, but he didn't think anyone would be interested because "it isn't what they idealize."

Land Rights Versus Tenure Security: A Perspective from ORAM, the Rural Mutual Aid Association

In response to the abuses of colonization and the long civil war, the Mozambican Constitution provides protection for community tenure even though all land in the country technically belongs to the state. But land laws are only as good as the local community's power to demarcate and defend their rights, and recognized local communities are not always indications of real collaboration between households in any given area—there is too much possibility that these communities date back to the authority given to local chiefs to secure their labor tribute. Individuals therefore need not only land security but also the right to choose whether or not to be represented by the local leader.

Providing tenure security for everyone means going beyond the discourse of "community rights" to enable both access to land and the entitlements required to benefit from it. On December 5, 2016, Wendy met with one of the leaders of the Rural Self-Help Organization (ORAM) who described the organization's experience with ProSavana and their efforts to address the insecurity of land tenure by mapping out community areas:

> We first heard about ProSavana in the middle of the second half of 2012, three years after the agreement between the three countries was signed. At first, we heard a somewhat more general statement by the Government of Mozambique, saying that they would implement a very ambitious program in the agricultural sector . . . in the Nacala Corridor. The program was going to be implemented by the three countries, Mozambique, Japan, and Brazil, and they required the occupation or exploitation of several areas in the region for the production of commodities. We [ORAM] did not immediately issue a statement denouncing ProSavana, as UNAC did; rather we commissioned a study of the Nacala Corridor to try to understand what the objectives of the program were, whether or not local governments and local communities knew about it, and how it would be set up in the region. In Nampula, they organized the Provincial Platform of Civil Society Organizations of Nampula. We brought to the table several issues we thought were key, such as land rights, how would these be protected, and environmental rights. We wanted investors to guarantee that their projects would adhere to environmental standards because we knew that the program before it in Brazil had had negative environmental impacts. We also questioned the impact of the project on food security of local people, and we raised the question of native seeds.

Members of ORAM went to Brazil with UNAC to see the Brazilian cerrado and perhaps understand what a similar program would mean for Mozambique. When asked what he thought of the experience, the ORAM leader said:

> We felt very threatened because we saw large stretches of land, large fields of crops, soya, sugar cane. . . . [E]ach field is about 5,000 meters by 5,000 meters. . . . [T]here were so many fields. And the irrigation system was aerial and creating serious impacts on people's health because of the chemicals that were being applied, so the rivers were polluted. . . . If this is ProSavana, that is, if it is that model that is being applied here, what will become of us! At that time we were talking about 14.5 million hectares [for ProSavana in Mozambique]. So, we said, well, if you leave Nacala, in fact from Nampula to Cuamba . . . you cannot travel a distance of little more than 500 meters without people. I mean, there is no free space, so how is this program going to be implemented in Nampula over an area of 14,500,000 hectares? Where will this land come from? And what will be the fate of those people, of those assets that are there? So, we felt very threatened, very much so.

ORAM leaders agreed with UNAC that there were problems with Pro-Savana, but ORAM believed the program could be modified to represent the interests of the rural poor and potentially to be a "positive force for change." As the activist said, "It's not that the peasant doesn't want development. The peasant wants development, but the peasant cannot enter the development game when he doesn't know what the rules are."

Even with the progressive Land Law on the books, the problem with land consultations in Mozambique was that "even at this time, the régulo, which is a historical figure, still has the power to make decisions. Despite the fact that the land law says that the power to make decisions about land management belongs to the community, in most cases it is the régulo who makes the decisions." The other issue was that when an investor arrived in a rural community, they found the community *contra-pé*, as he said, or on the wrong foot, unprepared. "An investor comes and makes a deal and the communities don't know how to negotiate, they don't have land use plans ready, they don't know how to ensure that their farms are protected." ORAM began to assist communities in mapping their land in order to prepare them for negotiations with investors who might show up and want a part of it.

ORAM may have taken a different approach than UNAC, but its basic demand was the same: local communities needed to be included in the design and the output; the plan had to be for local development. ORAM believed that out-grower or contract farming models were potentially a good way forward as long as they were organized by the communities themselves. Unlike UNAC, however, this activist suggested that colonial history provided examples that could be emulated:

> I think that many of the rural communities [in Nampula] want opportunities to develop, but with clear models, with models that create benefits for them. They don't want development to come in the form of threats. I think they want outgrower or ingrower models. . . . for example, where they have their land, the area that belongs to the community, they can produce and sell or supply to the investor, whether it is a factory or some other producer. They want this and this model has always worked even since colonial times. The big companies that have existed in Mozambique have also used this model, cotton production companies, and production of other crops such as soybeans, sesame, rice, copra, coconut—all of them worked like this. The companies had their areas, where they produced with tractors and everything, the peasants had their areas, but they produced and sold their surplus to this company and it worked.

The suggestion that Mozambique would benefit from a vertically integrated out-grower system, in which distributors contracted with smallholders, was a common one, even though it had clear parallels to the colonial period, when local residents had little autonomy and no authority. The difference for ORAM was that the organization worked with the smallholders to give them more power and voice in the agreements with corporate partners or external investors.

Monitoring Investors, Protecting the Future

Uacitissa Mandamule is a researcher at the OMR in Mozambique. She has a master's degree in political science and a PhD in sociology from Aix-Marseille Université. She has worked on a variety of topics at OMR, including land tenure and conflicts, disaster management, resettlement, and social and environmental justice. Uacitissa argues that Mozambique is rich, but those riches go to a small minority.

> Extractivism in Mozambique is part of a global political, socioeconomic, environmental and structural context. Historically, it is the result of the political will of the elites in power to carry out an "authoritarian modernization," previously from a "Marxist-Leninist" perspective, now from a neoliberal capitalist perspective, but with a certain continuity: political preference continues to be given to the large companies with high fixed capital, to the detriment of the revitalization of peasant agriculture. Furthermore, this attempt to "modernize" the country is carried out in an authoritarian manner. Policies are designed centrally, from top to bottom, without considering the interests of the majority of the local population, the group directly affected by the investments.
>
> Resources exist and are abundant, and Independence was achieved forty-eight years ago. Despite this, the country remains among the ten countries with low Human Development Index numbers. Investments are taking place in a context where the impacts of climate change further aggravate the vulnerabilities of local populations, increasing land tenure insecurity for women and other vulnerable groups in particular. In this context, it is necessary to transform the available resources into wealth-generating assets capable of satisfying the vital and basic needs of the population: education, health, public transport, employment, food security, etc. Other alternatives to land acquisition may be possible, such as temporarily leasing part of the land, without removing people from their land, when there is neither the financial nor technical capacity to adequately exploit large tracts of land.
>
> As stated in the Land Law, the local population must be involved in the country's development process, respecting the population's ecological knowledge. It is possible to imagine systems in which land ownership will always remain with the local community, where community members will be able to cultivate and sell the final product to investors who will provide various production inputs (tractors, fertilizers, etc.), ensuring

that this does not harm their normal activities and, in particular, without endangering their food production, since, in most cases, these are intensive agricultural projects, or even monocultures.

Opportunities for "the country to prosper" will only arise in a context in which the country is prepared to face investment and is able to derive real benefits from it. But if these opportunities are not combined with central political will and the allocation of local powers for the use of resources, the officially desired integrated development will be difficult to achieve. The government must monitor the activities of investors and ensure that they fulfill their promises, control the size of projects and impose a code of conduct to promote responsible investment. Furthermore, instead of propagating the idea that there is supposedly unoccupied land, the State should ask itself why, of the 36 million hectares of land available, only a small part of the land (9%) is under production, and what means and strategies can be mobilized to increase productivity and expand the productive area of national producers. We also need a global policy that allows farmers to remain farmers, is concerned with future generations and is environmentally sustainable.

Uacitissa argues that foreign investment should not be blamed for being extractive. External funds could promote rural development if investments were accompanied by government oversight driven first and foremost by support for local communities.

Democratizing Democracy: Building Strong Institutions and Grassroots Governance

Teresa Cunha has a PhD in sociology from the University of Coimbra in Coimbra, Portugal. She is a researcher at the Center for Social Studies at the University of Coimbra, where she teaches several PhD courses and also serves as a professor and coordinator of the Higher School of Education of the Polytechnic Institute of Coimbra. Teresa is also a researcher at the Centro de Investigación por la Paz Gernika Gogoratuz, Basque Country, and associate researcher at the Council for the Development of Social Science Research in Africa (CODESRIA). In 2017 Teresa was awarded the Order of Timor-Leste by the president of the Democratic Republic of Timor-Leste. Her research interests are feminisms and postcolonialisms; postwar transition, peace, and memories; and women's human rights in the Indian Ocean. She has published several books and scientific articles in different countries and languages.

In Mozambique, many of the popular ideals and aspirations can be translated as follows: to be masters of their lives and their own things, governing themselves and redistributing the sacrifices and benefits of what they can achieve together, to live in peace and live well. Therefore, it is extremely striking to realize that the country has been between positions 5 and 8 (from the bottom) in the UNDP Human Development Index tables since these data were published, being one of the poorest countries—in more appropriate words, impoverished. Remembering this helps me reflect and justify what I think will be necessary for the country to prosper. I focus only on three areas that I consider critical and must be addressed in an articulated, concerted and comprehensive way as this is the only way to achieve structural and lasting changes.

Firstly, I argue that, for Mozambique to prosper, it needs to seriously invest in the democratization of social, political and economic relations. I am not defending here more low-intensity liberal democracy. The institutions for that already exist and are moderately functional in Mozambique. What I defend is the deepening of democratization through: the reconstruction of vertical and horizontal trust relationships, valuing and respecting differences; the inclusion in decision-making processes of the greatest possible diversity of people and ideas, particularly those that have been silenced, namely women and young people, without manipulated quotas; and accountability for processes and results.

Secondly, the Mozambican and foreign scientists need to recognize the productive capacity of local populations and the importance of their agroecological techniques for the country's food security and sovereignty. Despite all the difficulties they face, peasant women produce significant quantities of food and often surpluses. Creating and protecting proximate and, in some cases, long-distance marketing circuits for local products of great value and quality (honey, cashew nuts, seasonal fruits, vegetables, fish, among others) presupposes access to roads and adequate transportation, access to trainings around harvesting, conservation and storage techniques, and the creation of production and marketing cooperatives that in the medium term can eliminate the weight of intermediary and import networks that impose prices and conditions and reproduce impoverishment and dismantle the productive fabric and income generation from below.

Finally, clear and strong regulation is necessary, supported by mechanisms to control its effective implementation regarding land occupation. In many cases, concessionary terms [for external investment] are not very different from those given to colonial royal companies of the past for the purposes of mono-crop production (cotton, soybeans, eucalyptus and others), intensive extraction of minerals, energy, food, timber, heavy sands, and other resources, and, to a lesser extent, but clearly expanding, for the tourism sector. This regulation must contain more robust environmental care measures, territorial planning that respects and protects the local, regional and national productive fabric through respect for individual and community rights on the land, temporal limitation and extension of land concessions for exploitation purposes, whether by national or transnational corporations, and a strong tax burden on profits obtained and the use of the amounts collected for comprehensive social policies.

For these reasons, a strong Land Policy and Land Law are fundamental. These legal structures need to be democratic, guaranteeing sovereignty, promoting agrarian reform based on effective land and environmental justice.

Teresa's vision for change has three components: democracy, locally appropriate economic support, and strong land laws, but they all require deepening political participation and democratizing access to state resources and oversight.

Musings on Mozambique's Development Alternatives to Plantation Agriculture: Looking Ahead by Looking Back

Bernhard Weimer passed away in February 2025. He was an economist and held a doctorate in political science from the Free University of Berlin, RFA.[3] He was a senior researcher at the Institute of International Relations and Security (Stiftung Wissenschaft und Politik, SWP) in Germany and worked in Mozambique since 1992, where he was, among other things, resident director of the Friedrich Ebert Foundation, adviser and coordinator of a decentralization project at the Ministry of State Administration (Ministério de Administração Estatal, MAE), researcher and university professor (Universidade Eduardo Mondlane), and manager of several decentralization projects. He has published on socio-economic development, governance, and political economy in Mozambique, Botswana and regional integration in Southern Africa. For several years he worked as a freelance consultant in Southern Africa, Southeast Asia, and Melanesia.

> Sugar and food or food and honey? If we assume what an individual, indigenous perception of "development" in Southern Mozambique holds, namely that 'development is like the movement of a chameleon, slowly motioning ahead, alert, adjusted to the colors of the environment, looking forward with one eye and back with the other' then looking back is part of analyzing the trajectory of development.[4] In doing so, what do we see in relation to our theme: sugar and food?
>
> From an African perspective this dynamic of plantation agriculture for export-oriented production and commercialization is intrinsically associated with slavery, forced labor, the dispossession from land resources and violation of human rights, on a continental, regional and global scale. As this book shows, colonial and post-colonial Mozambique obviously has not been able to escape the integration into the plantation and trade based the world economy, suffering the same features of dispossession and impoverishment of large parts of the rural population. Examples such as

cotton, sugar and tobacco plantation and, more recently, the timber plantations for fast growing trees designed for the pulp and paper industries in the global North show the integration of the agricultural sector into the world economy. Despite the resistance of the affected population in the plantation areas (e.g., setting on fire of tree plantations or turning cotton seeds infertile by roasting before sowing), plantation agriculture and extractive forestry projects dominate the primary sector, at the cost of food production and self-sufficiency in domestic food supplies and nutritional security. Thus, Mozambique came to produce what it does not consume and consumes what it does not produce.

First, the diversity, in terms of quality, fertility, accessibility of resources for innovative integrated agricultural activity (land, water, forests, climatic conditions, etc.) needs to be recognized as point of departure. What may work in one area, may not work in others. This implies that a localized, decentralized approach is needed. . . . Second, in terms of 'models of agrarian development,' an innovative, environmentally and socially conscious approach to sustainable agricultural production needs to focus on the family sector, the small producer. Neither large-scale investments associated with international agribusiness nor the national private, cash crops producing sector are options. . . . Third, within this segment of agrarian systems, the focus should be on rural women. In a recent evaluation of women-driven agricultural activities in Nampula province by Balane and Feijó (2022), the authors find 'an increase in market integration, expressed through access to credit, inputs, extension support and labor contracting, increased production, pluri-activity, income and possibilities of consumption of durable goods' and point out the "improvements in literacy and housing conditions" (3). Despite noting the persistence of high levels of socio-economic vulnerability, the authors conclude that "the project had an impact on reducing consumer and multidimensional poverty" (3).

Fourthly, innovative support to improve woman driven and environmentally conscious food producing and marketing systems risks would need to follow a holistic, integrated approach which emphasizes diversification, the use of natural fertilizers such as animal dung and compost, and preferably locally procured and fabricated inputs and tools. Producing nutritionally valuable food for schools feeding schemes and for hospitals should be a priority. . . . Fifth, security of land tenure for all small-scale producers, men and women, and protection against eviction and resettlement in case of capital-intensive investment, e.g., in projects of an extractive nature, is a pre-condition of innovative agrarian development driven by the family sector. Sixth, coming back to localization and decentralization, assuring sustainable and ecologically viable and diversified food production should be the exclusive function of local (municipal and district) governments. This not only implies devolving authority, functions, and responsibility for food production to those local governments, but also the consequential transfer of finances ("finance follows function"). And it includes the creation and cultivation of what, in the terminology of John Gaventa's (2006) analyis of local power relations, [are] referred to as "conquered" and 'invited" spaces for socio-economic change, in which the primary producers have voice and the capacity to monitor action by local governments and hold them to account. Finally, providing technical, institutional, research, and financial support for family sector–based, small-scale agriculture, for lobbying and advocacy should be the prerogative of NGOs, associations, religious organizations, etc., which subscribe, in principle, to those criteria enumerated above, including the international exchange of experiences and learning.

Given the manyfold issues and challenges, nationally and globally, particularly those which result from the dominant globalized extractive paradigm, one might feel discouraged to choose and pursue the sketched alternative path to agricultural development which emphasizes "food and honey" instead of "sugar and food." However, with the wisdom of Samuel Beckett, to whom we owe the motto, "Ever tried. Ever failed. No matter. Try again. Fail again. Fail better," we can start by thinking about alternatives, putting them into practice and testing them, and attempting to accomplish what we set out to do, even if "failing better" is a necessary part of the learning process.

The emphasis in Bernard's analysis is on holistic approaches, each one fairly straightforward on its own but together transformative for Mozambique.

Agroecology: System Change Is Not a Utopia, but a Necessity

Anabela Lemos has been an environmental justice activist since 1998. In 2004 she started the most important advocacy organization in Mozambique, Justiça Ambiental (JA!, Environmental Justice). She has served in a volunteer capacity as board director of that organization for almost twenty years. Working with JA!, Anabela coordinated the campaign to stop the proposed Mphanda Nkuwa Dam, which has been contested since 2015 because it would dislocate approximately fourteen hundred families. She has been on the Executive Board of Friends of the Earth International since 2019 and was the first environmental activist to be awarded the Per Anger Prize, which she won in 2022. Anabela's vision for the future emphasizes the need for an agroecological transformation of the system of food production and social reproduction.

> There is a clear urgent need for a change in the system, for a transition from our current socio-economic system to a more fair, more inclusive model focused on the country's needs. But how? In Global

South countries such as Mozambique, where the majority of the population lives in rural areas and depends directly on natural resources, and
particularly on peasant agriculture, this paradigm change is actually not
hard to imagine. A new paradigm involves rescuing and valuing good
ancestral practices, implementing agroecology, and conserving and using
native seeds and crops, all of which will help to diversify food production and the maintain biodiversity. To achieve that it is important to
guarantee support to smallholders and family farmers so that they can
transport and sell their produce outside of their villages, supplying local
and national markets. It is also important to promote and support the
creation of small food processing facilities, in order to create more value
for smallholders, guaranteeing the proper utilization of produce.

However, in the last ten years, there have been numerous government programs and projects implemented in the agricultural sector, with
large foreign direct investments but without visible positive results, as
the Government of Mozambique continues to prioritize industrial agriculture to respond to international demands. These demands not only
fail to support the local peasantry, they exert greater pressure on the
resource that is most fundamental to them: land.

To [create a true alternative], it is necessary and urgent to build food
systems based on diverse and local agricultural solutions, based on the
principles of agroecology, human rights, and ecological balance. People
must be allowed to decide and control their own food systems, define
their priorities and seek support, thus effectively and simultaneously
reducing poverty, malnutrition, unemployment, among other serious
crises that we have as a country.

Another strategy involves supporting and effectively promoting community forest conservation, thus valuing traditional knowledge and the
ancestral relationship between rural communities and their forests. The
global climate crisis leaves no doubt about the important role of native
forests in regulating the climate and mitigating its impacts, which are
already so serious and visible. The case of Mabu Forest can serve as an
example. This forest, located at the top of Mount Mabu, is one of the
largest and best preserved high-altitude humid forests, a "hotspot" of
biodiversity, much of which has yet to be studied. The Mabu Forest is
home to a huge variety of species, more than 250 plant species, numerous
bird species, butterflies, snakes, and chameleons, among others. In 2016,
after a long process of discussion where local communities evaluated
the various options, and an Environmental Impact Assessment was conducted, they submitted a request to obtain the Right to Use the Land (a
DUAT) as a Community Conservation Area. Since that time, and despite
JA! insistently following the process, only after the Environmental
License (valid for five years) had expired did we receive information necessary to correct some details of the request, which again involves huge
costs and redoing a large part of the process.

In this example, it is evident that community forest conservation, despite being provided for in the law, appearing in the political discourse, and being relatively simple to implement, is not a priority for the government. We continue to fight to ensure that the Mabu Forest is declared a community conservation area under the direct management of local communities, and that it is not just another instrument for carbon markets, which only serve to make pretend solutions for the climate crisis.

For an organization that fights for social, environmental and climate justice like JA!, it is more than evident that the neoliberal capitalist economic model is largely responsible for the multiple crises we are experiencing today in Mozambique. This model is based on the exploitation of extractive resources, which itself depends on the usurpation of land and the exploitation of workers, with environmental and climate impacts seen as externalities. The destruction of the environment and our forests, the pollution of the air, rivers and soil, the degradation of health, the constant violations of human rights, the closure of civic space, the increase in inequality, militarization, are all indicators of a failed socio-economic model, and its distorted vision of "development."

A better world is not a utopia, it is a necessity. And it can only come about through a socially just transition. A change of system is urgent so that we can together construct a country that we are proud of, committed to food sovereignty, as well as energy and economic sovereignty, where we see our resources as commons that should be used, preserved and protected, and not privatized. We want a country where everybody, with no exception, has the right to a healthy life, land, freedom and environment. Such a country is possible, not a dream, and we can imagine it better if we free ourselves from blindly following neocolonial development theories.

What is noteworthy in Anabela's essay is how closely her sentiments resemble the writings and philosophy of Samora Machel, the first president of independent Mozambique. Once freed of colonial rule, Mozambican policymakers argued that socialist and collective ownership of the land and other natural resources was the only way to forge an alternative, postcolonial, independent African nation. Current policies and annual plans contain echoes of this rhetoric but little of the same substance.

Plantations as an Obstacle for the Development of Smallholders: The Case of Zambezia

Johannes Godefridus Maria (Jan) de Moor is originally from a farm in the south of the Netherlands. He studied irrigation at the Agricultural University of Wageningen and did his practical work in Indonesia and Kosovo in the former Yugoslavia. He has worked since 1984 in Mozambique; his work in Homoine (Inhambane province) was interrupted by the massacre om July 18, 1987. Since that time, he has worked in the province of Zambezia. He contributed to the implementation of the legal lands right framework, guaranteeing the use rights of agricultural communities. He is currently helping to build the cooperative movement in central Mozambique. Since 2012 he has also been a manager in a consultancy company for the development of irrigation, drainage, and water control in the Zambézia River Delta, especially for rice cultivation.

Zambezia emerged mutilated from colonial occupation. During colonial times, plantations were set up in Zambezia—unlike in any other province in Mozambique. The absolute authoritarian plantation culture that has been imposed on the population still has an effect on the social consciousness of the rural communities. At the end of the nineteenth and beginning of the twentieth century, the people of Zambezia resisted colonial rule. An example is the movement Matchingiri from Morrumbala that attacked the opium plantations in Mopeia, but also decades later the uprisings in Maganja da Costa. This resistance was brutally suppressed, after which the population could only execute passive resistance.

In 1975, at the time of Independence, Zambézia—with an estimated population of 1.7 million inhabitants, the majority of whom could not read and write—inherited an export-oriented agriculture and a rural economy damaged by the brutal extraction of labor. After the 1997 legal framework for land was completed, civil society organizations started facilitating the "delimitation" of community land.

In total, the land of 67 communities has been delimited with an area of 1.8 million hectares (18%). A major flaw in land registration was the failure to draw up land use plans and mobilize capital for their implementation. However, after the community had formalized their land rights, the question was ". . . and what now?" The market for their products was mentioned as the next important topic. Based on this historical outline and recent developments in Zambezia, an attempt will now be made to define an alternative rural development process. The starting point here is the socio-economic emancipation of the agricultural rural population. In addition to the countless difficulties that farmers face, three things are very essential, namely:

1. Security regarding the use of the land.

2. Security for the sale of agricultural products at good prices.

3. Financial resources to increase production.

The alternative development strategy therefore has three elements:

1. Delimitation and formal registration of community lands, developing plans for community use of the land and natural resources

such as water, forests, and minerals. With regard to the latter, a connection will have to be made between the legal frameworks for land use and the exploitation of mineral raw materials. These community land use plans can be accumulated at the district level.

2. On the basis of "clusters" of communities given their geographical location and shared interests in the various value chains, the formation of commercialization cooperatives.

3. Based on the commercialization cooperatives, setting up a farmers' loan and savings bank at provincial level. The bank must have capacity to give small loans for example to finance the weeding of the crops. Electronic transfer of money will be important in this case.

This process must be supported and driven by the farmers themselves. In this context, the introduction of the "iron triangle" model is important. This would consist of a farmers' interest or advocacy organization that stands up for the rights of farmers; a network of commercialization cooperatives; and a cooperative farmers' loan and savings bank.

Farmers will have to establish and manage these three elements of the triangle themselves. Every farmer can be a member of these three organizations. It will be clear that this emancipation process is a long-term affair and that it must be tolerated by the government and supported by social organizations in the short and medium term. As far as sustainability is concerned, farmers will have to insure the costs of the interest group through their increased income.

Jan's alternative answer to the question "and what now" turns on finding very different market opportunities for local production. While elements of Jan's plan have been implemented before in Mozambique, what distinguishes his ideas from current practice is the coordinated, comprehensive approach in which local residents have security and appropriate assistance as they begin to increase production.

From the Plantation to Transnational Food Sovereignty

Bernardo Mançano Fernandes is a professor of geography at the Universidade Estadual Paulista (UNESP) in the state of São Paulo, Brazil, and a researcher with the National Council for Scientific and Technological Development (CNPq). He is also coordinator of the UNESCO Chair in Territorial Development and Rural Education. His work analyzes the socio-territorial dimensions of agrarian movements in several countries. Bernardo has worked with the MST since the early 1980s, and it was this interest that first brought him to Mozambique. Bernardo argues that the experience of the MST in Brazil is an important one for rural residents in Mozambique.

Wendy agrees that one of the most important achievements of the MST is its record in promoting and providing education, from primary school to advanced degrees and ongoing adult learning (Tarlau 2021). Education starts in the encampments that MST members establish as part of their strategy of occupying unused land with the goal of being granted permission to stay and farm. In these occupation camps, as they are called, activists set up spaces for child and adult classes. Most of these are simple literacy classes, and they provide a space for people to talk about what is happening in the occupation while also organizing classwork around those experiences. Grounding education in everyday life is a key part of the "pedagogy of the oppressed" articulated by Paulo Freire (perhaps a better Brazilian to be reading than Gilberto Freyre). Once the land occupation is over, if it has been successful, then the MST fights to establish schools on the new settlement sites. It has been successful in working with the government to find teachers and run these schools (Tarlau 2021; Meek and Simonian 2017). Key individuals have had their postgraduate education sponsored by the MST, including legal scholars who then fight for the movement. The MST also runs a university that holds workshops, regular meetings, and seminars: named after the radical Brazilian sociologist Florestan Fernandes, the school is an important symbol of the struggle for land and the value of education for the rural peasant.

Bernardo muses on the differences and similarities between Mozambique and Brazil, as well as the potential for rural social mobilization in both.

Mozambique and Brazil are references to the world as examples of agricultural models created from the logic that produces inequalities. These two nations are trapped in the hegemonic model of agrarian capitalism, in which countries and their corporations in the Global North have, for more than five centuries, used plantations to control the agrarian territories of countries in the Global South. Subordination to the plantation model keeps Brazil and Mozambique in poverty and hunger, even as they export food and concentrate wealth, perpetuating the predatory exploitation of natural resources and social relations. The long, exploitative rule of plantations should have convinced the governments of these countries that this model is an illusion and does not overcome the problems it creates.

[Both PRODECER in the Brazilian cerrado and ProSavana in Mozambique] contain the predatory logic of colonization because in order to produce monocultures, they devastate vegetation, contaminate rivers and deterritorialize peasants and indigenous peoples. From the perspective of sustainable development, these two projects failed in both countries, because they concentrated land and wealth and did not eliminate poverty and hunger. But the impacts of this predatory model do not only affect the countries that are exploited, they affect the world because they contribute to worsening climate change. Another negative characteristic of this subaltern model is the extreme violence used against people to promote the development of plantations.

There are ways out of this situation of subordination. There are prospects for prosperity for both of our countries. . . . The hegemonic model of agrarian capitalism can be interrupted with the advancement of food sovereignty policies. Brazil and Mozambique first adopted public food sovereignty policies at the beginning of the 21st century. The Food Acquisition Program (PAA), whereby government offices and institutions promise to purchase food from local smallholders for hospitals and schools, has been implemented in both countries and is an excellent initiative to support agroecological production and promote the sustainable development of rural regions. The PAA is one of a set of public policies that can be created grassroots prosperity that will reverberate across an entire country.

Other policies are needed to promote the agroecological transition and guarantee the processing and industrialization process as well as the necessary logistics for transporting food and the creation of new markets to serve all regions of the countries. It is also necessary for universities to offer training courses for professionals in relation to peasant communities, to create new technologies aimed at administration, production, marketing, etc. The 21st century is the century of great change in food systems. We have the potential to free ourselves from a predatory system and move towards a sustainable system. This change is necessary for people, nature, and even the world. The plantation is dying, it has gone beyond its limits, but we do not need to die with it.

In his essay and in his work, Bernardo promotes a set of public policies that support smallholder production by creating and subsidizing appropriate markets. As UNAC argues, smallholders and the organizations that support them are not "against development," but they need policies, regulation, and oversight that will support markets that are reliable, transparent, and fair.

Transforming Food Systems: From Food Security to Food Sovereignty

Máriam Abbas has a PhD in development studies from the School of Agronomy (Instituto Superior de Agronomia, ISA) at the University of Lisbon. Her PhD research focused on farming systems and food security in Mozambique in the context of climate change. She is a researcher at the OMR in Maputo, where she coordinates the environment and rural areas line of research. Her main areas of interest include food security and sovereignty, farming systems, biodiversity, climate change, rural development, and agrarian and climate policies.

In Mozambique, the idea that a food system has to be productive above all else still prevails. This means that the peasant must be transformed into an emerging producer inserted in value chains, often dominated by capital and external interests. This productivity paradigm promotes monoculture and encourages farmers to focus on high-yield varieties, which are not necessarily nutritious and do not meet the population's food needs (see Abbas et al. 2021).

Additionally, in the long term, climate change is expected to lead to an expansion of the country's semi-arid and arid zones, which will imply significant changes in production systems and, consequently, in the subsistence of small producers and levels of food security. Projections indicate that the amount of land dedicated to basic food crops and small livestock will need to expand to provide local subsistence, but this form of production is not often prioritized in public policies (Abbas et al. 2023). Public policies have essentially focused on medium and large producers, and on the production of cash crops for export, based on a concept of rural development that expropriates peasants from their own land and ignores the specific needs of producers. Small (family) producers constitute the backbone of agricultural production systems and food production in the country; therefore policies, strategies and action plans must focus on this group and facilitate long-term adaptation strategies that are sensitive to climate change.

A prosperous Mozambique requires the adoption of public policies that prioritize the family sector and food production for domestic consumption. A prosperous Mozambique must be based on the transformation of food and agricultural systems into sovereign systems that are sustainable, inclusive and resilient, based on the principles of food sovereignty. Food sovereignty places the aspirations and needs of food producers and the general population at the center of food policies and systems, rather than the demands of international markets and the private sector.

In a country like Mozambique, where a large part of the population depends on agriculture and natural resources for their subsistence and food, we cannot talk about development without talking about food sovereignty. Blind, short-term analysis and momentary indicators of food security do not allow the establishment of long-term policies and programs that aim to develop local communities and solve the problem of hunger in the country. Hence, the focus of policies must go beyond the issue of food and nutritional security and focus on the food sovereignty of the Mozambican people.

When Máriam says *sovereignty*, she doesn't mean *national* sovereignty, which Mozambique already has in theory. She means autonomy from the plantation model of production and imperatives of the global market. She is describing a move toward local, regional, and national control over the production, consumption, and distribution of food, one that would prioritize local rural development above other goals.

Without Democracy, There Is No Development

Boaventura Monjane holds a PhD on postcolonialisms and global citizenship (sociology) from the Faculty of Economics in the University of Coimbra. He is a research associate at the Institute for Poverty, Land and Agrarian Studies (PLAAS, University of the Western Cape) and a fellow of the International Research Group on Authoritarianism and Counter-Strategies of the Rosa Luxemburg Stiftung (RLS). He is also an associate fellow at the Centre for African Studies (CEA) at Eduardo Mondlane University in Maputo. His areas of interest and research include agrarian movements, rural politics, food sovereignty, and climate justice. He has been involved in agrarian social movements, both locally and internationally, working with UNAC and the International Secretariat of La Via Campesina. Boaventura is also the solidarity program officer for west Africa and Haiti at Grassroots International. In his essay, Boaventura highlights the importance of transparent, participatory democracy for the realization of sustainable and inclusive development.

> In recent years, I have dedicated my attention to the in-depth study of authoritarianism, especially given the notorious increase in authoritarian populism in the world. In the Mozambican context, I focused on the top-down imposition of policies, especially in the agrarian sphere, and argued that the consolidation of neoliberal agrarian authoritarianism was underway (Monjane 2023). The controversial program, ProSavana, widely resisted by agrarian civil society, including the peasant movement, is an intrinsic example of this imposition (Monjane and Bruna 2019). ProSavana, like other agrarian and rural development policies, resulted from the recurring failures of successive governments in Mozambique to understand the nature of the agrarian question in the country (Wuyts 2001), which is at the root of the persistence of poverty in rural areas, along with substantial obstacles to generating economic development both within and outside the agricultural sector. The absence of a national development agenda that results from a national consensus seems to be the main characteristic of post-colonial Mozambique, which further complicates the aporias that characterize it (Monjane and Conrado 2022). The construction of a national agenda will only be achieved with the consolidation of democracy, not with authoritarianism.
>
> Development and democracy represent two inseparable facets of the same sociopolitical coin. The interconnection between the two

manifests itself in a positive feedback relationship. An efficient democratic system encourages the creation of public policies that are more
inclusive and sensitive to the needs of the population, thus boosting
equitable development. On the other hand, economic and social progress strengthens the foundations of democracy, providing stability
and opportunities for more informed and active citizen participation.
Peasantry(ies), even recognizing their internal differences, constitute
the majority of the economically active population in Mozambique.
The paradox is that political and government decision-makers rely
on the exploitation of the peasantry even as they consider them less-
than-full subjects. The way out is to conceptualize the peasantry as an
active subject of development, worthy of prioritization in the design
and implementation of development policies. In the field of investment
and modernization, Mozambique needs to invest in the industrialization of the countryside, implementing small and medium-sized industries processing and manufacturing agricultural and other consumer
goods, considering the national and regional market and the needs of
Mozambicans. Since authoritarianism in Mozambique will undermine
development, Mozambicans have no other option than to face authoritarianism and fight for a country where true democracy prevails, since
the renunciation of democracy will lead to barbarism.

Boaventura points out that the increasingly authoritarian, one-party state
is not just bad for political vibrancy and expression; it is also bad for the
economy. Selling Mozambique's land and people to the highest bidder is a
strategy that results in wealth for a few at the expense of the many. Perhaps
when there is sufficient evidence of the connection between the plantation
ideal, autocracy, and poverty, calls for genuine political change will be taken
seriously.

CONCLUSION: BEYOND THE PLANTATION

This book argues that in order to understand current landscapes of extraction, we need to pay attention to the differentiated legacies of colonial histories; we should examine the material implications of plantations but without
losing sight of the economic and political ideals that have sustained them.
Forged over a century of colonial and postcolonial rule, the plantation ideal
has systematically justified plantations as a privileged solution for poverty
in Mozambique and made it difficult to put forward coherent counter-
narratives and alternative imaginaries.

The alternatives in the previous section likely sound simplistic to readers
more accustomed to the plantation projects Wendy described in this book,

with their high-yielding seed varieties, fertilizer optimization tools, tractors, and large-scale investment opportunities. But they aren't simplistic; they're simple, and that is very different. Implementing any of these ideas would mean focusing inward on local economies first instead of looking outward toward the global market. It would mean prioritizing communities, villages, towns, urban and regional markets, and local residents. It would mean putting funds into the hands of communities and ensuring that every member of the community had a voice and that communities had some measure of autonomy. It would mean allowing for the matrix of diversified farms that observers wrote about during the precolonial period before cotton plantations and forced labor simplified the landscape. It would mean relying on governments—rather than private corporations, investors, aid agencies, or NGOs—to use external funding and fiscal revenues to deliver the services that are fundamental to the practice of effective citizenship, such as access to health care and education. All of these things require money and political will, both of which are in short supply. But almost fifty years after independence, maybe it is time to prioritize Mozambicans and find out what would happen.

If the focus on discovery and extraction were to change, it might be possible to create relationships that repair the alienation fostered by plantations. Several of the contributors to this chapter suggest that agroecology and food sovereignty are critical to an alternative vision for Mozambique. Agroecology is a set of farming practices based in the local ecology rather than on abstract universals of Western science—almost the exact opposite of those that define the plantation (Bezner Kerr 2023). Where plantations seek to standardize plants and crop rows, making them more amenable to mechanized harvesting, and try to prevent the intrusion of local genes, flora, fauna, or microbes, agroecology begins with diversification as a strategy to maximize resilience and encourages experimentation to understand what works best on any given plot of land. Agroecology seeks solutions to problems of low yield, pests, or disease in the local environment and in changes to land management: well-placed hedgerows or repellent grasses to reduce pests, productive plant combinations to increase soil nitrogen, mulch to help soil retain water, crop rotations, plant-animal integration to improve fertility and soil compaction, and so on.

Prioritizing people and local ecologies instead of plantations would require a rethinking of agricultural science (Perfecto and Vandermeer 2010), given that almost all public funding for agricultural research goes to the six most widely produced commodity crops (Pingali 2015). Participatory plant breeding and attention to adoption and impact happen in many institutions, but most scientists are highly specialized, and agricultural science departments at major universities and national research institutes are divided by nutrient, crop, or organism (Henke 2008). In Mozambique, as Wendy detailed in chapter 3, researchers have funding to develop new varieties but not to follow those through to the communities. If knowledge production is to move away from the plantation ideal, then it needs to be driven by local people and contexts. One way to do this would be to encourage (facilitate, fund, reward) science to be or require (mandate) that it be done with teams made up of life scientists well versed in plant-soil-water dynamics; social scientists who understand the regional history, social norms, and traditional practices; and local farmers. Prestige and awards would go to those who could demonstrate uptake and livelihood improvement rather than (or in addition to) the discovery of a new variety. If we were to build this future, our educational systems would need to change; science would need to be done both for intellectual curiosity and for the well-being of the broader public (Nelson and Coe 2014; Goldstein et al. 2019).

Ambitious? Naive? Simplistic? Maybe, but less so than the plans for ProSavana. Imagine if ProSavana had been done differently. What if people from across Mozambique—like the ones who contributed to this conclusion—had gotten together and listed all of the things they would need to make their visions of a better life come true: community-led land rights; investments in regional processing facilities and markets; support for diversified farming that took advantage of local ecologies, flora, and fauna; access to research that helped them understand why some of their traditional varieties and practices worked, and why some didn't; and access to scientific materials and resources so they could experiment themselves with new products, plant combinations, and local fertilizers. And once they had built up a surplus—like the families who participated in the P&S project Wendy described in chapter 5—they might go to investors like the Brazilians and apply for a tractor or say they had some land they were not using if there were investors in Brazil who might want a short-term lease (see Smart and Hanlon 2014). Once their subsistence needs had been met, they might even decide to produce soy for traders from Japan who would negotiate honestly for fair contracts. That is what ProSavana might have looked like if the plantation hadn't been lurking underneath.

But how will such simple and necessary alternatives materialize in a country that is economically dependent on extraction? Given that Mozambique's developmental path is intertwined with the global market, external investors and creditors, and an authoritarian state, imagining alternatives is not enough. As important as imagining alternatives is thinking about the preconditions that would make their implementation possible. Based on our research and the contributions from the scholars and activists in this conclusion, we suggest that three preconditions are essential to bring about alternatives in Mozambique: decolonial transnational alliances, economic sovereignty, and democracy.

First, a long history of dependence on the global market means that external interests have considerable influence in Mozambique. These interests do not always prioritize Mozambique's well-being, but transnational alliances will be necessary to help defend Mozambique's own interests.[5] The experience with ProSavana revealed the importance of transnational alliances in helping to shape and fortify domestic resistance and the articulation of alternatives. The role of Japanese and Brazilian social movements and civil society helped local activists influence the conversation with the Mozambican government and resulted in the suspension of land allocations to foreign farmers. If Mozambican civil society is to continue applying pressure on the government, aid agencies, and investors, then decolonial transnational alliances will be necessary. Transnational pressure could provide the space for a discussion about progressive policy change as long as agendas are collaboratively set and local challenges are addressed.

Second, a critical mechanism for moving beyond the plantation is to make visible the colonial legacies of poverty and inequality. This book unveils the shortcomings of the plantation ideal and its implications on the ground, particularly its inability to promote transformative pathways in Mozambique. But most importantly, the book reveals the worrying silence regarding the connection with colonial history and its current effects in the country. Post-independence choices of development were not made in a vacuum; they were constrained by the limits of colonial extraction and knowledge. This is not to absolve Frelimo of the party's role in building ineffective and corrupt governance. Rather, the knowledge constitutes a call to recognize that developmental options were narrowed down by the plantation ideal. Incorporating this knowledge into the development debate is a starting point to demand accountability and reparation. Promoting internal debates, presenting a coherent progressive national agenda for inclusive conversations about well-being, and intensifying transnational resistance movements would be valuable contributions to deconstructing the plantation ideal and one step closer to effective implementation of alternatives.

Even if those two preconditions are met, a third is needed to make the materialization of imagined alternatives possible: democracy. ProSavana showed that it is easier to influence external actors than it is to influence actors within the authoritarian one-party state in Mozambique. Frelimo's loss of popularity has gone hand in hand with the intensification of repression. This reflects a "democratic backsliding" evident across the globe (Riedl et al. 2024). After half a century of authoritarianism resulting in increased poverty levels and the rising cost of living, uprisings against authoritarian governance are becoming more common in the country. The outpouring of resentment after the Constitutional Court declared Frelimo's candidate, Daniel Chapo, the officially-proclaimed victor in the 2024 presidential election suggests that people in Mozambique are no longer willing to ignore repression and corruption in the name of national unity. Whether or not alternatives will be implemented depends on what happens next.

From Brazil to Mozambique, there are proposals like the ones in this conclusion, proposals that would counter the hegemony of plantations, giving people the tools to grow, eat, and exchange in diversified, sustainable communities. There is reason to believe that because of the work that rural peoples and advocates and activists have done around the world, this vision for an alternative future—one that moves away from the plantation to a diversified, independent vision focused on thriving for all—may be more and more mainstream (Borras et al. 2008). The United Nations Declaration on the Rights of Peasants was one step, even if just a document on paper (Claeys and Edelman 2020; de Schutter 2014). There is a worldwide movement coalescing around the global food system (Gugganig et al. 2023; HLPE 2013), driven in part by the ecological and health risks of large-scale industrial agriculture (Guthman 2019) and widespread objection to multi-lateral support for industrial commodity production (Canfield et al. 2021). Not everyone wants to work on the land, and not every small-scale agrarian society is progressive, but disrupting decades of the plantation ideal and reorganizing the economy to provide space for these alternatives would be the basis of an alternative to colonial or capitalist forms of extraction and exploitation. Equitable, inclusive, and diversified alternatives might pull local residents in Mozambique out of the shadow of the plantation and serve as a form of both repair and reparation today.

Notes

CHAPTER 1. THE PLANTATION IDEAL

1. Villaça was a well-regarded Portuguese politician who served as the minister of foreign affairs before moving to the Mozambique Company. His letter is similar in content and form to other responses to requests for information about land in Mozambique in the early 1900s.

2. In its correspondence with prospective colonists, the Mozambique Company emphasized that "while we help morally in all we can, we don't give monetary subsidy." The offer to help secure labor was a constant, however. In a similar letter the company stated that it "limits its material assistance to helping you recruit the necessary native labor" (see Villaça 1909, 1913).

3. Under King Manuel I, who reigned from 1495 to 1521, the Portuguese crown claimed dominion over the sea that was "made navigable" by Portuguese technology and capacity and granted to the Portuguese by the Treaty of Tordesillas (Newitt 2001).

4. Seed compares the Portuguese to the British, arguing that the latter defined a legitimate territorial claim as one that made the land productive. Perhaps Seed's most compelling illustration of this argument is her observation that the Portuguese claimed their new possessions in terms of latitude, fixed on an abstract mathematical grid, while the British described their possessions in reference to landscape features such as rivers and mountains (1995: 141–42). Lauren Benton argues that the Portuguese invoked Roman law to argue ownership on the basis of "possession" rather than "occupation" but that such "persistent referencing of signs of possession" (2012, 22) was common across European empires (see also Bhandar 2016 for a discussion of the articulation of possession, occupation, and registration, as forms of claiming and signaling ownership in settler colonies).

5. Discovery is connected to moments of disruption and transformation. One could argue that property was "discovered" in pre-capitalist Europe and property claims imposed on rural inhabitants generated the initial accumulation

needed for the development of capitalism and industrialization (Perelman 2000). See Aston and Philpin (1995) and Brenner (1976) for a discussion of how agrarian class relations shaped the nature of industrial development in Europe, with implications for both the development of global capitalism and the colonial endeavor.

6. The *Cambridge Portuguese-English Dictionary* (https://dictionary.cambridge .org/dictionary/portuguese-english/explorar) defines *explorar* as to explore (as in to explore a region; synonym: to analyze), to exploit (as in to exploit workers; synonym: to abuse), and to utilize a natural resource (as in to explore a coal mine; synonym: to extract).

7. See "Mozambique—Human Development Index—HDI," accessed January 17, 2024, https://countryeconomy.com/hdi/mozambique. For poverty levels, including multidimensional poverty, see "The World Bank in Mozambique," Overview, accessed July 16, 2024, https://www.worldbank.org/en /country/mozambique/overview#1.

8. For statistics on hunger in Mozambique, see World Food Programme, "Mozambique," accessed January 17, 2024, https://www.wfp.org/countries /mozambique.

9. The GINI is a widely-used statistical measurement of inequality, in which 0 indicates perfect equality (all wealth or income is shared equally) and 1 indicates perfect inequality (all wealth or income is held by one person).

10. There is a nuanced scholarly debate over the value of the concept of Lusotropicalism, in which Cláudia Castelo's (1999, 2012) work is key. It is clear that it was politically opportunistic for political elites to claim that ideological and cultural affinities tied Portuguese-descended people together (including those in the former colonies), but I heard iterations of the beliefs described by the term when my family and I lived in Portugal in 2017. We heard many casual observations about the valuable contributions Portugal had made around the world, particularly in Africa. People we talked to seemed genuinely upset that Portugal had been forced out of its African colonies before the colonies were "ready" for democracy (see Pereira 2022 for an excellent overview).

11. As Gabriel Paquette writes in his excellent history of imperial Portugal, "The Portuguese . . . joined the 'myth of El Dorado' to a second 'myth of national inheritance,' conceiving of African colonization—whether of South or West Africa—as a long-overdue reprise of the military adventurism, martial glory, and geopolitical *grandeza* of Portugal's fifteenth- and sixteenth-century forebears" (2013: 331).

12. This is not a full list of the classic literature. It is a short list of references that were important for my understanding of plantation systems.

13. Plantations were, of course, not the only form of land acquisition that resulted in dispossession under colonial rule. Settler colonialism relied on white bodies from Europe colonizing land in areas where indigenous peoples lived, and this took the form of individuals or families moving onto land with the backing of the colonial regime (Banner 2005; Elkins and Pedersen 2005).

14. The fascination with plantations as sites of wealth and excess continues today with the popularity of "plantation tours" and plantation weddings in the United States—tours that continue despite growing recognition that they glorify a violent and shameful history of capture, enslavement, and torture.

15. See United Nations (2009). US national security is often linked to global food security (see BIFAD, IFPRI, and APLU 2019: 10).

16. There is a considerable literature on ProSavana now. On the relationship and comparison between Brazil and Mozambique, see Shankland and Gonçalves (2016), Ferrando (2015), Cabral (2015), Ekman, Stensrud, and Macamo (2014) and Cabral and Shankland (2009). For a specific focus on the impact of the project on rural inhabitants in Brazil and Mozambique, see Monjane and Bruna (2019) and Clements and Fernandes (2013). On the discourse surrounding ProSavana, see Kirshner and Baptista (2023), Mosca and Bruna (2015), Fingermann (2013), Cabral et al. (2013), and Wolford and Nehring (2015). On ProSavana as an agricultural project, see Perin (2023, 2020) and Gonçalves (2020). On Japan's role, see Funada-Classen (2013a, 2013b). For a "trove" of ProSavana documents, some official and some leaked, see GRAIN, "The Global Rush for Farmland and People's Struggles Against It," accessed January 12, 2025, https://www.farmlandgrab.org/post/26158-prosavana-files.

17. When I refer to the rapid growth of Brazilian agriculture and agroindustry after 1950, I use the word *miracle* and put it in quotes. I use this word because people often say that the growth in agricultural production (land area planted to crops) and productivity (yield) is the real miracle of Brazilian postwar development, as opposed to manufacturing. I put the word in quotes because many people would argue that agricultural "modernization" came at a steep price: many small farmers were expelled from their land, and growth exacerbated the already extreme inequality in landownership, and input-intensive production methods led to environmental degradation throughout much of the most productive areas but particularly the center-west, commonly known as the cerrado (Graziano da Silva 1982).

18. "Integrating Food Security and Resources Conservation in Rural Mozambique," Case Study, accessed January 12, 2025, http://www.conservationbridge .org/casestudy/integrating-food-security-and-resource-conservation-in-rural -mozambique/.

19. In Lisbon, repositories I consulted include the Torre do Tombo, the Geographic Society of Lisbon (SGL), the historical archive of the National Overseas Bank (BNU), the Superior Institute for the Social and Political Sciences (ISCSP), and the Lisbon School of Economics and Management (ISEG). The last two are both affiliated with the University of Lisbon.

20. A note on terminology: throughout the manuscript the term *native* appears, although it is used so negatively by elites from outside Mozambique that it is essentially a slur. I therefore use the word only when I am quoting a historical source directly. Otherwise, I use terms such as *indigenous persons*, *indigenous peoples*, or *local residents*, even though the latter can create

confusion given that it can refer to Portuguese settlers as well as indigenous residents.

CHAPTER 2. "NOW IS THE TIME FOR NEW INNOVATIONS"

Inaugural address, Primeiro Congresso Agrário de Moçambique. Lourenço Marques, June 4–9, 1962, Associação de Fomento Agrícola e industrial de Moçambique. Presiding over the session, Governor-General Almirante Manuel Maria Sarmento Rodrigues continued: "In this Congress and beyond, we need to find new systems of work and methods of doing business, the discovery of new sources of fertilizer, [and] the creation of new seeds."

1. Before the Portuguese explorations, Chinese ships had engaged in long voyages overseas. For a variety of reasons the Ming rulers ordered the destruction of all seafaring vessels after 1433, leaving the seas open for the Portuguese (Levathes 1994).

2. I have been asked why and how Brazil managed to develop a more successful economy than Mozambique when both were colonized by Portugal and dominated by plantations for the colonial period. There is not space to do justice to this question, but in brief, the differences between Brazil and Mozambique are considerable. Brazil has been able to develop a stronger economy in part because (1) Portuguese colonization there ended two hundred years ago; (2) colonization in Brazil was much less sophisticated and brutal than in Mozambique; (3) where Brazil was dominated by plantations, they suffered very similar dynamics as Mozambique—it was in the 1930s, when the former began to industrialize, that "associated dependent development" (to invoke Peter Evans 1979) began to materialize; and (4) Brazil is much larger than Mozambique and has more of both an internal market and regional connections.

3. The British were instrumental in establishing a doctrine of effective occupation that depicted tropical land as "empty" (*terra nullius*; see Makki 2013) or a wasteland. Isenberg (2017) writes that the English were "obsessed with waste": wastelands were equated with the commons, positing them as shared resources that would not be used efficiently by the enterprising (Fitzmaurice 2014). Particular people—diseased, racialized, dangerously mobile, unattached, or dark-skinned people—were also often perceived as waste, requiring government oversight to be *made* productive.

4. Britain and Portugal both had designs on southern Africa. Portugal hoped to control a wide swath of land from west (Angola) to east (Mozambique), while Britain laid claim to present-day Malawi. Britain issued what came to be known as the "Ultimatum," forcing Portugal to withdraw from Malawi and deepen its control of both Angola and Mozambique. In 1890 the Portuguese acceded, which forced them to vacate the Slure region between Mozambique and Angola (Moçambique Documentário Trimestral, published by the Governo Geral de Moçambique, No. 001, 1935, article titled "A Evolução Agrícola," 107; see Newitt 1995). The Ultimatum ultimately weakened the monarchy in

Portugal; in 1910 the king was overthrown and the First Portuguese Republic was instituted. Republicans believed in more autonomy for the colonial territories, an attitude that was not reversed until the 1930s under Salazar.

5. Between 1870 and 1936, less than 6 percent of all the foreign (colonial) investment in sub–Saharan Africa was invested in Angola or Mozambique, most of which went to plantation agriculture (Serra 2000: 193).

6. The Mozambique Company, created in 1888, was largely funded with British capital, with some French and South African capital. The Zambezia Company was created in 1892 with South African capital. The Nyassa Company was founded with German capital in 1891 but after 1908 operated under South African control.

7. Companhia de Moçambique (1910). In a 1901 report on Moribane, Senhor Canto e Castro judged the small Colony of Meyrelles in Manica to be a poor attempt at colonization: no one ever thought they would do well, he wrote, because they were "exported colonists [*colonos d'exportação*] who, because they were incapable in their own land were sent here" (Canto e Castro 1901). He added that "the proof is in the way they have set themselves up all on top of one another under the care of the Director of the Grange."

8. The largest producer of sugar (the most successful export from the territory) was a British company, Sena Sugar, run by J. J. Hornung. Hornung & Co. requested 100,000 contiguous hectares of land on November 17, 1913, for cattle raising, from the Mozambique Company. This was considered a large amount of land, but authorization was granted because the land was not very good and was full of tsetse sickness, and Hornung was considered a valuable friend to the company.

9. This was actually the title of the article: "The First Time That a Governor (Augusto de Castilho) Looked to This Land with Interest Was on July 14, 1885," by Director of Agriculture Egídio Inso (Inso 1929: 5–15).

10. See Santos (1934). On the Superior Institute of Agriculture, see Ferrão (1990).

11. Decree no. 21, "Basis for the Organization of the Agricultural Services in the Colonies," January 27, 1906.

12. March 18, 1908, Portaria no. 148, listed in the Reconhecimento Agricola-Económico do Distrito de Lourenço Marques, "Relatórios do Agrónomo do Distrito: 1916–1917," Lourenço Marques: Imprensa Nacional, 1918.

13. Provisions for the experiment stations were fairly limited; each was supposed to have an Agriculture Regent (a title that requires less training than an engineer), a farmhand, a supervisor for the warehouses, five "European workers," and fifty indigenous people.

14. Freire de Andrade is noteworthy for his support of indigenous landownership in Mozambique. He helped to draft a new land law, approved in 1909, that outlined how local residents could acquire land (Direito 2013: 357). The requirements for accessing land were so onerous, however, that by 1944, Director of Agricultural Services Monteiro Grilo noted that only three hundred indigenous

individuals had been awarded official use rights, and the "native reserves" in general were far from roads and in precarious condition (Grilo 1946: 299).

15. The *Boletim da Sociedade de Geografia de Lisboa*, 1908, series 26, no. 8, p. 263. The veterinarians fought for equal status within the agricultural services and received more funding from the colonial government (and from the aid program MONAP implemented during the socialist period), but establishing livestock was difficult in Mozambique as the presence of the tsetse fly made it tricky to sustain large herds of domesticated animals.

16. This journal ran from 1908 to 1915 and then reappeared as the *Boletim Agrícola e Pecuário* in 1928, which ran until 1933.

17. *Boletim da Repartição de Agricultura*, no. 3 (September 1910) concluded with "Guia Prático do Agricultor Colonial" by Miguel de Jesus Valladas Paes (219–44), in which Valladas Paes referred to António Enes and his sponsoring of the Quintas. Valladas Paes's guide was created out of this, because establishing the garden gave rise to a "treacherous war" (220). Inso (1929) said that Valladas Paes's guide should be reissued because there was still considerable interest in it (5–15).

18. In using the term "explorador," Valladas Paes deploys the double meaning of the word in Portuguese (explorer/exploiter) that I referenced in the introduction.

19. The survey questions in full and responses from across the territory were published in the department's regular journal, the *Boletim da Repartição de Agricultura*, nos. 13–15 (April/June 1914): 85–107.

20. In a passage that sums up his disregard of local ecologies and lives, Maugham writes: "Thus it will one day come to pass, I doubt not, that the region of Zambezia—its marshes drained, its riverbanks reclaimed and cultivated, its malaria stamped out, and its administration based upon modern and improved methods—will take its place among the most valuable of African possessions. This, however, is a result only to be achieved by years of patient toil, by the expenditure of large sums of money on agriculture and experiments, and last, but not least, by the sacrifice of European lives" (1910: 10).

21. "We have been condemned in recent years to constant and profound modifications." This was the subtitle of the article: "Relatórios e Informações: Projecto de reorganização e orçamento da Repartição de Agriculture," *Boletim da Repartição de Agricultura*, no. 5 (August 1913).

22. Meireles's name is sometimes spelled Mayreles.

23. At that time, there were very few employees working at the Experiment Station: Meireles (a certified agricultural technician, or *agricultor diplomado*), an agricultural regent, a warehouse overseer, a locksmith, a field hand, one indigenous carpenter, two indigenous foremen, and roughly 150 other indigenous persons.

24. *Boletim da Repartição de Agricultura*, no. 5 (August 1913): 24–27. This was a common complaint from managers of the various experiment stations; Ferraz (1915) lamented the time spent planting corn when the station should have been studying and introducing new and exotic crops.

25. Portaria No. 223, Governo Geral, Lourenço Marques, October 7, 1916.

26. Preamble of Decree No. 235, March 4, 1922.

27. *Boletim Agricolo-Pecuário*, no. 1 (1928): 5.

28. From *Boletim Agricolo-Pecuário*, no. 2 (1928). "South Africa has many experiment stations. Portugal does too and Angola has some. Mozambique only has the Experiment Station of Umbeluzi."

29. *Boletim Agricolo-Pecuário*, no. 2 (1928).

30. Authors writing about Mozambique under Portuguese rule sometimes deploy different terms, but in general Mozambique was called a province or a territory until the Colonial Act of 1930, when it was formally designated a colony. In 1951 Mozambique was renamed a province to indicate that it was not a separate entity but an extension of the Portuguese nation.

31. See also Direito (2013: 782) for a discussion of Carlos de Melo Vieira and his role in promoting the "checkerboard" approach to integrating indigenous and colonial agriculture.

32. The entomologist Hardenberg and Professor José J. de Almeida were pointed to as having done good work, but "the lack of organization of the services did not permit this work to continue on [after the two scientists left]" (Grilo 1926: 3).

33. Inso (1929: 12–13).

34. Inso (1929: 15).

35. Gomes e Sousa published regularly in various bulletins of Angola and Mozambique and was awarded the Thomas Sim Prize for his study of botany and forest biology. For more on his life and accomplishments across the Portuguese empire, see the biographical notes in Figueiredo et al. (2017).

36. "Primeiro Congresso de Agricultura Colonial: Agosto–Setembro: Regulamento e Programa" [First Congress of Colonial Agriculture: August–September: Regulation and Program], Porto, Exposição Colonial Portuguesa, 1934, Arquivo Histórico Ultramarino (ULT), Banco Nacional Ultramarino (BNU), ULT 788 BNU.

37. Gomes e Sousa argued against maintaining agricultural stations and instead for allowing specialists to roam the countryside, conducting experiments on farmers' land where conditions were best. The agricultural stations were too expensive and "for the most part useless" because of the lack of qualified people, such that "it is not without reason that the native calls the agricultural station 'government farms' [*machambas do governo*]" (1939: 11).

38. For more information on cotton production, specifically, see Isaacman et al. (1980), Isaacman (1996), and Mosca (2011). On coconut production under the Portuguese and then independence, see Adalima (2022). On tobacco, see Nguenha et al. (2021) and Pérez Niño (2016, 2017). On tree plantations, see Bruna (2017) and Calengo et al. (2016). For a historical and contemporary overview of tea production, see Matusse (2023), and on sugarcane, see Joaquim et al. (2022).

39. One of the most comprehensive reports on the agricultural services comes from the two-volume, detailed review by Grilo (1946). The 160 people in the Services included twenty agronomists and others with universities degrees,

twenty-five agricultural regents and equippers, seventy-seven assistants, and thirty-eight indigenous workers. Excluding the latter, 18 percent of the workers were political nominees, 30 percent were contracted, and 52 percent were salaried.

40. There was only one functioning station in 1945, along with a small number of smaller "posts," including the Agronomic Post of Ribáuè, Agricultural Post of Mogovolas, Agricultural Post of Mocuba, Irrigated Crop Post of the Vale do Limpopo, and the (experimental) Field of Chongoene and Cinco Matas of Lourenço Marques.

41. The Cotton Board (Junta de Exportação de Algodão) was established in Lisbon in 1938, with the result that concession companies had to sell their cotton to Portuguese manufacturers (who also had to buy from the colonies). On August 5 of the same year, the Junta de Cereias das Colônias was created with the right to intervene in the development of corn and wheat.

42. From the introductory note, "Our First Anniversary," *Gazeta Agricultor* 2, no. 13 (June 1950): 122.

43. The results of the survey have been collected and published in two volumes; see Centro de Investigação Científica Algodoeira (1995).

44. The first research team was directed by an agronomist and included three other scientists (a general agronomist, an agronomist who specialized in botany, and a soil scientist), a certified agronomy technician (a person with similar emphasis as an agronomist but less training), and three staff members. As they worked, an impatient administration allotted several more people to the effort, including a specialist in vegetal ecology and phytogeography, a botanist, a forestry specialist, and another pedologist.

45. The section on vegetation was the longest, with 160 pages and 62 references (17 in Portuguese); the physiography section was 102 pages long, with 21 references, 17 of which were in Portuguese; the climate section was 98 pages with 12 references, only 1 of which was in Portuguese; and the section on soils was 64 pages with 43 references, 24 of which were in Portuguese. The demography section stood out at only 12 pages, with 17 references, 16 of which were in Portuguese.

46. The Instituto de Investigação Agronómica de Angola (IIAA) was created four years earlier (on October 25, 1961) by the Diploma Legislativo Ministerial, while the "províncias de governo simples" of Cabo Verde, Guiné, S. Tome and Príncipe, Estado da India, and Macau and Timor were all covered by the Missão de Estudos Agronómicos do Ultramar in the Junta de Investigações do Ultramar (created in 1960).

47. IIAM Communique 05, *Agronomia Moçambicana*, no. 5 (1967), included a plan for the year of structuring the network of experimental stations in the province. According to a January 19, 1967, memo from the governor-general of Mozambique, the ideal would be to have thirty-eight research stations, but in 1967 they were just beginning to work with sixteen stations and subordinate stations (*postos*). When IIAM went to investigate the legal situation of the land on which these stations were located, only two were legalized:

Umbeluzi and the Agrarian Posto of Nametil (see also IIAM Communique 01, *Agronomia Moçambicana*, no. 1 [1967]).

48. Given that armed resistance was expanding in the countryside, the Portuguese managed to widen the reach of the agricultural services considerably in the late development period. In 1972 Martins Santareno documented the distribution of 180,200 fruit trees, 1,100,000 forest trees, more than 1 million plant cuttings (particularly manioc), approximately 18,000 tons of seeds, 2,000 tons of fertilizer, and pesticides to cover approximately 65,000 hectares (Martins Santareno 1973: 20–21).

CHAPTER 3. "A QUESTION OF HABIT"

1. All of the scientists and the research station director mentioned here worked under the director of IIAM. The extension agents were organized into a separate department, the National Directorate of Agrarian Extension (Direcção Nacional de Extensão Agrária, DNEA). Both IIAM and DNEA were in the Ministry of Agriculture.

2. Isaacman and Isaacman (1983: 91–93) discuss the divisive issue of women within Frelimo. They argue that gender became less problematic as Frelimo matured in the late 1960s, although official agricultural support programs still focused primarily on men, even though most household farming in Mozambique was done by women. During the colonial period, a report from the Head of Agricultural Services in 1944 read: "The agriculture that is practiced in Mozambique by the natives is very rudimentary, as you can see by the fact that it is a woman's job. . . . We need to combat this rationally. What needs to happen [to attract men] is to bring in cattle, machines and irrigation, adequately organize production, and objectively and progressively invest in professional preparation that will help, by association, to establish a more lucrative production regime [*um regime mais lucrativo de exploração*]" (Grilo 1946: 193). In spite of the fact that most of the farming in the country, particularly after the Portuguese left, was done by women, gender was also left out of the specific objectives of the major funding program, MONAP. "Women's issues" were regarded as the business of the Organization of Mozambican Women (Organização da Mulher Moçambicana, OMM), which was "entirely unintegrated" with the Ministry of Agriculture or the Department of Extension (Adam et al. 1991: 97).

3. Aid reports, particularly those from the United States, suggest that Mozambique's move toward socialism was a product of Soviet influence and the promise of financial support. See, for example, the desk study of extension services from 2020: "[Mozambique] made ties with and received a lot of economic and military support from the USSR and Eastern Bloc Countries on condition of becoming a socialist country. The one-party state that resulted because of the assistance from the communist bloc of countries sparked protests within Mozambique, resulting in a civil war that erupted a year after independence that ended with the peace accords signed in 1992" (Cunguara

and Thompson 2018: 11). But the new colony received very little support from socialist allies. It is more likely that Frelimo's early philosophy was an endogenous African socialism inspired by Marx, Mao, Nyerere, and African notions of indigenous communalism (Isaacman and Isaacman 1983).

4. MONAP I ran from 1977 to 1980, MONAP II from 1981 to 1984, and MONAP III from 1985 to 1990.

5. In Chokwe, for example, the MONAP report described the "family sector" as a quite "heterogenous population," comprising peasants, displaced indigenous people, resident immigrants, and workers on the state farms, as well as both men and women and those experienced with irrigated rice production and those not. Such diversity presented complex challenges: "A coherent extension strategy which respects the differences between these different enterprises does not yet seem to have emerged" (Adam et al. 1991: 92).

6. Prior to PROAGRI, donors funded about 90 percent of public expenditure in agriculture, but through more than fifty separate projects (Compton 2000, cited in Cabral 2009).

7. Notwithstanding the millions of dollars poured into PROAGRI, it was difficult to evaluate the program objectively (without relying on participant interviews) because very little standardized information on its projects was collected either before the program started or along the way. As Lídia Cabral writes, "Despite the good intentions, M&E [Monitoring and Evaluation] has been a problem since the start of PROAGRI. The mid-term evaluation of PROAGRI I documented a complete lack of progress which was later confirmed by the final evaluation conducted in 2007" (2009: 34).

8. Most English-language organizations translate the name as "Agricultural" rather than "Agrarian," although the word in Portuguese is "Agrária." *Agricultural* is an adequate translation, but it is a narrower word, referring to the cultivation of crops rather than the more holistic farm system implied by *agrarian*.

9. Even missionaries—usually a reliable source of fraternization with local people—were concentrated primarily in the capital city (Newitt 1995: 436).

10. Most of the farmers in Mozambique are organized into producer associations. These associations are eligible for credit, extension assistance, and other services from the government. They are also usually the first in line to receive any funding or other resources from one of the many foreign NGOs that work in the countryside. Having a well-organized association is often the most important characteristic in being chosen for a new well, latrine, or farmer field school.

11. Although the official language of Mozambique is Portuguese, only 10 percent of the population speaks Portuguese as their first language, and only 50 percent speak it at all. Bantu languages are much more common, with Emakhuwa the most common, covering nearly 25 percent of the population in 1998; see Ethnologue, "Republic of Mozambique: Mozambique," accessed January 5, 2025, https://www.ethnologue.com/country/MZ.

12. When I talked to families about cooking or food, it was often the woman who answered, but when one of the dishes people ate most often—*chima*, a

meal made out of manioc or corn flour and water, boiled and often flavored with herbs, meat, or snails (depending on where one was)—came up in discussions, there was usually tittering and embarrassed laughter. People thought it was funny to hear "poor people's food" discussed in public.

13. Changalane was described as yielding between 3 and 6 tons per hectare, SP-1 between 2 and 10 tons per hectare, Gogoma between 2 and 5 tons per hectare, Gema between 2 and 6 tons per hectare, Chinaca between 2.5 and 7 tons per hectare, and Tsangano between 3 and 8 tons per hectare.

14. In northeastern Mozambique (see chapter 5), we watched a community perform a skit they wrote and acted out to illustrate the difficulty of irrigating their fields by hand. They had performed the skit for local political officials in an as yet unsuccessful plea for assistance. Irrigation was one of the most difficult problems facing rural farming communities in coastal Nampula.

15. In Portuguese, the terms used for seeds along the development process were *genetic seed* (*semente genética*) for the original breeder seed, pure in its genetic composition; *pre-basic seed* (*semente pré-básica*) for the progeny of the original; *basic seed* (*semente básica*) for seeds two generations removed, registered with the national certification agency and developed for distribution to commercial breeders and distributors; and *certified seed* (*semente certificada*) for seed available for commercial use.

16. Vertical traits are acquired by transferring genes between plants that are related, while horizontal traits are acquired by transferring genes from non-relatives.

17. Whether the lack of a seed market was due to a shortage of firms that would sell seed was debatable, however. One of the IIAM scientists who worked in the socioeconomic study unit believed that there were no private sector actors in the seed industry in Mozambique because the farmers wanted open pollination plants, and that was a losing proposition for private companies (Interview 14, September 15, 2016).

CHAPTER 4. "INCOMPATIBLE WITH
A PROGRESSIVE AGRICULTURE"

1. Key sources on indigenous labor include Direito (2013), which focuses particularly on colonization and land in Mozambique, Brito (2019), Isaacman and Isaacman (1983), Pitcher (2002), Gengenbach (2005), Guthrie (2018), O'Laughlin (1995, 1996), Allina (2012), Cahen (2013), and Penvenne (2015).

2. The territory was administratively divided into distinct areas for Europeans and indigenous residents. *Conselhos* were usually urban centers populated by citizens, and *circunscrições* were rural administrative units governed by Portuguese administrators; the latter were subdivided into posts and then smaller *regadorias* headed by *régulos* (O'Laughlin 2000: 16; see Mamdani 2018, for a discussion of the rural/urban divide in African colonies).

3. Indigenous voices are rare in the archives. As Marvin Harris ([1960] 2021) and Michael Cahen (2013) note, Portugal was under a fascist dictatorship

for the last fifty years of colonial rule in Mozambique, and thus the voices captured in the archives are mostly those that laud the national enterprise.

4. *Indolence* was the word most commonly used to describe indigenous peoples in Mozambique, particularly those in the central and northern reaches of the territory. Robert Nunez Lyne, the second director of the colonial agricultural research agency, wrote as follows, for example: "One of the limiting factors to the development of agriculture in East Africa is the difficulty of procuring labour, a difficulty which arises from three causes: a sparse population, indolent disposition of the people, and inexperience of white employers" (1913: 206).

5. Ernesto Jardim de Vilhena had a long career in Portuguese Africa. He was a naval officer who became chief administrator or governor over multiple charter companies and districts in Timor, Angola, and Mozambique, becoming minister of the colonies in 1917.

6. This did not generate a class of indigenous landholders. By the 1960s, three thousand European planters and farmers controlled more land than 1.5 million African peasants (Isaacman and Isaacman 1983: 43). In 1962, 94 percent of Mozambique's population lived in the rural areas (57).

7. In 1915, Artur de Almeida de Eça (*agricultor diplomado*) was asked to survey Mozambique District to "first, study the possibilities for planting cotton and, second, acquire products for the 1915 Agricultural and Industrial Exposition" (183). In addition to his charge, he recorded some details about indigenous agriculture in the district and described the utility of regular movement for agriculture: "The native does have a notion of soil fertility and that is why they move to new places regularly. They move differently for different crops – manioc and beans they will do regularly in the same place, but sesame, corn, mapira [sorghum] they generally only plant two years in a row in the same place" (193–94).

8. J. Mousinho de Albuquerque, "Moçambique: 1896–1898", 2nd ed., 1913 (published by his wife). Joaquim Augusto Mousinho de Albuquerque was Governor-General from 1896 to 1898. He also claimed credit for winning the armed battle with the local ruler of the Empire of Gaza, Gungunhana. Albuquerque (1898: 115).

9. Portaria 2126 (signed October 17, 1914).

10. Paiva's essays were originally published in the national Brazilian newspaper *A Folha de São Paulo* and subsequently gathered into a book, *A Agricultura na África*, published by the Secretary of Agriculture for the state of São Paulo in 1952. In the introduction, Paiva describes the purpose of his trip thus: "Looking to attend to the interests of the rural classes, who were worried by the notices regarding the increase in production from the African colonies, the government of the state of São Paulo decided to send a commission of *técnicos* to the black continent to observe the relevant programs" (1952: 3).

11. Paiva wrote of the connection to the Portuguese in Africa in ways that Gilberto Freyre would echo. Paiva felt an immediate connection with his Luso-tropical brothers: "For us, Brazilians, arriving in Lisbon after a stay in London,

Brussels and Paris is more or less like arriving at home" (1952: 42). He later wrote of his conviction that "the Portuguese has a profound admiration and friendship for Brazil" (149).

12. Of the British, Paiva wrote: "The British have trouble with their natives because they treat them like children but not like children they like—they treat them like idiots because the natives don't demonstrate the same values as the British (punctuality, honor, dedication to work) while the natives seek status, a good lunch, or a good nap, so the British treat them badly—when the natives get a bit of education, it's even worse because this doesn't really get them much, just an awareness of how badly they're being treated" (1952: 160).

13. The mission had only a head (*engenheiro agrónomo*), three agricultural regents, one agricultural practitioner, thirty-two collectors (whose schooling varied from second grade of primary school to fifth year), one mechanic, and one driver.

14. Many commodity studies trace a single commodity and argue that this commodity illustrates the workings of global capitalism; Sidney Mintz (1986) wrote the classic example of this kind of study, but there are other noteworthy ones, such as Sven Beckert on cotton (2015) and Arturo Warman on corn (2003). In this chapter, I focus on a very modest crop that does not dominate regional or global markets (although it is gaining popularity as a gluten-free alternative to wheat flour), but I argue that focusing on manioc shows us what work is done to prop up the dominant tropical commodity markets (O'Connor 2013). Manioc production was vital to cotton production in Mozambique, I argue, and a focus on this highlights the importance of social reproduction, not just production. See Heidi Gengenbach's (2005, 2019) excellent work on manioc in Mozambique; Delêtre et al. (2011) on marriage exchanges and manioc; Rachel Bezner Kerr's (2014) work on lost and found crops in Malawi; and Marygold Walsh-Dilley (2013) and Andrew Ofstehage (2012) on quinoa in Bolivia.

15. The Portuguese brought manioc from Brazil to West Africa (as well as tobacco, corn, and groundnuts) sometime in the 1500s, probably to the Upper Guinea Coast and to the kingdom of Kongo in northern Angola (Karasch 2000: 183). According to the article in the *Boletim da Repartição de Agricultura*, nos. 13–15 (April/June 1914) written by Sub-Director Ferraz and cited in chapter 2, it is likely that the former governor and captain-general of Mozambique, Manuel Baltasar Pereira Lago (1765–1779), brought manioc to Mozambique along with coffee (99). It isn't clear whether Pereira Lago went to Brazil and brought the seeds or plants back himself or ordered them to be brought back by others.

16. See, for example, the comprehensive study of Mozambican agriculture by Martins Santareno (1973), which lists the various crops grown and land ceded for such purposes but suggests that the figures given do not include fallow land for traditional agriculture, which represented upward of 2 million hectares when total land occupied was approximately 10 million hectares (5).

17. The indigenous person, it was said in a compendium of local habits (Lopes), had no meaningful institution of property, in part because of "the facility with which the native cultivates the free land he inhabits."

18. Vilhena added, "Manioc is planted in succession, without real concern as to season" (1910: 10).

19. Manioc was also planted at military command sites. As one agronomist said of the military command of Massinga, in southeastern Mozambique, "There was a beautiful planting of manioc there, which the commander had had done to feed the locals. I told the commander to get me a pan to roast the flour, but he couldn't because they do not do that here" (Mayreles 1909: 319).

CHAPTER 5. "IT'S A SHAME IT'S SO DIFFICULT"

1. The short-handled hoe—or "devil's arm"—has a bad reputation in farming communities around the world. It was one of the most hated agricultural tools in California in the mid-1900s until it was outlawed by the California Supreme Court in 1975 after intensive organizing by the local legal assistance office (California Rural Legal Assistance, CLRA), the United Farm Workers (UFW), Cesar Chavez, Maurice Jourdane, and others (see Cozzens 2015; Jain 2006).

2. The most well-known references on extension in Mozambique are from Helder Gêmo (2009), a former extensionist and longtime member of DNEA; see also Mosca (1999, 2016) and Mosca and Bruna (2015). Mosca argues that extensionists in general were often enrolled in politics as local officials augmented their meager salaries with additional subsidies for political campaigning.

3. On extension and contemporary cotton production, see Boughton et al. (2003). The Cunguara and Thompson report previously cited includes a DNEA assessment of private extension services in Mozambique and puts the total number of these agents at 1,479—175 more agents than were employed by the public sector at that time (2018: 24). A year later, however, a leading administrator at DNEA told me that the agency did not know how many private extension agents were in the country, as they did not always fulfill the requirement of informing the government when they came or left.

4. In order to compete, officials in DNEA were developing a "career plan" that would provide for long-term employment, specific metrics, and promotion. Once this career plan was developed, all existing extension agents would need to take a qualifying course to be entitled to the new status, and their positions would be geared toward specific production areas in specific agroecological zones. This targeting was indicative of a broader turn toward specialization along crop lines, which was deemed necessary for farmer and extension agent alike. According to DNEA, this new hiring plan would mean increased competition for extension positions, better pay and benefits, and clearer paths for promotion. This new career plan was supposed to be announced in 2019 but was delayed by a lack of resources.

5. The divide between IIAM and DNEA was widely recognized, but there was also overlap. When IIAM was created, it established a department for technology transfer that had the same educational purpose as extension. A former DNEA director called the IIAM department "redundant": "We already had these same areas. But when they created IIAM out of [the other institutions

in 2004], they created a department that repeated extension. Don't think we didn't know this was happening and that it was stupid! We were told to do this by the donor [the World Bank]. Some reforms are forced, pushed through; the donors wanted IIAM to be created" (Interview 23, December 16, 2016).

6. In 2018 it was estimated that approximately 15 percent of extension agents were female (Cunguara and Thompson 2018: 22).

7. Most group meetings in rural Mozambique featured a collective chant or story to motivate participants. The majority of these that I saw were about the weather, often an invocation of rain. At the opening of REPETE in 2016, the senior official's opening comments were a formal version of what in other settings would have been done with hand clapping, a story, or a call and response.

8. As the review by Cuangara and Thompson noted, "Many extension officers did not clear their land because they understood that the Ministry of Agriculture and Food Security would support them in land preparation and provide free seeds and other inputs. However, such inputs and support in general never came, and the full potential of PITTA was not achieved. PITTA was a pilot project that received a lot of criticism" (2018: 32).

9. Although the data are not highly reliable, the World Bank draws on data for 2021 from the Instituto Nacional de Estatística (Mozambique) to estimate that approximately 17 percent of all Mozambicans had access to the internet. "Individuals Using the Internet (% of Population)—Mozambique," accessed January 5, 2025, https://data.worldbank.org/indicator/IT.NET.USER.ZS?locations =MZ. Given that Wi-Fi and cell coverage is concentrated in urban areas, and based on my own observations, it's likely that very few rural farmers were able to access the internet on a regular basis.

10. I asked one other question: whether the technology could still work if one used the Cinema Clubs instead of smartphones, since communities in the rural areas congregated in clubs to watch films on large screens. The researcher said yes, of course it would work, but he already knew it would work on a large screen, and he wanted to do his research on something innovative.

11. Initial claims that Chinese investors were some of the main actors grabbing land in Africa proved misleading (see Brautigam 2015). Lila Buckley (2013) has written on Chinese technical assistance programs in Africa; see Chichava et al. (2013) for a discussion of Brazilian and Chinese interventions in Mozambique.

12. I was told that when the Chinese had come to Mozambique to help train Mozambicans in agricultural techniques, they were originally going to be paired with scientists from IIAM on a regular basis. IIAM scientists who suggested this told me it was "impossible" because the Chinese were not qualified, since many of them didn't even have master's degrees. The lead scientist from Mozambique for the Brazilian horticulture project was highly offended at the idea that a technician without a university degree would presume to teach Mozambicans.

13. Twenty-nine participants answered the questions, and the responses were instructive. Eight people had already taught farmers how to make forage;

an additional four had taught other extension agents how to work with forage. Five people had experience with nutritional blocks or salt blocks, and two already taught silage practices. Fifteen people said that techniques for making forage were among the most important things that farmers needed to learn now. Only eight of the twenty-nine respondents indicated that IIAM was a place where they could receive information about these or other technologies. Finally, sixteen people said they received information about these or similar technologies from other extension agents rather than researchers. No one said that they received information about any of these techniques from the farmers themselves.

14. Contract farming of this sort increased in agricultural powerhouse producers after World War II, when many large farms vertically integrated, particularly in the United States in the 1940s and Brazil in the 1970s. Large family chicken producers in both countries, for example, consolidated grain farms to produce feed and diversified into consumer products with different cuts of chicken and other more highly processed goods like pizza (with chicken topping) and so on.

15. This poster is available at ResearchGate, Figure 2, accessed January 11, 2025, https://www.researchgate.net/figure/Figura-2-Poster-de-divulgacao-do -ProSavana_fig1_335093729.

16. CARE worked with the poorest communities but not necessarily the poorest people in those communities, because its theory of change suggested that the poorest people were unlikely to respond well to interventions.

17. See the FAO knowledge repository on FSS, "Global Farmer Field School Platform," accessed July 30, 2024, https://www.fao.org/farmer-field-schools /home/en/.

18. I was surprised when I met this person and he introduced himself as an extension agent who worked for IIAM and promoted conservation agriculture. He did not have a connection to researchers in IIAM but did act like a public extension agent, creating FFS and "testing" participants for their knowledge of key inputs in order to graduate.

19. The description of community that follows is based on themes that were repeated across interviews conducted in five rural communities in the coastal region of Nampula from 2014 to 2016. In 2014 we conducted oral histories of each community with small groups of people who were presented to us as the "elders." These were usually older men, and that shaped the histories they presented, providing more of a focus on national events than household dynamics.

20. This complaint echoes the file from the official hearings of Chefe do Mocuque Anibal Rezende, who had on more than one occasion "the audacity to order a black to take off the very boots he had put on, telling him that no black could enter the office with shoes on." In 1935, after many years of abuses, Rezende was tried and found guilty in the Judicial Tribunal of the Câmara da Beira (Companhia de Moçambique 1928).

21. For an excellent analysis of coconut production in central Mozambique during the colonial period, see Adalima (2022b).

22. In one community we visited, there was a rift between the families because aid organizations had incorporated some families in their projects and not others. One particular point of contention was the water pumps that were built in the community "seat," because that location was close to the road. A group of families farther from the road considered themselves the true heart of the community, and when that group saw the other families near the road receive funds, including water pumps from external donors, they decided to start their own association.

CHAPTER 6. AWAKENING THE SLEEPING GIANT

1. In his role as official spokesperson, Américo successfully deflected many requests for information (Mosca and Bruna 2015).

2. This quote is from a daylong public seminar held in Brasília with representatives of ProSavana and civil society from all three countries. A summary can be found in the response the Brazilian government provided to a request for information on activities that took place between Brazil, Japan, and Mozambique from April 12 to June 31, 2016, at "Pedido documentos pesquisa acadêmica Brasil Moçambique agricultura 2016," Pedido 09200000722201658o, February 8, https://buscalai.cgu.gov.br/PedidosLai/DetalhePedido?id= 1969969. The meeting took place May 30–June 3, and the response is dated August 18, 2016. Other quotations in this chapter are from my transcription of a recording of the meeting.

3. See note 2.

4. The FAO estimates that there are 3.2 million small farmers and 400 commercial farmers in Mozambique; see the Mozambique Factsheet, accessed August 2, 2024, http://www.fao.org/mozambique/fao-in-mozambique /mozambique-at-a-glance/en. The Agricultural and Livestock Census in Mozambique classifies a farm as belonging to smallholders (*pequena exploração*) when the cultivated area is smaller than 10 hectares. Of the total number of smallholders, approximately 70 percent have less than 2 hectares. "Censo Agropecuário, 2009–2010," accessed January 2, 2025, https://mozdata.ine.gov .mz/index.php/catalog/37.

5. In 2017 the Mozambican Constitution did not allow for land transfers of this sort. This is the revision that was under discussion in 2023 and 2024, and it is clear that the MCC's work helped usher in a new acceptance of legalized land transfers.

6. A long literature on land rights in Brazil suggests that lack of clarity in ownership or access is often the product of deliberate attempts on the part of the government to let possession be decided by force or other displays of power (see Holston 1991).

7. This study was conducted over several months in 2012 by three Japanese consulting firms (Oriental Consultants Co. Ltd., NTC International Co. Ltd., and Task Co Ltd.) in consultation with the Ministry of Agriculture and provincial agricultural offices.

8. Incredibly, the study calculates the carrying capacity of the Nacala Corridor under swidden farming by referring to the Japanese book *Inasaku Izen* (Komei 1971).

9. UNAC et al., "Open Letter from Mozambican Civil Society Organisations and Movements to the Presidents of Mozambique and Brazil and the Prime Minister of Japan," June 3, 2013, GRAIN, https://www.grain.org/bulletin _board/entries/4738-open-letter-from-mozambican-civil-society-organisations -and-movements-to-the-presidents-of-mozambique-and-brazil-and-the-prime -minister-of-japan.

CHAPTER 7. AFTERWARD

1. The authors of the OMR research report on Sustenta suggested that instead of the familiar top-down, outward-oriented programs, Mozambique would benefit from integrated, participatory, decentralized development responsive to the demands of the producers themselves, along with the provision of basic public goods oriented toward, and accessible to, the most vulnerable.

2. See the full report on land rights in Mozambique: *Mozambique*, USAID, 2018, accessed January 5, 2025, https://www.land-links.org/country-profile /Mozambique/#land.

3. The author owes inspiration and gratitude to conversations with Djamila Andrade, Universidade de Coimbra, Portugal, who also commented on the first draft, as well as with Heidrun Merk, an anthropologist and honorary director of the Schwälmer Dorfmuseum Holzburg e.V. Hesse, Germany.

4. Author's conversation with N. N., a man just slightly older than seventy-five, in Chitobe, Machaze District, Manica Province, in Mozambique on July 7, 2004, during a research stay within the framework of the project titled Capacity Building for Participatory District Planning and Financing, financed by Concern International, Dublin/Mozambique.

5. In the last several years, the United States has become an important investor in Mozambique. Those who live in the United States could push that government to insist on investment projects that honor transparency, inclusion, and pro-poor markets.

References

SECONDARY SOURCES

Abbas, Máriam, Boaventura Manjata, Isidro Macaringue, Mateus Costa Santos, René Machoco, and Vanessa Cabanelas. 2021. Sistemas alimentares em Moçambique: Rumo a uma política alimentar para Moçambique. Maputo, Moçambique. https://omrmz.org/wp-content/uploads/2022/08/Rumo-a -uma-politica-1.pdf.

Abbas, Máriam, Paulo Flores Ribeiro, and José Lima Santos. 2023. "Farming System Change Under Different Climate Scenarios and Its Impact on Food Security: An Analytical Framework to Inform Adaptation Policy In Developing Countries." *Mitigation and Adaptation Strategies for Global Change* 28, no. 43. https://doi.org/10.1007/s11027-023-10082-5.

Abreu, Fernando. 2013. "O Brasil e a cooperação Sul-Sul." Presentation at the BRICS Policy Centre, Rio de Janeiro.

Adalima, José Laimone. 2022a. "Connecting Livelihood Discourses to Land Conflicts in Central Mozambique." *Journal of Contemporary African Studies* 40, no. 3 (June): 384–99. https://doi.org/10.1080/02589001.2020.1774521.

Adalima, José Laimone. 2022b. "From Coconut to Land: Changing Livelihoods in Micaúne, Central Mozambique." *Etnográfica* 26, no. 1 (February): 29–50. https://doi.org/10.4000/etnografica.11067.

Adam, Yussuf, Robin Goodyear, Martin Greeley, Mick Moore, Julio Munguambe, Miguel Neves, Penelope Roberts, Gulamo Taju, and Sergio Vieira. 1991. *Aid Under Fire: An Evaluation of the Mozambique-Nordic Agricultural Programme (MONAP).* SIDA Evaluation Report no. 1. Swedish International Development Authority.

Adas, Michael. 1989. *Machines as the Measure of Men: Science, Technology, and Ideologies of Western Dominance.* Cornell University Press.

Agência Brasileira de Cooperação (ABC). 2010. "Catálogo ABC de cooperação técnica do Brasil para a África." Agência Brasileira de Cooperação. chrome -extension://efaidnbmnnnibpcajpcglclefindmkaj/https://www.abc.gov.br /content/abc/docs/catalogoabcafrica2010_p.pdf.

Agência Brasileira de Cooperação (ABC). "Moçambique." 2012. Agência de Cooperação Brasileira. https://www.abc.gov.br/projetos/cooperacaosulsul/mocambique.

Aikens, Natalie, Amy Clukey, Amy King, and Isadora Wagner. 2019. "South to the Plantationocene." *ASAP Journal* (October). http://asapjournal.com/south-to-the-plantationocene-natalie-aikens-amy-clukey-amy-k-king-and-isadora-wagner/.

Albuquerque, Mousinho de. 1898. *Moçambique: 1896–1898*. Ministério da Colonias, Sociedade de Geographia de Lisboa.

Ali, Rosamina, and Sara Stevano. 2022. "Work in Agro-Industry and the Social Reproduction of Labour in Mozambique: Contradictions in the Current Accumulation System." *Review of African Political Economy* 49 (171): 67–86. https://doi.org/10.1080/03056244.2022.1990624.

allAfrica. 2012. "Mozambique: Agreement on Nacala Fund." Accessed September 17, 2012. http://allafrica.com/stories/201207061132.html.

Allewaert, Monique. 2013. *Ariel's Ecology: Plantations, Personhood, and Colonialism in the American Tropics*. University of Minnesota Press.

Allina, Eric. 2012. *Slavery by Any Other Name: African Life Under Company Rule in Colonial Mozambique*. University of Virginia Press.

Almeida, José de. 1914. "Project of Reorganizing the Agronomic and Livestock Services." *Boletim da Repartição de Agricultura*, nos. 13–15 (April–June).

Anderson, Perry. 1962a. "Portugal and the End of Ultra-Colonialism, Part I." *New Left Review* 1, no. 15 (May/June): 83–102.

Anderson, Perry. 1962b. "Portugal and the End of Ultra-Colonialism, Part II." *New Left Review* 1, no. 16 (May/June): 88–123.

Anderson, Perry. 1962c. "Portugal and the End of Ultra-Colonialism, Part III." *New Left Review* 1, no. 17 (May/June): 85–114.

Anderson, Warwick. 2006. *Colonial Pathologies: American Tropical Medicine, Race, and Hygiene in the Philippines*. Duke University Press.

Arezki, Rabah, Klaus Deininger, and Harris Selod. 2011. "What Drives the Global 'Land Rush'?" World Bank Policy Research Working Paper No. 5864.

Aston, Trevor H., and C. H. E. Philpin. 1995. *The Brenner Debate: Agrarian Class Structure and Economic Development in Pre-Industrial Europe*. Cambridge University Press,

Baird, Ian, and Keith Barney. 2017. "The Political Ecology of Cross-Sectoral Cumulative Impacts: Modern Landscapes, Large Hydropower Dams and Industrial Tree Plantations in Laos and Cambodia." *Journal of Peasant Studies* 44, no. 4 (April): 769–95. https://doi.org/10.1080/03066150.2017.1289921.

Baird, Ian G. 2020. "Problems for the Plantations: Challenges for Large-Scale Land Concessions in Laos and Cambodia." *Journal of Agrarian Change* 20, no. 3 (July): 387–407. https://doi.org/10.1111/joac.12355.

Baka, Jennifer. 2017. "Making Space for Energy: Wasteland Development, Enclosures, and Energy Dispossessions." *Antipode* 49, no. 4 (September): 977–96. https://doi.org/10.1111/anti.12219.

Balane, Neusa, and João Feijó. 2022. *Agricultural Production and Women's Empowerment in Rural Contexts: Analysis of The Agrimulheres Project in Three Villages of Nampula Province (2018–2021).* Observador Rural no. 130. Observatório do Meio Rural.

Banner, Stuart. 2005. *How the Indians Lost Their Land: Law and Power on the Frontier.* Harvard University Press.

Barradas, Lereno Antunes. 1962. *Esboço agrológico do sul de Moçambique II plano de fomento.* Maputo: Instituto de Investigação Científica de Moçambique, Lourenço Marques.

Barrett, Otis W. 1910. "Impressions and Scenes of Mozambique." *National Geographic Magazine* 21, no. 10 (October): 807–30.

Barros, Alfredo Baptista. 1965. "Aspectos da produtividade da agricultura em Moçambique." PhD diss., Instituto Superior de Ciências Sociais e Políticas, University of Lisbon. Self-published in Lisbon.

Bassett, Thomas J., and Koli Bi Zuéli. 2000. "Environmental Discourses and the Ivorian Savanna." *Annals of the Association of American Geographers* 90, no. 1 (March): 67–95. https://doi.org/10.1111/0004-5608.00184.

Bastos, Cristiana. 2018. "Portuguese in the Cane: The Racialization of Labour in Hawaiian Plantations." In *Changing Societies: Legacies and Challenges,* vol. 1, *Ambiguous Inclusions: Inside Out, Inside In,* edited by Sofia Aboim, Paulo Granjo, and Alice Ramos. Imprensa de Ciências Sociais. https://doi.org/10.31447/ics9789726715030.03.

Batistella, Mateus, and Luis E. Bolfe. 2010. *Paralelos: Corredor de Nacala.* Embrapa Monitoramento por Satélite.

Beckert, Sven. 2015. *Empire of Cotton: A Global History.* Vintage.

Beckford, George. L. 1977. *Persistent Poverty: Underdevelopment in Plantation Economies of the Third World.* University of the West Indies Press.

Behal, Rana P. 2014. *One Hundred Years of Servitude: Political Economy of Tea Plantations in Colonial Assam.* Columbia University Press.

Benton, Lauren. 2012. "Possessing Empire: Iberian Claims and Interpolity Law." In *Native Claims: Indigenous Law against Empire 1500–1920,* edited by Sahila Belmessous. Oxford University Press.

Bernstein, Henry, Tom Brass, and E. Valentine Daniel, eds. 1993. *Plantations, Proletarians and Peasants in Colonial Asia.* Routledge. https://doi.org/10.4324/9781315827889.

Berry, Sara. 1992. "Hegemony on a Shoestring: Indirect Rule and Access to Agricultural Land." *Africa: Journal of the International African Institute* 62 (3): 327–55.

Besky, Sarah. 2014. *The Darjeeling Distinction: Labor and Justice on Fair-Trade Tea Plantations in India.* University of California Press.

Besky, Sarah. 2017. "Fixity: On the Inheritance and Maintenance of Tea Plantation Houses in Darjeeling, India." *American Ethnologist* 44, no. 4 (November): 617–31. https://doi.org/10.1111/amet.12561.

Besky, Sarah. 2022. "Reproducing the Plantation." *Annals of the American Association of Geographers* 114, no. 10 (December): 2212–15. https://doi.org/10.1080/24694452.2022.2147050.

Bezner Kerr, Rachel. 2013. "Seed Struggles and Food Sovereignty in Northern Malawi." *Journal of Peasant Studies* 40, no. 5 (November): 867–97. https://doi.org/10.1080/03066150.2013.848428.

Bezner Kerr, Rachel. 2014. "Lost and Found Crops: Agrobiodiversity, Indigenous Knowledge, and a Feminist Political Ecology of Sorghum and Finger Millet in Northern Malawi." *Annals of the Association of American Geographers* 104, no. 3 (April): 577–93. https://doi.org/10.1080/00045608.2014.892346.

Bezner Kerr, Rachel. 2023. "Feminist Agroecology Viewed Through the Lens of the Plantationocene." *Annals of the American Association of Geographers* 1, no. 8 (July): 2204–21. https://doi.org/10.1080/24694452.2023.2216779.

Bhandar, Brenna. 2016. "Possession, Occupation and Registration: Recombinant Ownership in the Settler Colony." *Settler Colonial Studies* 6 (2): 119–32.

Biggs, David. 2008. "Breaking from the Colonial Mold: Water Engineering and the Failure of Nation Building in the Plain of Reeds, Vietnam." *Technology and Culture* 49, no. 3 (July): 599–623.

Bledsoe, Adam. 2018. "The Present Imperative of Marronage." *Afro-Hispanic Review* 37, no. 2 (Fall): 45–58. https://www.jstor.org/stable/26875105.

Board for International Food and Agricultural Development (BIFAD), International Food Policy Research Institute (IFPRI), and Association of Public and Land-Grant Universities (APLU). 2019. *How the United States Benefits from Agricultural and Food Security Investments in Developing Countries.* Washington, DC: International Food Policy Research Institute. https://doi.org/10.2499/p15738coll2.133419.

Boletim da Repartição de Agricultura. 1914. "Inquérito sôbre a produção de géneros agrícolas coloniais." Nos. 13–15 (April/June): 85–107.

Boone, Catherine. 2014. *Property and Political Order in Africa: Land Rights and the Structure of Politics.* Cambridge University Press.

Borras, Saturnino, Jr., Marc Edelman, and Cristobal Kay. 2008. *Transnational Agrarian Movements.* Wiley-Blackwell.

Borras, Saturnino, Jr., David Fig, and Sofia Monsalve Suarez. 2011. "The Politics of Agrofuels and Mega-Land and Water Deals: Insights from the Pro-Cana Case, Mozambique." *Review of African Political Economy* 38, no. 128 (June): 215–34. https://doi.org/10.1080/03056244.2011.582758.

Borras, Saturnino, Jr., and Jennifer C. Franco. 2012. "Global Land Grabbing and Trajectories of Agrarian Change: A Preliminary Analysis." *Journal of Agrarian Change* 12, no. 1 (January): 34–59. https://doi.org/10.1111/j.1471-0366.2011.00339.x.

Borras, Saturnino, Jr., Ruth Hall, Ian Scoones, Ben White, and Wendy Wolford. 2011. "Towards a Better Understanding of Global Land-Grabbing:

An Editorial Introduction." *Journal of Peasant Studies* 38, no. 2 (March): 209–16. https://doi.org/10.1080/03066150.2011.559005.

Borras, Saturnino M., Jr., Jennifer C. Franco, S. Ryan Isakson, Les Levidow, and Pietje Vervest. 2016. "The Rise of Flex Crops and Commodities: Implications for Research." *Journal of Peasant Studies* 43 (1): 93–115. https://doi .org/10.1080/03066150.2015.1036417.

Boughton, Duncan, David L. Tschirley, Ballard Zulu, Afonso Osorio Ofico, and Higino Francisco de Marrule. 2003. "Cotton Sector Policies and Performance in Sub-Saharan Africa: Lessons Behind the Numbers in Mozambique and Zambia." Paper presented at 2003 Annual Meeting of the International Association of Agricultural Economists, Durban, South Africa, August 16–22. https://doi.org/10.22004/ag.econ.25855.

Bowen, Merle L. 2000. *The State Against the Peasantry: Rural Struggles in Colonial and Postcolonial Mozambique.* University of Virginia Press.

Bowen, Merle L., Arlindo Chilundo, and Cesar A. Tique. 2003. "Social Differentiation, Farming Practices, and Environmental Change in Mozambique." In *African Savannas: Global Narratives and Local Knowledge of Environmental Change,* edited by Thomas J. Bassett and Donald Crummey. James Currey.

Boyd, William, and Michael Watts. 1997. "Agro-Industrial Just-in-Time: The Chicken Industry and Postwar American Capitalism." In *Globalising Food: Agrarian Questions and Global Restructuring,* edited by David Goodman and Michael Watts. Routledge.

Brass, Tom, and Henry Bernstein. 1992. "Introduction: Proletarianisation and Deproletarianisation on the Colonial Plantation." In *Plantations, Proletarians and Peasants in Colonial Asia,* edited by E. Valentine Daniel, Henry Bernstein, and Tom Brass. Frank Cass.

Brautigam, Deborah. 2015. *Will Africa Feed China?* Oxford University Press.

Bray, Francesca, Barbara Hahn, John Lourdusamy and Tiago Saraiva. 2023. *Moving Crops and the Scales of History.* Yale Agrarian Studies Series. Yale University Press.

Brenner, Robert. 1976. "Agrarian Class Structure and Economic Development in Pre-Industrial Europe." *Past & Present* 70, no. 1 (February): 30–75. https://doi.org/10.1093/past/70.1.30.

Brito, Luís. 2009. *Moçambique: De uma economia de serviços a uma economia de renda.* IDEIAS, Bulletin no. 13. IESE.

Brito, Luís. 2019. *A Frelimo, o Marxismo e a Construção do Estado Nacional 1962–1983.* IESE.

Brockway, Lucile H. 1979. "Science and Colonial Expansion: The Role of the British Royal Botanic Gardens." *American Ethnologist* 6, no. 3 (August): 449–65. https://doi.org/10.1525/ae.1979.6.3.02a00030.

Bruna, Natacha, Alberto Tovele, Uacitissa Mandamule, René Machoco, Vanessa Cabanelas, Issufo Tankar, Daniel Ribeiro, Boaventura Monjane, and Isidro Macaringue. 2022. *Directrizes Para um Quadro Legal Sobre Terras*

Inclusivo e Sustentável: Políticas Redistributivas, Pró-Pobre e Transformativas. OMR, CTV, JA!, UNAC, and Alternactiva.

Bruna, Natacha. 2017. *Plantações florestais e a instrumentalização do Estado em Moçambique.* Observador Rural no. 53. Observatório do Meio Rural.

Buckley, Lila. 2013. "Chinese Land-Based Interventions in Senegal." *Development and Change* 44, no. 2 (March): 429–50. https://doi.org/10.1111/dech.12016.

Buur, Lars, and Celso Marcos Monjane. 2016. "Elite Capture and the Development of Natural Resource Linkages in Mozambique." In *Fairness and Justice in Natural Resource Politics,* edited by Melanie Pichler, Cornelia Staritz, Karin Küblböck, Christina Plank, Werner Raza, and Fernando Ruiz Peyré. Routledge.

Cabral, António Augusto Pereira. 1925. *Raças, Usos e Costumes dos Indígenas.* Imprensa Nacional.

Cabral, Lídia. 2009. *Sector Budget Support in Practice: Desk Study, Agriculture Sector in Mozambique.* London: Overseas Development Institute; Oxford: Mokoro, November 2009. http://cdn-odi-production.s3-website-eu-west-1.amazonaws.com/media/documents/5577.pdf.

Cabral, Lídia. 2015. "Priests, Technicians and Traders? The Discursive Politics of Brazil's Agricultural Cooperation in Mozambique." Future Agricultures Working Paper No. 110. Institute of Development Studies.

Cabral, Lídia, and Alex Shankland. 2012. "Transferring Brazilian Agricultural Successes to African Soil: A Reality Check for South-South Cooperation." In Leisa Perch, Anmad Bahalim, Lidia Cabral, and Alex Shankland, eds., "The Role of South-South Cooperation in Inclusive and Sustainable Agricultural Development: Focus on Africa." *Poverty in Focus,* no. 24. https://hdl.handle.net/10419/77968.

Cabral, Lídia, Alex Shankland, Arilson Favareto, and Alcides Costa Vaz. 2013. "Africa Agricultural Cooperation Encounters: Drivers, Narratives and Imaginaries of Africa and Development." *IDS Bulletin* 44 (4): 1–17.

Caetano, Marcelo. 1951. *Tradições, principios e métodos da Colonização Portuguesa.* Agência geral do Ultramar.

Cahen, Michel. 1987. *Mozambique, La révolution implosée: Etudes sur 12 ans d'indépendance (1975–1987).* L'Harmattan.

Cahen, Michel. 2013. "Slavery, Enslaved Labour and Forced Labour in Mozambique: Review Essay of Eric Allina, Slavery by Any Other Name: African Life Under Company Rule in Colonial Mozambique." *Portuguese Studies Review* 21, no. 1: 253–65.

Calengo, André, Fernando Machava, Judite Vendo, Rajabo Simalawonga, Raphgaiel Kabuna, and Sosdito Mananze. 2016. *O avanço das plantações florestais sobre os territórios dos camponeses no corredor de Nacala: O caso da Green Resources Moçambique.* LEXTERRA, JA! Justiça Ambiental e União Nacional de Camponeses.

Calmon, Daniela. 2020. "Shifting Frontiers: The Making of Matopiba in Brazil and Global Redirected Land Use and Control Change." *Journal of Peasant*

Studies 49, no. 2 (November): 263–87. https://doi.org/10.1080/03066150 .2020.1824183.

Camana, Ângela, and Jalcione Almeida. 2019. "Da insustentabilidade do desenvolvimento: Os discursos da produção de 'vazios' no âmbito de um programa de cooperação internacional." *Revista de Ciências Sociais* 19 (2): 391–408. https://doi.org/10.15448/1984-7289.2019.2.32057.

Canfield, Matthew, Molly D. Anderson, and Philip McMichael. 2021. "UN Food Systems Summit 2021: Dismantling Democracy and Resetting Corporate Control of Food Systems." *Frontiers in Sustainable Food Systems* 5 (April): 1–15. https://doi.org/10.3389/fsufs.2021.661552.

Captain, Yvonne. 2010. "Brazil's Africa Policy Under Lula." *The Global South* 4, no. 1 (Spring): 183–98. https://doi.org/10.2979/gso.2010.4.1.183.

Cardozo, Augusto. 1915. "Economia colonial: O aproveitamento do solo." *Boletim da Agricultura*, 3rd series, nos. 1–3 (January–to March): 19–29.

Carrilho, João. 1994. *Case Studies on Customary and Formal Administration of Land and Natural Resources in Mozambique.* Consultant report no. 2, FAO- UNDP TSS-1 Project, Advisory Policy on Rural Resettlement and Land Tenure.

Carmody, Pádraig. 2011. *The New Scramble for Africa.* Polity Press.

Carney, Judith. 2020. "Subsistence in the Plantationocene: Dooryard Gardens, Agrobiodiversity, and the Subaltern Economies of Slavery." *Journal of Peasant Studies* 48, no. 5 (April): 1075–99. https://doi.org/10.1080 /03066150.2020.1725488.

Carse, Ashley. 2012. "Nature as Infrastructure: Making and Managing the Panama Canal Watershed." *Social Studies of Science* 42 (4): 539–63. https:// doi.org/10.1177/0306312712440166.

Castel-Branco, Carlos. 2014. "Growth, Capital Accumulation and Economic Porosity in Mozambique: Social Losses, Private Gains." *Review of African Political Economy* 41 (supp. 1): S26–S48. https://doi.org/10.1080/03056244 .2014.976363.

Castel-Branco, Carlos. 2022. "The Historical Logic of the Mode of Capital Accumulation in Mozambique." *Review of African Political Economy* 49 (171): 11–45.

Castel-Branco, Ruth. 2022. "The Machamba Is for Life: navigating a precarious labour market in rural Mozambique." Future of Work(ers) SCIS Working Paper No. 47. Southern Centre for Inequality Studies, University of the Witwatersrand.

Castelo, Cláudia. 1999. *"O Modo Português de Estar no Mundo": O Luso-Tropicalismo e a Ideologia Colonial Portuguesa (1933–1961).* Edições Afrontamento.

Castelo, Cláudia. 2006. "Gilberto Freyre's View of Miscegenation and Its Circulation in the Portuguese Empire, 1930s–1960s." In *Luso-Tropicalism and Its Discontents,* edited by Warwick Anderson, Ricardo Roque, and Ricardo Ventura Santos. Berghahn.

Castelo, Cláudia. 2007. *Passagens para África, O Povoamento de Angola e Moçambique com Naturais da Metrópole (1920–1974).* Edições Afrontamento.

Castelo, Cláudia. 2012. "Investigação científica e política colonial portuguesa: Evolução e articulações, 1936–1974." *História, Ciências, Saúde—Manguinhos* 19, no. 2 (June): 391–408. https://doi.org/10.1590/S0104-59702012000200003.

Castelo, Cláudia. 2016. "Reproducing Portuguese Villages in Africa: Agricultural Science, Ideology and Empire." *Journal of Southern African Studies* 42, no. 2 (March): 267–81. https://doi.org/10.1080/03057070.2016.1142732.

Censo Agro-Pecuário (CAP). 2011. *Censo Agro-Pecuário 2009–2010: Resultados Definitivos.* Instituto Nacional de Estatística.

Centro de Integridade Pública (CIP). 2021. "Corrupção no Sector de Terras no Meio Rural: Práticas, actores e implicações—Análise dos casos de Nampula, Cabo Delgado e Manica." Centro de Integridade Pública.

Centro de Investigação Científica Algodeira (CICA). 1995. *Esboço do reconhecimento ecológico-agrícola de Moçambique.* Vols. 1 and 2. Memórias e Trabalhos no. 23. Lourenco Marques: Imprensa Nacional de Moçambique.

Cesarino, Letícia. 2017a. "Anthropology and the South-South Encounter: On 'Culture' in Brazil–Africa Relations." *American Anthropologist* 119, no. 2 (March): 333–58. https://doi.org/10.1111/aman.12874.

Cesarino, Letícia. 2017b. "O 'camponês' enquanto contexto: transferência de tecnologia em um projeto de cooperação sul-sul." In *Técnica e Transformação: Perspectivas antropológicas,* edited by Carlos Emanuel Sautchuk. ABA publicações.

Chagnon, Christopher W., Francesco Durante, Barry K. Gills, Sophia E. Hagolani-Albov, Saana Hokkanen, Sohvi M. J. Kangasluoma, Heidi Konttinen, Markus Kröger, William LaFleur, Ossi Ollinaho, and Marketta P. S. Vuola. 2022. "From Extractivism to Global Extractivism: The Evolution of an Organizing Concept." *Journal of Peasant Studies* 49, no. 4: 760–92. https://doi.org/10.1080/03066150.2022.2069015.

Chao, Sophie. 2022a. "Plantation." *Environmental Humanities* 14, no. 2 (July): 361–66. https://doi.org/10.1215/22011919-9712423.

Chao, Sophie. 2022b. "(Un)Worlding the Plantationocene: Extraction, Extinction, Emergence." *Etropic: Electronic Journal of Studies in the Tropics* 21 (1): 165–91. https://doi.org/10.25120/etropic.21.1.2022.3838.

Chao, Sophie, Wendy Wolford, Andrew Ofstehage, Shalmali Guttal, Euclides Gonçalves, and Fernanda Ayala. 2023. "The Plantationocene as Analytical Concept: A Forum for Dialogue and Reflection." *Journal of Peasant Studies* 51 (3): 541–63. https://doi.org/10.1080/03066150.2023.2228212.

Chari, Sharad. 2023. "Subalternization of a Postplantation City." *Annals of the American Association of Geographers* 114, no. 10 (January): 2189–93. https://doi.org/10.1080/24694452.2022.2149463.

Chichava, Sérgio. 2013. "'They Can Kill Us, but We Won't Go to the Communal Villages': Peasants and the Policy of 'Socialisation of the Countryside' in Zambezia." *Kronos* 39, no. 1 (January): 112–30.

Chichava, Sérgio, Jimena Duran, Lídia Cabral, Alex Shankland, Lila Buckely, Tang Lixia, and Zhang Yue. 2013. "Brazil and China in Mozambican Agriculture: Emerging Insights from the Field." *IDS Bulletin* 44, no. 4 (June): 101–15. https://doi.org/10.1111/1759-5436.12046.

Chiziane, Eduardo. 2015. *Legislação sobre os Recursos Naturais em Moçambique: Convergências e Conflitos na relação com a Terra.* Observador Rural No 28. OMR.

Chung, Youjin B. 2019. "The Grass Beneath: Conservation, Agro-Industrialization, and Land-Water Enclosures in Postcolonial Tanzania." *Annals of the American Association of Geographers* 109 (1): 1–17. https://doi.org/10.1080/24694452.2018.1484685.

Chung, Youjin B. 2023. *Sweet Deal, Bitter Landscape: Gender Politics and Liminality in Tanzania's New Enclosures.* Cornell University Press.

Claeys, Priscilla, and Marc Edelman. 2020. "The United Nations Declaration on the Rights of Peasants and Other People Working in Rural Areas." *Journal of Peasant Studies* 47 (1): 1–68. https://doi.org/10.1080/03066150.2019.1672665.

Clements, Elizabeth A., and Bernardo Mançano Fernandes. 2013. "Land Grabbing, Agribusiness and the Peasantry in Brazil and Mozambique." *Agrarian South: Journal of Political Economy* 2, no. 1 (June): 41–69. https://doi.org/10.1177/2277976013477185.

Compton, James. 2000. "Case Study: Mozambique PROAGRI." Paper presented at the DIFD Natural Resource Advisers Conference, London, England.

Cooper, Frederick. 1982. *From Slaves to Squatters. Plantation Labour and Agriculture in Zanzibar and Coastal Kenya, 1890–1925.* Yale University Press.

Cordeiro Dias, José Daniel. 1909. "Agricultural colonial: Relatórios do regent agrícola, dirigidos ao governador do districto de Quelimane." Relatórios e Informações, *Annexo ao Boletim Official,* Anno de 1909. Lourenço Marques: Imprensa Nacional.

Costa, Camilo M. Silveira da, and Homero Martins Ferrinho. 1964. *Agricultura, silvicultura, piscicultura, apicultura.* Lourenço Marques.

Cotula, Lorenzo, Sonja Vermeulen, Paul Mathieu, and Camilla Toulmin. 2011. "Agricultural Investment and International Land Deals: Evidence from a Multi-Country Study in Africa." *Food Security* 3 (February): 99–113. https://doi.org/10.1007/s12571-010-0096-x.

Cowen, Michael, and Robert W. Shenton. 1996. *Doctrines of Development.* Routledge.

Cozzens, Taylor. 2015. "Defeating the Devil's Arm: The Victory over the Short-Handled Hoe in California Agriculture." *Agricultural History* 89, no. 4 (October): 494–512. https://doi.org/10.3098/ah.2015.089.4.494.

Craib, Raymond. 2004. *Cartographic Mexico: A History of State Fixations and Fugitive Landscapes.* Duke University Press.

Crehan, Kate. 2016. *Gramsci's "Common Sense" Inequality and Its Narratives.* Duke University Press.

Cronon, William. 1996. "The Trouble with Wilderness: Or, Getting Back to the Wrong Nature." *Environmental History* 1, no. 1 (January): 7–28. https://doi.org/10.2307/3985059.

Cruz, Patrick. 2012. "Embrapa busca inspiração capitalista para crescer." Exame. http://exame.abril.com.br/revista-exame/edicoes/1024/noticias/embrapa-busca-inspiracao-capitalista-para-crescer?page=1.

Cunguara, Benedito, and Joseph Hanlon. 2012. "Whose Wealth Is It Anyway? Mozambique's Outstanding Economic Growth with Worsening Rural Poverty." *Development and Change* 43, no. 3 (May): 623–47. https://doi.org/10.1111/j.1467-7660.2012.01779.x.

Cunguara, Benedito, and Todd Thompson, in collaboration with Kristin Davis of IFPRI. 2018. "Mozambique: Desk Study of Extension and Advisory Services." Developing Local Extension Capacity (DLEC) Project, USAID Cooperative Agreement No. AID-OAAL-16-00002.

Curley, Andrew. 2019. "T'áá hwó ají t'éego and the Moral Economy of Navajo Coal Workers." *Annals of the American Association of Geographers* 109 (1): 71–86. https://doi.org/10.1080/24694452.2018.1488576.

Curley, Andrew, and Sara Smith. 2023. "Unruly River and Plantation Logics." *Annals of the American Association of Geographers* 114, no. 10 (November): 2182–88. https://doi.org/10.1080/24694452.2023.2266014.

Curtin, Philip D. 1990. *The Rise and Fall of the Plantation Complex: Essays in Atlantic History.* Cambridge University Press.

Cusicanqui, Silvia R. 2012. "Ch'ixinakax utxiwa: A Reflection on the Practices and Discourses of Decolonization." *South Atlantic Quarterly* 111 (1): 95–109. https://doi.org/10.1215/00382876-1472612.

Daniel, E. Valentine, Henry Bernstein, and Tom Brass, eds. 1992. *Plantations, Proletarians and Peasants in Colonial Asia.* Frank Cass.

Dávila, Jerry. 2010. *Hotel Trópico: Brazil and the Challenge of African Decolonization, 1950–1980.* Duke University Press.

Davis, Janae, Alex A. Moulton, Levi Van Sant, and Brian Williams. 2019. "Anthropocene, Capitalocene, . . . Plantationocene? A Manifesto for Ecological Justice in an Age of Global Crises." *Geography Compass* 13, no. 5 (May): 1–15. https://doi.org/10.1111/gec3.12438.

De Carli, Carlos Ricardo, and Magda E. S. de F. Wehrmann. 2007. "Embrapa: Precursora da Parceria Público Privada no Brasil." *Cadernos de Estudos e Pesquisas* 11 (26): 73–83.

De Carvalho, Mário. 1969. *A agricultura tradicional de Moçambique.* Lourenço Marques: Missão de Inquérito Agrícola de Moçambique.

De Carvalho, Mário. 1989. "Acção dos técnicos agrários portugueses em Mozambique e seu possível papel no âmbito de eventual cooperação com aquele País." *Revista de Ciencias Agrarias* 12 (2): 107–16.

de Schutter, Olivier. 2014. *Report of the Special Rapporteur on the Right to Food: Final Report; The Transformative Potential of the Right to Food.* United Nations General Assembly. https://digitallibrary.un.org/record/766914?ln=en&v=pdf.

Deininger, Klaus, and Derek Byerlee. 2011. *Rising Global Interest in Farmland: Can It Yield Sustainable and Equitable Benefits?* The International Bank for Reconstruction and Development/The World Bank. https://documents1 .worldbank.org/curated/en/998581468184149953/pdf/594630PUBoID 1810Box358282Bo1PUBLIC1.pdf?_gl=1*gd6ea9*_gcl_au*MTY1 MzA5NTU4Ni4xNzIzMzI3NjUy.

Delêtre, Marc, Doyle B. McKey, and Trevor R. Hodkinson. 2011. "Marriage Exchanges, Seed Exchanges, and the Dynamics of Manioc Diversity." *Proceedings of the National Academy of Sciences* 108, no. 45 (October): 18249–54. https://doi.org/10.1073/pnas.1106259108.

Desmond, Mathew. 2019. "American Capitalism Is Brutal, You Have to Trace That Back to the Plantation." *New York Times Magazine*, August 14.

Dinerman, Alice. 2006. *Revolution, Counter-Revolution and Revisionism in Postcolonial Africa: The Case of Mozambique, 1975–1994.* Routledge.

Direito, Bárbara. 2013. "Land and Colonialism in Mozambique-Policies and Practice in Inhambane, c. 1900–c. 1940." *Journal of Southern African Studies* 39, no. 2 (June): 353–69. http://dx.doi.org/10.1080/03057070.2013.795812.

Drayton, Richard. 2000. *Nature's Government: Science, Imperial Britain, and the "Improvement" of the World.* Yale University Press.

Eça, Artur de Almeida de. 1915. "Comissão de serviço desempenhado no Distrito de Moçambique (Nampula)." *Boletim da Repartição de Agricultura,* 3rd series, nos. 7–9 (July–September).

Eddens, Aaron. 2024. *Seeding Empire: American Philanthrocapital and the Roots of the Green Revolution.* University of California Press.

Edelman, Marc. 2013. "Messy Hectares: Questions About the Epistemology of Land Grabbing Data." *Journal of Peasant Studies* 40, no. 3 (June): 485–501. https://doi.org/10.1080/03066150.2013.801340.

Elden, Stuart. 2010. "Land, Terrain, Territory." *Progress in Human Geography* 34, no. 6 (April): 799–817. https://doi.org/10.1177/0309132510362603.

Elkins, Caroline, and Susan Pedersen. 2005. *Settler Colonialism in the Twentieth Century: Projects, Practices, Legacies.* Taylor and Francis Group.

Ekman, Sigrid, Marianella Stensrud, and Carmen Stella Macamo. 2014. *Brazilian Development Cooperation in Agriculture: A Scoping Study on ProSavana in Mozambique, with Implications for Forests Report.* Center for International Forestry Research.

Embrapa. n.d. "Africa, a Continent Full of Opportunities for Agricultural Research." Accessed September 12, 2012. www.cnpmf.embrapa.br/destaques /AFRICA.pdf.

Embrapa. 2010. *Paralelos: Corredo de Nacala.* Embrapa Monitoramento por Satélite.

Escobar, Arturo. 1995. *Encountering Development: The Making and Unmaking of the Third World.* Princeton University Press.

Escobar, Arturo. 2007. "Worlds and Knowledges Otherwise: The Latin American Modernity/Coloniality Research Program." *Cultural Studies* 21, nos. 2–3 (April): 179–210. https://doi.org/10.1080/09502380601162506.

Escobar, Arturo. 2010. "Latin America at a Crossroads: Alternative Modernizations, Post-Liberalism, or Post-Development?" *Cultural Studies* 24, no. 1 (January): 1–65. https://doi.org/10.1080/09502380903424208.

Esteves, A. Baião. 1967. "Planeamento e Organização do Instituto de Investigação Agronómica de Moçambique." *Agronomia Moçambicana* 1, no. 1 (January–March): 3.

Esteves, A. Baião, and V. Dantas da Silva. 1967. "Engenheiros Agrónomos e Silvicultores ao Serviço de Moçambique." *Agronomia Moçambicana* 1 (2): 55–56.

Esteves, João Damas. 1957. "A agricultura não Indígena de Moçambique—vista através da Estatística (1941/2 a 1951/52)." *Edição da Gazeta do Agricultor, Lourenço Marques*, série B, Divulgação no. 3: 11.

Evans, Peter. 1979. *Dependent Development: The Alliance of Multinational, State, and Local Capital in Brazil*. Princeton University Press.

Ewing, Reese. 2011. "Mozambique Offers Brazilian Farmers Land to Plant," Reuters, August 15. https://www.reuters.com/article/world/mozambique -offers-brazilian-farmers-land-to-plant-idUSJOE77E0O1/.

Fairbairn, Madeleine. 2013. "Indirect Dispossession: Domestic Power Imbalances and Foreign Access to Land in Mozambique." *Development and Change* 44, no. 2 (August): 335–56. https://doi.org/10.1002/9781118688229 .ch7.

Fairbairn, Madeleine. 2014. "Like Gold with Yield: Evolving Intersections Between Finance and Farmland." *Journal of Peasant Studies* 41 (5): 777–95.

Fairbairn, Madeleine. 2021. *Fields of Gold: Financing the Global Land Rush*. Cornell University Press.

Fairhead, James, and Melissa Leach. 1996. *Misreading the African Landscape: Society and Ecology in a Forest-Savanna Mosaic*. Cambridge University Press.

FAOSTAT. 2022. Food and Agriculture Organization of the United Nations. https://www.fao.org/faostat/en/.

Feldman, Shelley, and Charles Geisler. 2012. "Land Expropriation and Displacement in Bangladesh." *Journal of Peasant Studies* 39 (3–4): 971–93.

Ferguson, James. 1994. *The Anti-Politics Machine: Development, Depoliticization, and Bureaucratic Power in Lesotho*. University of Minnesota Press.

Ferrando, Tomaso. 2015. "Dr. Brasília and Mr. Nacala: The Apparent Duality Behind the Brazilian State-Capital Nexus." *Revista de Economia Política* 35, no. 2 (April–June): 343–59. https://doi.org/10.1590/0101-31572015v35 no2a08.

Ferrão, José Eduardo Mendes. 1990. "A evolução do ensino agrícola colonial." *Anais do Instituto Superior de Agronomia* 43: 35–73. http://hdl.handle.net /10400.5/17236.

Ferraz, J. Oliveira. 1914. Response to "Inquérito sôbre a produção de géneros agrícolas coloniais," *Boletim da Repartição de Agricultura*, 3rd series, nos. 13–15 (January–March): 89–90.

Ferraz, J. Oliveira. 1918. Response to request for a survey of agriculture in the district of Lourenço Marques. Reconhecimento Agrícola-Eonomico, Distrito de Lourenço Marques: Manhiça, Sabiè, Magude, e Bilene. In *Relatórios do Agronomo do Distrito 1916–1917*. Lourenço Marques: Emprensa Nacional.

Figueiredo, Estrela, Gideon F. Smith, and Pedro Bingre do Amaral. 2017. "Notes on António de Figueiredo Gomes e Sousa, a Near-Forgotten Collector of Succulent Plants in Mozambique." *Bradleya* 35 (August 1): 186–94. https://doi.org/10.25223/brad.n35.2017.a21.

Fingermann, Natalia. 2013. *Os mitos por trás do ProSAVANA*. IdeIAS No. 49. IESE.

First, Ruth. 1977. "O Mineiro Moçambicano: Um estudo sobre a exportação de mão de obra." Ruth First Papers Project. https://sas-space.sas.ac.uk/4140/.

Fischer, Klara, Jostein Jakobsen, and Ola T. Westengen. 2022. "The Political Ecology of Crops: From Seed to State and Capital." *Geoforum* 130 (March): 92–95. https://doi.org/10.1016/j.geoforum.2021.12.011

Fitzgerald, Deborah Kay. 2005. *Every Farm a Factory*. Yale University Press.

Fitzmaurice, Andrew. 2014. *Sovereignty, Property, and Empire, 1500–2000*. Cambridge University Press.

Flachs, Andrew. 2017. "'Show Farmers': Transformation and Performance in Telangana, India." *Culture, Agriculture, Food, and Environment* 39, no. 1 (June): 25–34. https://doi.org/10.1111/cuag.12085.

Flachs, Andrew, and Paul Richards. 2018. "Playing Development Roles: The Political Ecology of Performance in Agricultural Development." *Journal of Political Ecology* 25 (1): 638–46. https://doi.org/10.2458/v25i1.23089.

Foucault, Michael. 1980. *Power/Knowledge: Selected Interviews and Other Writings, 1972–1977*. Vintage Press.

Freyre, Gilberto. 1933. *Casa-grande & senzala*. Maia & Schmidt.

Freyre, Gilberto. 1940. *O mundo que o português criou: Aspectos das relações sociaes e de cultura do Brasil com Portugal e as colonias portuguesas*. J. Olympio.

Freyre, Gilberto. 1953. *Um Brasileiro em Terras Portuguêses*. Livraria José Olympio.

Funada-Classen, Sayaka. 2013a. *Analysis of the Discourse and Background of the ProSAVANA Programme in Mozambique—Focusing on Japan's Role*. University of Foreign Studies. Tokyo. https://university.open.ac.uk/technology/mozambique/sites/www.open.ac.uk.technology.mozambique/files/files/ProSavana%20Analysis%20based%20on%20Japanese%20source%20(FUNADA2013).pdf.

Funada-Classen, Sayaka. 2013b. "Anatomia Pós-Fukushima dos Estudos sobre o ProSAVANA: Focalizando no 'Os mitos por trás do ProSavana' de Natalia Fingermann." Working Paper No. 12. Observatório do Meio Rural.

Garcia, Francisco Proença. 2003. "Análise Global de uma Guerra (Moçambique 1964-1974)." PhD diss., Universidade Portucalense, Porto, Portugal.

Garcia, Ana, and Karina Kato. 2016. "Políticas públicas e interesses privados: Uma análise a partir do Corredor de Nacala em Moçambique." *Cadernos CRH* 29, no. 76 (January–April): 69–86. https://doi.org/10.1590/S0103-497 92016000100005.

Gaventa, John. 2006. "Finding the Spaces for Change: A Power Analysis." *IDS Bulletin* 37, no. 6 (November). https://doi.org/10.1111/j.1759-5436.2006.tb00320.x.

Geffray, Christian. 1990. *La Cause des armes au Mozambique: Anthropologie d'une guerre civile*. Editions Karthala.

Gêmo, Helder. 2009. "Extensão Rural em Moçambique: Evolução, desafios e perspectivas (1975–2006)." In *Políticas Públicas e Desenvolvimento Rural: Percepções e Perspectivas no Brasil e em Moçambique*, edited by Jalcione Almeida. Editora Popular.

Gengenbach, H., R. A. Schurman, T. J. Bassett, W. A. Munro, and W. G. Moseley. 2018. "Limits of the New Green Revolution for Africa: Reconceptualising Gendered Agricultural Value Chains." *The Geographical Journal* 184 (2): 208–14. https://doi.org/10.1111/geoj.12233.

Gengenbach, Heidi. 2005. *Binding Memories: Women as Tellers and Makers of History in Magude, Mozambique*. Gutenberg-e Electronic Book, joint publication of the American Historical Association and Columbia University Press.

Gengenbach, Heidi. 2019. "From Cradle to Chain? Gendered Struggles for Cassava Commercialisation in Mozambique." *Canadian Journal of Development Studies* 41 (2): 224–42. https://doi.org/10.1080/02255189.2019.1570088.

German, Laura. 2022. *Power/Knowledge/Land: Contested Ontologies of Land and Its Governance in Africa*. University of Michigan Press.

Gerschenkron, Alexander. 1962. *Economic Backwardness in Historical Perspective*. Harvard University Press.

Gill, Bikrum. 2016. "Can the River Speak? Epistemological Confrontation in the Rise and Fall of the Land Grab in Gambella, Ethiopia." *Environment and Planning A: Economy and Space* 48 (4): 699–717. https://doi.org/10.1177/0308518X15610243.

Goldman, Michael. 2005. *Imperial Nature: The World Bank and Struggles for Social Justice in the Age of Globalization*. Yale University Press.

Goldstein, Jenny E., Kasia Paprocki, and Tracy Osborne. 2019. "A Manifesto for a Progressive Land-Grant Mission in an Authoritarian Populist Era." *Annals of the American Association of Geographers* 109, no. 2 (February): 673–84. https://doi.org/10.1080/24694452.2018.1539648.

Gomes e Sousa, Antonio de Figueiredo. 1932. "Elementos para a organização dos serviços agrícolas de Moçambique." *Boletim da Sociedade de Estudos da Colónia de Moçambique* 1, no. 6 (December): 3–25.

Gomes e Sousa, Antonio de Figueiredo. 1939. "Exploradores e Naturalistas da Flora de Moçambique." *Documentário Trimestral* 18: 49–85.

Gonçalves, Euclides. 2020. "Agricultural Corridors as 'Demonstration Fields': Infrastructure, Fairs and Associations Along the Beira and Nacala Corridors of Mozambique." *Journal of Eastern African Studies* 14, no. 2 (March): 354–74. https://doi.org/10.1080/17531055.2020.1743094.

Gorman, Timothy. 2014. "Moral Economy and the Upper Peasant: The Dynamics of Land Privatization in the Mekong Delta." *Journal of Agrarian Change* 14 (4): 501–21.

GRAIN. 2008. "Seized! The 2008 Land Grab for Food and Financial Security." Grain Briefing. https://www.grain.org/article/entries/93-seized-the-2008-landgrab-for-food-and-financial-security.

Grandin, Greg. 2009. *Fordlandia: The Rise and Fall of Henry Ford's Forgotten Jungle City*. Macmillan.

Graziano da Silva, José. 1982. *A Modernização Dolorosa: Estrutura Agrária, Fronteira Agrícola e Trabalhadores Rurais no Brasil*. Zahar Editores.

Griffin, Keith. 1979. *The Political Economy of Agrarian Change: An Essay on the Green Revolution*. Macmillan.

Grilo, Francisco Monteiro. 1926. "O Problema Agrícola de Moçambique" [The problem of agriculture in Mozambique]. Conferência feita pelo engenheiro-agrónomo FMG na Associação dos Lojistas de Lourenço Marques em Março. Cota 5710, ISCSP. Lourenço Marques: Imprensa Nacional.

Grilo, Francisco Monteiro. 1946. *Relatório do chefe dos serviços de Moçambique, Part I and II*. Lourenço Marques: Imprensa Nacional.

Guerreiro, Manuel Gomes. 1964–1965. "A Investigação Científica como Factor de Progresso." *Sociedade de Estudos de Moçambique* 34: 33–34.

Gugganig, Mascha, Karly Ann Burch, Julie Guthman, and Kelly Bronson. 2023. "Contested Agri-Food Futures: Introduction to the Special Issue." *Agriculture and Human Values* 40 (September): 787–98. https://doi.org/10.1007/s10460-023-10493-9.

Gupta, Akhil. 2003. *Postcolonial Developments: Agriculture in the Making of Modern India*. Duke University Press.

Guthman, Julie. 2019. *Wilted: Pathogens, Chemicals, and the Fragile Future of the Strawberry Industry*. University of California Press.

Guthrie, Zachary Kagan. 2018. *Bound for Work: Labor, Mobility and Colonial Rule in Central Mozambique, 1940–1965*. University of Virginia Press.

Hall, Derek. 2013. *Land*. Wiley.

Hall, Derek. 2020a. "National Food Security Through Corporate Globalization: Japan's Changing Place in the Global Grain Trade." *Journal of Peasant Studies* 47 (5): 993–1029. https://doi.org/10.1080/03066150.2019.1615459.

Hall, Derek. 2020b. "Where Is Japan in the Land Rush Debate?" *Canadian Journal of Development Studies* 41 (1): 1–19. https://doi.org/10.1080/02255189.2020.1678461.

Hall, Ruth, Marc Edelman, Saturnino M. Borras Jr., Ian Scoones, Ben White, and Wendy Wolford. 2015. "Resistance, Acquiescence or Incorporation? An Introduction to Land Grabbing and Political Reactions 'from Below.'" *Journal of Peasant Studies* 42 (3–4): 467–88.

Hall, Ruth, and G. Paradza. 2012. "Foxes Guarding the Hen-House: The Fragmentation of 'the State' in Negotiations over Land Deals in Congo and Mozambique." Paper presented at the International Conference on Global Land Grabbing II, October 17–19, Cornell University, Ithaca, NY.

Hanlon, Joseph. 1984. *Mozambique: The Revolution Under Fire*. Zed Press.

Hanlon, Joseph. 2002. "Are Donors to Mozambique Promoting Corruption?" Working Paper No. 15, Open University.

Hanlon, Joseph. 2004. "Renewed Land Debate and the "Cargo Cult" in Mozambique." *Journal of Southern African Studies* 30 (3): 603–25. https://doi.org/10.1080/0305707042000254128.

Haraway, Donna. 2015. "Anthropocene, Capitalocene, Plantationocene, Chthulucene: Making Kin." *Environmental Humanities* 6 (May): 159–65. https://doi.org/10.1215/22011919-3615934.

Haraway, Donna, Noboru Ishikawa, Scott F. Gilbert, Kenneth Olwig, Anna L. Tsing, and Nils Bubandt. 2016. "Anthropologists Are Talking—About the Anthropocene." *Ethnos* 81 (3): 535–64. https://doi.org/10.1080/00141844.2015.1105838.

Harris, Marvin. 1959. "Labour Migration among the Mozambique Thonga: Cultural and Political Factors," *Africa: Journal of the International African Institute*, January, 29(1): 50 – 66.

Harris, Marvin. (1960) 2021. "As 'Alas' Africanas de Portugal." *GUARIMÃ, Revista de Antropologia e Política* 1 (2): 81–108.

Harrison, Graham. 1999. "Corruption as "Boundary Politics": The State, Democratisation, and Mozambique's Unstable Liberalization." *Third World Quarterly* 20 (3): 537–50. https://doi.org/10.1080/01436599913677.

Hart, Gillian. 2001. "Development Critiques in the 1990s: Culs de Sac and Promising Paths." *Progress in Human Geography* 25 (4): 649–58. https://doi.org/10.1191/030913201682689002.

Hart, Gillian. 2002. "Geography and Development: Development/s Beyond Neoliberalism? Power, Culture, Political Economy." *Progress in Human Geography* 26 (6): 812–22.

Hayami, Yujiro, and Vernon W. Ruttan. 1971. *Induced Innovation in Agricultural Development*. Center for Economic Research, Department of Economics, University of Minnesota. University of Minnesota Digital Conservancy. https://hdl.handle.net/11299/54243.

Hayden, Cori. 2003a. "From Market to Market: Bioprospecting's Idioms of Inclusion." *American Ethnologist* 30 (3): 359–71. https://doi.org/10.1525/ae.2003.30.3.359.

Hayden, Cori. 2003b. *When Nature Goes Public: The Making and Unmaking of Bioprospecting in Mexico*. Princeton University Press.

Headrick, Daniel R. 1988. *The Tentacles of Progress: Technology Transfer in the Age of Imperialism, 1850–1940*. Oxford University Press.

Heckler, Serena L. 2004. "Tedium and Creativity: The Valorization of Manioc Cultivation and Piaroa Women." *Journal of the Royal Anthropological Institute* 10 (2): 241–59. https://doi.org/10.1111/j.1467-9655.2004.00188.x.

Heckler, Serena L., and Stanford Zent. 2008. "Piaroa Manioc Varietals: Hyperdiversity or Social Currency?" *Human Ecology* 36, no. 5 (October): 679–97. https://doi.org/10.1007/s10745-008-9193-2.

Henke, Christopher R. 2008. *Cultivating Science, Harvesting Power*. MIT Press.

Henriksen, Thomas H. 1975. "End of an Empire: Portugal's Collapse in Africa." *Current History* 68, no. 405 (May): 211–15. https://www.jstor.org/stable/45313292.

Hetherington, Kregg. 2020. *The Government of Beans: Regulating Life in the Age of Monocrops*. Duke University Press.

Hickey, Amanda, Katherine Young, and Wendy Wolford. 2015. *Building Sustainable Alliances: A Study of Participation in Farmer Fields Schools in Northern Mozambique*. Report for the CARE-WWF Alliance.

High Level Panel of Experts (HLPE). 2013. *Investing in Smallholder Agriculture for Food Security*. A report by The High Level Panel of Experts on Food Security and Nutrition, Vol. 6. FAO, Rome. http://www.fao.org/family-farming/detail/en/c/273868/.

Hillocks, Rory J. 2004. *Research Protocols for Cassava Brown Streak Disease*. Food and Agriculture Organization. https://www.researchgate.net/publication/242197510_RESEARCH_PROTOCOLS_FOR_CASSAVA_BROWN_STREAK_DISEASE.

Hirschman, Albert. 1958. *The Strategy of Economic Development*. Yale University Press.

Hobson, Joseph A. (1902) 1978. *Imperialism: A Study*. University of Michigan Press.

Hodge, Joseph Morgan. 2007. *Triumph of the Expert: Agrarian Doctrines of Development and the Legacies of British Colonialism*. Ohio University Press.

Holston, James. 1991. "The Misrule of Law: Land and Usurpation in Brazil." *Comparative Studies in Society and History* 33 (4): 695–725. https://doi.org/10.1017/S0010417500017291.

Howard, Julie, Eric Crawford, Valerie Kelly, Mulat Demeke, and Jose Jaime Jeje. 2003. "Promoting High-Input Maize Technologies in Africa: The Sasakawa-Global 2000 Experience in Ethiopia and Mozambique." *Food Policy* A28, no. 4 (August): 335–48. https://doi.org/10.1016/j.foodpol.2003.08.008.

Iles, Alistair, Garrett Graddy-Lovelace, Maywa Montenegro, and Ryan Galt. 2016. "Agricultural Systems: Co-Producing Knowledge and Food." In *The Science and Technology Studies Handbook*, 4th ed., edited by Ulrike Felt, Rayvon Fouché, Clark A. Miller, and Laurel Smith-Doerr. MIT Press.

Inso, Egídio. 1929. "A Agricultura na Colónia de Moçambique." *Boletim Agrícola e Pecuário*, nos. 1–2 (January–June).

Instituto de Investigação Agrária de Moçambique (IIAM). 1968. *Relatório Anual*. Maputo: Ministério de Agricultura.

Instituto de Investigação Agrária de Moçambique (IIAM). 2011. *Plano Estratégico 2011–2015*. Maputo: Ministério de Agricultura.

Interim Report. August 2012. *Support Agriculture Development Master Plan in the Nacala Corridor in Mozambique*. For Mozambique: MINAG, DPAs; for Japan: Oriental Consultants Co. Ltd., NTC International Co. Ltd., Task Co. Ltd. https://farmlandgrab.org/uploads/attachment/Prosavana_Report1.pdf.

Isaacman, Allen, Michael Stephen, Yussuf Adam, Maria João Homen, Eugénio Macamo, and Augustinho. 1980. "'Cotton Is the Mother of Poverty': Peasant Resistance to Forced Cotton Production in Mozambique, 1938–1961." *The International Journal of African Historical Studies* 13 (4): 581–615. https://www.jstor.org/stable/218197.

Isaacman Allen F. 1996. *Cotton Is the Mother of Poverty: Peasants, Work, and Rural Struggle in Colonial Mozambique, 1938–1961.* Heinemann.

Isaacman, Allen F., and Barbara Isaacman. 1983. *Mozambique: From Colonialism to Revolution, 1900–1982.* Westview Press.

Isaacman, Allen F., and Barbara S. Isaacman. 2013. *Dams, Displacement, and the Delusion of Development: Cahora Bassa and Its Legacies in Mozambique, 1965–2007.* Ohio University Press.

Isenberg, Nancy. 2017. *White Trash: The 400-Year Untold History of Class in America.* Penguin.

Jain, Lochlann. 2006. *Injury: The Politics of Product Design and Safety Law in the United States.* Princeton University Press.

James, Cyril Lionel Robert. 1963. *The Black Jacobins: Toussaint L'Ouverture and the San Domingo Revolution.* Vintage Books.

Jasanoff, Sheila, ed. 2004. *States of Knowledge: The Co-Production of Science and the Social Order.* Routledge.

Jegathesan, Mythra. 2021. "Black Feminist Plots Before the Plantationocene and Anthropology's 'Regional Closets.'" *Feminist Anthropology* 2, no. 1 (March): 78–93. https://doi.org/10.1002/fea2.12037.

Joaquim, Joana Manuel Matusse, João Mosca, and Ana Sampaio. 2022. "Mudanças nos padrões tradicionais de exploração da terra e do trabalho: o caso da açucareira de Xinavane em Moçambique" [Changes in traditional patterns of land and labor exploitation: The case of the Xinavane sugar mill in Moçambique]. *Brazilian Journal of Development* 8, no. 7 (July): 49052–90. https://doi.org/10.34117/bjdv8n7-028.

Jones, William O. 1959. *Manioc in Africa.* Stanford University Press.

Kajisa, Kei, and Ellen Payongayong. 2011. "Potential of and Constraints to the Rice Green Revolution in Mozambique: A Case Study of the Chokwe Irrigation Scheme." *Food Policy* 36, no. 5 (October): 615–26. https://doi.org/10.1016/j.foodpol.2011.07.002.

Kamm, Henry. 1977. "Portugal's Absurd Empire." *New York Times*, August 18, 204.

Karasch, Mary. 2000. "Manioc." In *The Cambridge World History of Food*, edited by K. Kiple and K. Ornelas. Cambridge University Press. https://doi.org/10.1017/CHOL9780521402149.022.

Kay, Kelly, Chris Knudson, and Alida Cantor. 2023. "Plantation Pasts, Plantation Futures: Resisting Zombie Water Infrastructures in Maui, Hawai'i." *Journal of Peasant Studies* 51, no. 2 (March): 1–24. https://doi.org/10.1080/03066150.2023.2185140.

Kenney-Lazar, Miles, and Noboru Ishikawa. 2019. "Mega-Plantations in Southeast Asia." *Environment and Society* 10 (1): 63–82. https://doi.org/10.3167/ares.2019.100105.

King, Tiffany L. 2016. "The Labor of (Re)Reading Plantation Landscapes Fungible(ly)." *Antipode* 48, no. 4 (September): 1022–39. https://doi.org/10.1111/anti.12227.

Kirshner, Joshua, and Idalina Baptista. 2023. "Corridors as Empty Signifiers: The Entanglement of Mozambique's Colonial Past and Present in its

Development Corridors." *Planning Perspectives* 38, no. 6 (February): 1163–84. https://doi.org/10.1080/02665433.2023.2173636.

Kleibl, Tanja, and Ronaldo Munck. 2016. "Civil Society in Mozambique: NGOs, Religion, Politics and Witchcraft." *Third World Quarterly* 38, no. 1 (August): 203–18. https://doi.org/10.1080/01436597.2016.1217738.

Kloppenburg, Jack. 1988. *First the Seed: The Political Economy of Plant Biotechnology*. University of Cambridge Press.

Komei, Sasaki. 1971. *Inasaku izen* [Farming Practices in Japan Before Rice Farming Came]. NHK Books No. 147. Nippon Hoso Shuppan Kyokai.

Krause, Monika. 2014. *The Good Project: Humanitarian Relief NGOs and the Fragmentation of Reason*. University of Chicago Press.

Kröger, Markus. 2012. "The Expansion of Industrial Tree Plantations and Dispossession in Brazil." *Development and Change* 43, no. 4 (July): 947–73. https://doi.org/10.1111/j.1467-7660.2012.01787.x.

Krupa, Christopher. 2022. *A Feast of Flowers: Race, Labor, and Postcolonial Capitalism in Ecuador*. University of Pennsylvania Press.

Kuhn, Thomas. 1962. *The Structure of Scientific Revolutions*. University of Chicago Press.

Kull, Christian. 2004. *Isle of Fire: The Political Ecology of Landscape Burning in Madagascar*. University of Chicago Press.

Lacerda e Almeida, Dr. Franscisco José de. 1889. *Diário da Viagem: Moçambique para os Rios da Senna feita pelo Governador dos mesmos rios*. Documentos Para a História das Colónias Portuguesas. Lisbon: Imprensa Nacional.

Latham, Michael C. 1984. "International Nutrition and Problems and Policies." In *World Food Issues*, edited by Matthew Drosdoff. Center for the Analysis of World Food Issues, Program in International Agriculture, Cornell University.

Latour, Bruno, Isabelle Stengers, Anna Tsing, and Nils Bubandt. 2018. "Anthropologists Are Talking—About Capitalism, Ecology, and Apocalypse." *Ethnos* 83, no. 3 (April): 587–606. https://doi.org/10.1080/00141844.2018.1457703.

Leitão, A. Borges. 1971. *Ensaios realizados e em curso sobre a cultura da mandioca*. Informação Técnica No. 20. Lourenço Marques: Instituto de Investigação Agronómica de Moçambique.

Levathes, Louise. 1994. *When China Ruled the Seas: The Treasure Fleet of the Dragon Throne, 1405–1433*. Oxford University Press.

Lewis, Arthur. 1954. *The Theory of Economic Growth*. R. D. Irwin.

Li, Tania Murray. 2007. *The Will to Improve: Governmentality, Development, and the Practice of Politics*. Duke University Press.

Li, Tania Murray. 2014. *Land's End: Capitalist Relations on an Indigenous Frontier*. Duke University Press.

Li, Tania Murray. 2018. "After the Land Grab: Infrastructural Violence and the 'Mafia System' in Indonesia's Oil Palm Plantation Zones." *Geoforum* 96 (November): 328–37. https://doi.org/10.1016/j.geoforum.2017.10.012.

Li, Tania Murray. 2023. "Indonesia's Plantationocene." *Annals of the American Association of Geographers* 114, no. 10 (May): 2194–98. https://doi.org/10.1080/24694452.2023.2201633.

Li, Tania Murray, and Pujo Semedi. 2021. *Plantation Life: Corporate Occupation in Indonesia's Oil Palm Zone*. Duke University Press.

Little, Peter D., and Michael Watts. 1994. *Living Under Contract: Contract Farming and Agrarian Transition in Sub-Saharan Africa*. University of Wisconsin Press.

Lopes, Gabriela R., Mairon G. Bastos Lima, and Tiago N. P. dos Reis. 2021. "Maldevelopment Revisited: Inclusiveness and Social Impacts of Soy Expansion over Brazil's Cerrado in Matopiba." *World Development* 139: 105316. https://doi.org/10.1016/j.worlddev.2020.105316.

Lowder, Sarah, Marco V. Sánchez, and Raffaele Bertini. 2021. "Which Farms Feed the World and Has Farmland Become More Concentrated?" *World Development* 142: 105455. https://www.sciencedirect.com/science/article/pii/S0305750X2100067X.

Lowder, Sarah K., Jakob Skoet, and Terri Raney. 2016. "The Number, Size, and Distribution of Farms, Smallholder Farms, and Family Farms Worldwide." *World Development* 87: 16–29.

Lowe, Celia. 2006. *Wild Profusion: Biodiversity Conservation in an Indonesian Archipelago*. Princeton University Press.

Lu, Flora, Gabriela Valdivia, and Wendy Wolford. 2013. "Local Perceptions of Environmental Crisis in the Galápagos Islands, Ecuador." *Conservation and Society* 11 (1): 83–95.

Lugard, Frederick D. 1926. "The White Man's Task in Tropical Africa." *Foreign Affairs* 5 (1): 57–69.

Lund, Christian, and Catherine Boone. 2013. "Introduction: Land Politics in Africa—Constituting Authority over Territory, Property and Persons." *Africa* 83 (1): 1–13.

Lunstrum, Elizabeth. 2011. "State Rationality, Development, and the Making of Sovereign Territory: From Colonial Extraction to Postcolonial Conservation in Mozambique's Massingir District." In *Cultivating the Colonies: Colonial States and Their Environmental Legacies*, edited by Christina Folke Ax, Niels Brimnes, Niklas Thode Jensen, and Karen Oslund. Ohio University Press.

Lyne, Robert Nunez. 1913. *Mozambique: Its Agricultural Development*. T. Fisher Unwin.

Macamo, Elísio. 2005. "Denying Modernity: The Regulation of Native Labour in Colonial Mozambique and Its Postcolonial Aftermath." In *Negotiating Modernity: Africa's Ambivalent Experience*, edited by Elísio Macamo. Africa in the New Millennium. Bloomsbury.

Mahoney, Michael. 2003. "Estado Novo, Homem Novo (New State, New Man): Colonial and Anticolonial Development Ideologies in Mozambique, 1930–1977." In *Staging Growth: Modernization, Development and the*

Global Cold War, edited by David C. Engerman, Nils Gilman, Mark H. Haefele, and Michael E. Latham. University of Massachusetts Press.

Makki, Fouad. 2013. "Development by Dispossession: Terra Nullius and the Social-Ecology of New Enclosures in Ethiopia." *Rural Sociology* 79 (1): 79–103.

Mamdani, Mahmood. 2018. *Citizen and Subject: Contemporary Africa and the Legacy of Late Colonialism*. Princeton University Press.

"Manual de iniciação ao conhecimento económico, agrícola, florestal e pecuário de Moçambique." 1962. Mimeograph. Serviços de Economia e Estatística Geral, Lourenço Marques.

Marchesi, Greta. 2016. "The Blood of Heroes: Nationalist Bodies, National Soils, and the Scientific Conservation of the Federation of Colombian Coffee-Growers (1927–1946)." *Environment and Planning A* 48, no. 4 (August): 736–53. https://doi.org/10.1177/0308518X155974.

Marassiro, Mateus J., Marcelo L. R. de Oliveira, and Sergio F. Come. 2020. "Three Decades of Agricultural Extension in Mozambique: Between Advances and Setbacks." *Journal of Agricultural Studies* 8 (2): 418–39. https://doi.org/10.5296/jas.v8i2.16647.

Martins Santareno, J. A. L. 1973. *Agricultura moçambicana*. Imprensa Nacional de Moçambique.

Mason, Olivia, and James Riding. 2023. "Reimagining Landscape: Materiality, Decoloniality, and Creativity." *Progress in Human Geography* 47, no. 6: 769–89. https://doi.org/10.1177/03091325231205093.

Matusse, Anselmo. 2023. "From Colonial Tea to Postcolonial Rubber Plantations: Tracking the Plantationocene in Lugela District, Mozambique." *Journal of Peasant Studies* 51 (3): 586–602. https://doi.org/10.1080/03066150.2023.2225423.

Maugham, R. C. F. 1906. *Portuguese East Africa*. E. P. Dutton.

Maugham, R. C. F. 1910. *Zambezia: A General Description of the Valley of the Zembezi River, from Its Delta to the River Aroangwa, with Its History, Agriculture, Flora, Fauna and Ethnography*. J. Murray.

Mayreles, Francisco. 1909. "Relatórios do regent Agrícola, Francisco de Mayrelles, dirigidos ao governador do distrito de Inhambane." *Relatórios e Informações*, 307–20. Annexo ao Boletim Official. Lourenço Marques: Imprensa Nacional.

McKay, Ben M. and Henry Veltmeyer. 2021. "Industrial Agriculture and Agrarian Extractivism." In *Handbook of Critical Agrarian Studies*, edited by Aroon H. Akram-Lodhi, Kristina Dietz, Bettina Engels, and Ben M. McKay. ElgarOnline. https://doi.org/10.4337/9781788972468.00065.

McKittrick, Katherine. 2011. "On Plantations, Prisons, and a Black Sense of Place." *Social & Cultural Geography* 12, no. 8 (October): 947–63. https://doi.org/10.1080/14649365.2011.624280.

McKittrick, Katherine. 2013. "Plantation Futures." *Small Axe: A Caribbean Journal of Criticism* 17, no. 3 (November): 1–15. https://doi.org/10.1215/07990537-2378892.

McMichael, Philip. 2000. "World-Systems Analysis, Globalization, and Incorporated Comparison." *Journal of World-Systems Research* 1, no. 3 (November): 68–99. https://doi.org/10.5195/jwsr.2000.192.

McMichael, Philip. 2012. "The Land Grab and Corporate Food Regime Restructuring." *Journal of Peasant Studies* 39 (3, 4): 681–701.

McMichael, Philip. 2014. "Rethinking Land Grab Ontology." *Rural Sociology* 79, no. 1 (March): 34–55. https://doi.org/10.1111/ruso.12021.

McSween, S., Tom Walker, Venâncio Salegua, and Raul Pitoro. 2006. *Economic Impact on Food Security of Varietal Tolerance to Cassava Brown Streak Disease in Coastal Mozambique*. Research Report No. 1E, Institute of Agricultural Research of Mozambique.

Medeiros, Carmen. 2005. "The 'Right to Know How to Understand': Coloniality and Contesting Visions of Development and Citizenship in the Times of Neo-Liberal Civility." PhD diss., City University of New York.

Medeiros, Leonilde. 1989. *A História dos Movimentos Sociais no Campo*. FASE.

Meek, David, and Ligia T. L. Simonian. 2017. "Transforming Space and Society? The Political Ecology of Education in the Brazilian Landless Workers' Movement's Jornada de Agroecología," *Environment and Planning D: Society and Space* 35 (3): 513–32. https://doi.org/10.1177/0263775816667073.

Meemken, Eva-Marie, and Marc F. Bellemare. 2019. "Smallholder Farmers and Contract Farming in Developing Countries." *Proceedings of the National Academy of Sciences, PNAS* 117 (1): 259–64.

Meireles, Francisco de. 1915. *Relatório Sobre a Estação Experimental do Umbeluzi no Ano de 1913*. Lourenço Marques: Imprensa Nacional.

Millennium Challenge Corporation (MCC). n.d.-a. "Mozambique Compact." Accessed April 1, 2015. http://www.mcc.gov/pages/countries/program/mozambique-compact.

Millennium Challenge Corporation (MCC). n.d.-b. "Mozambique's Land Tenure Services Project," Excel spreadsheet in "Mozambique Compact: Spreadsheet Files." Accessed November 7, 2014. http://www.mcc.gov/pages/countries/err/mozambique-compact.

Mintz, Sidney W. 1986. *Sweetness and Power: The Place of Sugar in Modern History*. Penguin.

"The Miracle of the Cerrado," 2010. *The Economist*, August 26.

Missiaen, Edmond. 1969. *Mozambique's Agriculturappppl Economy in Brief*. ERS-USDA. https://ageconsearch.umn.edu/record/316394.

Mitchell, Don. 2021. "Geography Sculpts the Future, or: Escaping—and Falling Back into—the Tyranny of Absolute Space." *Studia Neophilologica* 93, no. 2: 136–54.

Mitchell, Timothy. 2002. *Rule of Experts: Egypt, Techno-Politics, Modernity*. University of California Press.

Mitchell, Timothy. 2011. *Carbon Democracy: Political Power in the Age of Oil*. Verso.

Mitmann, Gregg. 2017. "President's Address: Forgotten Paths of Empire; Ecology, Disease, and Commerce in the Making of Liberia's Plantation

Economy." *Environmental History* 22, no. 1 (January): 1–22. https://doi.org/10.1093/envhis/emw097.

Mitmann, Gregg. 2023. *Empire of Rubber: Firestone's Scramble for Land and Power in Liberia.* The New Press.

Moçambique: Documentário trimestral. 1939. "Número especial comemorativo da viagem de S. Ex.a o Presidente da República, General Óscar de Fragoso Carmona a Moçambique." Portugal, Colónia de Moçambique, E1939.

Monjane, Boaventura. 2023. "Resisting Agrarian Neoliberalism and Authoritarianism: Struggles Towards a Progressive Rural Future in Mozambique." *Journal of Agrarian Change* 23, no. 1 (January): 185–203. https://doi.org/10.1111/joac.12525.

Monjane, Boaventura, and Natacha Bruna. 2019. "Confronting Agrarian Authoritarianism: Dynamics of Resistance to PROSAVANA in Mozambique." *Journal of Peasant Studies* 47 (1): 69–94. https://doi.org/10.1080/03066150.2019.1671357.

Monjane, Boaventura, and Régio Conrado. 2022. *Aporias do Moçambique póscolonial: Estado, Sociedade e Capital.* Daraja Press.

Moore, Jason W. 2017. "The Capitalocene, Part I: On the Nature and Origins of Our Ecological Crisis." *Journal of Peasant Studies* 44, no. 3 (March): 594–630. https://doi.org/10.1080/03066150.2016.1235036.

Moore, Jason W. 2018. "The Capitalocene Part II: Accumulation by Appropriation and the Centrality of Unpaid Work/Energy." *Journal of Peasant Studies* 45 (2): 237–79. https://doi.org/10.1080/03066150.2016.1272587.

Mosca, João. 1999. *A experiência "socialista" em Moçambique (1975–1986).* Instituto Piaget.

Mosca, João. 2005. *Economia de Moçambique: Século XX.* Instituto Piaget.

Mosca, João. 2011. *Políticas agrárias de (em) Moçambique (1975–2009).* Escolar Editora.

Mosca, João, ed. 2016. *Políticas Públicas e Agricultura em Moçambique.* Escolar Editora.

Mosca, João, ed. 2019. *Agro-negócio em Moçambique.* Escolar Editora.

Mosca, João, and Natacha Bruna. 2015. *ProSAVANA: Discursos, práticas e realidades.* Observador Rural No. 31. Observatório do Meio Rural.

Mosca, João, Yara Nova, and Nelson Capaina. 2023. *Sustenta (Resumo): (In)Sustentável?!* Destaque Rural No. 210. Observatório do Meio Rural.

Mosse, David. 2005. "Global Governance and the Ethnography of International Aid." In *The Aid Effect: Giving and Governing in International Development,* edited by David Mosse and David Lewis. Pluto Press.

Mota, Teresa P. 1970. "Características Químico-Analíticas de Algumas Mandiocas em Ensaio: Contribuição para o estudo *Agronomia Mocambicana* 4, no. 1 (January–March): 21–29.

Moyo, Sam, Paris Yeros, and Praveen Jha. 2012. "Imperialism and Primitive Accumulation: Notes on the New Scramble for Africa." *Agrarian South: Journal of Political Economy* 1 (2): 181–203.

"Mozambican Accused in $2 Billion 'Tuna' Scandal Is Extradited to New York." 2023. *New York Times,* July 12.

Navaro, Yael, Zerrin Özlem Biner, Alice von Bieberstein, and Seda Altuğ. 2021. *Reverberations.* University of Pennsylvania Press.

Negrão, José. 2002. "Land in Africa: An Indispensable Element Towards Increasing the Wealth of the Poor." Document Aggregated from the Mokoro Land Rights in Africa publications archive. https://www.landportal.org/library /resources/mokoro5458/land-africa-%E2%80%93-indispensable-element -towards-increasing-wealth-poor.

Nehring, Ryan. 2016. "Yield of Dreams: Marching West and the Politics of Scientific Knowledge at the Brazilian Agricultural Research Corporation (EMBRAPA)." *Geoforum* 77 (December): 206–17. https://doi.org/10.1016 /j.geoforum.2016.11.006.

Nelson, Rebecca, and Richard Coe. 2014. "Transforming Research and Development Practice to Support Agroecological Intensification of Smallholder Farming." *Journal of International Affairs* 67 (2): 107. https://www .jstor.org/stable/24461738.

Newitt, Malyn. 1995. *A History of Mozambique.* Indiana University Press.

Newitt, Malyn. 2001. "Formal and Informal Empire in the History of Portuguese Expansion." *Portuguese Studies* 17 (1): 1–21.

Nguenha, Nicole, Benedito Cunguara, Stella Bialous, Jeffrey Drope, and Raphael Lencucha. 2021. "An Overview of the Policy and Market Landscape of Tobacco Production and Control in Mozambique." *International Journal of Environmental Research and Public Health* 18 (1): 343. https://doi.org /10.3390/ijerph18010343.

Nicholson, Fred T. 1910. "Agriculture in Mozambique: Vast Agricultural and Pastoral Possibilities." *Boletim da Repartição de Agricultura de Moçambique,* no. 1.

Nogueira, Isabela, Ossi Ollinaho, Grasiela Baruco, Alexis Saludjian, José Guedes Pinto, Paulo Balanco, Eduardo Pinto, and Carlos Schonerwald. 2017. "Investimentos e Cooperação do Brasil e o Padrão de Acumulação em Moçambique: Reforçando Dependência e Porosidade?" *Revista NERA* 20, no. 38: 220–54. https://doi.org/10.47946/rnera.v0i38.5299.

Norfolk, Simon, and Christopher Tanner. 2007. *Improving Tenure Security for the Rural Poor.* FAO.

Nunes, Salvador, A. R. 1964. "Contribuição para o estudo da qualidade das mandiocas em ensaio no posto Agrícola da Mahalamba." Separata do *Boletim da Sociedade de Estudos de Moçambique.* 6664 COTA ISCP.

O'Connor, K. 2013. "Beyond 'Exotic Groceries': Tapioca/Cassava/Manioc, a Hidden Commodity of Empires and Globalisation." In *Global Histories, Imperial Commodities, Local Interactions,* edited by J. Curry-Machado. Cambridge Imperial and Post-Colonial Studies Series. Palgrave Macmillan.

Ofstehage, Andrew. 2012. "The Construction of an Alternative Quinoa Economy: Balancing Solidarity, Household Needs, and Profit in San Agustín,

Bolivia." *Agriculture and Human Values* 29 (4): 441–54. https://doi.org/10.1007/s10460-012-9371-0.

Ofstehage, Andrew. 2018. "Farming Out of Place: Transnational Family Farmers, Flexible Farming, and the Rupture of Rural Life in Bahia, Brazil." *American Ethnologist* 45, no. 3 (August): 317–29. https://doi.org/10.1111/amet.12667.

O'Laughlin, Bridget. 1995. "Past and Present Options: Land Reform in Mozambique." *Review of African Political Economy* 22 (63): 99–106. https://doi.org/10.1080/03056249508704104.

O'Laughlin, Bridget. 1996. "Through a Divided Glass: Dualism, Class and the Agrarian Question in Mozambique." *Journal of Peasant Studies* 23 (4): 1–39. https://doi.org/10.1080/03066159608438618.

O'Laughlin, Bridget. 2000. "Class and the Customary: The Ambiguous Legacy of the Indigenato in Mozambique." *African Affairs* 99 (January): 5–42. https://doi.org/10.1093/afraf/99.394.5.

O'Laughlin, Bridget. 2002. "Proletarianisation, Agency and Changing Rural Livelihoods: Forced Labour and Resistance in Colonial Mozambique." *Journal of Southern African Studies* 28 (3): 511–30. https://doi.org/10.1080/0305707022000006495.

Paiva, Ruí Miller. 1952. *A Agricultura na África*. São Paulo: The Secretary of Agriculture for the State of São Paulo.

Paprocki, Kasia. 2018. "Threatening Dystopias: Development and Adaption Regimes in Bangladesh." *Annals of the American Association of Geographers* 108, no. 4 (Janeiro): 955–73. https://doi.org/10.1080/24694452.2017.1406330.

Paprocki, Kasia. 2021. *Threatening Dystopias: The Global Politics of Climate Change Adaptation in Bangladesh*. Cornell University Press.

Paquette, Gabriel B. 2013. *Imperial Portugal in the Age of Atlantic Revolutions: The Luso-Brazilian World, c. 1770–1850*. Cambridge University Press.

Paredes, Alyssa. 2021. "Experimental Science for the 'Bananapocalypse': Counter Politics in the Plantationocene." *Ethnos* 88 (4): 837–63. https://doi.org/10.1080/00141844.2021.1919172.

Patel, Raj. 2012. "ProSavana, Anti-Peasant." http://rajpatel.org/2012/10/24/prosavana-antipeasant/.

Peet, Richard, and Michael Watts. 1996. "Liberation Ecology: Development, Sustainability and Environment in an Age of Market Triumphalis." In *Liberation Ecologies: Environment, Development, Social Movements*, edited by R. Peet and M. Watts. Routledge.

Peluso, Nancy, and Jesse Ribot. 2009. "A Theory of Access." *Rural Sociology* 68, no. 2 (October): 153–81. https://doi.org/10.1111/j.1549-0831.2003.tb00133.x.

Peluso, Nancy L., and Christian Lund. 2011. "New Frontiers of Land Control: Introduction." *Journal of Peasant Studies* 38 (4): 667–81.

Penvenne, Jeanne Marie. 2005. "Settling Against the Tide: The Layered Contradictions of Twentieth-Century Portuguese Settlement in Mozambique."

In *Settler Colonialism in the Twentieth Century: Projects, Practices, Legacies,* edited by C. Elkins and S. Pedersen. Taylor and Francis Group.

Penvenne, Jeanne Marie. 2015. *Women, Migration and the Cashew Economy in Southern Mozambique.* James Currey.

Pereira, Pedro Schacht. 2022. "The (in)Tangible Legacy of 'Generic Lusotropicalism': Unexamined Links in the Textual History of 'Portuguese Humane Colonialism.'" *Portuguese Literary and Cultural Studies* 36/37: 53–80.

Perelman, Michael. 2000. *The Invention of Capitalism: Classical Political Economy and the Secret History of Primitive Accumulation.* Duke University Press.

Pérez Niño, Helena. 2016. "Class Dynamics in Contract Farming: The Case of Tobacco Production in Mozambique." *Third World Quarterly* 37 (10): 1787–1808.

Pérez Ninõ, Helena. 2017. "Migrant Workers into Contract Farmers: Processes of Labour Mobilization in Colonial and Contemporary Mozambique." *Africa* 87, no. 1: 79–99. https://doi.org/10.1017/S000197201600070X

Perfecto, Ivette, and John Vandermeer. 2010. "The Agroecological Matrix as Alternative to the Land-Sparing/Agriculture Intensification Model." *Proceedings of the National Academy of Sciences of the United States of America* 107, no. 13 (March): 5786–91. https://doi.org/10.1073/pnas.0905455107.

Perin, Vanessa Parreira. 2020. "'The Speed of the Political Is Not That of the Scientific': On the Time of Development in an Agricultural Technology Transfer Program," *Vibrant: Virtual Brazilian Anthropology* 17. https://doi.org/10.1590/1809-43412020v17a356.

Perin, Vanessa Parreira. 2023. "Plantation Designs in Northern Mozambique: Development, Struggles and (Re)compositions Facing the ProSAVANA Program." *Tapuya: Latin American Science, Technology and Society* 6 (1). https://doi.org/10.1080/25729861.2023.2252122.

Perkins, John H. 1997. *Geopolitics and the Green Revolution: Wheat, Genes, and the Cold War.* Oxford University Press.

Petitcorps, Colette Le, Marta Macedo, and Irene Peano, eds. 2023. *Global Plantations in the Modern World: Sovereignties, Ecologies, Afterlives.* Palgrave Macmillan.

Pingali, Prabhu. 2015. "Agricultural Policy and Nutrition Outcomes—Getting Beyond the Preoccupation with Staple Grains." *Food Security* 7 (3): 583–91. https://doi.org/10.1007/s12571-015-0461-x.

Pitcher, Anne. 1998. "Disruption Without Transformation: Agrarian Relations and Livelihoods in Nampula Province, Mozambique 1975–1995." *Journal of Southern African Studies* 24 (1): 115–40. https://doi.org/10.1080/03057079808708569.

Pitcher, Anne. 2002. *Transforming Mozambique: The Politics of Privatization.* Cambridge University Press.

Polanyi, Karl. 1945. *The Great Transformation: The Political and Economic Origins of Our Time.* Beacon Press.

Pritchard, Sara. 2012. "From Hydroimperialism to Hydrocapitalism: 'French' Hydraulics in France, North Africa, and Beyond." *Social Studies of Science* 42, no. 4 (April): 591–615. https://doi.org/10.1177/0306312712443018.

Pritchard, Sara, Steven Wolf, and Wendy Wolford. 2016. "Knowledge and the Politics of Land." *Environment and Planning A: Economy and Space* 48 (4): 616–25. https://doi.org/10.1177/0308518X1560417.

PROAGRI Final Evaluation. 2007. *Final Evaluation of the First Phase of the National Agriculture Development Programme PROAGRI (1999–2005)*. Main Report.

ProSavana. 2009. "Minutes of Meeting on Triangular Cooperation for Agricultural Development of the Tropical Savannah in Mozambique." Maputo, September 17. https://farmlandgrab.org/uploads/attachment/5.pdf.

PROSAVANA-PD. 2013. *Agriculture Development Master Plans in the Nacala Corridor in Mozambique*. Report No. 2, Quick Impact Projects, Triangular Cooperation for Agricultural Development of the Tropical Savannah in Mozambique. Mimeo. MINAG.

Quijano, Anibal. 2008. "Coloniality of Power, Eurocentrism, and Social Classification." In *Coloniality at Large: Latin America and the Postcolonial Debate*, edited by Mabel Moraña, Enrique Dussel, and Carlos A. Jáuregui. Duke University Press.

Quijano, Anibal. 2000. "Coloniality of Power, Eurocentrism and Latin America." *Nepantla* 1 (3): 533–80.

Ramisch, Joshua J. 2011. "Experiments as 'Performances': Interpreting Farmers' Soil Fertility Management Practices in Western Kenya." In *Knowing Nature, Transforming Ecologies: Science, Power, and Practice*, edited by Mara J. Goldman, Paul Nadasdy, and Matthew Turner. University of Chicago Press.

Rasmussen, Mattias B., and Christian Lund. 2018. "Reconfiguring Frontier Spaces: The Territorialization of Resource Control." *World Development* 101 (January): 388–99. https://doi.org/10.1016/j.worlddev.2017.01.018.

"Relatórios e informações: Projecto de reorganização e orçamento da Repartição de Agriculture." 1913. *Boletim da Repartição de Agricultura*, no. 5 (August).

Ribeiro, Darcy. 2006. *O povo brasileiro*. Companhia de Bolso.

Ribeiro Da Silva, Filipa. 2016. "Political Changes and Shifts in Labour Relations in Mozambique, 1820s–1920s." *International Review of Social History* 61: 115–35.

Ribeiro, Ruy. 1962. "Temos de produzir mais, melhor, e mais depressa, aumentando os rendimentos." Sessão de encerramento do I Congresso Agrário de Moçambique. *Gazeta do Agricultor* 14, no. 157 (June): 169–70.

Riedl, Rachel Beatty, Paul Friesen, Jennifer McCoy, and Kenneth Roberts. 2024. "Democratic Backsliding, Resilience, and Resistance." *World Politics* 77: 151–77. https://dx.doi.org/10.1353/wp.0.a917802.

Rivera, Willian, and Gary Alex, eds. 2004. "National Strategy and Reform Process: Agriculture and Rural Development." World Bank, Discussion Paper 12.

Robbins, Paul. 2001a. "Fixed Categories in a Portable Landscape: The Causes and Consequences of Land-Cover Categorization." *Environment and Planning A Economy and Space* 33, no. 1 (January): 161–79. https://doi.org/10.1068/a3379.

Robbins, Paul. 2001b. "Tracking Invasive Land Covers in India, or Why Our Landscapes Have Never Been Modern." *Annals of the Association of American Geographers* 91 (4): 637–59. https://doi.org/10.1111/0004-5608.00263.

Rodrigues, Almirante Manuel Maria Sarmento. 1962. "Inaugural Address, Primeiro Congresso Agrário de Moçambique." Lourenço Marques, June 4–9.

Rodrigues, Armando Lourenço. 1960. "A Produção no Sector Indígena de Moçambique." PhD diss., Instituto Superior de Estudos Ultramarinos.

Rogers, Everett M. 1983. *Diffusion of Innovations*. 3rd ed. The Free Press.

Ruttan, Vernon. 1960. "Research on the Economics of Technological Change in American Agriculture." *Journal of Farm Economics* 42: 735–54. https://www.jstor.org/stable/1235109.

Ryan, Bryce, and Neal C. Gross. 1943. "The Diffusion of Hybrid Seed Corn in Two Iowa Communities." *Rural Sociology* 8, no. 1 (March): 15.

Sachs, Jeffrey. 2005. *The End of Poverty: Economic Possibilities for Our Time*. Penguin Press.

Santos, Paulo Cavique. 1934. "Os Serviços de Agricultura e o Jardim Colonial: Quais São, nas condições presentes, as ligações do Jardim com os Serviços de Agricultura das Colônias." In "The First Colonial Exposition of Portugal, Porto." Thesis presented by the Eng Agron and Silvicultor. Arquivo Histórico Ultramarino 781.

Saraiva, Tiago. 2009. "Laboratories and Landscapes: The Fascist New State and the Colonization of Portugal and Mozambique." *Journal of History of Science and Technology* 3 (Fall): 35–61.

Saraiva, Tiago. 2016a. *Fascist Pigs: Technoscientific Organisms and the History of Fascism*. MIT Press.

Saraiva, Tiago. 2016b. "Fascist Modernist Landscapes: Wheat, Dams, Forests, and the Making of the Portuguese New State." *Environmental History* 21, no. 1 (January): 54–75. https://doi.org/10.1093/envhis/emv116.

Sassen, Saskia. 2013. "Land Grabs Today: Feeding the Disassembling of National Territory." *Globalizations* 10 (1): 25–46.

Saul, John S. 1985. "Briefing: Socialist Transition and External Intervention; Mozambique and South Africa's War." *LABOUR, Capital and Society* 18, no. 1 (April): 153–70.

Schumacher, Ernst F. 1973. *Small Is Beautiful: Economics as If People Mattered*. Harper and Row.

Schurman, Rachel. 2017. "Building an Alliance for Biotechnology in Africa." *Journal of Agrarian Change* 17, no. 3 (July): 441–58. https://doi.org/10.1111/joac.12167.

Schwartz, Stuart B. 1986. *Sugar Plantations in the Formation of Brazilian Society: Bahia, 1550–1835*. Cambridge University Press.

Scott, James. C. 2017. *Against the Grain: A Deep History of the Earliest States.* Yale University Press.

Scoones, Ian, Lídia Cabral, and H. Tugendhat. 2013. "New Development Encounters: China and Brazil in African Agriculture." *IDS Bulletin* 44, no. 4 (June): 1–19. https://doi.org/10.1111/1759-5436.12038.

Scoones, Ian, Ruth Hall, Saturnino M. Borras Jr., Ben White, and Wendy Wolford. 2013. "The Politics of Evidence: Methodologies for Understanding the Global Land Rush." *Journal of Peasant Studies* 40, no. 3 (June): 469–83. https://doi.org/10.1080/03066150.2013.801341.

Seed, Patricia. 1995. *Ceremonies of Possession in Europe's Conquest of the New World, 1492–1640.* Cambridge University Press.

Serra, Carlos. 2000. *História de Moçambique: Primeiras sociedades sedentárias e impacto dos mercadores (200/300–1885) e Agressão Imperialista, 1886–1930.* Vol. 1. Imprensa Universitária.

Shankland, Alex, and Euclides Gonçalves. 2016. "Imagining Agricultural Development in South–South Cooperation: The Contestation and Transformation of ProSAVANA." *World Development* 81 (May): 35–46. https://doi.org/10.1016/j.worlddev.2016.01.002.

Sheldon, Kathleen Eddy, and Jeanne Marie Penvenne, 2025. "Mozambique." *Encyclopedia Britannica.* https://www.britannica.com/place/Mozambique, Accessed June 05, 2025.

Sigaud, Lygia. 1979. *Os clandestinos e os direitos.* Duas Cidades.

Sim, T. R. 1910. "Our Natural Resources: The Rich Limpopo Valley." *Boletim da Repartição de Agricultura de Moçambique*, no. 1.

Slater, Candace. 2001. *Entangled Edens: Visions of the Amazon.* University of California Press.

Smart, Teresa, and Joseph Hanlon. 2014. *Galinhas e Cerveja: Uma receita para o crescimento.* Kapicua.

Sneddon, Christopher. 2015. *Concrete Revolution: Large Dams, Cold War Geopolitics, and the US Bureau of Reclamation.* University of Chicago Press.

Staatz, John M., and Carl K. Eicher. 1998. "Agricultural Development Ideas in Historical Perspective." In *International Agricultural Development*, 3rd ed., edited by C. K. Eicher and J. M. Staatz. Johns Hopkins University Press.

"State Loans at Heart of Mozambique Debt Scandal." 2017. *Financial Times,* June 25.

Stein, Stanley. 1986. *Vassouras: A Brazilian Coffee County, 1850–1900.* The Roles of Planter and Slave in a Plantation Society. Princeton University Press.

Stock, Ryan. 2023. "Power for the Plantationocene: Solar Parks as the Colonial Form of an Energy Plantation." *Journal of Peasant Studies* 50 (1): 162–84. https://doi.org/10.1080/03066150.2022.2120812.

Stolcke, Verena. 1988. *Coffee Planters, Workers and Wives.* St. Martin's Press.

Stoler, Ann L. 1985. *Capitalism and Confrontation in Sumatra's Plantation Belt, 1870–1979.* Yale University Press.

Sumich, Jason. 2010. "The Party and the State: Frelimo and Social Stratification in Post-Socialist Mozambique." *Development and Change* 41, no. 4 (August): 679–98. https://doi.org/10.1111/j.1467-7660.2010.01653.x.

Sundberg, Juanita. 2003. "Conservation and Democratization: Constituting Citizenship in the Maya Biospehere Reserve, Guatemala." *Political Geography* 22, no. 7 (September): 715–40. https://doi.org/10.1016/S0962-6298(03)00076-3.

Tanner, Christopher. 2010. "Land Rights and Enclosures: Implementing the Mozambican Land Law in Practice." In *The Struggle over Land in Africa Conflicts, Politics*, edited by W. Anseeuw and C. Alden. HSRC Press.

Tarlau, Rebecca. 2021. *Occupying Schools, Occupying Land: How the Landless Workers Movement Transformed Brazilian Education*. Global and Comparative Ethnography Series. Oxford University Press.

Tarp, Finn, Channing Arndt, Henning Jensen, Sherman Robinson, and Rasmus Heltberg. 2002. *Facing the Development Challenge in Mozambique: An Economywide Perspective*. Research Reports No. 126, International Food Policy Research Institute (IFPRI).

Teisch, Jessica B. 2011. *Engineering Nature: Water, Development, and the Global Spread of American Environmental Expertise*. University of North Carolina Press.

Thomas, Deborah. 2016. "Time and the Otherwise: Plantations, Garrisons, and Being Human in the Caribbean." *Anthropological Theory* 16, nos. 2–3 (March): 177–200. https://doi.org/10.1177/1463499616636269.

Thomas, Deborah. 2023. "Afterlives: The Recursive Plantation." In *Global Plantations in the Modern World: Sovereignties, Ecologies, Afterlives*, edited by Colette Le Petitcorps, Marta Macedo, and Irene Peano. Palgrave Macmillan.

Thomas, Stephen. 1992. "Sustainability in NGO Relief and Development Work: Further Thoughts from Mozambique." *Development in Practice* 2 (1): 37–46. https://doi.org/10.1080/096145249100076531.

Thompson, Edward P. 1971. "The Moral Economy of the English Crowd in the 18th Century." *Past and Present* 50: 76–136.

Tilley, Helen. 2011. *Africa as a Living Laboratory: Empire, Development, and the Problem of Scientific Knowledge, 1870–1950*. University of Chicago Press.

Tomás, António. 2016. "Introduction: Decolonising the 'Undecolonisable'? Portugal and the Independence of Lusophone Africa." *Social Dynamics* 42, no. 1 (April): 1–11. https://doi.org/10.1080/02533952.2016.1164956.

Trindade, João Carlos, and Alda Salamão, eds. 2016. *Avaliação da Governação de Terras em Moçambique*. LGAF-Moçambique/2015–2016. Maputo.

Tsing, Anna L., Andrew S. Mathews, and Nils Bubandt. 2019. "Patchy Anthropocene: Landscape Structure, Multispecies History, and the Retooling of Anthropology." *Current Anthropology* 60: S186–97. https://doi.org/10.1086/703391.

"Tuna and Gunships: How 850$ Million in Bonds Went Bad in Mozambique." 2016. *Wall Street Journal*, April 3.

United Nations. 2009. "Food Production Must Double by 2050 to Meet Demand from World's Growing Population, Innovative Strategies Needed to Combat Hunger, Experts Tell Second Committee." https://www.un.org/press/en/2009/gaef3242.doc.htm.

United States Agency for International Development (USAID). 2011. *AgCLIR Mozambique: Commercial, Legal, and Institutional Reforms in Mozambique's Agriculture Sector.* Washington.

Vail, Leroy. 1976. "Mozambique's Chartered Companies: The Rule of the Feeble." *The Journal of African History* 17 (3): 389–416. https://doi.org/10.1017/S0021853700000505.

Vail, Leroy, and Landeg White. 1978. "Plantation Protest: The History of a Mozambican Song." *Journal of Southern African Studies* 5 (1): 1–25. https://www.jstor.org/stable/2636763.

Valladas Paes, Miguel de Jesus. 1910. "Guia prático do agricultor colonial" [Practical guide for the colonial farmer]. *Boletim da Repartição de Agricultura de Moçambique,* no. 3: 219–44.

Veltmeyer, Henry, and Arturo Ezquerro-Cañete. 2023. "Agro-extractivism." *Journal of Peasant Studies* 50, no. 5: 1673–86. https://doi.org/10.1080/03066150.2023.2218802.

Vergès, Françoise. 2017. "Racial Capitalocene." In *Futures of Black Radicalism,* edited by Gaye T. Johnson and Alex Lubin. Verso.

Viana, A. Fragoso. 1938. *Moçambique documentação trimestral 16.* Lisbon.

Vieira, Carlos de Melo. 1936. "Aproveitamento e desenvolvimento das culturas mais apropriadas para definir e manter um regime de economia indígena baseado na riqueza Agrícola, natural, da Colônia, definindo a forma de o impulsionar e organização de instituições de previdência indígena destinadas a concorrer para esse impulse e para o aperfeiçoamento do sistema." Ppresentation at the Primeira Conferência Económica do Império Colonial Português, Third Commission, on Indigenous Agriculture, Lisboa.

Vilhena, Ernesto Jardim de. 1910. *A Mão de Obra Agrícola em Moçambique.* Memorial to be presented to the International Congress of Colonial Agronomy in Brussels. Lisboa: A Editora (Ministério da Marinha e Ultramar).

Wainwright, Joel. 2008. *Decolonizing Development: Colonial Power and the Maya.* Wiley-Blackwell.

Walker, Cherryl. 2008. *Landmarked: Land Claims and Land Restitution in South Africa.* Jacana Press; Ohio University Press.

Walsh-Dilley, Marygold. 2013. "Negotiating Hybridity in Highland Bolivia: Indigenous Moral Economy and the Expanding Market for Quinoa." *Journal of Peasant Studies* 40, no. 4 (September): 659–82. https://doi.org/10.1080/03066150.2013.825770.

Warman, Arturo. 2003. *Corn and Capitalism: How a Botanical Bastard Grew to Global Dominance.* University of North Carolina Press.

Watts, Michael. 2003. "Development and Governmentality." *Singapore Journal of Tropical Geography* 24 (1): 6–34.

Watts, Michael. 2004. "Resource Curse? Governmentality, Oil and Power in the Niger Delta, Nigeria." *Geopolitics* 9 (1): 50–80. https://doi.org/10.1080/14650040412331307832.

Watts, Michael. (1983) 2013. *Silent Violence: Food, Famine, and Peasantry in Northern Nigeria*. University of Georgia Press.

Welker, Marina. 2012. "The Green Revolution's Ghost: Unruly Subjects of Participatory Development in Rural Indonesia." *American Ethnologist* 39, no. 2 (May): 389–406. https://doi.org/10.1111/j.1548-1425.2012.01371.x.

Whatmore, Sarah. 2002. *Hybrid Geographies: Natures Cultures Spaces*. University of Oxford Press.

White, Ben, Saturnino M. Borras Jr., Ruth Hall, Ian Scoones, and Wendy Wolford. 2012. "The New Enclosures: Critical Perspectives on Corporate Land Deals." *Journal of Peasant Studies* 39, nos. 3–4 (May): 619–47. https://doi.org/10.1080/03066150.2012.691879.

Wise, Timothy. 2014. "What Happened to the Biggest Land Grab in Africa? Searching for ProSavana in Mozambique." Food Tank. https://foodtank.com/news/2014/12/what-happened-to-the-biggest-land-grab-in-africa-searching-for-prosavana-in/.

Wolford, Wendy. 2004. "This Land Is Ours Now: Spatial Imaginaries and the Struggle for Land in Brazil." *Annals of the Association of American Geographers* 94 (2): 409–24. https://doi.org/10.1111/j.1467-8306.2004.09402015.x.

Wolford, Wendy. 2005. "Agrarian Moral Economies and Neoliberalism in Brazil: Competing Worldviews and the State in the Struggle for Land." *Environment and Planning A* 37, no. 2 (February): 241–61. https://doi.org/10.1068/a3745.

Wolford, Wendy. 2008. "Environmental Justice and the Construction of Scale in Brazilian Agriculture." *Society and Natural Resources* 21, no. 7 (July): 641–55. https://doi.org/10.1080/08941920802096432.

Wolford, Wendy. 2010. *This Land Is Ours Now: Social Mobilization and the Meanings of Land in Brazil*. Duke University Press.

Wolford, Wendy. 2015. "From Pangaea to Partnership: The Many Fields of Rural Development." *Sociology of Development* 1, no. 2 (June): 210–32. https://doi.org/10.1525/sod.2015.1.2.210.

Wolford, Wendy. 2021a. "The Plantationocene: A Lusotropical Contribution to the Theory." *Annals of the American Association of Geographers* 111, no. 6 (February): 1622–39. https://doi.org/10.1080/24694452.2020.1850231.

Wolford, Wendy. 2021b. "The Colonial Roots of Agricultural Modernization in Mozambique: The Role of Research from Portugal to ProSavana." *Journal of Peasant Studies* 48 (2): 254–73. https://doi.org/10.1080/03066150.2019.1680541.

Wolford, Wendy, Saturnino M. Borras Jr., Ruth Hall, Ian Scoones, and Ben White. 2014. "Governing Global Land Deals: The Role of the State in the

Rush for Land." *Development and Change* 44 (2): 189–210. https://doi.org/10.1002/9781118688229.ch1.

Wolford, Wendy, and R. Nehring. 2015. "Constructing Parallels: Brazilian Expertise and the Commodification of Land, Labour and Money in Mozambique." *Canadian Journal of Development Studies/Revue canadienne d'études du développement* 36 (2): 208–23. https://doi.org/10.1080/02255189.2015.1036010.

Wolford, Wendy W., Ben White, Ian Scoones, Ruth Hall, Marc Edelman, and Saturnino M. Borras. 2024. "Global Land Deals: What Has Been Done, What Has Changed, and What's Next?" *Journal of Peasant Studies* 1–38. https://doi.org/10.1080/03066150.2024.2325685.

Woods, Clive. 1998. *Development Arrested: The Blues and Plantation Power in the Mississippi Delta.* Verso Books.

World Bank. 1997. *PROAGRI—Joint Donor Pre-Appraisal Mission, 1997.* Aide Memoire, Final Draft, March 6, 1997. Mozambique: Agricultural Sector Memorandum, vol. 2, Main Report. Report No. 16529 Moz.

World Bank. 1999. *Project Appraisal Document on a Proposed Adaptable Program Credit in the Amount of SDR 21.7 Million to the Republic of Mozambique in Support of the First Phase of an Agricultural Sector Public Expenditure Program (PROAGRI).* Report No. 18862 MOZ, January 22.

World Bank. 2009. *Awakening Africa's Sleeping Giant: Prospects for Commercial Agriculture in the Guinea Savannah Zone and Beyond.* Agriculture and Rural Development Notes, No. 48. http://documents.worldbank.org/curated/en/312591468004457911.

World Bank. 2011. *Bridging the Atlantic: Brazil and Sub-Saharan Africa, South-South Partnering for Growth.* World Bank.

Wuyts, Marc. 2001. *The Agrarian Question in Mozambique's Transition and Reconstruction.* United Nations University, World Institute for Development Economics Research Helsinki.

Wynter, Sylvia. 1971. "Novel and History, Plot and Plantation." *Savacou* 5 (June): 95–102.

Young, Thomas. 1988. "The Politics of Development in Angola and Mozambique." *African Affairs* 87 (347): 165–84. https://www.jstor.org/stable/722399.

Zoomers, Annelies. 2010. "Globalisation and the Foreignisation of Space: Seven Processes Driving the Current Global Land Grab." *Journal of Peasant Studies* 37, no. 2 (April): 429–47. https://doi.org/10.1080/03066151003595325.

ARCHIVAL MATERIALS

Repositories consulted in Lisbon:

Geographic Society of Lisbon (SGL)

Lisbon School of Economics and Management (ISEG)

National Overseas Bank (BNU) historical archive

Superior Institute for the Social and Political Sciences (ISCSP)

Torre do Tombo National Archives

Canto e Castro. 1901. "Visita aos palmares de Sofala, Chiloane e Govuro." Beira, July 24. Companhia de Moçambique, 963 Mç. 543, Cx. 527, Cap. 5. PT/TT/CMZ-ADGL/H-B-E/02/29. Arquivo Nacional Torre do Tombo, Lisbon, Portugal.

Companhia de Moçambique. 1902. "O território de Manica e Sofala e a administração de Companhia de Moçambique (1892–1900)." Monographia para ser presente ao Congresso colonial promovido pela Sociedade de Geographia de Lisboa em 1901. Companhia Nacional Editora, Lisbon.

Companhia de Moçambique. 1910. "Aos Senhores Chefes de Circumscripção: Concessões de Terenos." July 15. Companhia de Moçambique, Lisbon, Portugal. No. de Ordem 2168, no. 476 AJ28, Circular no. 8/1650, Beira. PT/TT/CMZ-ADGL/H-F-A/001/0010/28, Arquivo Nacional, Torre do Tombo, Lisbon, Portugal.

Companhia de Moçambique. 1913a. Letter from José Emílio Pinheiro de Azevedo about a concession in Mozambique. March 14. Companhia de Moçambique, Lisbon, Portugal. Mç. 524, Cap. 21, Cx. 508, N.R. 392. PT/TT/CMZ-ADGL/H-B-E/01/05, Arquivo Nacional, Torre do Tombo, Lisbon, Portugal.

Companhia de Moçambique. 1913b. Letter from L. M. Wyllie to Governor General. March 31. Companhia de Moçambique, Lisbon, Portugal. 958 Mç 538 Cx. 522, Cap. 8. 120 Cap. no. 1, doc. no. 2. PT/TT/CMZ-ADGL/H-B-E/02/21, Arquivo Nacional, Torre do Tombo, Lisbon, Portugal.

Companhia de Moçambique. 1928. Communication about Anibal Rezende, local official tried and found guilty of mistreating the local régulo. September 11. Companhia de Moçambique, Lisbon, Portugal. No. de Ordem 1246 Cx, 792, Mç. 826. PT/TT/CMZ-ADGL/H-C/2/424, Arquivo Nacional, Torre do Tombo, Lisbon, Portugal.

Coulombier, F. 1903. "Annual Report from the Experimental Garden of Mambone: Company of Moçambique Document on Mambone." Companhia de Moçambique, Lisbon, Portugal. ca-PTT-TT-CM-ordem2179-No853-AV2_c0001, Arquivo Nacional, Torre do Tombo, Lisbon, Portugal.

de Azevedo, José Emílio Pinheiro de. 1913. "Letter to the Territorial Governor." January 31. Companhia de Moçambique, Lisbon, Portugal. Mç. 524, Cap. 21, Cx. 508. Arquivo Nacional, Torre do Tombo, Lisbon, Portugal.

Lopes, Manuel Monteiro. 1907. Alguns Usos e Costumes Indígenas da Circunscrição de Sofala. March 22. Companhia de Moçambique. No. de Ordem 2193, RA23. PT/TT/CMZ-ADGL/H-F-A/001/0035/23, Arquivo Nacional Torre do Tombo, Lisbon, Portugal.

Villaça, A. Eduardo. 1909. "Letter to A. J. Gonçalves." July 13. Companhia de Moçambique, Lisbon, Portugal. Companhia de Moçambique Collection

944, Mç 524, Cx. 508, Cap. 8. PT/TT/CMZ-ADGL/H-B-E/01/01, Arquivo Nacional, Torre do Tombo, Lisbon, Portugal.

Villaça, A. Eduardo. 1913. "Letter to José Emílio Pinheiro de Azevedo." February 6. Companhia de Moçambique, Lisbon, Portugal. Concessões Proc. no. 146, Cap. no. 1, doc. no. 2. Arquivo Nacional, Torre do Tombo, Lisbon, Portugal.

Index

Founded in 1893,
UNIVERSITY OF CALIFORNIA PRESS
publishes bold, progressive books and journals
on topics in the arts, humanities, social sciences,
and natural sciences—with a focus on social
justice issues—that inspire thought and action
among readers worldwide.

The UC PRESS FOUNDATION
raises funds to uphold the press's vital role
as an independent, nonprofit publisher, and
receives philanthropic support from a wide
range of individuals and institutions—and from
committed readers like you. To learn more, visit
ucpress.edu/supportus.

www.ingramcontent.com/pod-product-compliance
Lightning Source LLC
Chambersburg PA
CBHW031056280326
41928CB00049B/489